Physical Distribution Management

PHYSICAL

DISTRIBUTION

MANAGEMENT

LOGISTICS PROBLEMS OF THE FIRM

REVISED EDITION BY **Donald J. Bowersox**

Edward W. Smykay / Bernard J. La Londe

Graduate School of Business Administration, Michigan State University

Foreword by WENDELL R. SMITH

THE MACMILLAN COMPANY, NEW YORK

COLLIER-MACMILLAN LIMITED, LONDON

Library of Congress catalog card number: 68–15264

THE MACMILLAN COMPANY, NEW YORK
COLLIER-MACMILLAN CANADA, LTD., TORONTO, ONTARIO

Printed in the United States of America

Foreword

Since the appearance of the first edition of *Physical Distribution Management* interest in this area of marketing has increased substantially. The communications explosion brought about by the declining cost of telecommunications and high-speed transportation and by the computer has both influenced and been influenced by the development of physical distribution management as a professional field.

It is not enough, however, that specialists in physical distribution management be developed. Rather, general knowledge of the field must be available to executives responsible for the development of marketing strategies and the tactical implementation of these strategies in specific markets both at home and abroad.

Otherwise effective marketing plans can be frustrated if they have been designed without reference to their implications from the physical distribution point of view. Similarly, important marketing opportunities may be overlooked if the feasibility of serving markets once thought to be beyond reach is not known and taken into account.

The first edition did an important pioneering job in calling attention to what was then the "gray area between manufacturing and marketing"; the revised edition documents the important developments that have occurred and provides insights concerning what may be expected in the future.

Wendell R. Smith, Dean
School of Business Administration
University of Massachusetts
Amherst, Massachusetts

Preface

Physical distribution has come a long way since the first edition of this book appeared in early 1961. Therefore, in considering this revision, the authors were in fact confronted with the need to substantially write a new book. The intent of the authors, in the initial work, was to present broad outlines of physical distribution system analysis. This objective remains the same for the revised edition. The first edition appeared as the initial attempt to develop the integration of corporate physical distribution activities into a single text. In that sense, the authors consider the initial text a pioneer work. The revised edition is but one of a large number of books devoted to the subject of physical distribution management.

The original book was the result of investigations in the practical arena of business decisionmaking. The long period of cooperative research and consultation between the academic and business communities was identified as its underlying bedrock. This valuable interrelation is intensified by seven additional years in this edition. Valuable assistance and advice were freely given the authors by many academic colleagues and by business executives. It is impossible to indicate all of the persons who extended these kindnesses.

In particular, the authors wish to acknowledge the continuing influence of Professor Frank Mossman. Professor Mossman was a coauthor in the original text. He elected to forgo this revision in order to author a new text on macro and micro distribution systems. His contribution in concept and organization of the initial work has influenced the revised edition.

All of this edition's authors are or have been officers of the National Council of Physical Distribution Management. Professors Bowersox and Smykay are past presidents of N.C.P.D.M. Association with all members of the Council has been of valuable assistance in preparation of the manuscript. In order to recognize the contribution of so many different individuals, this book is dedicated to the principles and objectives of N.C.P.D.M. and its many members.

The authors wish to acknowledge the following for their able assistance and encouragement: Dean Alfred Seelye and Professor Thomas A. Staudt, both of Michigan State University; Professor Merrill J. Roberts of the University of Pittsburgh; Professor Robert Pashek of the Pennsylvania State University; and Walter L. Jeffrey, Vice Chairman of the E. F. Mac-Donald Company.

We wish to single out Fay Rogers and Lloyd Mitchell for their assistance in manuscript preparation, and also Miss Julie Adcock and Mrs. Avis Skalland for their contribution to manuscript typing. We also wish to acknowledge the valued comments of students in physical distribution courses at Michigan State University.

D. J. B.

E. W. S.

B. J. L.

Contents

ENDING APPENDIXES

PART I Physical Distribution and

the Market Environment

CHAPTER 1 Physical

Distribution Management

FROM the earliest of civilizations to the dynamic market place of twentieth-century world commerce, geographically-separated buyers and sellers have required a capability to move or physically transfer goods and commodities. Although the physical transfer of merchandise is traceable to the most primitive of people, a broad based requirement to overcome spatial separation between production and consumption did not exist until specialization of labor became commonplace and did not become of prime importance until the industrial revolution. As one might expect, the field of physical distribution did not gain general acceptance until complex operating systems became necessary for business management. Thus, whereas the process of physical distribution is as old as organized trade, the scientific study of integrated physical distribution systems has only emerged in the past few decades.

In a free society, management enjoys wide latitude regarding selection among systems of physical distribution. One firm may select a system to provide all customers overnight delivery. Another firm, in the same industry, may decide that delivery within two weeks of order receipt is sufficient to maintain market position. The determination of "how much" service to provide customers is a central issue in physical distribution planning. Service costs money. In all firms there exists a desire to save money. However, without adequate customer service, there may be no sales, no profit, and no survival.

The problem in seeking a balance between physical distribution cost and service is one of precise analysis of market and production requirements, resource availability, and operational capability. The choice is not one of to do, or not to do, the physical distribution job. Rather, the opportunity is one of performing the future physical distribution mission better than in the past and better than competition.

During the last two decades, it has become increasingly apparent that a substantial difference in return on investment can result from how resources allocated to physical distribution are administered. This book is concerned with the process of physical distribution management by the individual firm. This introductory chapter establishes the basic framework within which the study of physical distribution management is developed. The initial point of penetration is the establishment of working definitions for "physical distribution" and "physical distribution management."

Physical Distribution Defined

The National Council of Physical Distribution Management (NCPDM) has broadly defined physical distribution as follows:[1]

A term employed in manufacturing and commerce to describe the broad range of activities concerned with efficient movement of finished products from the end of the production line to the consumer, and in some cases includes the movement of raw materials from the source of supply to the beginning of the production line. These activities include freight transportation, warehousing, material handling, protective packaging, inventory control, plant and warehouse site selection, order processing, market forecasting, and customer service.

This NCPDM definition clearly identifies physical distribution as the link between resources committed to manufacturing and marketing. The activities of physical distribution are concerned with the creation of time and place utility. It is the job of physical distribution to get the right assortment of raw materials and finished products to the right location in an efficient manner timely to marketing and manufacturing requirements. If the physical distribution mission is aborted, little happens of a profitable nature. Thus, physical distribution is concerned with a vital area of corporate activity. The totality of the physical distribution process constitutes one of the main operational efforts of the firm.

In general, the authors find the NCPDM definition of physical distribution acceptable. Two areas of managerial concern implied by the above definition are not sufficiently highlighted. The first is the broad area of distribution communications. For a physical distribution system to function properly it must enjoy timely and accurate dissemination and feedback of distribution information. Little of any importance happens in a logistical system without continuous and distortion-free information flow. Conversely, ambiguous communiqúes can initiate a flurry of unproductive and duplicated logistical

[1]This definition obtained from the National Council of Physical Distribution Management Executive Offices, 307 N. Michigan Ave., Chicago, Ill.

activity. Logistical mistakes are costly, because they must be undone. Most firms have a long history of interbranch transfers of inventory initially shipped to the wrong location. Thus, the area of distribution communication must be studied in great detail in order to properly design and manage a physical distribution system.

The NCPDM definition also neglects to place proper emphasis upon the joint activities between firms linked together in the physical distribution of a single assortment of products. Most physical distribution systems utilize the resources of more than one independently owned firm to complete the physical distribution process. Such firms couple forces in the pursuit of joint economic opportunity. Less obvious and well understood is the fact that such marriages may either stimulate or hinder the flow of physical products in the marketing channel. The true scope of physical distribution penetrates corporate legal boundaries to become multifirm in terms of distribution cost commitment. The value added in the process of physical distribution is seldom paid for or accomplished by a single firm. The linkage of more than one firm opens the door to duplication and waste and often hinders antici- pated operational results. Such obstacles must be eliminated to achieve a multifirm competitive advantage.

Given the above two expansions and modifications the NCPDM definition is adopted for this book. Various other authors and speakers have utilized different terms to describe what is primarily called physical distribution in this book. The terms *business logistics*, *physical supply*, *materials manage- ment*, *market supply*, *logistics of distribution*, and *total distribution* are com- monly found in the literature dealing with this broad area of corporate activity.

In the present treatment the terms *physical distribution* and *business logistics* are considered synonymous and are freely interchanged. During the past decade the term *physical distribution* has gained the widest acceptance in business practice and educational circles and throughout the general liter- ature dealing with product and raw material flow management.

Physical Distribution Management Defined

Within the broad area of corporate physical distribution activity, the ma- terial that follows is further structured by a precise definition of physical distribution management.

Physical distribution management is defined as that responsibility to design and administer systems to control raw material and finished goods flow.

Paramount to the management of physical distribution is the concept of in- tegrated planning and administration. The scope of activities included in physical distribution consists of a wide range of management responsibilities normally or traditionally administered by a variety of different departments within a typical firm. Herein lies one of the major advantages of the integrated physical distribution concept. Coordinated management of all logistical activity centers as a single performance system offers a potential of improved customer service and often significant reductions in required dollar expenditures.

From the corporate viewpoint the performance of specific activities is only significant to the degree that overall objectives or goals of the firm are consistently satisfied. Such a holistic viewpoint is often lost when individual logistical activities are planned and administered by separate departments. In fact, decisions that appear efficiently based at a single department level may lead to costly mistakes when viewed from a corporate or total firm vantage point.

Consider the following examples of isolated physical distribution decisions:

(1) The case of the traffic manager who insisted that salesmen hold customer orders that characteristically were irregular until sufficient volume was available to ship consolidated carloads to the general market area. *Result: a significant lowering of transportation cost as a percent of sales, coupled with a reputation for inconsistent delivery and a gradual erosion of market position,*

or

(2) The case of the firm that utilized outbound data transmission of orders to warehouses coupled with air freight distribution to customers in order to support a policy of consistent two-day delivery once the order was received in the distribution department. *Result: only a minor decrease in actual delivery times coupled with a substantial increase in total distribution cost because it took an average of ten days for a customer's order to clear sales, credit, and data processing,*

or

(3) The case of the purchasing agent who developed the habit of ordering in multiples of 25 units without any consideration of standard pallet patterns used in material handling. *Result: 100 cases purchased, which consisted of two pallets containing 44 cases each. The pallets were efficiently handled, and the 12 individual cases were moved at five times the cost by hand in a highly mechanized warehouse facility.*

These examples illustrate typical interfaces that exist when the management of physical distribution is not coordinated. In final analysis, the job of implementing physical distribution principles requires detailed balancing and integration of disparate functions. In a managerial sense, such highly integrated performance is accomplished through system design and administration.

SYSTEM DESIGN RESPONSIBILITY

The design responsibility in physical distribution management is to develop the desired structure of facilities to achieve logistical goals. To a significant degree, the structure of a distribution system determines or limits the ultimate obtainable operational results.

The physical distribution system of a firm includes the location of production plant and distribution warehouse facilities, the selection of transportation mode, the allocation of inventory, and the development of a communication network. The structure of these elements must be designed to meet specific standards of customer order delivery at approved expenditures.

A wide range of alternatives exist in physical distribution system design. No ideal, perfect, or so-called optimum system exists that will fit the requirements of all firms. Two firms in the same industry may find widely divergent systems most suitable to their specific requirements. Each firm will find that the physical distribution system best fitted to its particular circumstances and objectives will depend upon the nature of marketing and manufacturing capabilities, their financial resources, and the geographical arrangement of current and potential customers.

The above comments may have falsely created the impression that design of a distribution system is a once-and-for-all responsibility on the part of management. Such is not the case. Although it is true that major revamping of the total system structure is not a common occurrence, modifications should be constantly under consideration and frequently implemented. The dynamics of modern business require frequent adjustments to accommodate changing patterns of customers' requirements and competitive tactics. Over a period of time, change may reach sufficient magnitude to occasion a complete study of the existing physical distribution structure. Both modification and complete revamping of the distribution system design is a responsibility of physical distribution management.

SYSTEM ADMINISTRATION RESPONSIBILITY

The administration of physical distribution systems is primarily concerned with control. Regardless of how fundamentally right a system is in design, the end results may be disappointing unless the ever present human element is properly directed. Whereas it is often the case that good management can make a poor distribution system achieve management objectives, it is rare when poor management can make even the best of systems function in a near satisfactory manner.

A great deal of physical distribution administration is concerned with day-to-day operations. In final analysis effective operational control is checking — checking essential details of every plan to assure proper implementation.

Checking, however, must be disciplined. It must be soundly based on a system of surveillance that fully utilizes management by objectives coupled with exception-reporting. The concept of integrated physical distribution — coordinated management of all related activities as a single performance system — creates some pressing problems in corporate organization. Operational experience argues for centralization of a great deal of distribution record keeping and policy formulation. In many cases, the greatest benefit from the integrated management of physical distribution result from joint operational programs between separate corporate divisions. This process of centralization may be difficult in a firm that has traditionally been structured around profit responsibility in a decentralized or divisionalized organization.

The problem of physical distribution administration is further complicated by the lack of relevant methods of performance measurement in most firms. Performance measurement is difficult because most business managers are trained, organized, and evaluated on the basis of traditional management functions. They are geared to independent action by the fact that they are allocated resources by isolated budgets and their performance is measured by traditional accounting. Thus, the action of one activity center in the total physical distribution effort may be either condemned or praised simply because the firm has not established techniques of integrated control. The development of such control techniques and related performance measurement devices requires a major reorientation in management philosophy. Such reorientation may or may not include formal reorganization.

Historical Development of Physical Distribution in the American Economy

Although formal definitions have a tendency to stifle the feel for a particular subject, the foregoing definitions and descriptions provide a basis for study of physical distribution management. Less than two short decades ago, physical distribution management, "as currently conceived," was virtually unheard of in the business society.[2]

To understand the need for physical distribution planning in the modern firm, one must realize that American industrial development has passed through a number of definable stages each characterized by a general type of business orientation. These orientations have, to a large extent, determined what factors historically received primary emphasis in business planning.

In the initial stages of American industrial development, the most significant problems revolved around the scarcity of goods and services. This resulted in the application of organizational principles and technological de-

[2]To the knowledge of the authors the term *physical distribution* was first used by Fred E. Clark, *Readings in Marketing* (New York: The Macmillan Co., 1924), Chapter XV.

velopments to problems of production.[3] In these early stages, the dynamics of economic development encouraged broad market expansion and techno-logical improvement. This need tended to place the engineer and innovator at the forefront of business organization. The Carnegies, Whitneys, and Astors were characteristic of this period. Continued technological improve-ment resulted in the need for larger aggregates of capital. The total increase in productivity, combined with the closing of the domestic frontier, increased the vulnerability of industry to business fluctuations and government control.

The entrance of the American economic system into its next stage became apparent with the need for rationalization and control of the production orientation. This resulted in the financier, the lawyer, and the professional administrator gaining dominant positions in the organization structure. Perhaps the story of this era will never be told better than Sloan's personal report contained in *My Years with General Motors*.[4] During this period the major financial and industrial amalgamations of the early twentieth century developed. Such amalgamations were aimed at market stability and the long-run health of the individual enterprise.

Finally, the domestic market could no longer regularly absorb increased output. Although the capacity to absorb was relatively untapped, the desire to absorb a steady stream of standard products was checked by the highest standard of living ever known to civilized man. To realize continued growth it became necessary to cultivate world markets and to stimulate domestic markets with specialized products aimed for purchase by smaller groups of consumers. The business arena had become multinational in scope. Domestic business had entered the era of product differentiation and market segmenta-tion. It was at this stage that business began to utilize the specialized knowl-edge of the marketing expert. To maintain or expand its competitive position, it became increasingly necessary for the individual firm to obtain reliable and complete information on alternative courses of marketing action. These alternatives involved programs aimed at demand cultivation and supply per-formance. From the marketing viewpoint, demand embodied opportunity and supply required organized effort.[5]

Business entered into and still remains in the marketing era. It seems safe to conclude that the marketing viewpoint will persist as a dominant philos-ophy among firms engaged in global competition. During the early stages of marketing awareness, progress centered around the application of scientific

[3] For one of the earliest published works in this field, see Frederick W. Taylor, *Scientific Management* (New York: Harper and Brothers, 1957). This volume contains two of Taylor's major works, *Shop Management* (1902) and *Principles of Scientific Management* (1911).

[4] Alfred P. Sloan Jr., *My Years With General Motors* (New York: Doubleday and Co., Inc., 1963).

[5] Wroe Alderson, *Marketing Behavior and Executive Action*, p. 355 (Homewood, Ill.: Richard D. Irwin, Inc., 1957), and Wendell Smith, "Product Differentiation and Market Segmentation as Alternative Marketing Strategies," *Journal of Marketing*, July, 1956., pp. 3–8.

methods to the field of demand analysis. For example, the scientific techniques of market research were first applied immediately following World War I.[6] The application of statistical techniques began during the 1920's. In later years substantial progress was made in applying the contributions of sociology and psychology to the problem of identifying and understanding qualitative market information.[7] Each of these advances to varying degrees, was aimed at supplementing the basic assumption of "economic rationality." The concept of "economic man" was modified by a view of the consumer as a purchasing unit having a variety of wants and normally imperfect information concerning product and service offerings. The executive was viewed as molding total corporate offerings in an effort to capitalize upon market opportunity. This philosophy embodied demand analysis in order to achieve the goal of maximum consumer satisfaction. The customer was assumed to represent the focal point of business activity. The market was viewed as holding veto power over the business enterprise.[8]

Initially the advances of integrated marketing centered on the areas of product development, price strategies, and promotional programs. Lesser attention was directed to supply and problems of marketing channels, transportation, and inventory management. In part, this can be attributed to the newness of integrated marketing and the lack of outstanding improvements in techniques of physical distribution.

Firms have always faced a need to physically distribute products. In the physical distribution function significant portions of corporate total dollar expenditures were incurred. Thus, all firms developed networks capable of moving goods. In many instances, these networks were inefficient causing high cost and poor customer service. These inefficiencies were most often passed on to the buyer without any detailed study of their cause or prevention. Thus, as recently as 1962, one year after the first edition of this text was published as the initial treatment of integrated physical distribution, Peter Drucker[9] writing in *Fortune* concluded,

We know little more about distribution today than Napoleon's contemporaries knew about the interior of Africa. We know it is there, and we know it is big; and that's about all.

However, by 1962 forces of fermentation were well at work regarding the opportunities of physical distribution. Innovation was forthcoming in the basic concepts of physical movement systems. It may appear illogical that

[6]C. S. Duncan, *Commercial Research* (New York: The Macmillan Co., 1924).

[7]For an example of the type and quality of information see Lincoln H. Clark (ed.), *Consumer Behavior: Research on Consumer Reactions* (New York: Harper and Brothers, 1958). For an example of research techniques that can be employed in qualitative market research see W. Lloyd Warner and William E. Henry, "The Radio Day Time Serial: A Symbolic Analysis," *Genetic Psychology Monographs*, Vol. XXXVII (1948), 3–71.

[8]For modern development of this concept see Thomas A. Staudt and Donald A. Taylor, *A Managerial Introduction to Marketing* (Englewood Cliffs, N. J.: Prentice-Hall, Inc., 1965), Chapter One.

[9]Peter F. Drucker, "The Economy's Dark Continent," *Fortune*, April, 1962, pp. 265–70.

physical distribution is referred to as a new managerial concern, because all integral parts are so firmly embedded in historical literature and business practice. The uniqueness of physical distribution is found in the integration of several related bodies of knowledge into a framework for managerial action. The perspectives of physical distribution allow plant location, inventory management, transportation, and distribution warehousing to become a basic part of total corporate strategy. As such, physical distribution is the logical extension of overall marketing orientation to a sophistication of physical supply systems. Such sophistication culminates in precise customer service at lowest financial expenditures.

In September, 1966, *Business Week* published a feature special report entitled "New Strategies to Move Goods."[10] This summary report clearly depicts development of the physical distribution concept through mid-1966 and highlights several current issues. From the early 1950's to the mid-1960's, a variety of forces had combined to create a timeliness for integrated physical distribution management. In succeeding paragraphs important forces are singled out to provide the student with a broader background for the study of physical distribution management.

THE COMPUTER AND HIGH-SPEED DATA TRANSMISSION

After World War II, we, as a nation, began to feel the initial impact of the computer age. Although a few years earlier the first computers had been a novelty, by the late 1950's their use in business management was commonplace. The development of physical distribution management during the period in which computers emerged from infancy provided the basis for a unique marriage. Rather than dealing with internal scheduling, accounting, or payroll, physical distribution offered the potential for placing high-speed digital computers to work in day-to-day operations.

Thus, the impact of the computer was not to be denied the fertility of integrated physical distribution. First, the computer, coupled with advancements in applied analytical tools, placed at the disposal of business a device that could be used to perform experimental analysis on alternative physical distribution system designs. Such experiments could be conducted by the use of mathematical modeling without any disruption in daily business operations. Controlled experimentation became a reality.

Perhaps the second impact of the computer tends to overshadow the major development of controlled experimentation. The computer became a device that allowed management to cope with millions of details in an orderly and systematic manner. This capability to process data coupled with high-speed data transmission allows information to flow from original documents at speeds that permit discovery and interpretation of a significant trend while it

[10]New Strategies to Move Goods," *Business Week*, September, 1966.

is still in the formation stage. Computers can be relied upon to maintain operational detail with unquestionable accuracy. In terms of data transmission, Paris and Tokyo are as close to New York City as Newark, New Jersey.

The comment is often made that the advent of written communications revolutionized man because it freed him from reliance upon personal memory. The advent of the high-speed computer altered the scope and capability of man's written memory by rendering the process of detailed record keeping an accepted way of life. Now man has high-speed data transmission. Without doubt the development of data transmission constitutes one of the most exciting technological advances of modern times. Speedy transmission of data on a multinational basis offers man the capacity of an expanded workable memory, because it eliminates the need to stop and place information into storage. To a significant degree the need to forecast uncertain future events is replaced by momentary reporting of current happenings.

At this early stage of development it is difficult to prophesy the final degree of physical distribution gain that will culminate from the computer and high-speed data transmission. The potential appears limited only by man's ability to develop and implement imaginative systems. It appears certain that future historians will view the simultaneous development of integrated physical distribution, computers, and high-speed data transmission as a most serendipitous event.

PROLONGED PROFIT SQUEEZE AND COST-REDUCTION POTENTIAL

It is a sad commentary that, despite the availability of new tools and techniques, little time or capital is applied toward development until some event or crisis creates an immediate need. The profit squeeze of the 1950's, highlighted by the recession of 1958, created a business environment conducive to the development of integrated physical distribution management. This environmental condition continues to act as a stimulant to logistical development, as the future holds no immediate relief to shrinking profit margins. After many years of increasing production economies, by the 1950's it was apparent that the point of diminishing returns had been reached for several industries. New methods of cost reduction had to be found. Physical distribution offered management one such area for cost reduction.

Once again it is appropriate to draw upon the comments of Peter Drucker to report this potential as viewed by one expert in corporate management.[11]

. . . [Physical distribution] is the big area in which one can still do anything about costs. We have been working for a hundred years on costs in manufacturing areas. I would imagine that 100 years ago, the physical distribution costs were as much

[11]Peter F. Drucker, Remarks made at spring meeting, National Council of Physical Distribution Management, April, 1965, Chicago, Illinois.

as they are today. But the total share in the cost was much less than it is today, simply because we have whittled down, and cut down and slit off so much of the manufacturing costs and a good many others. As a result, physical distribution has become the largest single cost element. It varies for economic processes and industries but it is very large.

This is, therefore, the area in which I hope you will see very, very big strides. They are needed because the costs are very high and because we can expect a period of continuing pressure on costs and profits. We can, in other words, anticipate a highly competitive period. The question is therefore what can give. Physical distribution is the one area where there is plenty of room. There is not much left in the other areas. In a well-managed plant, one cannot really cut costs of the machine work much. The trouble with sales expense is not that they are too high, but that salesmen are not productive enough. When it comes to costs, physical distribution is about the one area where efforts really pay off. A 10% improvement in physical distribution cost is probably worth a 40% improvement in true manufacturing costs. I have yet to see a situation where the costs of actually changing physical characteristics of a material is much higher than 10% of the price the customer pays, whereas physical distribution runs to 40% or 50%. And yet as all of you know, the industrial engineers are all where the machines are and very rarely does any of them poke his head into the shipping room.

What are the true costs of physical distribution? Depending upon the firm's specific product assortment, the total expenditure for all logistical activities appears to range between 20 and 50 percent of gross sales. In the economy in general, many experts estimate the aggregate annual expenditure on national physical distribution to be approaching 150 billion dollars. When one considers that the most recent estimate of our National Intercity Freight Expenditure is 62.6 billion dollars, it is easy to see why physical distribution represents much more than transportation.[12] The challenge to improve efficiency becomes of national concern when we consider that the distribution system of the United States will be required to support a 50-percent increase in productivity during the next decade if our current standard of living is to be maintained under conditions of an expanding population.

Thus, at a time when management needs to make significant reductions in cost, physical distribution is rapidly moving toward maturity. The potentials are great because so little has been done. The prospects are encouraging because physical distribution deals with tangible facets of material, space, and time. It is of little wonder that integrated physical distribution is commonly referred to as the last commercial frontier for cost reduction.

CONSISTENT SERVICE AND LONG-RANGE MARKET ENTRENCHMENT

Perhaps the potential for cost reduction tends to overshadow an even more potent reason for top-management interest in logistical capability. At

[12]Estimate provided by the United States Department of Commerce.

the end of all complex activity of the corporation rests the need to complete a transaction. The complexities of production, the problems of finance, the need for research, and the problems of marketing only gain importance to the degree to which a firm is able to culminate all efforts into a series of profitable transactions. The ability to achieve such transactions on a routine basis, and to a significant degree resultant profitably, rests in part with a firm's physical distribution capability. Thus, when viewed in terms of transaction capabilities, the logistical network of a firm constitutes a major element in the total customer offering of services and product assortments. Physical distribution exists for the sole purpose of market and production support. As such it is a cost center and never a profit center. Although it is desirable to hold physical distribution costs to a minimum, unless the degree of performance is sufficient to complement other efforts, all expenditures are in vain.

Firms, similar to actors, politicians, and women, have reputations in the eyes of their constituents. One aspect of any firm's reputation centers around physical distribution capability. One firm may be known as a fast shipper, whereas another may be plagued with the reputation of inconsistency in delivery. A particular firm may be known as a shipper who has few out-of-stocks and complete order information, whereas a competitor may have a reputation for constant stock-outs and hopeless backorders. Over a period of time, some firms gain the reputation of being easy to do efficient business with, and others drop by the wayside. Problems of logistical capability are more often felt at the level of daily operating decisions than at the level of top management. Unless top management makes a concerted effort to keep abreast of a firm's logistical reputation, serious problems may develop. The best-laid market and production plans are easily neutralized by erratic logistical support.

A firm's physical distribution capability is measured in terms of speed and consistency. Among those managers engaged in the operation of physical distribution systems, consistency of performance is a more noteworthy virtue than pure speed of service. A fast delivery cycle is of little value to customers unless it is consistently met from one order to the next. Development of both consistency and speed of service is dependent upon distribution system design and administration. However, potential speed is essentially a design factor, whereas performance consistency is always a responsibility of distribution administration.

The fact that early emphasis upon physical distribution centered around cost reduction is understandable in terms of the potential savings a firm could enjoy. It may well be that the long-range importance of integrated physical distribution will center around service capabilities. Although a competitor can react to a price cut over night and imitate a product in a short period of time, substantial creativity, training, and investment must proceed the introduction of an outstanding physical distribution system. Such a network represents a combination of management talent, systems, and distribution facilities hard to duplicate. Top-management recognition of this potential to differentiate offerings through logistical superiority is one prime reason for the explosive growth of physical distribution.

Approaches to the Study of Physical Distribution

As one would expect, when considering a commercial area as large as physical distribution, there are a number of different vantage points.[13] It is useful to briefly review the major areas of physical distribution study in order to structure clearly the approach used in this book.

The broadest and clearest divisions of the subject matter are between macro and micro approaches. Generally used in the study of formal economics, the prefix *macro* is used to describe the study of whole or large distribution systems. In this context, macrodistribution refers to the study of the total distribution system of the United States economy a region or a total industry. Included in a macro approach are all elements in the economy, individual firms, government, and other ecological factors which combine to make up a national movement system. In contrast, the microdistribution field is concerned with the study of management as it relates to a specific shipper or carriers' physical distribution system.

The study of physical distribution must include elements of both macro and micro analysis. The primary orientation of this book would be classified as one of microdistribution. The orientation is concerned with the efforts of an individual firm to develop an effective and efficient physical distribution system. The individual firm's objective is to develop the best possible system to support and encourage the achievement of profitable transactions. Such development requires a cognizance of macrodistribution forces at work in the economy. Such forces act as limiting factors, barriers, and opportunities.

In general, the development used in this book is classified as a systems approach. Emphasis is placed upon the design and administration of the individual firm's physical distribution. Concern is with the process by which the individual firm mobilizes, organizes, allocates, and controls resources to establish and achieve physical distribution objectives. To the extent the material does venture beyond the legal boundaries of the individual firm it is for the purpose of developing intercorporate dynamics at the supplier-customer level. Such relationships extend and have significant influence throughout the total distribution channel including activities of such service suppliers as transportation and public warehouse companies.

As such, this treatment does not tackle some of the vexing and challenging problems related to aggregate or macrophysical distribution. Such subjects as public policy, national capacity, regional development, and even service

[13]For a good review of alternative approaches to the study of physical distribution see J. L. Heskett, Robert M. Ivie, and Nicholas A. Glaskowsky, Jr., *Business Logistics* (New York: The Ronald Press, 1964), pp. 17–18.

facility structure are left for those with primarily a macrodistribution orientation. This omission in no way means that such issues are of any less importance than those developed in this book. In fact, the question of national physical distribution capacity may soon represent one of this nation's most serious problems.

Format for the Study of Physical Distribution Management

The purpose of this synopsis is to provide the student with an overview of the material that follows. The remainder of the book is devoted to a detailed treatment of physical distribution management. The general organization is from the broad to the specific. Development of subject matter is divided into three parts. It is important at the outset for the student to understand fully the relationship of each of these parts.

Part One, "Physical Distribution and the Market Environment," is concerned with the structure within which a firm plans, designs, and implements a physical distribution system. Chapter 2 is devoted to a detailed development of marketing and physical distribution interaction. Of primary concern is a discussion of marketing forces influencing the selection among distribution alternatives. This chapter highlights the fact that many forces shape the market effort of the individual firm. To a large extent these same forces influence physical distribution requirements and capabilities.

Chapter 3 moves beyond the area normally considered the domain of the firm and examines issues related to the total distribution channel as a single system of action. Firms engaged in channel relationships confront both barriers and opportunities greater than the scope of their own resources. The study of physical exchange between firms linked together in quest of joint opportunity raises some questions regarding traditional treatment of distribution channels.

In Chapter 4 attention is directed to the geographic basis of the entire logistical effort. Geomarket patterns of population and business activity are of critical importance in physical distribution planning. The fact that market potential is constantly shifting is of primary importance. This chapter also utilizes geomarket patterns for the development of georeference systems. Such reference systems are vital to strategic distribution planning.

The final chapter of Part One, Chapter 5, is devoted to a comprehensive treatment of physical distribution systems. As such, it is designed to integrate Part One and to serve as an introduction for material that follows. The activity centers of the physical distribution system are developed in a network concept followed by definition of the logistics mission and examples of typical physical distribution systems found in industry.

Part Two is devoted to development of primary activity centers included in physical distribution. Chapters 6 and 7 are concerned with transportation and Chapter 6 treats transportation institutions, regulatory framework and concludes with a treatment of unitization. The title *unitization* is adopted in an omnibus sense to group the subjects of material handling, packaging, and containerization. These subjects are directly related by their common objective of efficient product movement within a physical distribution system. Chapter 7 deals with transport costing. Chapter 8 deals with inventory allocations. In Chapter 9 the subject of distribution communications is explored. Chapter 10 deals with distribution warehousing. Although the subjects of Chapters 6 through 10 are developed on an individual basis, it is axiomatic to physical distribution that their subject matter be treated on an integrated system basis.

At the conclusion of Part Two, the stage has been set for treatment of the basic physical distribution management responsibilities of system design and administration. In Part Three, Chapter 11 introduces the total cost techniques of integrating physical distribution activity centers. Problems and approaches to distribution cost accounting and planning are discussed. Included are various methods of dividing fixed and variable expense for use in total cost integration. The chapter concludes with a treatment of alternative policies to guide system design.

Chapter 12 isolates the system design responsibility of physical distribution management. Basic principles of design are developed within the context of systems analysis. The essential assignment in design of physical distribution systems is to integrate all activity centers into a network of physical facilities. Such an integration requires development of distribution goals and a balance between service objectives and cost of resource commitments. The techniques of evaluating a total system from the viewpoint of service and cost integration are developed.

In Chapter 13 attention shifts from design responsibility to questions of administration. The orientation of this chapter is directed to management by objectives. The logistical information system is developed, attention is directed to operations planning, performance measurement, and reporting. The chapter concludes with a discussion of the vital issues of organization. Chapters 12 and 13 combine to complete treatment of the distribution manager's dual responsibilities to design and administer logistical systems.

The presentation of any subject matter contains a degree of bias resulting from beliefs and experience of the authors. In the case of this book several basic beliefs influence the entire work. Therefore, these underlying convictions are stated now so as to prearm the reader and disarm the critic.

First, the entire work is developed upon the premise that the physical distribution activities of a firm function within the scope of total marketing effort. This does not mean that physical distribution is a function of marketing to the extent that it should be administered in the marketing organization. Rather, a market-oriented position is assumed for the simple reason that the battle for corporate survival is fought in the market place, not in the plant or in the warehouse. Therefore, an overall market orientation must guide planning and implementation throughout total corporate organization including production, finance, and physical distribution. This viewpoint is widely accepted as the marketing concept.

Second, specific opinions concerning the proper role of quantitative techniques in predoctoral training and the practice of business management permeate subject matter development. Mathematics and statistics are tools of management which have many useful applications and many limitations. One serious limitation is the preoccupation of some users, and among several who develop these techniques, for arrival at optimum answers to business problems. Our philosophy concerning quantitative techniques is that they represent tools for better management. They are no substitute for good management. In the dynamic arena of business, management rarely has the time or resources to seek an optimum solution. More often than not the practicing manager must be willing to accept a satisfactory solution to an immediate problem. Therefore, treatment of advanced quantitative techniques is left for books dealing with such subjects. In this book, techniques are introduced on a descriptive basis where they can be applied to the problems of system design or administration. When it is desirable to develop a specific technique in greater detail, appendixes are used. As a result, the reader may engage appendixes if desired or merely read the text without interruption of the flow of the main material.

Third, the subject of location analysis and theory is difficult to integrate into a treatment of physical distribution management. Although location selection is a concern of physical distribution, it is a specialized responsibility limited to questions of system structure. However, individual location decisions are often confronted, with the result that all such decisions create a spatial network within which physical distribution resources must be allocated.

Therefore, location issues are considered in the following manner. In Chapter 4 some aspects of location theory are developed. In Chapter 5, the network concept of fixed facilities is introduced in a systems concept. In Part Two, when dealing with distribution activity centers, the distribution warehouse facility is singled out for treatment in Chapter 10. Analytical techniques for locating the single distribution warehouse facility are treated in Appendix 10A. The design of multiple facility networks is developed in Chapter 12 under the broad subject of systems design. The treatment of procedures and checklists to aid location selection is reserved for ending appendixes. This approach has the disadvantage of spreading treatment of fixed facility location throughout the text. The advantage gained is a treatment of specific aspects of location at points where it is most beneficial to development of overall subject matter.

Finally, illustrations and basic material developed in the text are selected for the most part from distribution of finished inventory. To some degree the logistics of raw material flow experiences different economics than the flow of finished inventories. However, basic principles of physical distribution are applicable to either raw material collection or finished goods dispersion.

Summary

In summary, the study of physical distribution has become timely in American business for a variety of technological and economic reasons. In the management of physical distribution, the firm finds a fertile area for cost reduction and customer service improvement. The area of physical distribution cuts across a great many traditional departments of a typical organization. The potential of integrated physical distribution is gained from mobilizing all resources of the firm into a single purpose system. The responsibility of physical distribution management is to design and then administer the performance of such an integrated system.

The present status of physical distribution is one of semimaturity. An analogy between mass production techniques in the 1930's and physical distribution in the 1960's is appropriate. There is little doubt that physical distribution will continue to grow in importance for one simple reason. In business a need exists for the development of exacting logistical networks. Physical distribution deals with the tangible facets of material, space, and time. The potential for efficient alignment of these tangible facets of a corporation is only limited by desire, resourcefulness, and imagination.

Discussion Questions

1. Why did the concept of physical distribution come to the attention of American industry in the 1950's?

2. Why is physical distribution of such importance to firms in the future?

3. Could physical distribution function as a profit center?

4. What factor of physical distribution normally has the most significance to a firm's customers?

5. What is meant by the term *physical distribution*? Would not the term *transportation* suffice to explain it? Why?

6. Why is feedback so important in a distribution system?

7. If a firm's transportation costs have been cut by 10% as a result of a recent management decision to use a different mode of transportation, is this necessarily a good thing or may this cause other problems?

CHAPTER 2 Marketing and Physical

Distribution Interaction

RALPH WALDO EMERSON was reported to have said: "If a man can write a better book, preach a better sermon, or make a better mouse trap than his neighbor, though he builds his house in the woods, the world will make a beaten path to his door." An early retailer commenting on this statement noted that it might be true, but he would still set his traps where the mice were thickest.

The present-day executive cannot afford to take Emerson's advice. Although it no doubt helps to offer the best product to the potential consumer, it is unlikely in today's mass production–mass distribution economy that the consumer will journey through the woods in search of a better mouse trap when more convenient locations exist. The business firm competing for a share of a mass market must produce a product satisfactory to customer needs and design a physical distribution system that places the right product at the right place at the right time.

A tendency exists to connect only the production process with creation of value. The distribution process is considered to add costs rather than value. However, four types of utility add value to a product: (1) form, (2) place, (3) possession, and (4) time. Form utility is the transformation of raw materials into want-satisfying goods. For example, an ingot of steel has some value, but its value as an automobile is substantially increased. Of course, marketing shares in the creation of form utility in that it relays consumer preferences concerning the type of automobile to build. However, ten million automobiles in Detroit have little practical use to a driver in Los Angeles, California. The automobile must be shipped to California (place utility) at the time the consumer wants to purchase the automobile (time utility), and arrangements must be made for a convenient transaction between buyer and seller (possession utility).

Physical distribution is concerned with creating time and place utility in the business systems. It is a function that is integral to achieving corporate goals. Marketing can specify the color, shape, and style of the product, as well as create a convenient and economical transaction between buyer and seller. Production can build a high-quality product at the lowest possible unit cost. It remains for physical distribution to insure that the right product is at the right place at the right time.

If the premise that the firm's objective is to provide customer satisfaction at a profit is accepted, it logically follows that the physical distribution plays a vital role in providing customer satisfaction. It is the purpose of Chapter 2 to (1) illustrate the relationships between physical distribution and marketing, and (2) demonstrate the strategic marketing implications of effective physical distribution management.

Marketing Management and Physical Distribution

In the 1950's, American business became more and more impressed with the importance of marketing as a focus for corporate activity. This corporate posture emerged out of the shift from a post-World War II sellers' market to a buyers' market. With this recognition of the role of marketing emerged a shift in corporate philosophy to that popularly termed *marketing concept*. The marketing concept is simply a market-focused corporate philosophy, which is based upon identifying consumer needs and mobilizing corporate resources to serve this need at a profit.[1]

The overall firm has four key elements of the marketing mix which must be developed and integrated to implement the marketing concept within the firm: (1) product, (2) price, (3) promotion, and (4) physical distribution.[2] These resources represent the marketing mix elements that can be altered or controlled by management in developing a total marketing plan.

Two important factors should be recognized at this point. First, these elements of the marketing mix are interdependent. That is, the type of product developed and the type of promotional program undertaken will obviously influence the price of a given product in the market place. Second, the management of resources contained in the marketing mix does not reside exclusively in the marketing department. To develop and maintain an effective product in the market place, full support from the engineer in the re-

[1] J. B. McKitterich, "What Is the Marketing Management Concept?" *The Frontiers of Marketing Thought and Science* (Chicago: American Marketing Association, 1957), pp. 77–82.

[2] E. J. McCarthy, *Basic Marketing: A Managerial Approach* (Homewood, Illinois: R. D. Irwin and Co., 1964), pp. 38–40.

search and development department and quality input on the asembly line are required. In the case of physical distribution, it is necessary to coordinate finished goods inventory and other distribution requirements, regardless of their geographic or organizational location within the firm, to the customer service requirements of the corporate marketing program.

In summary, the company has four elements with which to build a balanced marketing program: product, price, promotion, and physical distribution. The purpose of the marketing program is to achieve target market penetration at a profitable level of operation. The interrelationship between physical distribution and the other elements of the corporate marketing program are discussed below.

PRODUCT

The physical distribution support system should be designed to deliver the right product to the right place at the right time and at the lowest total cost consistent with targeted customer service levels. If this objective is not achieved within reasonable limits, two types of costs are incurred by the firm. The first cost is what might be termed a *stock-out cost*.[3] This cost comes from lost sales and in some cases lost customers. For example, if a consumer goes to a drugstore with the intention of purchasing a certain size and brand hairspray and finds that it is not available, she could decide either to go to another store or to purchase a substitute product. If she purchases a substitute product, the company has lost the revenue from one sale. The possibility also exists that she will be favorably impressed by the substitute product and the company will permanently lose her as a customer. The total cost of lost sales or lost customers (stock-out costs) is subject to considerable speculation and controversy. In today's mass merchandising environment, where repeat purchases are the objective of the basic marketing strategy of many firms, stock-out problems can be serious in terms of lost sales revenues. It should be recognized that almost no business attempts to provide 100 percent immediate availability of all products, because customer service exceeding 95 percent usually involves excessive investment in inventory.

The second type of cost is incurred when a firm moves the wrong product from one location to another. The wrong product can result from an error in size, color, or some physical attribute, or the right product can arrive damaged and thus be unacceptable to the potential consumer. In such cases, the manufacturer bears the risk of all of the stock-out costs plus the movement and handling costs incurred by putting the wrong product through the system. Although this might not appear to be a serious problem, inventory and shipment, double handling, repack costs, and paperwork charges can

[3]See Chapter 8, pp. 210, for a more detailed description of stock-out costs.

mount rapidly and serious inventory imbalance may occur within the firm's physical distribution network.

The problem of damage in transit is also a serious one for many industries. It has been estimated that over 25 percent of the furniture shipped in the United States arrives at final terminal point in damaged condition. This forces the furniture retailer to do one of two things. He can either scrap individual pieces or repair the product on site. The retailer or carrier and eventually the consumer is forced to bear the cost of damaged merchandise in all cases. These increased costs have led to some comprehensive re-evaluation of unit-loading characteristics and transportation equipment capability in an effort to reduce the incidence of damaged goods. Some industry associations and individual companies now cooperate with packaging, materials handling, and transportation suppliers in developing new and improved methods for delivering products.

It is important to note that this discussion revolves around physical distribution factors relating to the product and to the overall marketing program of the firm. Customer satisfaction, in both a quantitative and qualitative sense, is heavily dependent upon the capability of the logistical support system to deliver the right product in acceptable condition.

PROMOTION

Anyone who has visited an appliance store to purchase an advertised special and found that the company was sold out of the product has experienced the dramatic impact of breakdown between the physical distribution and the promotional programs of a firm. Perhaps even more significant, however, is the impact of the promotional program on the physical distribution activities of the firm. A loosely conceived promotional program may result in unrealistic demands, which in turn are amplified by communication lags and normal order accumulation processes. This may result in disrupted and economically expensive production schedule alterations, rush orders from suppliers, premium transportation costs, and strained manufacturer-supplier relationships. In Chapter 9, page 236, a more detailed description of this amplification effect is presented and discussed.

Some firms are developing computer models for new product introduction in which the physical distribution buildup and support is a critical element in the total planning process.[4]

The promotional decisions of the firm have an impact upon logistics in two ways. First, from the marketing view point, serious stock-outs at all levels in the distribution channel can occur from uncoordinated promotional programs. These stock-out costs, in addition to lost revenue, undermine the

---

[4]Warren Dusenbury, "CPM for New Product Introductions," *Harvard Business Review*, July–August, 1967, pp. 124–139.

basic marketing objectives of the firm by loss of customer and distributor satisfaction. A second impact is felt in internal operations where production scheduling, shipping commitments, and other routine logistically-related activities must adjust to an unanticipated crisis caused by sudden sales shifts. Such a crisis affects both the external image of the company with its suppliers and customers and the internal harmony between various areas of the business. For example, a salesman might become gun shy about cooperating with the next promotional program of his company due to a history of failure in physical distribution support. Similarly, production executives feel they must pay for poor planning on the part of marketing functions in terms of uneconomically scheduled production at overtime rates. A series of strained internal relationships can develop as a result of a breakdown between the promotional efforts and the anticipated physical distribution support required to fill the marketing objectives of the firm.

PRICE

It is axiomatic that the price of a product must cover all costs in the long run. It seems equally axiomatic that in the long run any wastes in physical distribution efficiency must be passed on to the consumer in the form of either a higher price or poor product quality. The inability of a firm to control costs in the physical distribution sector can impair profit in the short run and survival in the long run.

On the positive side, effective control of physical distribution costs can present the firm with a significant added advantage in the marketplace. Lower distribution costs can be passed on to the consumer in the form of reduced prices and lead to market expansion. Alternatively, cost saving from increased distributive efficiency can be allocated to strengthen other areas of business activity. It should, however, be recognized that for most companies a significant share of the final price is made up of physical distribution cost. This in turn makes price vulnerable to any upward or downward shift in such cost and thus directly influences the marketing mix of the individual firm.

PHYSICAL DISTRIBUTION AS A SALES AND MARKETING STRATEGY[5]

From the marketing viewpoint, there are at least two basic ways of viewing physical distribution capability. Physical distribution may be viewed in a passive way as the backup capability to support the marketing objectives of

[5]H. Jay Bullen, "New Competitive Selling Weapon — Physical Distribution Management," *Sales Management*, May 7, 1965, pp. 41–52.

the firm. It may also be viewed as a positive force in obtaining a competitive advantage in the marketplace. Utilizing this approach, efficient physical distribution is sold to potential customers as a major advantage of a firm.[6] This is a particularly powerful selling tool when the product in question is easily substitutable or sensitive to price changes.

Customer Service as a Competitive Advantage. In the past few decades American businessmen have become more scientific in their basic approach to business problems. Much of this scientific approach is due to the introduction and increasingly widespread use of the computer. Twenty or thirty years ago, the retailer did not evaluate the service performance of his suppliers. It was a cumbersome process and was undertaken only when a supplier flagrantly and repeatedly violated established service schedules. Today most manufacturers and wholesalers and many retailers have sophisticated inventory control systems, which determine service requirements for many thousands of products on a routine weekly or monthly basis. As more and more businesses adopt such inventory control systems, it will become increasingly routine to have analysis of customer service performance and evaluation of suppliers by purchasers. In summary, customer service has become measurable through application of computer technology and hence becomes a factor in the total marketing program.

The ability to provide quick delivery on a wide variety of items at specified times reduces customer inventory requirements. Such a program allows customers to cut safety stocks to a minimum. With annual inventory costs running as high as 25 percent of value, substantial savings can be passed on to the customer by an efficient physical distribution system. As noted previously, more and more companies are arriving at that point in management information systems where they can measure and appreciate the advantage of lower holding cost and inventory, better utilization of facilities, increased inventory turnover, and more efficient materials handling.

From the supplier's point of view, an efficient physical distribution system allows specific measurement of costs associated with different levels of customer service. Because more customers are demanding increased service, in terms of faster delivery or smaller and more frequent shipments, it is useful to be able to calculate the cost of increasing customer service and to weigh this cost against the possible loss of revenue. The impact of any new service or alteration in service pattern can be measured against cost and value of the strategy as a marketing tool.

Profit Leverage and Market Opportunity. In recent years, businessmen have been faced by increasing costs and more exacting competition. The increasing costs have stemmed mainly from a cost-push type of inflation.

[6]Wendell M. Stewart, "Physical Distribution: Key to Improved Volume and Profits," *Journal of Marketing*, January, 1965, pp. 65–70.

Increasing competition has stemmed from larger and more aggressive domestic and international competitors. As a result of these two factors, a so-called "profit squeeze" has occurred in most industries. This is simply a pressure on the profit position of the firm due to the fact that costs are rising and competition or some other factor prevents passing on the increasing costs to the consumer in the form of increased prices.

Businessmen confronted with this situation face a dilemma. Many believe that the path to increased profits and sales can always be achieved by adding a new product, or by adding another store, or by investing a few more dollars into advertising. However, shrinking profit margins have forced a re-evaluation of this belief. As marginal costs of securing additional sales increase, more and more manufacturers, wholesalers, and retailers are forced to look to reductions in physical distribution costs to protect profits. For example, in the supermarket industry with a 1.3 percent profit-to-sales ratio, a $150,000 savings in physical distribution cost would yield the same dollar profit as an approximately $18.5 million dollar increase in sales. For an individual supermarket, an approximately $10,000 savings in operations cost would equal more than half the net annual profit of the average store.

Physical distribution savings can also be used for market expansion. For example, for every one dollar reduction in existing total cost, the market area served can be profitably expanded. Large savings in cost can convert marginal markets into profitable markets for the individual firm. On the other side of the coin, manufacturers who use inefficient physical distribution methods are penalized by their reduced ability to penetrate geographically distant markets. If costs continue to rise, as they have during the last ten years, manufacturers with inefficient physical distribution systems will be forced to service a shrinking geographic market. It is interesting to note that even Wall Street financial analysts are becoming concerned with corporate physical distribution philosophies and procedures as one part of total analysis of the firm as a potential investment.[7]

Another alternative is that working capital released through the design and implementation of a more efficient physical distribution system can be devoted to other areas of the business. For example, funds can be diverted into new product development, marketing research, plant modernization, and so on. In summary, it appears that the profit squeeze of recent years coupled with increased competition has led many businesses to explore the alternatives of physical distribution cost reduction as a means of protecting their profit position. This is in marked contrast to the period in the 1950's where sales expansion and new product introduction were considered the best methods of maintaining the profit position of the firm. Funds saved through more effective physical distribution can be, and often are, diverted to

[7]Robert Hall, "Wall Street Looks at Physical Distribution." A paper presented at the Spring Conference of the National Council of Physical Distribution Management, April, 1965.

strengthening the overall marketing program either by tapping new geographic markets or by funneling additional funds into project development and marketing research efforts.

Supplier-Customer Relationships. The development of improved distribution systems or distribution methods by either customers or suppliers appears to have a generally beneficial effect upon the entire channel. Recently the Quaker Oats Company published a pamphlet for the retail trade entitled "Palletized Shipment from the Quaker Oats Company." In addition to outlining the advantages of palletized shipments, the publication included a "Buyer's Guide to Ordering" and a "Warehouseman's Guide to Handling Palletized Shipment."[8] Most large companies that embark on a comprehensive distribution program develop a physical distribution service division with the primary mission of coordinating customer systems with supplier systems. In some instances these departments act as consultants on customer problems. In such a service, customers are provided with ideals and help that usually result in cost savings. Hopefully, as a result of this coordinated effort, the relationship between the supplier and customer is strengthened.

An integrated physical distribution system will frequently require close cooperation between customer and supplier in such things as palletized unit loads, disposable pallets, and returnable containers. One promising new development is the experimental application of direct computer hookups between suppliers and large customers for full integration of forecasting, ordering, shipment, and inventory control.[9]

In summary, an effective physical distribution program at the supplier level can lead to a strengthening of ties with customers in the channel. Strengthening of relationships is achieved (1) physically, through the use of interchangeable equipment such as pallets and containers; (2) through the expansion of consulting services to the customer from the supplier; or (3) by the supplier's interest in making his customers more profitable.

An Example of Marketing-Physical Distribution Interaction

An illustration drawn from a case in the marketing of cut flowers may clarify the relationship of overall marketing and physical distribution.

A major production area for cut flowers is centered around California. In some cases, the blossom is considered a by-product of bulb production and therefore may be sold at relatively low prices and still yield a profit. Deterioration begins immediately after cutting. As a result, some method of blossom preservation must be applied immediately. The abundance of local

---

[8]"Palletized Shipping from the Quaker Oats Company," *Quaker Oats Company*, Chicago, 1967. A number of other companies including Pillsbury, Corning Glass, and Bobbie Brooks have developed similar types of customer programs.

[9]"Communications," *Modern Materials Handling*, January, 1967, pp. 53.

production creates an over-supply and thus requires sales to more distant markets. The only acceptable method of transportation over long distances is air freight because of rapid product deterioration. The "normal" channel of distribution for flowers has been the flower shop, which sells in traditional sprays, bunches, or dozens.

The problem of deterioration was solved by designing a special container that (a) precools blossoms as they are cut in the fields, (b) holds trays of flowers in different quantities, (c) fits aircraft dimensions, and (d) has good handling characteristics. Through expeditious handling, each container may be delivered the next morning to almost any point in the United States.

Flower shops were eliminated as a method of distribution, because they did not achieve the mass consumer exposure required to sell the stock rapidly. Department stores and food chains were selected as the final means of distribution. Large numbers of customers moving more or less regularly through each outlet were exposed to the product. The flower shop with its emphasis on marriage, funeral, and special-occasion orders did not seem to fit mass marketing requirements. But these traditional outlets could experience increased sales if consumers could be induced to buy flowers more or less regularly. The size of the untapped market was indicated by a study, which showed that only 2.5 percent of all families regularly had flowers in the home. It was considered extremely unlikely that traditional flower shops could reach any substantial portion of the untapped market.

One of the apparent resistances to regular flower purchases, as indicated in the market study, was the high unit price. This difficulty was overcome by abandoning the sales unit of a dozen. Instead, the number of flowers in a selling unit was aimed at bringing down the purchase price per package. Roses, for example, were sold in groups of three. Once the size of the sales unit was established, flowers were packed, at the field where they were cut, in the quantity of units desired.

The next problem was to induce the retailer to stock the product. At this point, flowers competed with other products for the limited floor space available. The net revenue contribution of flowers had to meet competition from existing products carried in the store. Two steps were taken to solve this problem. First, a case that would hold standard trays of cut flowers was designed to minimize use of floor space and to increase sales turnover and gross margins to the retailer. The second step was to induce the retailer to place the flowers near the end of the route that a customer would normally follow in the store. It had been discovered that, as a customer entered the store, planned purchases tended to overshadow impulse buying. The longer the duration of the customer's stay in the store, the more likely was the occurrence of impulse purchases. This characteristic was especially apparent in large food stores. Therefore, every attempt was made to induce the retailer to place flowers near prime impulse locations along the shopping route.

Thus, the physical distribution approach to this particular marketing problem resulted in a new method of distribution and marketing for the product. In some cases, this might result in a loss of trade to outlets by-passed in the new marketing program. However, here it appears that the traditional method of marketing may have benefited by introducing flowers to consumers who otherwise would have been permanently out of the market.

Market Forces Influencing Physical Distribution

During post-World War II, a number of market forces emerged that have an impact upon effective physical distribution management. This section briefly summarizes the more important market forces influencing the rate and nature of increased interest in physical distribution management by business firms. Many of the factors are developed in more detail in other sections.

GEOGRAPHIC SHIFTS

The marketplace is dynamic and constantly shifting in geography as workers, firms, and government seek to gain strategic and operational advantage. In recent years, the state of California outstripped the state of New York as the nation's most populous state. New industrial complexes have developed in the South and Southwest to take advantage of lower-priced resources. As concentrations of consumers or industrial users geographically shift within the marketplace, the physical distribution system of the firm must be adjusted to maintain an effective balance between customer service and costs.

NEW PRODUCT DEVELOPMENT

To maintain sales volume and profit position, most firms find it necessary to introduce new products regularly. In 1950, the average supermarket carried approximately 3,750 items in stock. By 1966, the number of items carried in stock more than doubled. This product proliferation experience of the supermarket is typical of most consumer and industrial markets. The net effect of expanded product line is an increase in the complexity and the scope of the logistics task. For example, consider the problem of the tobacco manufacturers. Prior to 1940, six major national brands accounted for over 90 percent of national sales. Today there are over 70 national brands with new product introductions occurring almost monthly. With this explosion in the number of brands, stock-outs, inventory investment, shipment size, and decentralized placement of inventory arise as serious physical distribution problems.

TRANSPORT AND UNIT-LOADING TECHNOLOGY

New technology in transportation, unit loading, and closely related functions continually causes business firms to re-evaluate the adequacy of present operations. The new interstate highway system has shortened both the time and cost of motor carrier movement of goods to the marketplace and of raw materials movement to the production site. The appearance of multilevel rail cars for auto transport significantly shifted the carrier selection for the distribution of new automobiles. Containerization, developments in packaging, and material handling innovations have introduced unit loading as a standard method of product movement. The introduction of specifically designed jet air freighters has caused shifts in finished goods and raw materials flow. New products, new applications, and new technology have caused alterations in cost, and management must constantly monitor innovations that will allow lower costs and/or improve customer service.

INTERNATIONAL MARKETING

Improvements in physical distribution technology have helped develop an emerging world market for United States products and services. This world market is two-sided, because the same developments make it possible for foreign businesses to compete for a share of the United States domestic market. As a result of this expanding market, the demands on physical distribution have considerably broadened. For example, it is not unusual for a company to purchase raw materials from one country and subassemblies from another, to assemble finished products in a third country's freeport, and then to export for sale in a fourth country. With variations in export-import documentation and regulation, carrier availability and reliability, taxes and business regulation, international physical distribution is a formidable task.

COMPETITION

In addition to multinational competition, a substantial increase in tempo between domestic firms has also developed in consumer and industrial markets. The increasing cost of new product introduction raises the cost of failure. One manufacturer recently spent 15 million dollars to launch a new consumer product. With this stake in the success of a new product, a manufacturer cannot afford failure in its logistical support. A soundly developed and administered physical distribution system also offers a means to gain advantages over competition in terms of delivery service. This is particularly true in industrial markets or in markets where there are alternatives between competitive products. In this sense, a superior physical distribution system provides a competitive tool for the firm.

CHANNEL PRESSURES

Institutions in the channel of distribution may be viewed as a competitive system with each element in the system attempting to gain an advantage over other channel members. For example, retailers would like instant delivery of mixed small orders and the highest possible margins and allowances. Wholesalers on the other hand would prefer to deliver large orders and enjoy the highest possible margins for their service.

The extent to which any member of the channel can exert pressure to achieve its objectives at the expense of other channel members depends upon economic power of the firm and government regulation of competitive and cooperative relationships. As the structure of distribution changes and middlemen at all levels in the channel become more scientific in their management of the physical distribution, some increased pressures can be expected to occur. For example, there is currently a great deal of pressure to push inventory stocks back from the retailer to the manufacturer. Some manufacturers are being pressured to locate inventory stocks in major metropolitan areas for daily replenishment of wholesalers and retailers. Other manufacturers have been forced to change case sizes, pallet sizes, shipment sizes, and carrier modes and schedules to meet customer needs more closely. These concepts and problems are discussed in more detail in Chapter 3.

General Foods: Distribution-Sales Service Division

It is appropriate to end the chapter with an example of the interrelationship between logistics and marketing, as structured by the General Foods Corporation. In Exhibit 1 excerpts from a description of the function and service goals of General Foods Distribution-Sales Service Division (D-SSD) are presented. Several significant points should be noted. First, the general description of the mission of D-SSD is clearly one of physical distribution support of the firm's marketing objectives. A second interesting factor is that the customer service standards are expressed in market-focused terms, and the performance of the division is measured in terms of customer service standards. Careful coordination between sales and physical distribution is maintained through a computerized information system and by location of the sales divisional offices in key distribution warehouses in the network.

EXHIBIT 1

The Role of the General Foods Distribution-Sales Service Division

The Distribution-Sales Services Division serves all of General Foods' domestic divisions doing business with grocery, institutional and military customers. The

International Division is also served by moving domestic grocery products and bilingual packs through the system to ports of embarkation.

GF management has designated D-SSD as the single, unified organization representing the company to customers in the areas of physical distribution and sales services. In essence, the services D-SSD provides include, but are not limited to, the functions necessary to complete a sale once a customer's order has been taken, plus service activities in support of the operating divisions' field sales organizations. Additionally, D-SSD has been assigned corporate responsibility for certain distribution, credit and sales accounting activities.

It is the division's goal to provide highly efficient and effective distribution and sales services for General Foods divisions and their domestic grocery, military and institutional customers. Attaining this objective requires a continuing search to identify and evaluate opportunities to provide constantly and significantly improved customer service. It also requires the division to build flexibility into its methods of operation and to remain alert to, and provide for, rapid and far-reaching changes in both customer and GF requirements.

Economical performance that meets or exceeds established standards is the division's objective for internal administrative and warehousing functions. In considering improvements in functions related to customer service, the potential value of the service to General Foods is always measured in relation to its cost.

D-SSD's responsibilities as the service organization for all domestic divisions include the administration of the Market-Centered Customer Service Plan. This plan is built around five basic guarantees to customers:
1. Individualized customer service.
2. Rapid and reliable order-taking and delivery procedures; prompt and accurate shipping and handling of GF products.
3. Receipt of products by customers on a dependable, rapid basis.
4. Ready and complete information on the status of orders, shipments, and related activities.
5. Greater inventory turnover with lower capital investment and reduced warehouse apace for customers.

D-SSD Standards of Performance

Customer orders received prior to 10 A.M. will be shipped the next workday. Customer emergency orders will be shipped the same day if possible.

All Bracket I, II and III orders are expedited to assure rapid, reliable delivery to customers. The performance standard is 90% or better on-time delivery to customers. (Because of the size of the shipment, it is not always possible to deliver back orders within the time specified for the delivery of original orders.)
1. The maximum rail transit time from the Distribution Service-Distribution Center to customers is three days. Performance is measured against the individual one-, two-, or three-day standard established for each customer.
2. Truck transit time from the DSDC to customers is one day.

Invoices are mailed to customers the workday following shipment.

Credits, promotional funds, and other payments to customers will be issued to meet the following standards:
1. Adjustments to invoices — two days after requirement is identified.
2. Credit memoranda and checks resulting from price declines — four days from date of decline.
3. Credit memoranda and checks for participation in promotions — five days from receipt of supporting data.

Issuance of timely and accurate sales, inventory and financial reports in accordance with established report schedules.

Summary

To fully implement the marketing concept, the business firm must produce a product that meets customer needs and physically move the product from the point of production to the point of consumption in a convenient and efficient manner. During the past two decades, management's attitude toward physical distribution has evolved from a passive, fragmented approach to one of systems integration. Further, the integrated system is viewed by an increasing number of companies as an important tool in the competitive struggle for market position.

In the following chapter, the dynamics of marketing interaction from a channel perspective are explored. The functions and structure of marketing channels are identified and analyzed within a logistical framework

Discussion Questions

1. Why is physical distribution important to the marketing program of a firm?

2. What types of costs may be incurred as a result of an inefficient physical distribution system? Which of these is the most damaging to an enterprise?

3. Is there any connection between promotion and physical distribution?

4. What effect does physical distribution have on price?

5. Assume that a firm has a ratio 10 percent profit to sales. How much would it be willing to expend to effect a $100,000 savings on distribution? A $10,000 savings?

6. Why would a geographical shift of consumers cause a change on a firm's cost and service standards?

7. Could a firm's distribution system ever be dictated to it by a customer? A supplier? A middleman? Explain, with examples of situations.

CHAPTER 3 Distribution Channels

and Exchange Action

ONE of the least understood areas of business centers around institutions and activities normally grouped under the encompassing labels of distribution or marketing channels. A great deal of descriptive material has been written about the purpose and functions of institutions normally found in distribution channels. In contrast, the literature is less abundant in terms of comprehensive treatments of channel dynamics, structure, and strategy.[1] At the outset it is clear that the distribution channel is of fundamental importance to a treatment of physical distribution, because the channel is the arena within which marketing and logistics culminate into customer transactions. Therefore, for a proper understanding of physical distribution, one should develop a sound insight into the overall nature of total distribution channels. Although this chapter does not present a comprehensive treatment of channels, it does provide sufficient development for purposes of describing the inter-relationship of physical distribution management to channel selection.

The initial section of this chapter is concerned with a broad discussion of differences in traditional distribution channel treatment between those concerned with marketing as contrasted to those with a physical distribution focus. Next, attention is directed to a discussion of channel structure. A general structural classification of channels is developed based upon separation of transaction and exchange activities. Given structure, the next section moves to a treatment of functions that must be performed by the total

[1]In the opinions of the authors, several notable exceptions exist, *i.e.*, Richard Clewett, ed., *Marketing Channels* (Homewood, Ill.: Richard D. Irwin, Inc., 1954); Roland Vaile, E. T. Grether, and Reavis Cox, *Marketing In The American Economy* (New York: The Ronald Press Co., 1952); Wroe Alderson, *Marketing Behavior and Executive Action* (Homewood, Ill.: Richard D. Irwin, Inc., 1957); and Bruce E. Mallen, ed., *The Marketing Channel* (New York: John Wiley and Sons, Inc., 1967).

exchange channel in the overall marketing process. Essential to this functional development is a consideration of interfirm relations with respect to total channel considerations. All channel members need not play an equally aggressive part in functional activities nor engage in equal risk. Thus, the final section of this chapter is devoted to a treatment of total channel direction with respect to tactics and strategy.

Traditional Development of Channel Structure

Considerable difference exists between the way in which distribution channels are normally treated by those concerned with marketing management in contrast to those who have a major interest in physical distribution. Neither traditional approach constitutes an adequate structure for physical distribution planning.

TYPICAL PHYSICAL DISTRIBUTION APPROACH TO DISTRIBUTION CHANNELS

The physical distribution of any product requires the utilization of corporate facilities and/or intermediary specialists. By definition, a facility is considered a company-owned and -operated unit engaged in the performance of all or some part of the physical distribution process. Thus, a distribution warehouse or a company-operated truck constitutes a distribution facility. However, either may also have the status of intermediary specialists.[2] For example, the warehouse may be of a public variety, and the truck may be owned and operated by a common carrier. The intermediary specialist is an independent business operated for profit. In the design of a physical distribution system, the services of an intermediary specialist can be substituted for those of a company facility. The objective is to select the proper combination of facilities and specialists to meet objectives at the lowest total cost.

One serious deficiency of the traditional physical distribution approach to system development is that planning considerations are limited to the individual firm. A second deficiency results from a general subordination of physical distribution specialists to those intermediaries selected for reasons of marketing competence. Each of these deficiencies is discussed in turn.

Deficiency of Legal Limits. Traditional physical distribution planning seldom extends beyond the legal boundaries of the firm because normal control and profit measurement end when the product is transferred to a new owner. Depending upon conditions and terms of sale, legal ownership ex-

---

[2]The term *middleman* is more commonly used in marketing literature. The authors prefer the use of the term *intermediary* because in the development that follows the role of specialists in the distribution channel is expanded beyond those normally classified as marketing middlemen.

change is normally accomplished immediately before or after the final physical transfer of the product. However, in some special cases such as consignment selling, a product's physical exchange may be completed long before the actual legal exchange.

The problem is expanded by the fact that physical distribution of a product does not end once ownership transfer occurs. It does not end when the product is turned over to the next level or firm in the distribution channel or even when it is delivered to a buyer unless all conditions of the transaction are satisfied. Ultimate responsibility for physical distribution does not end until the product in question is totally accepted by the person, family, or firm that will utilize it. All practitioners of physical distribution will agree that a product is not fully distributed until no additional physical transfer is possible. Some of the most difficult physical distribution problems are those of handling and moving return products. Such products may be returned for damage, improper performance, or even late delivery. Therefore, to properly direct physical distribution activities, planning horizons must transcend the total distribution channel.

Many significant costs of physical distribution occur between firms engaged in a distribution channel. To a large extent the control of such costs may rest with an intermediary specialist who has very little risk or vested interest in the overall success of the marketing and physical distribution process. For example, an infrequently used common carrier who actually takes 20 days to transfer a shipment scheduled for three-day delivery and who makes final delivery in split quantities of the original shipment may substantially increase total distribution costs.

In addition, a great many costs of physical distribution may accumulate by duplicate effort at various levels within a channel. Such duplication increases the cost of total marketing, thereby either influencing product price or channel participant profit. Activities on the part of one firm in a channel arrangement may be justified on the basis of that firm's cost control program, while at the same time such activities may increase the costs of all other firms in the channel and seriously hinder the ability of the total channel to survive. Physical distribution planning must be channel-wide in perspective.

As indicated above, the main reason for a firm's limitation of physical distribution considerations to legal boundaries results from control and profit measurement. Perhaps of the two, desire and capability of control is the primary reason. When a firm limits consideration to controllable limits within a channel, they, in effect, operate under conditions of vertical integration. In short, the physical distribution system is designed to include only vertically controlled operations.[3]

_____

[3]The term *vertically controlled* is adopted to describe a situation in which the next link of a channel is operationally controlled through purchase relationships to the extent that two independent firms function as a single entity — for example, the use of a public warehouse as an intermediary specialist.

In system design, captive facilities are controlled, because they represent a geographical extension of general office authority. Specialized intermediaries are controlled to various degrees through service purchase contracts and obligations. The activities of both can readily be subordinated and coordinated to overall performance of the firm's physical distribution system. Such control is normally severed when ownership transfer occurs. This deficiency of legal limits may be detrimental to all parties concerned.

Deficiency of Intermediary Selection. The second main deficiency in physical distribution treatment of channels evolves from the overall tendency to utilize the same specialized intermediary selected for reasons of marketing competence. Traditionally, when a firm decided to locate a branch or district sales office, it was almost axiomatic that a field inventory would also be located at the facility. If a firm selected a market plan to utilize a specific wholesaler, it was normally assumed that the same wholesaler would inventory a full line of the firm's product assortment. The designs of physical systems to support marketing systems, in more cases than not, have traditionally been identical with respect to specialized intermediaries.

The deficiency of this single structure system stems from the fact that a very effective marketing intermediary may not be either an effective or an efficient physical distribution intermediary. It is generally acknowledged that the successful marketing of a firm's product may require a wide range of different channels to effectively reach different market segments.[4] Utilizing the same structure for logistical flows has the inherent weakness of forcing small uneconomical shipments upon the physical distribution system. Substantial economies of scale and related advantages exist in physical flow. In later chapters such considerations will represent important factors in distribution system design. At this point it is sufficient to point out that the most suitable structure for marketing channels may not, and often is not, satisfactory for physical distribution channels.

TYPICAL MARKETING APPROACH TO DISTRIBUTION CHANNELS

Unlike those concerned with physical distribution, marketing has traditionally acknowledged that distribution channels consist of a fantastically complex network of organizations grouped together in a variety of combinations.[5] The American Marketing Association defined the distribution channel as the structure of intracompany organization units and extra-

---

[4]For a discussion of physical distribution complexity when markets become highly segmented see Thomas A. Staudt and Donald A. Taylor, *A Managerial Introduction To Marketing* (Englewood Cliffs, N. J.: Prentice Hall, Inc., 1965), p. 157.

[5]This point is well developed in Schuyler F. Otteson, William G. Panschar, and James M. Patterson, *Marketing* (New York: The Macmillan Company, 1964), pp. 302–22.

company agents and dealers, wholesale and retail, through which a commodity, product, or service is marketed.[6] Others have defined the distribution channel as a grouping of intermediaries from first owner to last owner, who take title to a product during the marketing process.[7]

The main advantage of the overall marketing approach is the basic acknowledgment of the complex process of marketing and the existence of a wide variety of organizational relationships. Each organization linked in a distribution channel exists for a reason and performs services in anticipation of a return on investment and effort. The marketing task is never considered complete until the final owner has been satisfied with respect to pretransaction anticipations. In fact, a considerable degree of marketing effort centers around measurement of pretransaction anticipations and post-transaction satisfactions. Thus, marketing horizons are not limited by legal boundaries of the firm. It is the basic acknowledgment of a wider spectrum of planning and the realistic approach to interorganizational relationships that renders the marketing approach to channel structure superior to single firm physical distribution planning. The marketing approach eliminates the limitation of dealing only with vertically controlled systems.

Four general approaches have been employed to study and describe channels by marketing writers: (1) descriptive institutional, (2) graphic, (3) commodity groupings, and (4) functional. A fifth and newer grouping, behavorial, will be treated later in the chapter. Although the first four groups are to various degrees concerned with structure as a primary focal point, the newer behavorial contributions expand structural considerations into a comprehensive treatment of interfirm strategies and relationships.

Descriptive Institutional.   The descriptive institutional approach to distribution channels identifies the many participants who may be found within a channel structure. Such institutions are grouped with respect to the marketing services they perform. A complete listing of all intermediaries and traditional classification is found in Appendix 3A to this chapter. As one would expect, considerable differences exist in the type of institution employed in the marketing of consumer, industrial, and government products. Considerable differences in intermediary selection also exist between the marketing of products and services.

Those who have undertaken research into the various institutions of marketing generally acknowledge that the broad classifications of wholesaling and retailing are descriptive of the structure within which marketing is accomplished. Naturally, the wholesale structure is substantially different among industrial, agricultural, and consumer products. In addition, various categories of middlemen do not fall into a strict definition of either retailer or wholesaler. In an effort to prescribe when various institutions should be

---

[6]American Marketing Association, *Marketing Definitions.*
[7]Theodore N. Beckman and William R. Davidson, *Marketing* (New York: Ronald Press Company, 1962), p. 44.

CHART 3–1 Typical Channels of Distribution

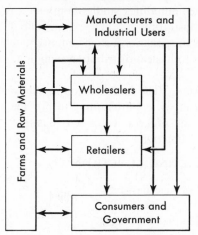

utilized, the basic descriptive institutional approach to channels has been expanded into the other treatments introduced below. Every student of marketing and physical distribution should have a detailed understanding of the institutional approach, because it serves as the basis for all other ways of studying channel structure.

Graphic. In an effort to identify the flow of title of raw materials and finished products, a useful technique utilized in marketing has been the development of flow graphs. Such graphs illustrate the range of alternatives in institutional selection at all levels of the marketing process.

Chart 3–1 illustrates the many different title levels products or raw materials may pass through between original owner and final buyer. For example, retail stores may purchase from all levels of supply ranging from farm to wholesalers. Several of the neat classification lines illustrated in Chart 3–1 have been reduced by the expanding tendency toward scrambled merchandising. What was once considered a wholesaler may now be a retailer as well as a wholesaler. Retailers and manufacturers in turn have assumed many traditional duties of wholesalers. This extension of activities has been referred to as integrated wholesaling.[8] Under integrated wholesaling, the retail operation performs the functions traditionally performed by the wholesale intermediary.

The main advantage of graphs is that they illustrate the many links engaged in modern marketing. By the use of graphs the multiplicity of institutions are focused into logical sequence. However, the simplicity of flow diagrams tends to understate some complexities of designing the proper channel structure for an individual firm.

Commodity Groupings. In an effort to limit the range of considerations in channel planning, several studies have been completed with the objective

[8]For a full discussion see *Ibid.*, pp. 348–64.

of defining in detail channel structure for specific commodities.[9] Generally empirical in nature, commodities studies combine a description of institutions with a graphic illustration of primary ownership flows.[10] Although they are very useful in specific situations, such commodity channel treatments are too specific for general physical distribution planning.

Functional Treatments.   The functional approach to channel structure has developed as a result of writers attempting to provide a logical explanation of the overall marketing process. Table 3–1 illustrates the most commonly agreed upon listing of functions.

TABLE 3–1   MARKETING FUNCTIONS[11]

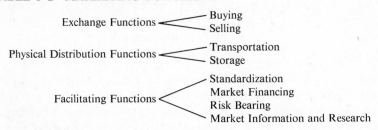

In general, a function in a marketing sense represents a major economic activity that must be performed to some degree in the marketing of all products. In the marketing of many products, a given function may be performed by a number of different institutions and intermediaries between the points of original sale and final sale. For example, storage may be performed by a producer, wholesaler, retailer, and even a user. On the other hand, market financing might be performed by only one institution in the total process of marketing a given product. Beckman and Davidson[12] have summarized these functional relationships as follows:

> Marketing has been defined as a process — one in which no person or institution is self-sufficient. It involves many participants and consists of various functional components. One must consider each of these functions and their interrelationships to understand the totality of the process.

The functional approach to marketing provides a framework for evaluation of alternate channel structures with respect to total channel capability.

Initial listing of marketing functions have been greatly expanded by subsequent developments of functional analysis. Functional analysis concentrates upon the interrelation of various functions in the total marketing process. Particularly noteworthy are the developments of Alderson with respect to the

---

[9]See Clewett, *op. cit.*

[10]Albert W. Frey, ed., *Marketing Handbook*, 2nd ed. (New York: Ronald Press Company, 1965), p. 20–25.

[11]Adapted from Beckman and Davidson, *op. cit.*, p. 390.

[12]*Ibid.*

CHART 3–2   Alderson's Process of Sorting

Sorting Out ⟶ Accumulation ⟶ Allocation ⟶ Assortment

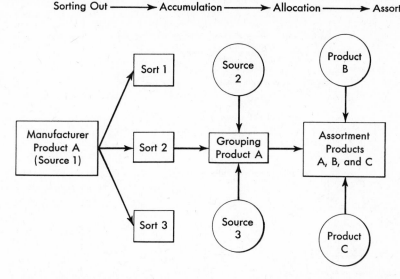

role of middlemen in the marketing process.[13] The essential role of marketing intermediary is, in the Alderson treatment, one of reconciling a narrow conglomeration of products from any one source into a wide assortment at the point of final sales. This involves several steps, which can be best accomplished by a specialized middleman.

The entire marketing process of changing conglomerations to assortments was labeled sorting in the Alderson treatment.[14] The marketing channel serves to perform the sorting activity which consists of four steps.

The initial step involves the sorting out of large conglomerations and results in one large supply being reclassified into smaller lots of various types of goods according to the requirements of the sorter. Next, a larger supply, perhaps from different locations, is accumulated over a period of time to provide a larger grouping of specialized but homogeneous goods. The third step in the sorting process consists of allocation. In allocation the total supply is apportioned either within corporate facilities or among market outlets. Finally, assorting takes place which constitutes the building of individual supplies into a combination of different products or an assortment in accordance with an anticipated pattern of demand. Alderson's process of sorting is illustrated in Chart 3–2. In Chart 3–2 the four aspects of sorting are illustrated in the sequence most commonly found in the marketing process.

Staudt and Taylor[15] have built upon Alderson's concept of sorting and have generalized three principles that justify the existence of marketing inter-

[13]Alderson, *op. cit.*, pp. 195–227.
[14]*Ibid.*
[15]Staudt and Taylor, *op. cit.*, pp. 223–26.

CHART 3–3   Principle of Minimum Total Transactions

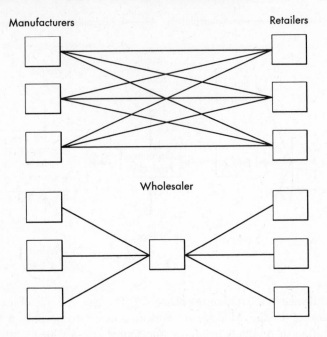

mediaries: (1) the principle of minimum total transactions, (2) the principle of massed reserves, and (3) the principle of proximity.

The principle of minimum total transactions acknowledges that the total process of sorting is reduced by having a limited number of middlemen. This principle has wide application in finished goods and agricultural commodity distribution. In essence, the principle advocates specialization in the marketing process. Chart 3–3 illustrates the principle of minimum total transactions.

The principle of massed reserves is concerned with the storage of goods in the distribution channel. Staudt and Taylor acknowledge that goods in the form of inventories exist at each stop in the concentration and dispersion of goods. Such stops are defined as the producer level, accumulation level, assortment level, and the household. They conclude that the amount of goods in inventory when intermediaries are used is less than would otherwise be required.[16] This principle assumes exacting inventory control and consistent product delivery.

The principle of proximity states that the specialized intermediary should be located closer to the market place. Close proximity provides better positioning to render final assortments in a manner most satisfactory and timely to market demands.

In total, the three principles provide credence to the inclusion of a specialized intermediary in the channel of distribution.

[16]*Ibid.*, p. 224.

Deficiency of Marketing Treatments. It should be apparent from the brief review of marketing approaches to channel structure that they overcome the limitations of typical physical distribution treatments and move toward a systematic analysis of the complex situation that exists. However, marketing approaches have some limitations with respect to physical distribution planning.

Two primary kinds of transactions take place between intermediaries in a distribution channel. One is the physical exchange of products, and the other is the legal exchange of title. A product may never move physically, although legal ownership changes hands several times. This is particularly true of an agricultural commodity as demonstrated by the grain markets. On the other hand, a product may be handled many times within a single corporation, even moving across the entire nation, without changing legal ownership.

It appears clear that the specialized institutions most capable of performing marketing functions may differ from those desired for performance of physical distribution activities. The typical scheme of marketing institutions provides no allowance for the existence of a very important class of physical distribution intermediaries — common, contract, and exempt transportation carriers. For example, the functional role of a public warehouse as an accumulation and dispersion intermediary is most often subordinated to the role of the storage specialist in marketing treatments. Thus, an integration of traditional marketing and physical distribution treatments is essential to the study of business logistics.

Channel Structure

The term structure is widely used to describe a number of interrelationships which are part of but subordinate to the whole.[17] In distribution channels, structure relates to the framework for classification of basic flows, which pass through the channel. A careful delineation of primary flows provides the basis for specialization of effort within the channel structure. In addition, it provides a logical framework to guide physical distribution planning.

THE CONCEPT OF SEPARATION

Several authors have developed the idea of flow separation within the overall structure of the distribution channel.[18] The present approach singles

[17]For a detailed discussion of marketing channel structure see Kenneth R. Davis, *Marketing Management* (New York: Ronald Press Company, 1961), pp. 131–3.

[18]In particular Vaile, Grether, and Cox, *op. cit.*; Ralph F. Breyer, "Some Observations on Structural Formation and the Growth of Marketing Channels," in Reavis Cox, Wroe Alderson, and Stanley J. Shapiro, eds., *Theory In Marketing* (Homewood, Ill.: Richard D. Irwin, Inc., 1964), pp. 163–75; and George Fisk, *Marketing Systems* (New York: Harper & Row, 1967), pp. 214–79.

out two flows. To accomplish a satisfactory marketing process, a flow of transaction-creating efforts and a flow of physical fulfillment efforts must exist and be coordinated. There is no logical reason why these two flows must sequentially transpire through the same network of intermediaries. These two flows — physical fulfillment and transaction creating — are considered primary; all other flows in the total distribution channel are considered secondary.

J. R. Commons differentiated elements of bargaining transaction in contrast with the process of physical exchange.[19] He viewed the bargaining transaction as containing three essential steps: (1) negotiation, i.e., reaching a satisfactory agreement; (2) contract, i.e., establishment of obligations; and (3) administration, i.e., performance of obligations. In the Commons scheme, exchange was viewed as the mechanical and labor process of physical delivery.[20]

The logic for separation of exchange fulfillment and transaction creation is based on the notion that no positive legal or economic laws require a simultaneous treatment or performance. Factors that tend to increase or decrease the total cost of physical flow have no real relationship to ownership boundaries, only an artificial one. Conversely, advertising, credit, personal selling, and other transaction-creating efforts of marketing have little influence upon the economics of physical flow. The responsiveness of each primary flow to specialization is unique to the circumstances surrounding that flow. In any given marketing situation, primary flows may best be accomplished by different middlemen. The most effective network for achieving profitable transactions may not be the most efficient arrangement of exchange intermediaries. Based upon specialization in primary flow, the total distribution channel is classified as containing transaction and exchange channels.

The transaction channel consists of a grouping of intermediaries engaged in the establishment of trading. The goal of the transaction channel is to negotiate, to contract, and to administer trading on a continuing basis. Thus, the full force of creative marketing action exists within the transaction channel. Participants in transaction channel activities are marketing specialists such as manufacturing agents, salesmen, jobbers, wholesalers, and retailers.

The exchange channel contains a network of intermediaries engaged in the functions of physical movement. Participants in the exchange channel are physical distribution specialists. Their concern is one of solving problems of time and space at a total expenditure consistent to trading specifications.

EXAMPLES OF SEPARATION

Chart 3–4 illustrates the concept of separation for the distribution of color television sets. In this situation the transaction channel consists of five links:

---

[19]John R. Commons, *The Economics of Collective Action* (New York: The Macmillan Co., 1950), p. 53.
[20]*Ibid.*, p. 45.

CHART 3–4　Distribution Channel — Exchange and Transaction Separation

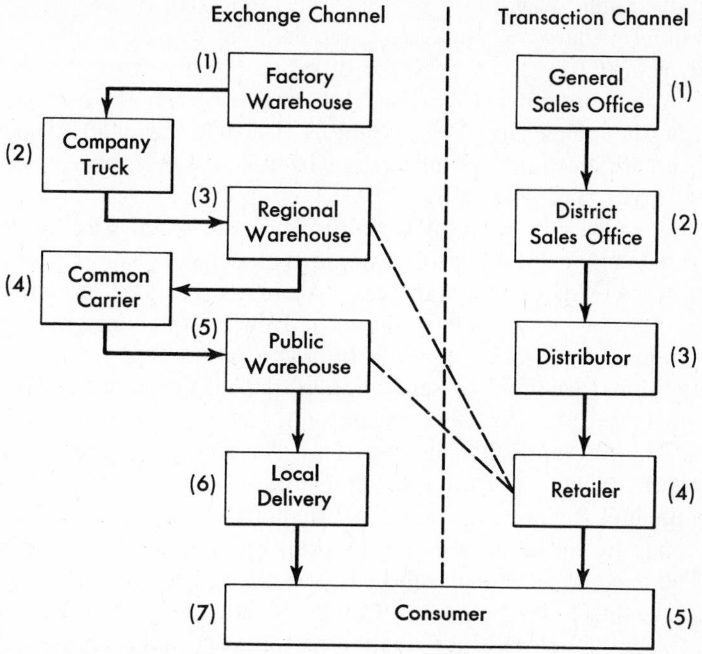

Exchange Channel　　｜　　Transaction Channel

(1) Factory Warehouse
(2) Company Truck
(3) Regional Warehouse
(4) Common Carrier
(5) Public Warehouse
(6) Local Delivery
(7) Consumer

General Sales Office (1)
District Sales Office (2)
Distributor (3)
Retailer (4)
Consumer (5)

(1) general sales office, (2) district sales office, (3) distributor, (4) retailer, and (5) consumer. The exchange channel design consists of seven links: (1) factory warehouse, (2) company truck, (3) regional warehouse, (4) common carrier motor, (5) public warehouse, (6) local delivery, and (7) consumer. Only at the point of final transaction completion, the consumer's home, do the two primary channels merge.

Chart 3–4 also illustrates additional significant points. Concerning the exchange channel, three different specialized intermediaries are engaged in the physical distribution of the product. These three specialists are at level 4, a common carrier motor firm; level 5, a public warehouse; and level 6, a specialized local delivery firm. Three levels of physical distribution take place in the exchange channel utilizing organizational facilities of the producing firm. The TV sets in question are warehoused at the factory, transported in company trucks, and stored in a regional warehouse before any specialized intermediary ever participates in the exchange channel.

The distributor, link 3 in the transaction channel, plays a unique role. He never physically handles the TV sets; however, he has legal title from the time they depart the company warehouse (link 4, exchange channel) until they are delivered to the consumer. Of course, the distributor could elect to warehouse in his own facility, but his preference is to use a public warehouse specialist to service the needs of all his retailers.

The retailer illustrated is only one of many who sell the line of TV sets. He displays limited sets offering next day delivery to consumers who enter into a transaction. Delivery is then made from the distributors stock being held in the public warehouse utilizing the services of a specialized local delivery intermediary. When sets are required for display in the retailer's store, they may be obtained by the distributor from either the factory's regional warehouse (link 3, exchange channel) or from his own stock in storage at the public warehouse (link 5, exchange channel). These two possibilities are illustrated as connections between the two channels utilizing common carrier transportation.

Retailers commonly limit stocks to display models. Sales are negotiated based on a commitment to deliver a specified model and color at a particular time and place. Although the transaction is initiated at a retail store, physical exchange may be completed by shipment from a warehouse strategically located many miles from the point of transaction.

An additional example of separation is the factory branch office that carries no inventory. The office exists for the sole purpose of transaction creation. The physical exchange between seller and buyer may move in a variety of combinations of transport and storage depending upon the value, the size, the bulk, the weight, and the perishability of the shipment. Generally no economic justification exists for locating warehouses with each branch office. The network of branch offices is best selected to facilitate maximum transaction impact. The selection of exchange intermediaries is designed to achieve the desired physical distribution performance and economies.

A final example of separation comes from the rapidly growing mail order industry. An order placed at a local catalog desk may be shipped from a distant factory direct to the buyer's home. Although the flow pattern described is only one of many observable arrangements in mail order, all such systems are designed to create separation and thereby the opportunity for specialization.

INTERDEPENDENCE OF TRANSACTION AND EXCHANGE ACTIONS

The concept of separation of transaction flows and exchange flows should not be interpreted to mean that either can stand alone. Both must be completed as the basis for a satisfactory sale; both are essential to the marketing process. The main argument for separation of transaction and exchange is that it increases the structural opportunities for development of specialization.

Separation does not necessarily require separate legal enterprises to enjoy the benefits of specialization. The same intermediary may be very capable of performing both transaction and exchange. Many wholesalers successfully combine the performance of both flows. The degree of individual enterprise separation depends upon the necessity for specialization, economies of scale, available resources, and managerial capabilities.

Transactions are never complete until physical exchange is fully administered. Depending upon the category of goods — convenience, shopping, or speciality — the exchange process may start in anticipation of, be simultaneous with, or follow after actual negotiation is initiated.[21] The final exchange act occurs in accord with specifications established during the negotiation phase of the transaction. Such exchange specifications relate to time, location, or terms of transfer. Given any set of specifications, minimizations of exchange expense is essential to achieve a mutually satisfactory transaction.

Contributions of efficient exchange are not limited to cost reduction. By achieving time and place utility, exchange can enhance transaction capabilities.[22] The ability to promise and provide dependable delivery of a proper assortment serves as a stimulant to purchase agreement. Actual performance according to specifications creates a tendency toward repeated transactions and the benefits of routinization. Thus, whereas present concern is with exchange mechanics, exchange capabilities may greatly enhance or dilute transaction potential.

Channel Functions of Exchange

Exchange channel goals are simply stated. The exchange channel exists to deliver the specified product assortment to the right location at the right time. A number of functions must be performed in the exchange process. From the viewpoint of the total channel, these functions should be performed with a minimum of duplication between firms linked in a given channel structure.

Exchange flow in a channel is analogous to the mechanical workings of a ratchet wrench. Physical movement is best designed for economies of one-way movement toward terminal user locations. Although it is a fact that products often have to be returned from retailer to manufacturer, such a reverse movement is an expensive exception rather than the rule.

ADJUSTMENT

The function of adjustment has received considerable treatment in marketing literature.[23] Some of the main contributions were reviewed earlier in this chapter.

[21]This classification is widely used in marketing to describe conditions surrounding the availability of consumer goods in the market place. Different exchange channel considerations relate to each which, in turn, may dictate different timing in actual physical distribution performance with respect to transaction.

[22]For two discussions of the impact of physical distribution on sales see Wendell M. Stewart, "Physical Distribution: Key to Improved Volume and Profits," *Journal of Marketing*, January, 1965, pp. 67–68, and Staudt and Taylor, *op. cit.*, p. 222.

[23]This concept has long standing in marketing literature. Two early treatments are found in Percival White, *Scientific Marketing Management* (New York: Harper and Brothers, 1927), and Fred E. Clark, *Readings in Marketing* (New York: The Macmillan Co., 1924).

Adjustment is the exchange function concerned with the creation of an assortment of goods. At some geographical point or points in the exchange process, goods must be concentrated, sorted, and dispersed to the next level in the exchange channel.

Concentration refers to the collection of large lots of a single good or large groupings of several goods earmarked for final sale in an assortment. A manufacturer's distribution warehouse is a prime example of a concentration point in the exchange channel. Large shipments of products produced at each factory may be transferred to the distribution warehouse. The distribution warehouse, in turn, may hold such concentrations until an order is received for a particular assortment. The process of grouping individual products into an assortment is referred to as sorting.

The sorting process results in a custom offering, which meets one customer's specifications. It has become a common service for manufacturers to offer mixed carloads or truckloads of all marketed products based upon the quantity specifications of the buyer. This service is based upon the functional capability of being able to sort in an economical manner. Such custom-sorted shipments allow customers to carry the minimum necessary inventory of all items in the product line and to retain the benefits of lower per unit freight rates resulting from volume shipments.

Dispersement consists of placing custom assortments at the proper time in the right place. The dispersement aspect of adjustment refers to the establishment of the overall specifications to guide the remainder of the exchange functions. Thus, dispersement is directive in nature and stimulates the performance of a given exchange process.

The particular facility performing the adjustment function may be either a company-operated facility or a specialized middleman. Wholesalers find economic justification by performing the adjustment function and thereby reducing some risk on the part of other channel members. A recent study indicates that merchant wholesalers have increased at the very time when vertical integration by large retailers and manufacturers was supposed to have eliminated their basis of economic justification.[24]

It would appear that the potential economies of integrated wholesaling by vertical expansion of the exchange channel may not offset the corresponding loss of innovative specialization and risk spreading. The strategically placed merchant wholesaler is able to perform the adjustment function for a number of different retailers and manufacturers, thereby reducing the number of transactions required in the total exchange channel.

TRANSFER

The transfer function consists of the mechanics of collection and dispersement. A single good or an assortment of goods must be physically transported

[24]Reavis Cox, *Distribution In A High-Level Economy* (Englewood Cliffs, N. J.: Prentice Hall, Inc., 1965), p. 56.

to achieve temporal and spatial fulfillment of exchange contracts. In the collection phase of the adjustment function, the typical transfer consists of large limited commodity shipments. In the dispersement phase of the adjustment function, the typical transfer will be smaller shipments of a variety or assortment of products. As a general rule, transfers related to dispersement will be more costly than transfers related to concentration.

In total, transfer costs are the highest of all functions of exchange. Each transfer in the exchange process is a singularly conclusive act with associated costs. A shipment sent to the wrong destination or at the wrong time is double costly to one completed in the proper manner. As such, the margin for error in transfer is narrow, and the related costs or penalties cannot be recovered.

It is not surprising to find a grouping of transfer intermediaries who specialize in the mechanics of movement. Such specialists, in the form of motor, rail, water, and air carriers, number in the thousands in the United States. Transfer specialists exist because of the high cost of investment in equipment which can be spread across many different shippers. In some cases, the performance of the transfer function is in part or total vertically integrated by the shipper through the purchase and operation of private transportation equipment. Normally the volume of movement must be heavy and balanced in both directions to justify the operation of private transfer facilities. In other cases, vertical control is achieved by establishment of contract commitments between the shipper and a specialized transfer intermediary.

However, the majority of transfer specialists, the common carriers, provide their services to all shippers at a specified charge. A typical common carrier is regulated by either the federal or state government within the territory authorized for performance of the transfer function. For a specified charge the carrier assumes the risk for performance of the transfer mechanics. The risks of timing and directing the strategy of transfer remain with other intermediaries in the exchange channel.

STORAGE

Storage occurs in the exchange channel because a great deal of concentration sorting and dispersement is performed in anticipation of future transactions. Given conditions of uncertainty in demand and supply, the exchange process must develop certain hedges to be able to satisfy future transaction requirements.

Accumulation of raw material or agricultural stockpiles in anticipation of future production requirements is a very common form of storage. Products produced the year around for sale during a very short period often require off-season storage; summer furniture and Christmas toys are examples of such products.

The risks of storage may be the greatest of all exchange functions, because damage and obsolescence can occur when inventories stand idle. Therefore, a continuous exchange flow from processing through adjustment and on to final consumption would contain less risk for all channel members. However, in a buyer's market, continuous movement seldom exists. At some point in the exchange channel, storage of at least a temporary nature must be performed.

Because of related risks, the function of storage is normally spread out among firms linked in a channel. Each firm is willing to assume the minimum amount of storage necessary to support its transaction activities. Because the total concentration of any one product tends to be reduced as the product moves through consecutive adjustments, it is not surprising to find that manufacturers are frequently forced to assume the largest share of product storage in a given exchange channel. Thus, in a given channel containing a manufacturer, a wholesaler, and a retailer, it appears logical that the retailer would perform the least amount and the manufacturer the greatest amount of storage.

Faced with the need to perform the lion's share of the storage, the manufacturer may elect to operate his own distribution warehouses. A common alternative is to purchase the use of storage space from an independent specialist called a public warehouseman. Historically, public warehouses were most commonly used for storage of off-season production. In more recent times, the public warehouse specialist has expanded his services to perform some additional exchange functions. The most common example is the performance of the adjustment function for manufacturers in a given market area or city.

As one would expect, the public warehouse specialist does not normally assume full risk for a product in storage. He does assume the risk for performance of the actual storage and related activities. The product in storage remains the property of the firm purchasing the specialized services of the public warehouse.

HANDLING

Handling is the least risky of exchange functions. However, expenses associated with handling are significant. Once a concentrated lot or an assortment of goods reaches a stopping point, shuffling begins. Cartons are moved in, placed, moved about, moved about some more, and finally moved out. The objective is to reduce handling in the exchange channel to an absolute minimum. Each handling has a separate and unique cost. Consequently, the fewer the total handlings in the exchange channel, the lower is the total cost.

Few specialized intermediaries exist for the sole purpose of performing the handling function. Handling is normally performed as part of adjustment, transfer, and storage functions. Therefore, handling must occur at all points in an exchange system through which the actual product passes. No function is more prone to duplication throughout the exchange channels than handling.

During the past decade substantial interest has developed around the use of containers and unitized loads. The basic idea of both is that products can be grouped together and handled as a single unit rather than multiple pieces. To the extent that products can be containerized from the manufacturer to the retailer, substantial handlings can be eliminated in the total exchange channel.

COMMUNICATIONS

Communications is a two-way function in the exchange channel. In one direction, messages relay the need for exchange action. In the other direction, communications serve to monitor progress toward desired end results. Channel communication is continuous as products are transferred, adjusted, and stored in anticipation of future transaction requirements. Communications also exist between the transaction channel and the exchange channel with respect to assortment, quantity, location, and time of exchange.

At the outset it was noted that the total exchange channel was similar to a ratchet wrench in design concept with primary emphasis on forward movement to terminal user locations. A forward movement that subsequently requires reversal can be very costly to the total channel of exchange. Thus, from initial stimulant to feedback, the direct costs of communications are overshadowed by the resultant cost of a faulty message.

Because a great deal of exchange action is initiated in anticipation of future transaction requirements, communication containing an overly optimistic appraisal of potential may stimulate an exchange channel into a fever of ultimately useless work. Recent analysis of communications between channel members suggests such anticipation has a tendency to increase in amplification as it proceeds between consecutive intermediaries in an exchange network[25]. Each such error in appraisal of transaction requirements has a tendency to introduce a disturbance for the total exchange channel. Faced with such a disturbance, the total channel may enter into an oscillatory corrective pattern resulting in a series of over- and underadjustments to real requirements.

By the nature of its basic mission, an exchange channel must be sensitive to transaction requirements. Therefore, the system stands ready to initiate the exchange process upon receipt of a stimulating message. Extreme care must be taken to structure communications in a manner that will result in a high degree of reliability.

[25]See Jay W. Forrester, *Industrial Dynamics* (Cambridge, Mass.: The M.I.T. Press, 1961), p. 62.

The Exchange Network

Because a sequence of functions must be performed in the exchange process, it is not surprising that a number of individual enterprise units combine to create a channel or network. Only through coordination of all exchange functions can transaction requirements be fully satisfied. To the extent that duplication of functions exist in the channel, the total efficiency of the combined network will be impaired. To various degrees each channel member enjoys rewards or suffers losses based upon the overall success of the total exchange channel.

Enterprises that make up the exchange channel are specialists in performing one or more exchange functions. Specialization by function has the end result of increasing efficiency and spreading risk. However, it is clear that risk in an exchange network is never equally spread among all participants. The greater the degree of specialization the intermediary has in the performance of exchange functions, the less risk he will assume in the overall performance of any given exchange channel.

A motor carrier performing a single transfer function in a channel has relatively little risk with respect to the ultimate transaction. To the extent possible, such carriers will attempt to hedge risk involvement in any one exchange channel by performing similar functions for a wide variety of different channels. A retailer or a merchant wholesaler has risk involvement related to the sale of a single manufacturer's product assortment. Each attempts to hedge this risk by offering a total assortment far broader than any single manufacturer's product mix.

In contrast, a processor or manufacturer of a single product line may risk his total survival on the capabilities of a single exchange network. This disproportionate spread of risk among channel members is of central importance in the exchange process. Some channel members have a deeper vested interest in the ultimate accomplishment of successful exchange than other members. Therefore, members with a vested interest are forced to play a more active role and assume greater responsibility for channel performance.

Without guidance, a great many exchange costs may be rapidly accumulated by functional duplication. In addition, costs may be unfavorably influenced by firms who have very little at stake in the channel. Such costs must be controlled if the channel is to realize maximum exchange capabilities. Control in an exchange channel is difficult to realize, because the only alternatives to ownership are persuasion or coercion.

Ownership control consists of vertical integration of two or more consecutive links in the exchange channel by a single enterprise. The ultimate of vertical integration in an exchange channel would be a manufacturer shipping via private transportation through his own storage points to his own retail outlets. Such complete vertical integration is rare. The exact extent to which vertical integration has materialized during the past two decades is difficult to appraise. As noted earlier, merchant wholesalers have tended to increase in number rather than decrease. There is increasing justification to conclude that the transaction channel has undergone more dramatic vertical integration than the exchange channel. The most radical shifts in intermediaries has been within the transfer channel between agents and factory sales branches.[26]

Even when a firm is vertically extended with respect to integrated wholesaling, rarely can the services of a specialized transfer intermediary be fully eliminated. Sears Roebuck and Montgomery Ward utilize a high degree of common carrier transportation in addition to the vast fleet of private transportation vehicles they own and operate. It is doubtful that a firm could ever be fully integrated with respect to complete performance of every function required in the total exchange channel.

Tactics of persuasion and coercion are the most practical methods of directing and controlling exchange activities. Within the exchange channel, this basic need for common action under leadership guidance has been referred to as super-organization management.[27] The benefit of spearheading coordinated activity often resides with the channel member who has the greatest economic power. Such economic power most often rests with the channel member who directs activities at the point of transaction creation. Earlier in the chapter, domination by virtue of economic leverage was termed *vertically controlled* in contrast to *vertically owned* operations. In a variety of situations, a firm is able to coordinate the activities of specialized intermediaries by virtue of market strength. The name of *channel captain* has been suggested for the firm that is economically able to stimulate interfirm coordination.[28]

Although all firms in a given exchange channel have a desire to cooperate, individual profit orientation and legal boundaries tend to create elements of conflict. In addition, there exists a degree of conflict over which member of a channel is willing to assume responsibility for performance of the more risky exchange functions. The firm having the greatest economic power may very well be the one least directly involved in the welfare of a specific exchange channel. The burden of economic power could very well be employed to shift risk rather than stimulate coordination.

The analysis of motivation for conflict and cooperation in both trading and exchange channels is currently receiving substantial attention in the litera-

[26]Cox, *op. cit.*, p. 55.

[27]J. L. Heskett, "Costing and Coordinating External and Internal Logistics Activities," unpublished paper before joint seminar, The Railway Systems and Management Association and The Transportation Research Forum, Chicago, October 6, 1964.

[28]E. Jerome McCarthy, *Basic Marketing: A Managerial Approach*, rev. ed. (Homewood, Ill.: Richard D. Irwin, Inc., 1964), pp. 460–62.

ture.[29] Detailed treatment of the techniques of leadership are beyond our scope of immediate interest. The essential point is that the ultimate survival of a channel may depend upon constructive leadership. In addition, a great deal of future improvement in marketing efficiency could depend upon a substantial increase in managerial concern with channel group objectives as opposed to the preoccupation of the firm as an individual channel member.

Exchange Channel Objectives

As a competitive group, all firms in an exchange channel have some common and definable objectives. A statement of objectives is useful to planning integrated activities of all firms involved. The objectives of the exchange channel are specified in part by transaction requirements with respect to time, place, and assortment and in part by the alternate exchange channel intermediary specialists available. Thus, the total exchange channel is subject to scrutiny by two measures: (1) capability in time, place, and assortment performance; and (2) evaluation of total cost expenditure between alternate structures capable of achieving performance.

The most durable channel is one capable of meeting the objectives of (1) minimum possible engagements, (2) maximum postponement in adjustment, and (3) minimum massed reserves. All these objectives must be satisfied at the lowest total cost expenditure.

MINIMUM POSSIBLE ENGAGEMENTS

The objective of minimum possible engagements encourages the least amount of possible duplication in transfer, handling, adjustment, and storage for the total exchange channel. Whereas each of these exchange functions is important to the total process, the costs of duplication rapidly accumulate. Thus, the less nodal points physical products are required to flow through, the more inherently efficient is the exchange channel.

MAXIMUM POSTPONEMENT IN ADJUSTMENT

The objective of maximum postponement in adjustment is aimed at retaining homogeneous concentrated lots of a product as long as possible in the

[29]For example see J. C. Palamountain, Jr., *The Politics of Distribution* (Cambridge: Harvard University Press, 1955); Valentine Ridgeway, "Administration of Manufacturer-Dealer Systems," *Administrative Science Quarterly*, March, 1957, pp. 464–483; Bruce Mallen, "Conflict and Cooperation in Marketing Channels," in L. George Smith (ed.), *Reflections on Progress in Marketing, Proceedings American Marketing Association* (Chicago: American Marketing Association, 1964), pp. 65–85; and Bert C. McCammon, Jr., "Alternative Explanations of Institutional Change and Channel Evolution," in Stephen A. Greyser (ed.), *Toward Scientific Marketing Proceedings* (Chicago: American Marketing Association, 1963), pp. 477–490.

exchange process. Because much exchange activity is initiated in anticipation of future transactions, the longer a concentration is maintained, the greater is the ability to adjust custom assortments when required.

The ideal degree of postponement is to concentrate products based upon transaction anticipation and hold sorting and dispersement until a firm commitment is at hand. The longer the total exchange channel can postpone final adjustment, the more flexible is the total exchange process.[30] Remolding a previous established assortment into a new assortment adds ancillary cost to the total exchange process.

MINIMUM MASSED RESERVES

In general, the exchange channel should attempt to hold the minimum reserve of products consistent with support of transaction creating activities. The objective of minimum massed reserves may appear to be in contrast with the objective of postponement. However, there is no reason to hold homogeneous product groupings at consecutive levels of the exchange channel.

It has been a long-standing practice to mass inventories at various levels of the exchange channel in anticipation of transaction. In practice, there has been extensive pressure on the part of trading groups for inventory assortments in each market as a prerequisite to transaction creation.

The tendency in exchange channels is toward the staging of a central supply geographically separated from the market as far as is economically feasible. The rapid extension of product offerings in all trade channels has created serious risks in holding reserves for each specialized market segment. Given conditions of erratic demand, the lowest total cost exchange process may well be the rapid shipment of custom assortments from a distant supply point as late in the transaction process as technologically possible. Transfer of the assortment may justify using air freight. Although the transfer cost may be higher than by other methods, the total cost of exchange may be lowest by this process.

The objective of minimum massed reserves differs in substance from the marketing principles of massed reserves and market proximity reviewed earlier in this chapter.[31] The contrast is one of traditional marketing orientation and exchange separation orientation. The total objective is to meet

---

[30]For a discussion of the relationship of postponement to the entry into a distribution channel for purposes of speculation see Louis P. Bucklin, "Postponement Speculation and the Structure of Distribution Channels," *Journal of Marketing Research*, February, 1965, pp. 26–31.

[31]In fact this is a basic dichotomy between the sales orientation for holding inventory near or in all primary markets and the physical distribution orientation for holding strategically located stocks. The amount of inventory held in the exchange channel is a key variable in physical distribution planning. It may well be that total physical distribution costs savings may support a reduction in service performance greater than the corresponding loss of sales revenue.

trading requirements at the lowest possible total cost. Inventories in the total exchange channel must be minimized without diluting transaction support capabilities. To the degree that transaction requirements are satisfied while the objective of minimum massed reserves is achieved, the total process will be accomplished at lowest possible cost.

Spatial-Temporal Relationships

Thus far, the treatment of exchange channels has been developed without proper acknowledgment of the geographical complexity of the entire network. In the physical distribution sense, an exchange channel is a series of nodal points having geographic dispersement over the entire market area involved. The total number of such nodal points consistent with exchange channel objectives is directly related to economies in the movement of goods. Generally, the larger the volumes that may be shipped through the exchange channel, the greater are the distribution economies. These economies are directly related to the geographic dispersion or concentration of nodal points involved.

Because physical distribution is fundamentally concerned with the spatial aspects of business operations, it is understandable that primary emphasis is placed upon geographical arrangements of exchange facilities. This preoccupation with georeference is intensified by the array of different markets a typical firm's exchange channel must logistically support. However, distance alone is not adequate in planning an exchange channel.

Time relationships have equal importance to effective product flow and in many cases will determine the degree of nodal point concentration possible.[32] The various objectives of the exchange channel can only be achieved with respect to response times to transaction demands. Therefore, the ideal network arrangement is one capable of meeting transaction time requirements and taking advantage of spatial arrangements that allow maximum flow economies through the network of nodal points.

Summary

Today, retailers sell wholesale, wholesalers sell retail, hardware stores sell soft goods, department stores sell food, food stores sell appliances — they all sell toys and discount stores sell everything. Channel jumping is not limited to retailing. Finished goods often move to the same retailer from wholesalers, distributors, jobbers, assemblers, and direct from producers. In some cases, goods bypass retailers altogether moving directly to consumers. These

[32]J. L. Heskett, "A Missing Link in Physical Distribution System Design," *Journal of Marketing*, October, 1966, pp. 37–41.

changing patterns have forced a careful review of the channels used in the physical distribution of products.

The entire notion of loosely aligned middlemen linked together in pursuit of joint opportunity is not consistent with the logic of efficient physical distribution systems. One promising way to increase marketing efficiency is to improve physical movement within the distribution channel. Advantages in operation result when physical flow is separated from other flows in the total distribution process. The development of a specialized network of exchange intermediaries allows maximum control and economies of specialization in physical flow.

Many corporate costs of replenishment are hidden between departments of an enterprise and not necessarily under the control of any given department. In addition, little consideration has been given to problems of coordinating and controlling physical distribution beyond the limits of legal control of an individual firm. Most physical distribution flow proceeds from production to consumption through specialized enterprises linked as an exchange channel. Each of these independent units or links may perform an excellent individual job of physical distribution, although, as a totality, the overall channel suffers from expensive duplication. Therefore, the proper planning of a firm's physical distribution effort must transcend the total exchange channel.

As a total grouping of enterprises, an exchange channel must perform a specific sequence of functions in order to support transaction-creating efforts. Thus, the total channel is in effect an integrated network with well-defined objectives. The most effective total channel is one capable of meeting objectives and controlling the flow of materials and finished goods in accordance with time and space demands.

The nature of the total physical flow of a firm is such that spatial and temporal relationships are of primary significance. Only through coordination of all exchange facilities can a firm's total logistics effort meet the highest standards of performance.

Peter Drucker recently concluded that physical distribution contributes little if anything to the physical characteristics of a material or a product. It does, however, create the attributes of time and place — it brings the product to the customer.[33]

Discussion Questions

1. What is the difference between the traditional physical distribution approach and the marketing approach to the concept of physical distribution?

2. What is a channel of distribution? What is its function?

[33]Peter F. Drucker, "The Economy's Dark Continent," *Fortune*, April, 1962, pp. 265–70.

3. Given the fact that middlemen increase costs, why do they continue to exist in American business today?

4. What is meant by sorting? What service does it perform?

5. What is channel jumping? Explain why it occurs.

6. What is meant by integrated wholesaling?

7. If the members of a channel are not integrated in their physical distribution system, what is the economic significance of this to ultimate consumers?

8. Why do manufacturers have a deeper vested interest in a channel than other members? For what reason does this occur?

9. How could a manufacturer gain greater control over his channel of distribution?

10. Define the following terms: channel captain; minimum possible engagements; maximum postponement in adjustments; minimum massed reserves; nodal point.

11. How can you reconcile the marketing principles of massed reserves and market proximity with the physical distribution principle of minimum massed reserves?

Appendix 3A

DEFINITION AND CHARACTERISTICS OF MIDDLEMEN

The conventional approach to channel structure focuses on the path taken by the title of a product from producer or manufacturer to ultimate user. Included in this path are all middlemen, whether they take title directly or merely facilitate the title's passage. The purpose of Appendix 3A is to provide a brief overview of the conventional approach to channel description.[1] Specifically, emphasis is placed on the wholesaling or middleman structure of distribution. It should be noted that the terms *wholesaler* or *middlemen* are used in this section to describe specialists in the channel of distribution rather than the term *intermediary* as used in Chapter 3.

The conventional approach to channel description focuses on the identification, description, and classification of middlemen. Chart 3A–1 typifies the analytical framework. At the first level, the distinction is made between merchant and functional middlemen. Merchant middlemen take title to the goods with all of the ownership risks. Functional middlemen escape the risks of ownership but provide some necessary service to both client and customer.

At the second level, the distinction between range and type of wholesale services is made. Full-function middlemen typically buy in large quantities, break bulk, assemble, assort, sell, and deliver. In performing these activities,

---

[1]*Note On Marketing Channels* (Cambridge: Harvard Business School, 1965), ICH 10M65, EA–M, 480. This note provides additional coverage of distribution channels.

**CHART 3A–1   An Analytical Framework of Middlemen in the
Structure of Distribution**

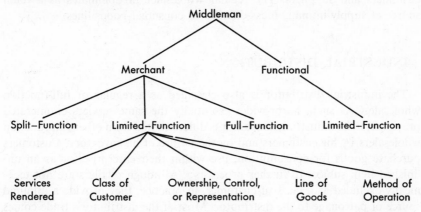

the full-function middleman maintains a warehouse; employs a sales force, which calls on the trade regularly; provides for physical distribution; extends trade credit; manages the collection of accounts; and serves in an advisory capacity or as an informational link to both suppliers and customers. The limited-function wholesaler is so designated because his range of services falls short of that provided by his full-function counterpart. On the other hand, the split-function middleman usually operates as both a retailer and wholesaler.

The third level of Chart 3A–1 represents descriptive criteria commonly applied to the various categories of wholesalers specified by the first two levels. The following section contains a more detailed description of the characteristics of specific classes of middlemen.

Merchant Middlemen

Included in this section are those wholesalers that buy and sell of their own initiative, thereby dealing with the risks of ownership.

REGULAR WHOLESALERS

The service or regular wholesaler operates a full-function enterprise. Most commonly, the firm is independently owned and handles consumer goods. The regular wholesaler purchases in large volume from producers and manufacturers, accepts delivery at one or more of his warehouses, breaks down and stores its purchases, sends out its sales force to canvass the trade, assembles orders in relatively small quantities, delivers orders to its customers, extends credit, assumes the risks of inventory and receivables, offers advisory service to its customers, and supplies marketing information to both customers and suppliers. The regular wholesaler predominates as a retail source of supply in many mass-distributed consumer-goods lines.

INDUSTRIAL DISTRIBUTION

The industrial distributor is also classified as a regular or full-function wholesaler. As such, he provides essentially the same services enumerated previously. The industrial distributor is differentiated from other full-function wholesalers by his customers and by the nature of his inventory. Customers purchase goods for consumption, use within their enterprise, or as an unfinished item subject to further processing. Although retailers are not technically excluded as a class of customer, in practice, they provide a minimal source of patronage to the distributor. Most of the distributor's trade comes from such concerns as manufacturing firms, public utilities, railroads, mines, and service establishments (e.g., doctors, barbers, beauticians, hotels, and restaurants). The industrial distributor often specializes in servicing one industry segment such as automotive or mining.

DROP SHIPPERS

Drop shippers are limited-function wholesalers in that they seldom take physical possession of the goods. Commodities such as coal, lumber, construction materials, agricultural products, and heavy machinery are bulky and require the economies of shipment by carload lots. The drop shipper typically purchases the carload from the supplier in anticipation of a future order. Once a buyer is found, the drop shipper assumes the responsibility and ownership of shipment until it is accepted by the customer. Because no warehouse facilities are maintained, the drop shipper's risk of title bearing varies with the time lag between purchase and sale of the carload. Apart from this risk, he also incurs the risks and costs of credit extension and receivables collection. This distinction between the practice of drop shipping and the drop shipper is important. Drop shipping is the practice of shipping an order direct from the supplier to the customer, although a middleman might be involved in the transactions. For example, headquarters purchasing might centrally purchase a large quantity of bulk merchandise. Instead of requiring shipment to the firm's distribution warehouse, the company might allocate portions of the shipment directly to its retail store. This practice is termed *drop shipping*. The drop shipper, on the other hand, is a distinct middleman who arranges for shipment, takes title, assumes responsibility for shipment, and functions as a merchant middleman in the overall distribution channel.

CASH-AND-CARRY WHOLESALERS

Cash-and-carry wholesalers are limited-function middlemen who operate on a cash basis with no merchandise delivery. Chiefly found in the grocery trade, they were established to serve small retailers whose order size was typically not large enough to justify delivery. By stocking staple merchandise, employing no salesman, and eliminating delivery services and credit, such middlemen can economically serve the small retailer. To take advantage of such services, the retailer must travel to the warehouse, find and assemble his order, carry it to a central check-out location, pay cash, load on his truck, and carry the order to his place of business.

WAGON DISTRIBUTORS (JOBBERS)

Principally utilized by the grocery trade, the wagon distributor is a limited-function wholesaler who specializes in high-margin speciality items or quick-turnover perishables. This middleman purchases from producers, may or may not maintain a warehouse, and employs one or more driver-salesmen to regularly call on the trade. Characteristically, sales and delivery are performed simultaneously. The customer fills his order from the truck's limited assortment and closes the transaction with a cash payment.

RACK JOBBERS

Rack jobbers or service merchandisers are classified as full-function intermediaries in that they perform all of the regular wholesaling functions plus some retailing functions. Dealing in extensive lines of nonfood merchandise, driver-salesmen regularly service grocer accounts. Typically, a salesman on call performs a stock control function in that he insures that his display racks are adequately stocked, properly price-marked, and arranged in an attractive manner. Generally, a rack jobber will replace upon request of the retailer or at his own initiative unsold or slow-moving items. The retailer is usually billed on a consignment basis, paying only for merchandise sold since the jobber's last visit.

ASSEMBLING WHOLESALERS

Principally dealing in agricultural products, the assembling wholesaler reverses the common procedure in terms of order size. He buys the output of many small farmers, assembles and grades the product, ships in economical quantities to central markets, and sells in larger quantities than those purchased.

SEMIJOBBERS

Semijobbers are designated split-function middlemen, because they operate at both the wholesale and retail level of the channel of distribution. Usually semijobbers are limited- or full-function wholesalers who indulge in some retail sales; or conversely, they are retailers who find it advantageous to be classified as wholesalers for at least a small portion of their operation. An illustration of the former is automotive suppliers. The second case is not typical of any particular retailing segment, but is illustrative of a strategy aimed at gaining lower prices or developing business in two separate market segments.

Functional Middlemen

The functional category of wholesalers do not take title but, nevertheless, perform many wholesale functions. All middlemen included in this classification are, by definition, limited-function wholesalers, because they are precluded from assuming the risks of ownership.

SELLING AGENTS

Selling agents serve their clients in lieu of a sales organization. They are contracted to sell output of one or more manufacturers, so long as the lines handled are supplementary and do not compete directly. Because their principals are generally small firms, as illustrated by the textile industry, they are often called upon for financial assistance in terms of loans, carrying credit for the client, or collecting receivables. Furthermore, agents serve as collectors, analysts, and dispensers of marketing data. For these services, selling agents are remunerated on a commission basis.

MANUFACTURERS' AGENTS

Manufacturers' agents are similar to selling agents in that they act as substitutes for a direct sales organization, are hired on a continuing contractual basis, represent relatively small enterprises, provide market intelligence, and are reimbursed by commissions. They differ from selling agents inasmuch as they do not sell the entire output of their clients, are limited to a specific geographic territory, and have little control over prices, discounts, and credit terms. A manufacturer's agent or representative usually represents a number of manufacturers who produce noncompetitive but related lines.

COMMISSION MERCHANTS

Unlike agents, commission merchants rarely are used on a regular contractual basis. Instead, they are engaged for a single transaction, or more
commonly, to facilitate the disposal of a particular lot of goods. Once
contracted, the commission merchant takes possession but not title of the
goods, provides warehousing facilities, and displays either a sample or the
entire lot to prospective purchasers. Once negotiations begin, the commission
merchant is usually empowered to accept what in his judgment will be the
best offer, so long as it exceeds a previously stipulated minimum price. To
facilitate good offerings and speed the closing of transactions, the commission
merchant may choose to extend credit at his own risk. In practice, he commonly extends credit, bills the customer, collects the account, provides a
final accounting, and remits the proceeds less commission to his principal.
Such a wholesaling operation is of vital importance to the marketing of
livestock, grain, and other agricultural products.

BROKERS

Brokers serve as catalytic agents to classes of buyers and sellers that would
normally have considerable difficulty in meeting for purposes of negotiation.
A broker's entire function is to stimulate and arrange contacts between the
two groups. It is commonly understood that brokers do not permanently
represent either buyer or seller. Furthermore, they do not handle the goods,
rarely take physical possession, nor do they provide financial assistance to
clients. The brokerage fee is paid by the principal, whether it is the buyer or
the seller. In no case can a broker legally receive a fee from both parties to a
transaction. Brokers are widely used in foreign trade by small manufacturers
of convenience goods and by wholesale grocers.

AUCTION COMPANIES

Auction companies are widely used in the marketing of fruit, tobacco, and
livestock. They provide a physical setting conducive to the marketing of
specific lots of commodities. Facilities are usually available to all those
offering commodities and to all those bidding for them. The auction company is paid usually by the seller at a flat fee per transaction or a percentage
of the sale.

PETROLEUM BULK STATIONS

Stations provide the storage and wholesale distribution for the petroleum
industry. Such establishments may be owned by refining companies and

CHART 3A–2   Typical Channel Structure Alternatives in
Consumer Goods Distribution

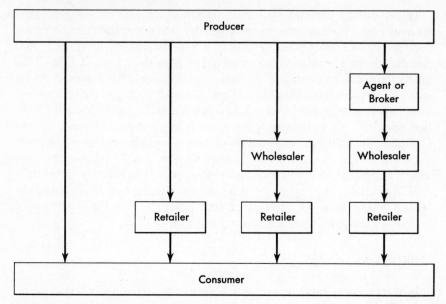

operated on a basis similar to manufacturers' sales branches; or they may be
owned and operated independently.

Structural Alternatives in a Distribution System

In the first section of this appendix a description of the function and
specific types of middlemen was presented. In this section a brief description
of structural alternatives in product distribution is presented. Both sections
treat structure in a graphic sense rather than in a strategic, dynamic context
as presented in Chapter 3.

The graphic approach to describing a structure of distribution is described
in Charts 3A–2 and 3A–3. In Chart 3A–2 the most common variations in
consumer goods channels are illustrated. Of the four channels shown the
most typical for the consumer is the wholesale-retail-consumer channel. Most
mass-produced consumer goods reach the market through a wholesaler and
retailer. The channel selected by the manufacturer depends upon the characteristics of the product, the buying habits of the consumer, and the overall
marketing strategy of the firm. For example, a large personal sales force is
required to market successfully a product nationwide directly to the consumer. Such companies as Avon Products and Fuller have selected this
method of distribution. On the other hand, a manufacturer with limited
capital resources and a limited product line might elect to hire a broker or
an agent to sell his products in consumer channels.

CHART 3A–3   Typical Channel Structure Alternatives in Industrial Goods Distribution

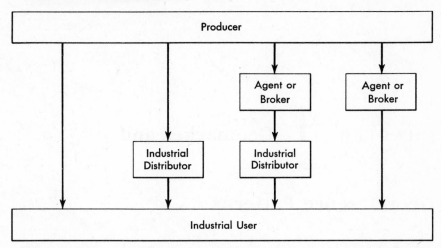

In Chart 3A–3, a description of alternative channels for industrial goods distribution is presented. Most high-volume items in industrial markets move directly from producer to consumer. Supplies, replacement parts, and small orders of bulk items often use the wholesaler. In this sense, the industrial middleman performs much the same function as the wholesaler in consumer channels. One major difference between consumer and industrial channels is that the incidence of functional middlemen such as selling agents, brokers, and manufacturers' agents is much greater in industrial than in commercial channels.

The structures described in Charts 3A–2 and 3A–3 should be regarded as typical patterns. There are a great number of possible variations in channel structure in addition to those shown in these charts depending on the product, the customer, and the entrepreneurial vision of the channel members.

CHAPTER **4** **Geomarket and**

Georeference Patterns

THE marketing analyst, like the traditional economist, often assumes away the problem of space in his analysis. If, indeed, it took the same time to move the same distance in every direction and the factors of production and demand were evenly spread in the marketplace, the spatial characteristics of physical distribution could be assumed away.

However, from a practical point of view, there are 13 million people living in the metropolitan New York area and 300 thousand in the state of Wyoming. There are variations in raw material supplies and in market demand. The imperfections created by natural and man-made barriers to free movement further complicate efforts to achieve spatial efficiency. The manufacturer, the middleman, and the consumer must overcome the spatial imperfections of the marketplace in order to match the manufacturer's product offering with the consumer's economic needs. The manufacturer must consider variation in the density of market demand and raw materials in designing a physical distribution system. The middleman must stock the appropriate mix of products in the right amount and at the right location to meet customer requirements. The consumer, too, must overcome the "friction of space" in satisfying most of his economic needs. He often must travel congested roads, make multiple stops, find adequate parking, and return home with his purchases.

The general purpose of this chapter is to identify those geographic factors which influence the physical distribution task of the firm. The first part briefly summarizes the historical contributions of the space economists and regional scientists. These pioneers were the first to recognize and analyze scientifically the relationship between space and business activity. The second part of the chapter presents and illustrates some of the key geographic variables that influence the design and evaluation of physical distribution systems. The third section of the chapter deals with coding methods for identifying geographic segments.

Some Preliminary Considerations

A number of preliminary considerations should be recognized prior to a discussion of geomarket patterns. These considerations center principally around imperfections in the marketplace and the dynamic aspects of geographic change.

GEOGRAPHIC IMPERFECTIONS AND TECHNOLOGICAL INNOVATION

If supply and demand were evenly distributed throughout the market, the problems of coping with space in a physical distribution system would be immeasurably simplified. In the real world this is not the case. Differences exist in supply availability, market density, mobility of raw materials, finished goods inventory, and people.

Basically, the imperfections in the marketplace may be classified into density or flow imperfections. The density imperfection refers to uneven geographic distribution of supply, demand, raw materials, and other economic inputs. Flow imperfection distorts equal time distance movement in any direction. For example, the existing patterns of railway tracks, interstate highways, and navigable waterways facilitate movement in certain directions and prohibit movement in other directions. To a significant degree, flow imperfections create density imperfections. In the long run, technological innovation may stimulate change in either density or flow imperfections. However, in the short run, the firm faces these two imperfections as limiting factors in physical distribution system design.

GEOMARKET DYNAMICS

Each year approximately 20 percent of American families move their place of residence. The center of population for the country has shifted constantly westward, but significant shifts between regions are also observable. To a large extent, demographic shifts can be forecast with some degree of reliability. In designing a physical distribution system, such shifts over time are critical to long-range planning. Thus, a physical distribution system with inventory locations and allocations designed for the 1970 market will require readjustment to serve the same demand equally well in 1975. Depending on the needs and objectives of the system, a geomarket forecast might be required for five to ten years in the future.

MARKET PENETRATION AND POTENTIAL

Another important geomarket factor is the relationship between current market penetration and future market potential. A physical distribution system can be designed on the basis of either current sales or future potential. A system designed to meet the needs of an individual firm's current market would probably not be satisfactory for the total industry. This is due to demand variation and differences in market penetration between firms and between different market areas. Planning, therefore, should include both present sales and future potential.

Some Early Contributions to Location and Space Economics

During the past several decades, businessmen, economists, regional scientists, economic geographers, and marketing men have become increasingly interested in the economics of space. Technology, a mass production and mass consumption environment, and increasing distances between producer and consumer have served to highlight the importance of efficiently overcoming the "friction of space."

Even before the current interest in the economics of space, farsighted economists and social scientists were concerned with the problem of spatial efficiency in the marketplace. In the following section, a brief overview of the contributions of the principal researchers are presented. This section is not designed to review their contribution comprehensively, bur rather to provide a background perspective for early work in the area of business activity and space economics.

THE GERMAN SCHOOL

Von Thünen. In the middle of the nineteenth century, von Thünen[1] addressed himself to the problem of explaining the distribution of various kinds of agricultural activity within a given homogeneous territory. His theoretical structure was oriented to cost considerations dominating the placement of various types of activity within this territory. Major costs were the price of land and transport expense. The price of land varied depending upon location relative to the market for its produce. But the primary determinant of the

[1]Joachim von Thünen, *The Isolated State* (Rostock, 1842–1863, reprinted Jena, 1921).

exact value of a product is its price less the transport expense necessary to bring it to market. Therefore, in von Thünen's system, transport expense is the primary factor explaining production locations of different agricultural commodities. Those commodities that cannot readily absorb transport expense will be located near the market and vice versa.

Given the assumptions of equal fertility and freight rates proportional to distance, different activities will take the form of a series of concentric rings. The type of production in each ring will be largely a function of transportation expense.

Weber. Von Thünen's early contributions to location theory were followed by those of Alfred Weber,[2] another German economist, who wrote his major work in 1909. From von Thünen's time to that of Weber's, a vast transition in economic activity had taken place. This transition consisted of a rapid acceleration of economic activity through industrialization. The dynamic quality of industrial growth patterns was Weber's major interest. Von Thünen's theory was agriculturally oriented; Weber's was primarily industrially oriented. Further, because von Thünen's theory dealt solely with agriculture, inbound transport costs of capital equipment and supplies were not included in the analysis. Weber concentrated on the total inbound raw materials and outbound finished products necessary to industrial production and marketing.[3] His major assumptions included (1) uniform freight rates as a function of distance, (2) equal costs of raw materials at the site of their deposit, (3) uneven distribution of raw material deposits, and (4) many consuming centers scattered through the economy.

From this starting point, Weber analyzed two general variable factors influencing location: regional and agglomerative. Regional factors are labor and transportation. Agglomerative factors consider the social conditions surrounding production such as population densities and industrial complexes. Regional factors explain, for example, the location of the steel industry in the Midwest portion of the United States. Agglomerative factors explain the concentration of steel production around Pittsburgh.

Weber next developed a measure termed the *material index*. It is defined as the ratio between the weight of the localized material (found at a unique location) and the weight of the finished product. The other important quantitative measure developed by Weber is the *locational weight*. This is defined as the total weight transported. Both measures are expressed per unit of product. By use of these measures, Weber illustrated that the location of an industry is primarily dependent upon transportation costs. The precise point at which an industry locates may be at (1) the point of consumption in

[2]Carl J. Friedrich (trans.), *Alfred Weber's Theory of the Location of Industries* (Chicago: University of Chicago Press, 1928).
[3]Weber is sometimes criticized for this assumption. However, at the time he wrote his book, freight rates in Germany were pretty much linear with distance.

weight-gaining processes, (2) the point of production in weight-losing processes, or (3) some point in between where the weight gain or weight loss is equal or not important in a particular case.

Mathematically, Weber's system could handle only three possible points resulting in what Weber termed a location figure. When considering more than three points, he was forced to use a Varignon plane. This device was a circular machine to which location weights were attached on a series of strings corresponding to their relative locations.[4] The resultant forces brought about an equilibrium position for least cost. As will be demonstrated in Appendix 10A, this cumbersome method is easily translated into more manageable mathematical techniques.

Losch. August Losch,[5] another of the German space theorists, was the first to include elements of imperfect competition in economic space analysis. In the same manner as the previous authors, he made some basic assumptions to provide a starting point for analysis. Specifically, these assumptions followed the homogeneous characteristics of von Thünen's model. Among his assumptions were (1) a transport network capable of moving products of any quantity in any direction at a constant rate per ton-mile, (2) agricultural population evenly distributed throughout a plane of uniform fertility, and (3) uniform tastes and technical knowledge.

Starting with a single self-sufficient producer in the above environment, Losch showed that if such a producer wishes to sell his surplus, his market will be circular. As other producers enter the market, this circular pattern takes on a hexagonal shape.[6] For any specific industry, the number of such hexagonal markets depends upon the production costs and market characteristics of each commodity. Where relatively large units of production are possible, the size of the market for each producing unit increases, and thus the number of hexagonal market areas for the industry decreases. Conversely, where small-sized producing units are characteristic, the size of the hexagon diminishes, and the number of market areas increases.

A single circular market results from a single producer located in a large homogeneous plane. If 20 producers attempted to serve the entire market, 20 spatially interconnected hexagons would cover the same territory. Each producer, in this case, would have a spatial monopoly within these hexagons. Assuming FOB mill pricing, a consumer located in the line separating two hexagonal territories would be indifferent as to the firm from which he

---

[4]Frederick, *op. cit.*, p. 216.

[5]A good review of Losch is contained in Melvin L. Greenhut, *Plant Location in Theory and Practice* (Chapel Hill: University of North Carolina Press, 1956), pp. 270–271.

[6]These early writers were concerned primarily with market territories served from a plant location. The warehouse, when conceived as a part of a distribution network and not a mere storage unit, will have a profound effect on territories that may be economically served from a given plant. See John H. Frederick. *Using Public Warehousing* (Philadelphia: Chilton Company, 1957), p. 81.

bought. For all consumers located within the hexagonal territories, only one firm would be a logical supplier, because land cost would be lower from the nearer source of supply.

SUMMARY OF THE GERMAN WRITERS

The German writers may be classified as indicating primary interest in optimum allocation of resources according to cost. In this sense, they do not differ fundamentally from the Anglo-Saxon classical economists. However, when optimum allocation problems are attacked from the point of view of classical Anglo-Saxon economics, it is strongly suggested that all firms in an industry are located at a point. Actual differences in cost of production because of location are conveniently equalized by considering economic rent as a cost factor.

AMERICAN WRITERS

Hoover.   In 1948, Edgar Hoover[7] wrote his text *The Location of Economic Activity*. Hoover followed in the footsteps of the German theorists in the sense that he focused attention on an optimum allocation model. His analysis, however, included a criticism of the homogeneous and therefore a simplified model of space economy. The nonlinear nature of freight rates was emphasized, as was the nonhomogeneous character of the distribution of economic factors. Hoover correctly assailed previous assumptions of complete flexibility of transport by emphasizing the nonuniform distribution of transport facilities and the institutional forces affecting specific rates. The result of Hoover's analysis was to show that these influences resulted in irregularly shaped market territories. Hoover, however, was similar to the German theorists in the sense that he placed primary emphasis upon the optimality based on cost considerations.

Greenhut.   The distinction of Greenhut[8] is that he is among the first of the theoretical writers to abandon optimum distribution of location based solely on cost considerations. Greenhut at the time of his basic work was practically alone in theoretical literature in pointing out that demand is the second important factor, along with cost, which has an important effect on location decisions and space allocation of economic factors of production.

---

[7]Edgar M. Hoover. *The Location of Economic Activity* (New York: McGraw-Hill Book Company, 1938).

[8]Greenhut, *op. cit.*, pp. 54–55. Another important American writer not reviewed here is Walter Isard. Isard's work is essentially an extension of the cost-oriented models of Weber and Losch with much added rigorous econometric analysis.

All previous writers, without notable exception, assumed a constant demand, which resulted in cost being the sole determinant of space allocation of plant locations.

The demand curve for an industry will depend on the aggregate demand of all spatially located markets taken together. Therefore, in pure competition of the nonspatial variety, all firms face the same elasticity of demand, i.e., demand will be perfectly elastic. However, once space is introduced into the system of analysis, the demand elasticity for any given spatial submarket will be something other than perfect. In competition, transfer costs make it impossible for any given producer to cross over demand for the individual firm indifference lines. As a result, the demand curve can never be perfectly elastic. The equilibrium position for any firm in an industry in spatial isolation must, therefore, more closely approximate the monopolistic competition of Chamberlin than the perfect competition of classical economic theory.[9] Location decisions then appear to be based not only on the centripetal force of minimum cost attraction but also on the centrifugal force of demand elasticities. Although cost tends to cause all firms to locate at a point of least cost, profit maximization causes individual firms to locate at points of maximum profit. For the individual firm's equilibrium there may appear to be no significant difference between the two goals, but for the long-run economic health of the enterprise, there is a substantial difference.[10] Furthermore, these unique conclusions need not be at issue with welfare principles derived from nonspace economics.

Isard. Walter Isard[11] has been a pioneer contributor to the rapidly developing discipline of regional science. The basic premise of regional science is that regions are not undifferentiated or homogeneous, but that patterns of space activity can be identified and measured. Regional science focuses on three types of decisions: (1) location, (2) scale of operations, and (3) flow. Regional analysis views the region as an integrated system where location, scale of operations, and flows are all interrelated. For example, a change in location within the region will cause corresponding changes in the location of spatial activity in other areas as well as flows between locations and scale of activity within the region.

[9]See especially Edward H. Chamberlin's statement of this point in his *The Theory of Monopolistic Competition*, 6th ed. (Boston: Harvard University Press, 1956), pp. 130–176 and 260–265.

[10]This principle has been used to explain the existence of large numbers of retail stores. In the food industry, for example, a store tends to experience minimum cost at points of high customer density. It is well known, however, that a store located at a lower density point near the periphery of the market may experience both higher costs and higher profits. In this case, it is demand which is the attraction; in the former, it is minimum cost. See Wroe Alderson, *Marketing Behavior and Executive Action* (Homewood, Ill.: Richard D. Irwin, Inc., 1957), pp. 336–341.

[11]For a more complete discussion see W. Isard *et al.*, *Methods of Regional Analysis: An Introduction to Regional Science* (New York: John Wiley and Sons, Inc., 1960).

CHART 4–1 A Synthesis of Regional Science Studies*

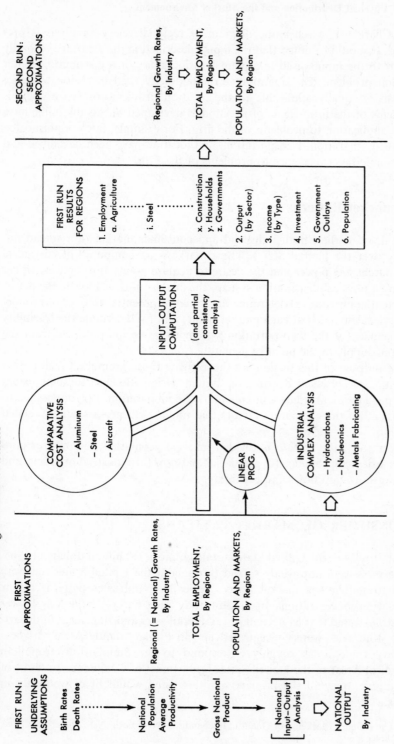

*SOURCE: *Theory in Marketing,* Reavis Cox *et al.,* eds. (Chicago: American Marketing Association, 1964), p. 393.

In Chart 4–1, a schematic diagram of regional science analysis is presented. It should be noted that the inputs described in the chart are generally similar to the inputs used in a plant location study or a distribution center location problem. The quantitative methodology used in regional science analysis is equally applicable to the location problems or space analysis problems of the firm. Some of the models developed in this discipline have direct application to problems of the firm. For example, fairly sophisticated models in migration, transportation, and location have been developed and have some direct relevance to problems of the firm.

Geomarket Patterns

As noted earlier, both industrial and consumer markets are spread unevenly over the United States. These markets are composed of customers with purchasing power and the desire to acquire goods and services. In designing a physical distribution system, the analyst must (1) locate the actual or potential market; (2) determine the actual or potential amount of product or service demanded at each market point; and (3) determine the feasibility or adequacy of the transportation system to move the products from the point of supply to the point of demand.

The purpose of this section is to investigate those geomarket factors that will influence physical distribution system design. Because to some extent each product or firm has a unique market configuration, it is impossible to discuss all of the geomarket factors that might influence a spatially related decision.

Specifically, the section is divided into (1) geomarket patterns for consumer-oriented products, (2) geomarket patterns for industrial products, and (3) transportation flows and capability.

CONSUMER GEOMARKET PATTERNS

Retail sales in the United States totaled almost 290 billion dollars in 1965. These sales were not evenly spread throughout the United States but were concentrated in key market areas. Typically, retail sales patterns follow population concentrations. In a recent study (see Chart 4–2), the *New Yorker Magazine* stated that 54 percent of total retail sales and 70 percent of department store sales were concentrated in "40 Primary Trade Areas.[12] These primary trade areas roughly correspond to the Standard Metropolitan Statistical Areas of the United States Department of Commerce. In terms of geographic area, all the primary markets listed would fit conveniently in Texas.

[12]"The Primary Markets For Quality Merchandise," New York, *New Yorker Magazine, Inc.,* 1966.

CHART 4–2   The 40 Primary Trade Areas

These areas are the 40 most important U.S. markets for quality merchandise. Their ranking has been determined by using seven indexes, each given equal weight: retail sales, women's ready-to-wear stores sales, department stores sales, registrations of new price class 5 cars, families with incomes of $15,000 and over, families with incomes of $25,000 and over, and character of stores.

RANK BY TRADE AREA

1. New York	11. St. Louis	21. Buffalo	31. New Orleans
2. Los Angeles	12. Dallas-Fort Worth	22. Indianapolis	32. Toledo
3. Chicago	13. Minneapolis-St. Paul	23. Atlanta	33. Louisville
4. Philadelphia	14. Houston	24. Denver	34. Providence
5. San Francisco-Oakland	15. Baltimore	25. San Diego	35. Charlotte
6. Detroit	16. Milwaukee	26. Portland	36. Syracuse
7. Boston	17. Seattle	27. Columbus	37. Phoenix
8. Cleveland	18. Miami	28. Rochester	38. Albany
9. Washington	19. Cincinnati	29. Hartford	39. Oklahoma City
10. Pittsburgh	20. Kansas City	30. Dayton	40. Grand Rapids

THESE 40 AREAS ACCOUNT FOR

54% of the U.S. Retail Sales
62% of the U.S. Women's Ready-to-Wear Stores Sales
70% of the U.S. Department Stores Sales
64% of the U.S. Registrations of New Price Class 5 Cars
69% of the U.S. Families with Incomes of $15,000 and Over
69% of the U.S. Families with Incomes of $25,000 and Over

*   *   *

50% of the U.S. Population
75% of The New Yorker's U.S. Circulation

SOURCE: *The Primary Markets For Quality Merchandise*, Revised Edition, *New Yorker Magazine*, 1966.

The primary measures of consumer markets are (1) population and its distribution, (2) purchasing power, and (3) potential changes in either population, its distribution, or in purchasing power.

In Chart 4–3 a distribution of United States Population for 1965 is presented. California has forged into the lead as the most populous state in the union. With the exceptions of California, Texas, and Florida, the ten most populous states in the United States are eastern, heavily industrialized states. These ten states had almost 55 percent of the total United States population. It is significant to note that there is virtually no relationship between geographic area and population density. In New York state, population density was 381 people per square mile; in the District of Columbia, population density reached 13,246 people per square mile; in Wyoming, population density was approximately three people per square mile (Table 4–1). Total population of the United States exceeded 200 million in 1967.

CHART 4–3   States Ranked by Population — 1965

States Ranked by Population: 1965

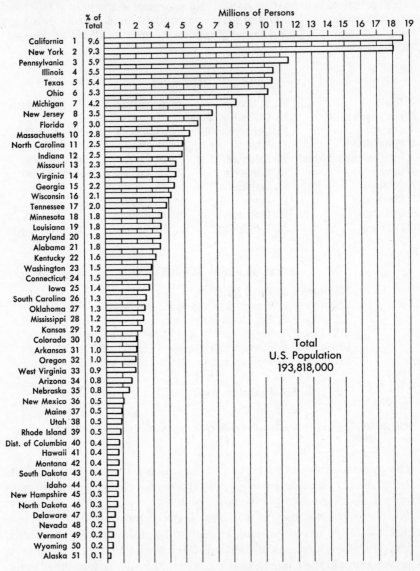

In addition to the number of residents in any given location, anticipated or forecasted changes in population can be important in the design of a logistics system. Population change occurs from two major sources: (1) net new population (births — deaths) and (2) migration in and out of an area. The first factor, new population, is generally a function of the present population base. The second factor, migration, is a function of the mobility of the population. Since the mid-1950's, mobility of the United States population

TABLE 4–1* POPULATION DISTRIBUTION

Area	Resident population as of July 1. 1960, total (1,000)	Average annual percent change 1950 to 1960	1966 Total (1,000)	Rank	Per square mile	Average annual percent change 1960 to 1966
UNITED STATES	179,992	1.7	195,857	(X)	55	1.5
Alabama	3,276	0.6	3,517	21	69	1.2
Alaska	228	5.6	272	51	(Z)	3.2
Arizona	1,321	5.5	1,618	34	14	3.8
Arkansas	1,792	−0.7	1,955	¹31	37	1.5
California	15,862	4.0	18,918	1	121	3.2
Colorado	1,768	2.8	1,977	30	19	2.0
Connecticut	2,543	2.3	2,875	24	590	2.2
Delaware	449	3.4	512	47	258	2.3
District of Columbia	766	−0.5	808	40	13,246	0.9
Florida	4,997	5.8	5,941	9	110	3.2
Georgia	3,958	1.4	4,459	15	77	2.1
Hawaii	641	2.4	718	41	112	2.0
Idaho	671	1.2	694	43	8	0.6
Illinois	10,083	1.5	10,722	5	192	1.1
Indiana	4,673	1.7	4,918	12	136	0.9
Iowa	2,757	0.5	2,747	25	49	−0.1
Kansas	2,180	1.3	2,250	29	27	0.5
Kentucky	3,045	0.3	3,183	22	80	0.8
Louisiana	3,263	1.9	3,603	19	80	1.7
Maine	974	0.6	983	38	32	0.2
Maryland	3,111	2.8	3,613	18	365	2.7
Massachusetts	5,157	0.9	5,383	10	687	0.7
Michigan	7,833	2.1	8,374	7	147	1.2
Minnesota	3,422	1.4	3,576	20	45	0.8
Mississippi	2,185	(Z)	2,327	28	49	1.1
Missouri	4,326	0.9	4,508	13	65	0.7
Montana	679	1.3	702	42	5	0.6
Nebraska	1,417	0.6	1,456	35	19	0.5
Nevada	291	5.8	454	48	4	9.3
New Hampshire	609	1.3	681	45	75	2.0
New Jersey	6,104	2.3	6,898	8	916	2.2
New Mexico	953	3.3	1,022	36	8	1.2
New York	16,855	1.2	18,258	2	381	1.4
North Carolina	4,576	1.2	5,000	11	102	1.6
North Dakota	634	0.2	650	46	9	0.4
Ohio	9,737	2.0	10,305	6	251	1.0
Oklahoma	2,337	0.4	2,458	27	36	0.9
Oregon	1,772	1.5	1,955	¹31	20	1.7
Pennsylvania	11,328	0.8	11,582	3	257	0.4
Rhode Island	858	0.8	898	39	854	0.8
South Carolina	2,395	1.2	2,586	26	85	1.3
South Dakota	683	0.4	682	44	9	−(Z)
Tennessee	3,577	0.8	3,883	17	94	1.4
Texas	9,631	2.2	10,752	4	41	1.9
Utah	900	2.6	1,008	37	12	2.0
Vermont	389	0.3	405	49	44	0.7
Virginia	3,986	1.8	4,507	14	113	2.2
Washington	2,855	1.8	2,980	23	45	0.7
West Virginia	1,855	−0.7	1,794	33	74	−0.6
Wisconsin	3,961	1.4	4,161	16	76	0.8
Wyoming	331	1.3	329	50	3	−0.1
Puerto Rico	2,362	0.6	2,668	(X)	780	2.0

X   Not applicable.   Z   Less than 0.05 percent or 0.5 per square mile.
¹Arkansas and Oregon are identical in rank — 31.

*SOURCE: U.S. Bureau of the Census.

**CHART 4–4   Flow of Migrants Between Regions:
Annual Average: 1955 to 1960 and 1960 to 1965**

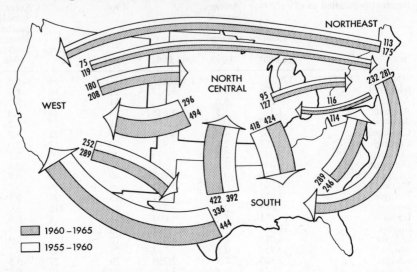

has stabilized at about 21 percent. That is, each year about one fifth of American families change their residence. In Chart 4–4 an overview of migration between the major United States census regions is presented. About 6 million people moved between states during the 12 months from March 1964 to March 1965, and about half of these moves involved inter-regional migration. The volume and the rate of migration reflected in these figures are typical of the pattern that has prevailed during the first half of the current decade and throughout the preceding decade of the 1950's. During the present decade, as in the 1950's, the West registered net gains from domestic migration and the other regions lost population. An average of one million persons per year moved into the West from other regions, and 600,000 persons migrated from the West, a ratio of 5 in-migrants to 3 out-migrants. Nearly a third of the total interregional migration had the West as its destination, with the largest streams of in-migrants coming from the South and the North Central regions.

Second in volume to the migration streams into the West were those be-tween the North Central region and the South, which resulted in a virtually equal exchange of population between the two regions. Movements between these two regions and the Northeast were smaller in volume but similar in nature in that they represented largely an exchange of population and pro-duced only minor net gains or losses.

Patterns of net migration for states did not always follow that of the re-gion in which they were located. Although the South as a whole lost popula-tion through migration, Maryland and Delaware had substantial gains, and Florida registered the second highest net in-migration in the country. Some alteration in the migration pattern of the late 1950's is apparent in the slight

TABLE 4–2* VARIATIONS IN REGIONAL EXPENDITURE PATTERNS: 1960–61

	North East	North Central	South	West
Expenditures for current consumption	$5,761	$5,028	$4,410	$5,677
Alcoholic beverages	110	81	43	102
Appliances	69	71	82	84
Transportation	775	783	703	924
Auto purchase	294	317	269	348
Dental services	58	42	33	62
Hunting and fishing equipment	6	8	10	13
Cameras	5	5	3	7
Newspapers	35	28	19	23
Men's clothing	158	130	119	143
Women's clothing	240	188	164	196

*SOURCE: *Expenditure Patterns of the American Family*, National Industrial Conference Board, New York, 1965.

acceleration of population movement into the West during the current decade and the lessening of the outward flow from the South to the Northeast.

Because consumer markets are composed of people with purchasing power, it is appropriate to consider variations in consumer income and spending patterns by state. In Chart 4–2, the prime retail markets in the United States are outlined. Variations for selected consumer spending categories are presented in Table 4–2, and changes in per capita personal income are detailed in Table 4–3. All of these charts and tables serve to illustrate the same general conclusions. First, demand expressed in terms of dollars or retail sales is concentrated in a limited number of key market areas. Second, there is some positive relationship between population density, degree of industrialization, and income levels. Third, the pattern of consumer income is both increasing and shifting. In Table 4–3, average per capita income as a percent of average United States income presents a type of index of consumer purchasing power. In general, the table illustrates increasing income concentration in the far western states, Nevada and Arizona. The South and much of the West are deficient in purchasing power when measured against the United States.

In Table 4–4, a summary of retail sales, wholesale sales, manufacturing value added, and land in farms is presented. The table demonstrates several basic relationships or tendencies. First, there is a positive relationship between value added by manufacturers and retail sales. Second, there is an inverse relationship between retail sales and land in farms by state. Third, there are significant variations between states in their importance, as wholesale-retail ratio in Missouri was 2.1, in New York 2.8, in Illinois 1.9, and 0.6 in Nevada and Alaska. The states with higher wholesale-retail ratios are typically the wholesale centers for the surrounding region.

TABLE 4–3* PERSONAL INCOME PER CAPITA

State personal income is current income received from all sources by the residents of each state.

State	1950 income per capita	1960 income per capita	1965 Income per capita	1965 Rank	1965 Percent of U.S.
UNITED STATES	$1,496	$2,215	$2,746	(X)	100
Alabama	880	1,488	1,910	47	70
Alaska	2,385	2,846	3,187	8	116
Arizona	1,331	2,032	2,370	32	86
Arkansas	825	1,372	1,845	49	67
California	1,852	2,710	3,258	6	119
Colorado	1,487	2,275	2,710	20	99
Connecticut	1,875	2,807	3,401	1	124
Delaware	2,131	2,757	3,392	2	124
District of Columbia	2,221	3,017	3,708	(X)	135
Florida	1,281	1,950	2,423	29	88
Georgia	1,034	1,639	2,159	41	79
Hawaii	1,387	2,369	2,879	13	105
Idaho	1,295	1,849	2,395	31	87
Illinois	1,825	2,650	3,280	4	119
Indiana	1,512	2,188	2,846	14	104
Iowa	1,485	1,986	2,676	21	97
Kansas	1,443	2,161	2,639	24	96
Kentucky	981	1,574	2,045	43	74
Louisiana	1,120	1,655	2,067	42	75
Maine	1,185	1,844	2,277	38	83
Maryland	1,602	2,343	3,001	11	109
Massachusetts	1,633	2,459	3,050	9	111
Michigan	1,700	2,324	3,010	10	110
Minnesota	1,410	2,116	2,666	22	97
Mississippi	755	1,205	1,608	50	59
Missouri	1,431	2,115	2,663	23	97
Montana	1,622	2,037	2,438	28	89
Nebraska	1,491	2,110	2,629	25	96
Nevada	2,019	2,856	3,311	3	121
New Hampshire	1,323	2,143	2,547	27	93
New Jersey	1,834	2,708	3,237	7	118
New Mexico	1,177	1,890	2,193	40	80
New York	1,873	2,746	3,278	5	119
North Carolina	1,037	1,561	2,041	44	74
North Dakota	1,263	1,715	2,279	37	83
Ohio	1,620	2,334	2,829	15	103
Oklahoma	1,143	1,861	2,289	36	83
Oregon	1,620	2,235	2,761	17	101
Pennsylvania	1,541	2,242	2,747	18	100
Rhode Island	1,606	2,211	2,823	16	103
South Carolina	893	1,377	1,846	48	67
South Dakota	1,243	1,782	2,213	39	81
Tennessee	994	1,543	2,013	46	73
Texas	1,349	1,925	2,338	34	85
Utah	1,309	1,968	2,355	33	86
Vermont	1,121	1,841	2,312	35	84
Virginia	1,228	1,841	2,419	30	88
Washington	1,674	2,349	2,906	12	106
West Virginia	1,065	1,594	2,027	45	74
Wisconsin	1,477	2,175	2,724	19	99
Wyoming	1,669	2,263	2,558	26	93

X   Not applicable.

*SOURCE: Dept. of Commerce, Office of Business Economics.

TABLE 4–4* SELECTED MANUFACTURING, WHOLESALE, RETAIL, AND AGRICULTURAL—FACTORS BY STATE

State	1963 Retail sales (mil. dollars)	1963 Wholesale sales (mil. dollars)	1963 Manufacturing value added (mil. dollars)	1959 Land in farms (mil. acres)
Alabama	$3,253	$3,395	$2,342	17
Alaska	284	181	89	1
Arizona	2,016	1,791	617	40
Arkansas	1,984	1,546	959	16
California	26,889	35,386	17,157	37
Colorado	2,649	3,623	1,203	39
Connecticut	3,929	3,476	4,478	1
Delaware	713	1,090	666	1
District of Columbia	1,418	2,059	261	
Florida	7,619	7,487	2,326	15
Georgia	4,570	8,100	3,239	20
Hawaii	751	735	254	2
Idaho	947	779	366	15
Illinois	15,190	29,135	14,557	30
Indiana	6,476	6,459	7,688	19
Iowa	3,888	4,724	2,276	34
Kansas	2,837	3,390	437	50
Kentucky	3,174	3,211	2,460	17
Louisiana	3,391	4,598	1,918	10
Maine	1,185	980	779	3
Maryland	4,237	4,474	2,978	3
Massachusetts	7,431	10,392	6,365	1
Michigan	10,855	14,055	13,004	15
Minnesota	4,541	8,390	2,828	31
Mississippi	1,914	1,787	1,022	19
Missouri	5,946	12,307	4,424	33
Montana	966	844	235	64
Nebraska	2,096	3,403	743	48
Nevada	707	390	112	11
New Hampshire	882	505	654	1
New Jersey	9,060	12,769	9,980	1
New Mexico	1,166	779	170	46
New York	23,977	66,208	19,510	13
North Carolina	4,975	6,983	4,618	16
North Dakota	871	1,220	72	41
Ohio	12,905	18,208	15,443	19
Oklahoma	2,900	3,465	965	36
Oregon	2,679	4,448	1,570	21
Pennsylvania	13,911	18,044	13,969	12
Rhode Island	1,126	1,199	950	(Z)
South Carolina	2,273	1,993	2,117	9
South Dakota	876	975	142	45
Tennessee	4,009	6,677	3,344	16
Texas	12,715	18,305	7,054	143
Utah	1,210	1,470	705	13
Vermont	535	264	309	3
Virginia	4,790	4,376	3,064	13
Washington	4,043	5,173	2,873	19
West Virginia	1,779	1,396	1,834	6
Wyoming	486	249	83	36
Total	$244,202	$358,386	$190,555	1,124

(Z) Less than 500 farms, 500,000 acres, or $500 million.

*SOURCE: Developed by authors from U.S. Bureau of Census data.

INDUSTRIAL GEOMARKET PATTERNS

There are basically three types of firms in the United States: (1) raw-materials oriented, (2) market-oriented, and (3) foot-loose. The raw-materials oriented firm is typically a *weight-loss* industrial enterprise. Products that lose a large proportion of the weight of raw materials in the manufacturing process typically locate close to the sources of raw materials in order to minimize transportation charges of raw materials. For example, the steel industry was historically developed in a geographical pattern, which places its manufacturing facilities close to large supplies of iron ore and coal reserves. Even high-grade iron ore loses substantial weight in the form of slag and other waste materials in the steel manufacturing process. It would be uneconomical to ship iron ore from the mining site to the market site because of the high concentration of waste material in the iron ore. There are exceptions to this pattern, of course, which are usually found in some historical market requirement strong enough to overcome the economics of transportation. A similar market pattern can be found in the agricultural processing of fruit, vegetables, and livestock. As consumers demand more and more processing in their utilization of agricultural products, the agricultural processor is forced to locate closer and closer to the actual agricultural production site.

A second type of industry is a manufacturing enterprise in which the product gains weight during the processing into a final product. The most obvious example of this type of manufacturing enterprise is the brewing or a similar type industry. The brewing industries produce a product, which is composed of approximately 95 percent water. Since it is prohibitively expensive to ship water, especially because it is available in most locations in suitable supply and quality, considerable decentralization of this industry has resulted. Manufacturing operations are now located in the most thickly populated areas, and the firm ships into these areas the malt, hops, and other materials necessary for the production of beer or carbonated beverages. This in effect results in the manufacturer shipping a smaller amount of the product weight instead of 100 percent of the product weight and gives significant reductions in transportation expense.

The pattern in these types of industries is to locate either in the center of the marketplace or to develop decentralized facilities positioned in key geographic submarket areas. There are, of course, exceptions to the market-oriented type of manufacturing enterprise. For example, some brands of beer are imported from Europe and elsewhere when brand preferences are strong enough to offset increased transportation costs to the consumer.

The third type of industry is what is generally termed a *foot-loose* industry. A foot-loose industry depends on neither raw materials nor market for its principal economic advantage. For example, a company manufacturing exotic electronic equipment might be more concerned with its ability to attract labor and scientific talent rather than raw materials or market position.

CHART 4–5   Relative Rank of States That Accounted for over One Percent of 1964 Machine Tool Shipments

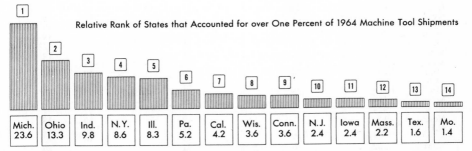

Mich.	Ohio	Ind.	N.Y.	Ill.	Pa.	Cal.	Wis.	Conn.	N.J.	Iowa	Mass.	Tex.	Mo.
23.6	13.3	9.8	8.6	8.3	5.2	4.2	3.6	3.6	2.4	2.4	2.2	1.6	1.4

SOURCE: Machinery's Geographical Pattern of the Metalworking Market, *Machinery*, 1965.

This is one of the reasons why many of these firms will be located close to universities with strong science and engineering programs and/or pleasant geographic and climatic surroundings. If $10,000 of a product will fit into a two-foot square box, this shipment can be air-freighted any place in the United States or overseas in one day. If the equipment is unique enough, the geographic distance between the production point and consumption point is generally not important.

These factors, along with some historical factors in the development of United States' industry, have caused some alterations in the concentration of industrialization by state. In 1963 almost half of the manufacturing value added occurred in the states of California, Illinois, Michigan, New York, Ohio, and Pennsylvania (Chart 4–5). Further, if one were to closely inspect each of these six states, you would find that over 80 percent of the manufacturing activity is located within 20 counties of the six states.

One measurement commonly used to identify industrial activity within states, counties, and regions is manufacturing employment. In Table 4–5 a

TABLE 4–5*   NONAGRICULTURAL EMPLOYMENT: 1965

State	Total (1,000)	Contract con- struction	Manu- facturing	Transporta- tion and public utilities	Wholesale and retail trade	Finance, insurance, and real estate	Service and miscel- laneous[1]	Govern- ment
U.S.	60,444	5	30	7	21	5	16	17
Ala.	884	6	31	6	19	4	14	20
Alaska	70	10	9	10	14	3	12	43
Ariz.	401	6	16	6	24	6	21	23
Ark.	454	6	29	7	21	4	14	19
Calif.	5,775	6	24	7	22	6	17	19
Colo.	586	6	15	8	24	5	19	24
Conn.	1,033	5	42	5	18	6	13	11
Del.	181	7	37	6	19	4	13	14
D.C.	618	4	3	5	14	5	18	50[2]
Fla.	1,625	9	15	7	27	6	18	18
Ga.	1,250	6	32	7	21	5	12	18
Hawaii	217	8	11	8	23	6	18	27
Idaho	175	6	19	8	24	4	16	23
Ill.	3,850	4	34	7	21	5	15	13
Ind.	1,625	5	41	6	19	4	11	14
Iowa	751	5	25	7	25	5	15	18
Kan.	600	6	20	8	23	4	16	22
Ky.	756	6	27	7	21	4	17	18
La.	900	9	17	9	22	5	19	19
Maine	293	5	37	6	19	3	12	19
Md.	1,058	8	25	7	22	5	16	17[2]
Mass.	2,034	4	33	5	21	5	18	14
Mich.	2,612	4	41	5	19	4	13	14
Minn.	1,073	5	24	7	24	5	17	18
Miss.	481	6	32	5	19	4	13	22
Mo.	1,465	5	28	8	23	5	15	15
Mont.	180	7	12	10	24	4	18	26
Nebr.	414	6	17	9	25	6	17	21
Nev.	156	8	5	8	19	4	39	18
N.H.	217	5	41	4	18	4	16	12
N.J.	2,253	5	37	7	19	4	14	13
N. Mex.	262	7	6	8	21	4	25	29
N.Y.	6,506	4	28	7	21	8	18	15
N.C.	1,416	6	41	5	18	4	11	14
N. Dak.	145	8	6	8	28	4	18	28
Ohio	3,356	4	39	6	19	4	13	14
Okla.	649	5	16	7	23	5	20	24
Oreg.	607	5	26	8	23	5	14	20
Pa.	3,922	4	38	7	18	4	15	13
R.I.	315	5	38	5	18	4	15	14
S.C.	684	6	43	4	17	3	10	16
S. Dak.	151	6	9	7	26	5	18	30
Tenn.	1,108	5	35	5	20	4	14	17
Tex.	2,913	7	20	8	25	5	18	18
Utah	301	5	16	7	23	4	18	26
Vt.	119	5	32	6	19	4	19	15
Va.	1,212	8	27	7	21	5	15	19[2]
Wash.	891	5	25	7	22	5	14	22
W. Va.	473	5	27	9	18	3	22	17
Wis.	1,329	5	37	6	21	4	14	15
Wyo.	97	8	7	10	22	4	22	27

[1]Includes mining.
[2]Maryland and Virginia parts of Washington, D.C., metropolitan area are included in D.C.

*SOURCE: U.S. Bureau of Labor Statistics.

distribution of nonagricultural employment by state is presented. The data indicate that the heavily industrialized states also tend to be retail and wholesale centers.

As specific products are singled out for geomarket analysis, the matter becomes even more concentrated. For example, in Chart 4–5 the geographic distribution of machine tool orders is presented. Almost 50 percent of the machine tool shipments in the United States were accounted for in the states of Michigan, Ohio, and Indiana. The state of Michigan alone accounted for almost one quarter of all machine tool shipments in 1964. This geographic concentration by type of manufacturing is also true for most types of agricultural raw materials.

TRANSPORTATION AND GEOMARKET PATTERNS

Historically, transportation has shaped market development in the United States. The earliest cities in the United States developed where good ports existed to receive freight and immigrants from Europe and the East. New York, Philadelphia, San Francisco, and New Orleans all owed their early growth as wholesale and retail centers to strategic port locations. As the frontier expanded into the interior of the United States, large cities developed on navigable inland waterways. Cities such as Chicago, Detroit, Saint Louis, and Kansas City owe a large part of their early growth to the availability of water transportation.

Transportation interacts with the economic environment to form geomarket patterns. As innovations in transportation occur, alternative methods of moving people and merchandise appear. Along with these innovations come less dependence upon traditional forms of transportation and more flexibility in integrating newer transportation methods such as air freight, unit train, and pipelines into a physical distribution system.

One method of identifying transport supply is to consider maps of facilities based upon route configurations. Of all modes, the most flexible in terms of routes is the motor carrier. By and large, it is the only mode that literally is not route bound and enjoys access to origin points and destinations that no other significant mode has. Although major arterial routes, such as the Interstate Highway System, account for the majority of motor carrier movements, it equally applies that a motor carrier can serve significant numbers of points beyond those connected by asphalt or concrete. In Chart 4–6 the major route configurations available to the motor carrier are shown.

Railroads have recently experienced a decline in route availability through abandonment of service and frequently notice a decline in their utilization. Exclusive rail use, therefore, requires sites adjacent to the track or easily accommodated to that purpose. To overcome this operational difficulty, railroads often agree to extend trackage to traffic-generating sites as an accommodation to customers. These trackage agreements usually require a demonstrable volume of traffic subject to rail transport. In Chart 4–7 the rail configurations of the United States railroad industry are illustrated in map form.

CHART 4-6 The American Highway System*

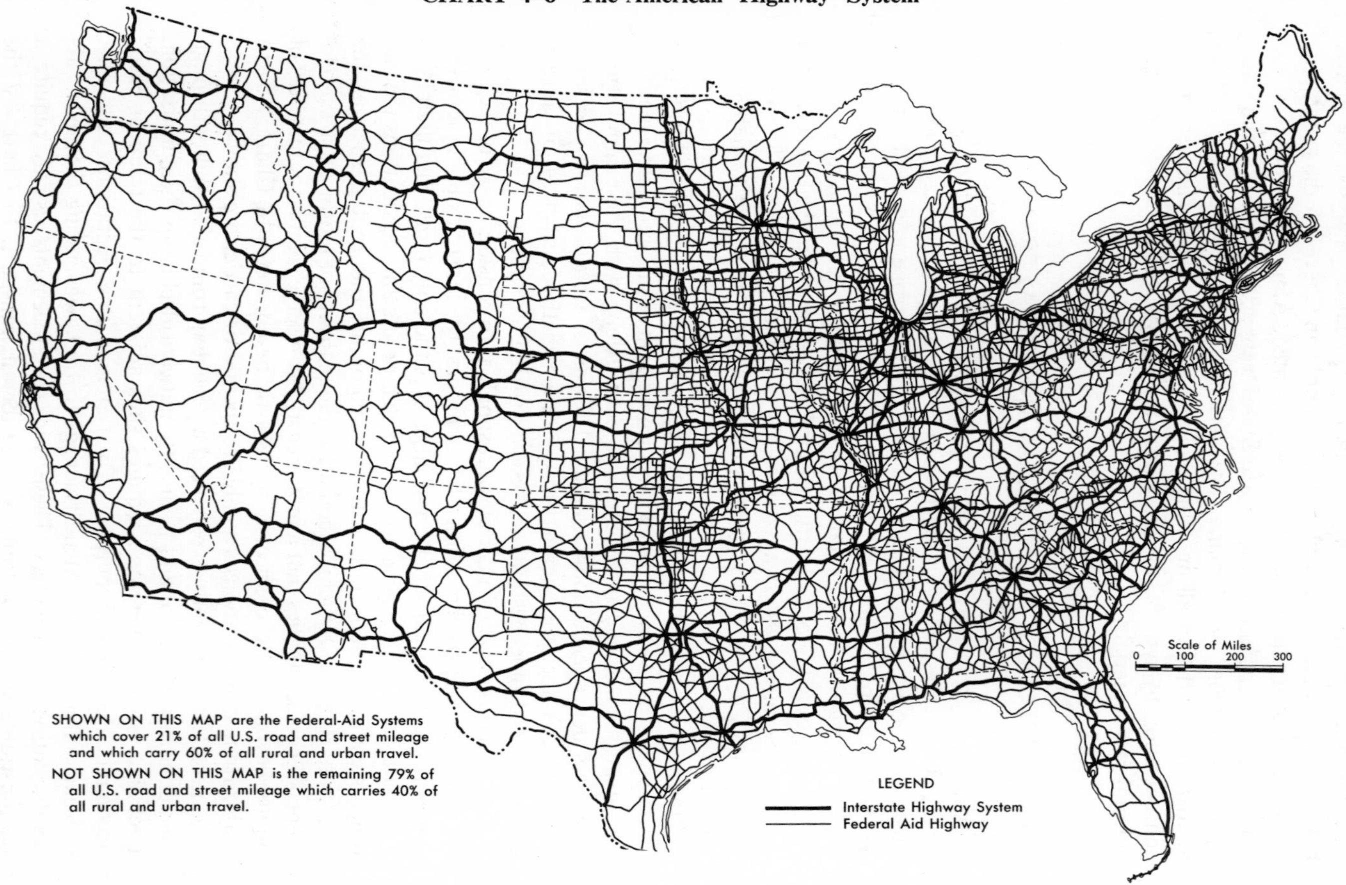

LEGEND

▬▬▬ Interstate Highway System
───── Federal Aid Highway

Scale of Miles
0 100 200 300

SHOWN ON THIS MAP are the Federal-Aid Systems
which cover 21% of all U.S. road and street mileage
and which carry 60% of all rural and urban travel.
NOT SHOWN ON THIS MAP is the remaining 79% of
all U.S. road and street mileage which carries 40% of
all rural and urban travel.

*Courtesy Bureau of Public Roads, U.S. Department of Commerce.

CHART 4–7   The American Railroad System*

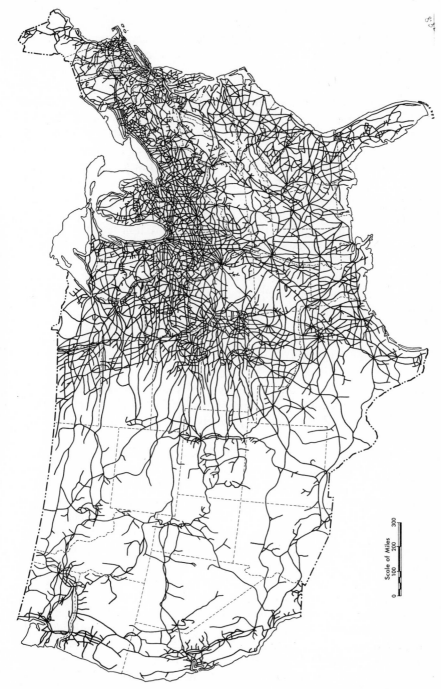

Scale of Miles
0   100   200   300

*Courtesy Association of American Railroads.

There are significant variations in transportation facilities between the states. In Table 4–6 a summary of selected transportation factors by state is presented. It should be recognized that there are some limitations to the data. For example, truck and bus registrations can be influenced by the taxes and operating restrictions imposed by a state. Aircraft registrations can be similarly affected by taxes and regulation. However, the table does serve to illustrate some significant variations between the states in transportation facilities. In 1964, New York, Illinois, and Texas each had more than five times as much federal highway miles as New Jersey. Almost 20 percent of the trucks and buses registered in the United States are registered in either California or Texas. Illinois and Texas have three times as much rail track as Oregon or Kentucky. Almost 20 percent of active civil aircraft are registered in Texas or California.

Although these facts might appear isolated, they are significant in that they provide general indicators of the type of transportation facilities available within the individual states. Extreme care must be taken to interpret Table 4–4 as an indicator rather than as a series of data that can be directly utilized in planning. For example, in the case of rail track mileage, equally important can be service levels, types of equipment, rates, terminal facilities, and so on, which are covered in greater detail in Chapters 6 and 7.

Georeference Systems

Almost any type of physical distribution study requires a method for establishing and identifying geographic boundaries in the marketplace. These geographic segments are used to precisely allocate, control, and evaluate corporate effort.

Historically, a number of states, counties, and other minor political subdivisions have emerged in the United States and elsewhere. Occasionally, boundaries were surveyed and carefully plotted, but often they became a matter of historical accident or geographic convenience. Rivers provided the boundaries between states and counties. Early land grants and frontier cattle trails were often used as boundaries between states or between states and territories. This somewhat random growth of state lines coupled with variations in population density, manufacturing activity, and raw materials availability has led to wide market variations between states, counties, and even standard metropolitan statistical areas.

Two factors have emerged in recent years which have altered much of management's thinking regarding appropriate geographic identification of market segments. First, the concept of information systems has been introduced. Most forward thinking firms are experimenting with information system feasibility and implementation. To develop successfully an effective internal information system, the firm engaged in national marketing effort

TABLE 4–6*   SELECTED TRANSPORTATION FACTORS BY STATE

State	1964 Federal aid highway systems (000)	1965 Truck & bus registrations (000)	1964 Railroad mileage (000)	1965 Active civil aircraft
Alabama	6.6	292	4.60	1,201
Alaska	3.3	33	0.02	1,702
Arizona	3.2	173	2.10	1,462
Arkansas	4.0	260	3.70	1,397
California	9.6	1,484	7.50	13,108
Colorado	4.5	259	3.80	1,458
Connecticut	1.3	151	0.70	694
Delaware	0.7	38	0.30	320
District of Columbia	0.2	19	0.03	599
Florida	5.5	356	4.60	3,630
Georgia	9.0	353	5.60	1,676
Hawaii	0.5	33	0.03	169
Idaho	3.3	126	2.70	929
Illinois	11.0	507	11.00	4,482
Indiana	6.0	435	6.50	2,560
Iowa	10.1	294	8.40	1,911
Kansas	7.8	352	8.10	2,782
Kentucky	4.6	289	3.50	704
Louisiana	3.3	279	3.90	1,530
Maine	2.0	79	1.70	438
Maryland	2.4	173	1.10	952
Massachusetts	2.3	203	1.60	1,253
Michigan	7.1	463	6.50	3,744
Minnesota	8.5	324	8.00	2,540
Mississippi	5.9	231	3.60	1,111
Missouri	8.9	418	6.50	2,472
Montana	6.5	132	4.90	1,199
Nebraska	5.9	206	5.60	1,363
Nevada	2.2	59	1.60	736
New Hampshire	1.3	51	0.80	263
New Jersey	2.2	299	1.90	2,074
New Mexico	4.1	126	2.20	1,089
New York	12.6	566	5.90	4,368
North Carolina	4.7	399	4.30	1,660
North Dakota	4.6	128	5.20	764
Ohio	8.1	496	8.10	4,148
Oklahoma	8.2	374	5.60	2,132
Oregon	4.1	192	3.20	1,925
Pennsylvania	8.5	588	8.70	3,048
Rhode Island	0.4	42	0.20	134
South Carolina	5.3	178	3.30	692
South Dakota	6.0	109	3.90	775
Tennessee	6.7	280	3.30	1,266
Texas	17.5	1,137	14.30	7,971
Utah	2.4	110	1.70	583
Vermont	1.7	36	0.70	172
Virginia	5.7	259	4.10	1,244
Washington	4.0	316	5.00	2,213
West Virginia	2.9	131	3.60	448
Wisconsin	6.4	279	6.10	1,834
Wyoming	3.9	72	1.80	534
Puerto Rico	0.5	N.A.	N.A.	282[1]
Total	267.8	14,188	212.06	97,741

[1]Includes Puerto Rico, American Samoa, Canton, Guam, Virgin Islands, and Wake.

*SOURCE: Developed by authors from U.S. Bureau of Census data.

must find some method of isolating geographic control units. Past experience has indicated that the state and county geographic sector is inadequate for this purpose, and a more effective technique must be developed.

A second development is the availability of computer technology to handle on a continuous basis large amounts of geographically identified data. When the quantitative tools of simulation and linear programming are combined with the high speed and high capacity of modern computers, it becomes possible and economically feasible to manipulate large masses of data to assist in marketing and physical distribution decisions. Out of this capability also emerges a closer integration of the functional areas of the business firm. That is, production, purchasing, physical distribution, and marketing are tied together through a core information system geared to modern high-speed computer technology.

In summary, progress in the geographical referencing of physical distribution and marketing data has come about from the recognition of the inadequacies of traditional methods of measuring geographic market segments and the development of computer technology to handle large amounts of geographically referenced input on a continuous basis. The movement toward standard geographic control units is also consistent with the concept of total management information systems. Firms utilizing this type of system can integrate sales, marketing procurement, and distribution information using a common georeference coding system.

GEOGRAPHIC CONTROL UNITS[13]

A geographic control unit may be defined as an area with definable geographic boundaries, which is used for gathering and analyzing marketing data. The geographic control unit should meet certain minimum criteria. Practically speaking, the selected geographic control units are usually a compromise between ideal criteria and inherent imperfections of the marketplace. The ideal criteria include (1) size, (2) homogeneity, (3) mutually exclusive, (4) stability, (5) flexibility, and (6) geographically continuous. These requirements are discussed in brief detail below.

Size.   The exact size of a geographical reference unit is of some considerable importance. If the size of the control unit becomes too large, the unit becomes almost invariably nonhomogeneous. For example, almost any six-county contiguous area in the United States would contain a mixture of urban and rural residence and industrial and nonindustrial land use. As the size of the geographic control unit becomes larger, differences between units

[13]For a more complete discussion and an application example see Richard J. Lewis, *A Business Logistics Information and Accounting System for Marketing Analysis*, unpublished Ph.D. dissertation, Michigan State University, East Lansing, Michigan, 1964.

tend to average out and significant variations in market and distribution requirements become obscured. On the other hand, if the geographic control units are too small, problems of collecting, coding, and analyzing data increase almost geometrically. Even with the assistance of a large capacity computer, for example, the problem of handling data on a quarter-mile square grid area as a geographic control unit would be a formidable task. It is obviously an oversimplification to say that the geographical control selected probably should be appropriate to the individual company. However, the size of the control unit selected should be based upon the nature of the product, distribution of customers, and shipment patterns, which will provide the most meaningful unit of analysis for management decision making.

Homogeneity. A corollary criterion to size is homogeneity. The geographic control unit should be as homogeneous as possible in order to prevent the averaging error noted above from wide variations within the cell. For example, a market for a consumer product might be considerably different both in density and in patterns of demand between a rural area and an urban area. A geographic control unit including both an urban and rural segment might result in an average sales or profit figure atypical of either segment. It is generally impossible except in large rural concentrations or large urban concentrations to get completely homogeneous units, but to the extent possible homogeneity is a desirable goal in building a geographic unit control system.

Mutually Exclusive. All geographic control units should be mutually exclusive. Any overlap between units results in double counting, increased record-keeping expense, and the general undermining of the entire concept of geographical control units.

Stability. A geographical control unit system should possess the characteristic of stability. Obviously, the market is dynamic, and activity within units will change as population and industrial concentration shifts. However, the selected unit should possess some stability in order that historical comparisons and continuous collection can be facilitated without costly and time-consuming reprogramming efforts. For example, over the past several decades the definition of the standard metropolitan area of the Bureau of Census has changed a number of times. To make meaningful comparisons between census years for Standard Metropolitan Statistical Areas (SMSA), time-consuming statistical adjustments are required. Similarly if city-limit boundaries are used, adjustments must be made for annexation of surrounding territories. The geographical reference system ultimately selected for use must have some degree of stability or constant reprogramming and statistical adjustment will be required to utilize effectively this system as an information base for marketing and distribution decisions.

Flexibility.   A geographical reference system should be flexible to accommodate any changes occurring in the marketplace without major recoding of historical data. For example, if a major new supplier of raw materials is found, it should not require any major changes in coding, classification, or flow of information. Similarly, if sales territories are realigned, systems should be flexible enough to accommodate these alterations in marketing patterns without serious interruption or expensive reprogramming. In the case of an individual company, time or financial constraints might dictate the establishment of a partial geographic identification system, which would usually be keyed to major market areas. As the market territory covered expands and/or new distribution facilities or patterns emerge, the system should be flexible enough to be expanded.

In a dynamic business environment, it is of considerable importance to develop a system tailored to individual company needs, yet flexible enough to accommodate the constant change in suppliers, customers, and distribution patterns characteristic of most industries in the United States.

Geographically Continuous.   A geographically continuous system is one wherein all geographical areas are identified. For example, the SMSA system is not a geographically continuous system, because it covers only the major metropolitan areas of the United States. Unless an area has a minimum amount of population, it is not identified in a geographic coding system that identifies SMSA's. With decentralization of production facilities and distribution facilities, many large facilities are not located in SMSA's and, therefore, a system must be developed to accommodate all present and potential production plants, distribution facilities, suppliers, and customers.

This, however, does not mean that the system selected must account for the entire geography of the continental United States. A firm operating exclusively in northeastern United States would not require a geographic identification code for the Far West. However, all of the market territory it serves should be identified in its geographic reference system consistent with the flexibility criteria noted above. In the event that it expands its operations to the West Coast, the company should be able to utilize a compatible system for such expansion.

BASIC TYPES OF GEOREFERENCE SYSTEMS

The two basic systems of geographic referencing are the point system and the grid system. In the point system, geographic points such as cities, customers, or terminal facilities within cities are assigned specific geographic identification. This geographic identification is usually in the form of some multiple digit code with a unique code number for each specific point within the system. A graphic example of a point system identification scheme is shown in Chart 4–8.

CHART 4–8   Point Reference System — Picadad

Picadad Key Points

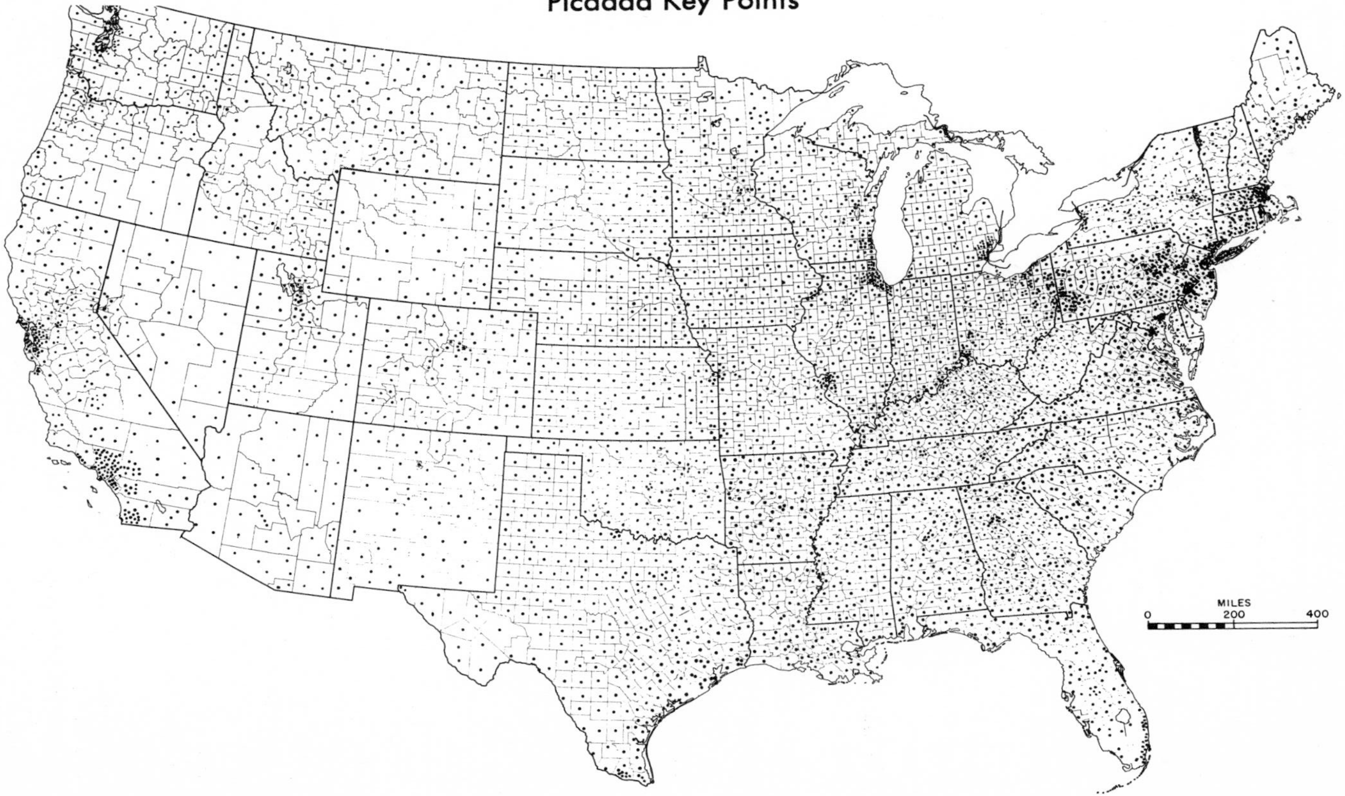

The grid approach to developing a georeference system involves gridding a geographic plane with horizontal and vertical lines. This approach results in a particular geographic area being subdivided into geographic segments or "cells." In this system, each specific cell receives a unique geographic identification code. A graphic example of this type of grid division is shown in Chart 4–9.

Within the past few years variations in both types of georeferencing systems have been developed by the Federal Government, business firms, carriers, and distribution consulting firms. Typically, however, the variations can be classified as one of the above types with relatively minor deviations to accommodate a company or industry need. Two such typical systems are briefly discussed below. The Picadad System is a point georeference system, and the Railway Express Agency System is a grid georeference system.

Point Reference System — Picadad.[14]   The Transportation Division of the Bureau of the Census, United States Department of Commerce, developed the Picadad System originally for use in the 1963 Census of Transportation. The word Picadad signifies the following: Pi(*p*lace *i*dentification), ca(*c*haracteristics of *a*rea), and dad(machine procedure for computing *d*istance *a*nd *d*irection). Place identification is composed of a four-digit number, which identifies the city or town and state of shipment, origin, and destination. The area characteristics are indicated by a four-digit code, which denotes the census division, the state, the city size, and any special area characteristics such as SMSA's. The computation of distance and direction is made through a vertical and horizontal coordinate system. Two basic lines, one vertical and one horizontal, are established and a four-digit code is used to designate the specific place location in relation to the vertical and horizontal base line. Distance can be calculated by using a computer program that utilizes the coordinates in relation to the vertical and horizontal base line to calculate exact distance between origin and destination of any two points in the system. This distance is calculated within a 1 percent accuracy. If one wishes to convert to over-the-road distance, motor carrier distance is 24 percent greater and rail distance is 21 percent greater than straight-line distance.

The Picadad System has several unique advantages. First, it is compatible with other data collected by the United States Department of Commerce. Because there is evidence that future census activity will be designed with data processing compatibility to business systems, this could represent a

---

[14]Donald E. Church, "Picadad: A System for Machine Processing of Geographic and Distance Factors in Transportation and Marketing Data," Bureau of the Census, U. S. Department of Commerce, 1965. There has been some interest and activity in using the U. S. Post Office Zip Code format as a geographic control unit for marketing analyses and evaluation; see Martin Baier, "Zip Code — New Tool for Marketeers," *Harvard Business Review*, February, 1967, pp. 136–140.

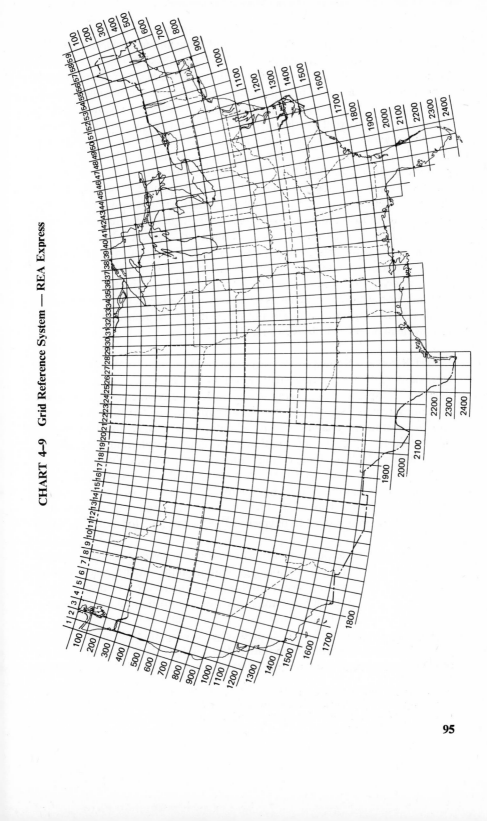

CHART 4–9   Grid Reference System — REA Express

95

distinct advantage.[15] For example, it may be possible to order a computer tape of the 1970 Census of Population and Housing which would be compatible with the place identification of the Picadad System. Similarly, it may be possible to obtain future censuses of business with a compatible coding format. The Bureau of Census is encouraging this type of planning both by business and local and regional planning groups. A second advantage of the Picadad System is that it allows relatively accurate measurements between two points within the georeference system. This represents an advantage over the grid system, in which system distance is typically estimated between blocks or cells rather than between specific points. The primary use of the Picadad System is to estimate flow of products, people, or transportation movement between two points or multiple points within the system. It is not generally used to estimate market density or demand characteristics of an area. It could be used only to estimate demand characteristics at a point. This probably represents the major disadvantage of this system as a marketing and distribution tool. Estimation of demand and supply at a point rather than within a given geographic area often tends to distort the true pattern of demand. For example, some cities serve as wholesale centers for surrounding areas, and because demand does not originate at the point some distortion in flow-demand relationships can result.

Grid Reference System — Railway Express Agency.   Point reference systems described earlier enjoy great flexibility, because they allow maximum data inputs expressed as geographic units. However, some cases arise where a point system lacks sufficient descriptive capability or flexibility with reference to marketing analytical requirements. Most marketing data require orientation to sources of information based upon predetermined geographic configurations. Among these configurations are (1) states, (2) census regions, (3) SMSA, (4) counties, and (5) Federal Reserve Bank Districts. Even with internal sources of information, nonhomogeneity occurs. Sales territories, for example, are designed for sales administrative purposes. Records may also be kept on a state basis for payment of sales tax and for other statutory reasons.

The grid system provides a convenient midpoint between point type systems on the one hand and conventional geographic units on the other. By this method, the unit under consideration can be aggregated into a series of blocks of equal size. Each block then becomes an information cell containing sales, production, customers, and other relevant data.

One long-existing block system used originally for transportation pricing, is the REA Express block map. In it, the United States is broken down into blocks one degree square (60 × 60 nautical miles). Each block is then

[15]William T. Fay and Robert L. Hagan, "Computer-Based Geographic Coding for the 1970 Census," U. S. Bureau of the Census, *Census Tract Conference Papers*, August 15, 1966. U. S. Government Printing Office, Washington, D.C., 1967, pp. 27–34.

further divided into 256 smaller squares, each containing an area of about 41 square miles. Pricing of REA class rated service is then calculated on a subblock to subblock basis reflecting the actual short-line mileages between blocks.

The basic REA grid-block system has been redesigned to grid-block sizes of 3 × 4 miles, increasing accuracy in required geographic information. Under either system (REA or modified), grid blocks may be aggregated to conform closely to state boundaries, counties, SMSA, sales territories, and so on. Through this aggregation, all the traditionally defined marketing and production information is still available and in the records, but homogeneity through the block system is maintained.

The purpose of block systems is to provide information in a form suitable for various types of analysis, especially the mathematical type of linear programming and simulation. In choosing to collect information on a grid-block system, collection of new data for linear programming or simulation solutions is not necessary. From an administrative point of view, only one additional piece of information is required to convert to a grid system consisting of a six-digit numerical code. This code ordinarily consists of a six-digit number, three indicating the horizontal position of the block and three indicating its vertical position. These six digits would be added to the present record-keeping system. A sample card layout for such a coding system is shown below:

```
240  316  42  26  54674  05  03
  240  Horizontal grid
  316  Vertical grid
   42  State
   26  County
54674  Customer number
   05  Warehouse best able to serve customer
   03  Next best warehouse to serve customer
```

Additional traditional information such as sales territory designation can be added as required.

Once a firm places its records on a grid system, significant features of its markets are usually discernible. For most firms, state sales territory and other methods of data collection obscure the fact that large areas of the United States consist of low-density demand areas. One such map for the sale of beans and peas is shown in Chart 4–10.

Note that in the chart only a surprisingly small number of blocks account for the large proportion of sales. This appears to be the typical case from firms studied by this method. With this knowledge, more precise planning and operation of not only physical distribution, but also of advertising, sales, and other factors can be formulated.[16]

[16]Mark E. Stern, *Marketing Planning: A Systems Approach* (New York: McGraw-Hill, Inc., 1966), pp. 92–104.

CHART 4-10 Sales Analysis Using Grid Identification System

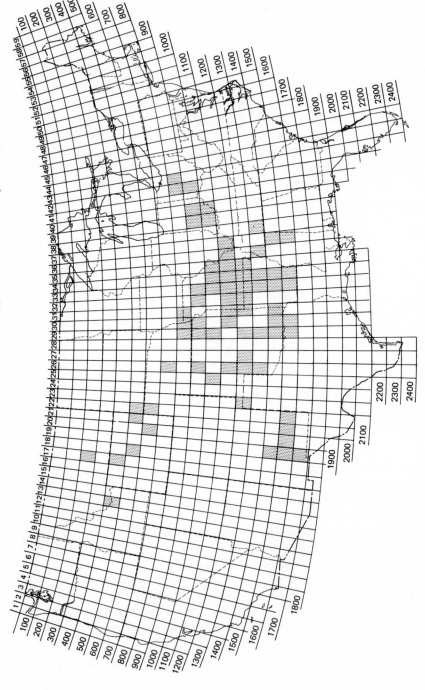

The grid system has the capability of providing a base for a total management information system. That is, such a system can be used in planning, controlling, and evaluating sales, distributor performance, and advertising performance; in locating production or distribution facilities; in selecting and evaluating transportation and raw materials vendors; and in basic distribution planning. Because input documents provide both the date and the location of activity involved, both temporal and spatial data can be provided in a system of this type. With proper design and implementation, all internal data are compatible. External data, such as government data, can be integrated in a system by aggregating the grid cells to approximate the political subdivision or by converting government data to compatible grid blocks.

Summary

In the American marketplace, there is freedom of movement of the mobile resources of production. This freedom of movement results in a constant pressure to re-evaluate the most appropriate system of physical distribution for the individual firm. As manufacturers seek a differential advantage in the marketplace and the consumers seek to more appropriately satisfy their economic wants, both in terms of income and expenditures, the face of the American market gradually changes. Assessing current and potential changes in market composition and adjusting production and physical distribution to these changes is an important continuing responsibility of management.

In recent years, this responsibility for continued control and evaluation of internal operations and external information has led to the increased management attention to total information systems. Because information systems must have both a temporal and spatial dimension, innovations have occurred in the georeferencing of procurement, production, marketing, and sales information. The management information system is designed as a total corporate system, which provides information for decision making on a wide variety of problems including the design of physical distribution systems.

Discussion Questions

1. Why would a firm consider using a geomarket forecast as part of its decision criteria on warehouse location?

2. What are the differences between the theories of von Thünen, Losch, and Weber?

3. Why are state and county lines inadequate for use in delineating market boundaries?

4. Why is homogeneity a factor to be considered in designing geographic control systems?

5. What is the major disadvantage of a point reference system?

6. How could a firm use a georeference system to aid it in differentiating itself from its competitors?

7. What are the problems associated with the using of data, such as that shown in this chapter, by a firm for part of its input into planning and forecasting decisions? Is there an alternative to using this type of data?

CHAPTER 5 Physical

Distribution Systems

IN Chapter 1, physical distribution management was defined as that portion of corporate management responsible for the design and administration of systems to control the flow of raw materials and finished inventories. Central to this definition is the key word *systems*. A system can be defined as "an assemblage or combination of things or parts forming a complex or unitary whole."[1] It is in this context that the term is applied to the field of physical distribution. To obtain a maximum integration of all activities related to physical distribution, it is desirable to consider total physical flow as a single system.

The objective of this chapter is to develop the basic logic of physical distribution systems. Thus far, chapters have been concerned with the business and market environments within which the firm's physical distribution must be completed. Emphasis is now shifted to the managerial task of developing an integrated physical distribution effort.

The initial section of this chapter is concerned with the development of the systems concept and the integration of basic components of a physical distribution system. Next, attention is directed to the basic physical distribution mission confronted by the firm. The basic question of cost and service balance is of primary importance in the development of an effective system. The final section reviews some basic physical distribution systems commonly found in industry. In total this chapter serves as a bridge from the general to the specifics of physical distribution management.

---

[1] *Webster's Collegiate Dictionary.*

Physical Distribution as an Integrated System

Earlier chapters have stressed that one major deficiency of traditional physical distribution management is the lack of integrated treatment. More often than not, management of segments of physical distribution have been under the direction and control of various departments within the corporation. Such diffusion of responsibility often resulted in duplication, waste, and sometimes hindrance of mission accomplishment. Likewise, information flow concerning physical distribution matters was often sufficiently fragmented to prohibit both planning and administration of the total system. Two developments of a technological nature have provided management with the proper tools to eliminate this undesirable segmentation.

First, the advent of high-speed digital computers provides a tool for use in integrated systems analysis. Although the computer is not a private servant of physical distribution, there appears little doubt that it has been put to work on an operating basis as well in physical distribution as in any other area of the corporation.[2]

The second major development, closely related to computer technology, was the development of systems logic. Once again physical distribution has no exclusive claim on the use of the systems approach to problem solving or administration. However, physical distribution managers are increasingly finding systems analysis an effective tool for development of physical flow control.

Some basic ideas of systems analysis are developed forthwith. First, a few comments regarding organization of physical distribution within the corporation will be helpful with respect to the material that follows.

Implicit in the statements regarding duplication and waste is the assumption that if all management responsibility for physical distribution were centralized in a single organizational group integrated control would automatically be improved. This assumption has the basic fallacy of placing emphasis upon structure rather than on results. Support for the fact that centralized organization alone is not sufficient to guarantee results can readily be found in actual business cases. Many of the most effective physical distribution operations function without formal organizational grouping under a single management unit. Others with centralized grouping also achieve superior results.

Individual organization structures vary depending upon the specific mission, the given personnel, and the resource capabilities. Some basic patterns of physical distribution organization are available to guide management; however, discussion and development is deferred until Chapter 13. At this stage the significant point is the development of a philosophy of operation

---

[2]For an expanded discussion of the operational use of computers in physical distribution management see "New Strategies to Move Goods," *Business Week*, September 24, 1966, p. 112.

that stimulates all levels of management within a firm to think and act in terms of integrated physical distribution capabilities and economies. Such a philosophy is found in the systems concept.

THE SYSTEMS CONCEPT

It is difficult to trace the exact origins of the systems approach to problem solving. The first significant applications of systems analysis can be traced to research developments during World War II. This does not mean that men lacked an appreciation of systems prior to World War II, because the concept of a system is closely related to all forms of organized activity. However, with the challenges of global war, scientists developed an organized methodology to guide the research and development of complex physical and organizational problems. This approach is referred to as systems analysis. Technical aspects of distribution system design are treated in Part Three. However, a basic understanding of the systems concept is essential for a proper appraisal of integrated logistics.

The systems concept is one of total integrated effort toward the accomplishment of a predetermined objective. Such an objective for a physical distribution system might be either the lowest possible cost method or the fastest method of product movement. Given the objective, a system capable of obtaining the desired results within the stated parameters can be designed.

Under the systems approach, basic acknowledgment is given to the importance of all activity centers included in the system. These activity centers are normally considered components of the system, each of which has a specific function to accomplish toward attainment of the basic objective of the total system. To illustrate, consider the classic example of a precision high-fidelity stereo-tape player. Many different components are combined into an integrated system for the single purpose of reproducing sound. The speakers, the transistors, the amplifier, and other parts only exist to the end that their combined performance results in the desired quality of sound.

From this basic illustration some principles can be stated concerning systems in general. First, it is the performance of the total system, which is singularly of importance. Components only exist and find justification to the extent that they enhance total system performance. Second, components need not have optimum design on an individual basis, because emphasis is based upon their integrated relationship with other components in the system. Third, there exists between components a functional relationship, which may stimulate or hinder combined performance. This relationship is commonly called trade-off. Finally, it is explicit that components linked together as a system can, on a combined basis, produce a result greater than that possible by individual performance. In fact, the desired result may not be attainable without integrated performance.

These principles are basic and logically consistent. There can be little doubt that a physical distribution system having balanced integration of all component parts should be able to attain greater results than one lacking coordinated performance. However, although logical and noncontroversial in concept, the effective implementation of a basic systems approach to physical distribution remains rather rare.

The various activities involved in physical distribution are more often than not performed within corporations as individual activities. For example, transportation and purchasing may be performed by separate units in the corporation without any real effort at integrating the activities. To the degree that such isolated performance exists, a serious void may also exist in total integrated capability. In final analysis, it makes very little difference whether a firm spends more or less for any individual distribution activity — warehousing for example — as long as the overall objectives are accomplished at the lowest cost expenditure for the integration of all critical activities.

One useful way to study the implications of physical distribution as a corporate-wide system is to disregard organizational arrangements. Placing primary emphasis upon the arrangement of system components on a corporate-wide basis allows substantial freedom in system design without involvement in matters of organizational control.

PHYSICAL DISTRIBUTION SYSTEM ACTIVITY CENTERS

The major components of a firm's physical distribution system are grouped into five broad areas: (1) facility locations, (2) transportation capability, (3) inventory allocations, (4) communication networks, and (5) unitization. These five activity centers combine to form a physical distribution control network, which constitutes the physical distribution system of the firm. Two factors relating to development of a firm's physical distribution system are important to keep in mind while reviewing the material that follows.

First, whereas a firm desires to maintain a high degree of congruency with all other firms engaged in the exchange channel, such alliances only extend to an agreement regarding common interfirm policies and programs. To a significant degree, firms will only accept risk for performance of exchange functions to the extent it corresponds with potential return on investment or counterbalance of power.[3] The decisions of who will perform what exchange functions are therefore matters of negotiation. Once these negotiations have stabilized, they in effect become operating parameters. Each firm involved in the exchange channel must make their own arrangements concerning implementation of their respective responsibility. The result of such negotiation becomes the basis for each firm's physical distribution system. It therefore

[3]See Chapter 3, page 53 for an expanded treatment.

follows that a firm may be more or less engaged in the various functions of channel exchange and as a result will require more or less involvement in each of the five activity areas outlined.

Second, those activity centers included in a firm's physical distribution system are considered under complete control. Such control includes all the aspects of the system under direct ownership of the firm as well as the intermediary specialists performing specified activities for a price. Thus, design of the distribution system includes for hire specialists such as transportation or public warehouse firms who perform a stated activity for a specified payment.

Facility Locations. One deficiency in classical economic analysis is a lack of attention to the role of facility location. In an effort to study supply and demand under a wide variety of market structures, economists in general have often assumed location advantages and transportation cost differentials to be either nonexistent or equal among competitive firms. Businessmen are not able to neglect the impact of location decisions upon the subsequent success or failure of their firm to realize an adequate return on investment. In many ways, the network of facilities selected by a firm's management represents one of their most important decisions with respect to ultimate results. In particular, the number, the size, and the geographical arrangement of facilities operated or used have a direct relationship to the customer service capabilities and corresponding logistics cost outlay of the firm.

In Chapters 2, 3, and 4, a significant number of basic differentials with respect to market potential and related cost of logistical support were noted. It is a fact of business life that a great deal of disparity exists between market areas. The top-ten trading markets in the United States account for at least 42 percent of the potential sale of any quality product or service.[4] It fairly well follows that any firm attempting to market on a national basis should give serious attention to the location of fixed facilities in these prime markets.

When one realistically views competition, it is clear that all marketing transactions must be developed within and between a given framework of location points. From the viewpoint of physical flows, the facility network represents a series of nodal points through which materials and finished inventories physically move. In a planning sense, such facilities include production plants, distribution warehouses, and retail stores operated by a firm. If the specialized services of transportation firms or public warehouses are utilized by a firm, the facilities of these specialists represent part of the network.

The primary importance of selecting the best possible network of facilities cannot be overemphasized. Although it is unlikely that any firm can relocate all facilities at any given time, considerable latitude remains in location selection and facility design over a period of time. From the viewpoint of

[4]See Chart 4–2 on page 75.

marketing impact, the selection of a superior set of locations can result in a substantial competitive advantage. Concerning the physical distribution support system, a superior network of locations can result in speedy delivery at a minimum dollar expenditure. The degree of distribution efficiency attainable by a given physical distribution system is directly related and limited by the network of facilities.

Transport Capability.   Given a network of facilities, the first connecting link in the system is the transport capability utilized by the firm. Transportation and traffic management has received considerable attention over the years both in industry and in academic circles. Almost every firm of any size has a traffic manager who is responsible for administration of the firm's transport program.

In a general sense, a firm has three alternatives in the establishment of a transport capability between facility locations. First, a private fleet of equipment may be purchased or leased. Second, specific contracts may be arranged with firms and individuals who are transport specialists to provide an exclusive movement service. Third, a firm may purchase the services of any legally authorized transport company that offers point-to-point transfer at specified charges. These three forms of transport are commonly called private, contract, and common carriage.

From the physical distribution system viewpoint the firm must establish a capability to move materials and finished inventories between facilities. Three factors are of primary importance in establishment of the transport capability: (1) cost of service, (2) speed of service, and (3) consistency of service.

The cost of transport results from the actual payment for a movement between two points plus the expense related to having inventory committed to transit. Physical distribution systems should be designed to minimize the transport cost in relation to the total system cost. As will be illustrated later, this does not necessarily mean that the lowest or cheapest method of movement between two facility points should be utilized.

Speed of service relates to the actual time required to complete a transfer between two facilities. Speed of service and cost of service are related in two ways. First, those transport specialists capable of providing fast service normally charge higher rates. Second, the faster the service the shorter is the interval that materials and inventories are frozen in movement between facilities.[5]

Consistency of service refers to measured performance over a range of transfers between two facilities. In essence, how dependable is a given method of transfer with respect to time? In many ways consistency of service is the most important characteristic of a transportation specialist. If a given move-

---

[5]This reduction in transit time results in a lower total system inventory investment. In many cases the savings from such inventory reductions will more than offset the higher rate required for fast transport.

ment takes two days one time and six the next, serious bottlenecks can develop in the flow of goods within the physical distribution system. To the degree that transport capability lacks consistency, safeguards in terms of extra inventory must be built into the system to prevent service breakdowns. Such impacts influence both sellers' and buyers' inventory control systems.

In the design of a physical distribution system, a delicate balance must be established between transfer cost and speed of service. The ultimate objective is to regulate and integrate speed of transfer into the total system. Under some circumstances, low-cost slow transfers are preferred, whereas under other conditions fast methods of transfer are desirable.[6] Finding the proper balance in transport capability is one of the primary objectives of physical distribution system analysis.

Three aspects of transport capability should be kept in mind as they relate to the physical distribution system. First, the selection of facilities forms a network which in fact limits the range of transport alternatives available and establishes the nature of the job to be accomplished. Second, the cost of physical transfer involves more than the freight bill received from a carrier for movement between two facilities.[7] Third, the entire effort to integrate transport capability into a total system may be defeated if the service received is sporadic and inconsistent.

Inventory Allocations.   The requirements for physical transfer between fixed facilities are determined by the inventory allocation program followed by a firm. In a broad sense a firm could stock every item carried in inventory at every facility. Few firms, however, follow such a luxurious inventory allocation program, because the total cost would be prohibitive. The objective of inventory integration into the physical distribution system is to employ the minimum quantities consistent with desired delivery capability and total cost expenditure. Excessive inventories can compensate for errors in the design of the basic system and may even help overcome poor administration of physical distribution activities. However, inventory used as a crutch can and normally will result in poor system performance.

Thus, inventory allocation programs should be initiated with the idea of the minimum practical commitment. The answer to a sound inventory program is found in selectivity. Such selective allocation centers around four factors: (1) customer qualities, (2) product qualities, (3) transport integration, and (4) competitor performance. Each is briefly discussed.

Every firm selling to a variety of different customers is confronted with an array of quality with respect to profitability. Some customers are very

---

[6]Techniques for evaluating transport capabilities in terms of total system balance are developed in Chapters 11 and 12.

[7]For a discussion of total cost related to freight movement see J. L. Heskett, Robert M. Ivie, and Nicholas A. Glaskowsky, Jr., *Business Logistics* (New York: The Ronald Press, 1964) p. 430.

profitable to do business with and others are not. Such profitability stems from range of product line purchases, volume of purchases, price, marketing services required, and the necessary supporting activities needed to maintain a repetitious relationship. Customers who are highly profitable to do business with constitute the core market of a firm. Inventory allocations should be designed to protect these customers with respect to rapid and consistent physical distribution.

Given a product line, most firms find that a substantial variance exists concerning the volume and profitability of individual products. It is often stated that most firms with a wide assortment find 20 percent of the products marketed account for 80 percent of a firm's profit. Given this variance, a realistic appraisal should be made of the reasons why low-profit items are carried in the assortment. On the surface it would seem obvious that a firm would want to provide a high degree of consistent delivery service on highly profitable products. The fallacy may be that many of the less-profitable items are carried to provide full-line service to a core customer. Therefore, it is necessary to consider all factors when selectively allocating inventory holdings among facilities. Many firms find it desirable to centralize inventories on slow-moving or low-profit items and then utilize the fastest method of transfer when such items are needed by a customer.

To a significant degree the selection of inventory assortments for given facilities is related to transport cost. Most charges of transportation specialists are directly related to size of shipment. Therefore, it may be sound policy to stock more items at a specific facility in order to generate larger volume shipments. The corresponding savings in unit transport cost may more than offset the increase in unit inventory holding cost.

Finally, inventory allocation programs are not created in a competitive vacuum. The ability of a firm to provide rapid delivery of a complete assortment of products may well render that firm cheaper and more desirable to do business with. Therefore, inventory may be allocated to a specific facility in order to improve the physical distribution impact even when such commitments may increase cost. Such allocations may result from an effort to gain a differential advantage over a competitor or to neutralize one that a competitor currently enjoys. The strategy of competitively stimulated allocations increases in tempo in direct relationship to the extent to which users can substitute competitive offerings.

Three managerial tasks are directly related to inventory allocation programs. The first is market forecasting, which constitutes an evaluation of all pertinent and known facts with respect to an estimate of anticipated future events. Inventory allocations would require very little effort and would involve very little risk, if the uncertainty of the future with respect to individual products could be eliminated. The second task is production scheduling. In essence this is the unit market forecast refined to a work program. The third management task is purchasing or procurement. Although primary emphasis throughout this book is placed upon finished goods flow, the inbound material flow constitutes a significant part of total corporate effort. Scheduling of the inbound flow of materials is harmonized with the outbound flow of finished goods via the coordination of market forecasting, production scheduling, and procurement.

It is apparent that an integral relationship exists between facilities, transport capability, and inventory allocations. With respect to inventory, it is desirable to be as selective as possible in development of an allocation program.

Communication Networks. Distribution communications represent the most neglected activity area in the physical distribution system. In part this neglect has resulted from the lack of data processing and data transmission equipment capable of handling the necessary flow of information. Equally the cause of neglect has been the lack of realistic understanding of the importance of rapid and correct communications with respect to physical distribution performance.

The total physical distribution system is designed to achieve an orderly flow of goods from the point of initial customer order to the time of product delivery. Distribution communications have a direct impact on system capability in two ways: (1) quality of information and (2) speed of information.

A deficiency in the quality of information can result in countless problems. Such deficiencies fall into two broad categories. First, information received may be incorrect with respect to appraisal of trends and events. Because a great deal of physical distribution flow takes place in anticipation of future transaction, an inaccurate appraisal can result in a deficiency or abundance of inventory commitments with all associated costs. Second, information may be incorrect with respect to a specific customer's needs. A firm who processes a wrong order confronts all of the costs of physical distribution without the resultant sale. In fact, the costs are often compounded by the need to absorb the cost of returning the order and, if the sales opportunity still exists, once more attempting to provide the proper assortment in an effort to maintain customer relations.

The speed of information flow is directly related to the integration of fixed facilities, transport capability, and inventory allocations. It makes little sense for a firm to accumulate orders at a local sales office for a week, mail them to a regional office, send them to data processing, finally assign them to a distribution warehouse, and then ship air express in order to give fast delivery. Perhaps a direct phone call would have been justified from the customer's office, if such speedy order transmittal would have resulted in faster delivery at a lower total cost. Once again it is a question of balance among all components of the physical distribution system.

Two managerial tasks are directly related to corporate distribution communications. The first is customer order processing. An order represents a critical information flow, which is the prime input of the total logistics system. The second managerial task relates to customer adjustment. The adjustment function constitutes administration of an order until it is fully received by a customer in a damage-free condition. Shipment of a customer order on time is not sufficient physical distribution performance. The order must be received as promised with respect to time, quality, and quantity.

In general, the more efficient the design of a firm's physical distribution system the more sensitive it is to disturbances in information flow. Finely balanced systems have no extra inventory holdings, and safety stocks are the minimum possible within the consistency of transport capability. Incorrect information can cause a serious disturbance in system performance, and delays in corrective communication flow can amplify the range of error resulting in a series of oscillations in over- and under-correction. It is communication that renders a physical distribution system dynamic, and the quality and timeliness of information is the prime determinant of systems stability.

Unitization.   The design of a basic physical distribution system is primarily concerned with the four activity centers consisting of facility locations, transport capacity, inventory allocations, and communication network. These areas are subject to a wide variety of alternate design arrangements, each of which has a degree of potential effectiveness and a limit in attainable efficiency. In essence, these four structural areas provide a systems framework for integrated product flow. One final area of design — unitization — also represents an integral part of the physical distribution system.

Unitization does not fit into the neat structural scheme of the other areas. Rather, unitization occurs throughout the system and is directly related to the physical flow of products. Thus, unitization involves inventory as it flows through facilities and as it is transported between locations. Such flow is only initiated in response to a message expressing a need at some point in the system.

In a broad sense, unitization involves material handling, packaging, and containerization. Material handling consumes a great deal of the cost of physical distribution in terms of operations and capital expenditure. It stands to reason that the fewer times a product has to be handled in the total exchange process the less restricted and the more potentially efficient will be the total physical flow.

To facilitate handling efficiency, individual products are combined into larger cartons containing a grouping of cans, bottles, boxes, or whatever. This master carton performs two functions. First, it serves to protect the product while the physical distribution process is underway. Second, the master carton serves as a primary load allowing the handling of one larger package as opposed to a multitude of individual units.

For purposes of efficient handling, the master cartons are normally grouped together into larger lots. These larger lots may be banded with steel strapping, combined with tape, stocked into a wire cage, or stacked on a wooden pallet to name a few common techniques. Each of these grouping devices provides a load of sufficient size to justify some form of specialized material handling equipment to assist in movement.

A container in the technical sense includes all devices used for grouping from the original can used to protect pineapple up to a 40-foot sea-truck box loaded on a ship in Hawaii for ultimate delivery in Lansing, Michigan. However, for ease of understanding the term *container* is commonly used to describe loadings containing more than one master carton.

Unitization effectively integrated into a firm's physical distribution system can substantially reduce problems related to time and ease of product flow throughout the total system. In fact, several firms have been able to design unit loads that move large assortments of products from the production line to a customer's shelf. Although such programs have a related expense, if properly developed they may more than pay for themselves by reduced handling, lower transport cost, improved customer relations, and general overall efficiency.

THE PHYSICAL DISTRIBUTION NETWORK, THE FIRM, AND COMPETITIVE ACTION

From the foregoing discussion it is apparent that the design of a physical distribution system is a very complex process. Chart 5-1 illustrates a firm's physical distribution network with respect to internal and external forces influential in system design. The main objective of system design is to integrate the five primary activity centers into a unified and balanced effort. Regardless of a firm's internal organization with respect to management responsibilities, the five activities must be harmonized. The total physical distribution system exists for the sole purpose of accomplishing spatial and temporal closure for the firm's product assortment. Until the utilities of time and place are achieved, little if any value has been added by the physical distribution process.

In Chart 5-1, the five main activity centers of the physical distribution system are linked together as part of a corporate system. External to physical distribution are the other primary systems of a typical corporation. In essence, the physical distribution system is but one of four basic systems comprising the corporation. As such, physical distribution, marketing, production, and finance are all parts of the master system — the firm. Just as the

CHART 5–1   Physical Distribution — The Firm — The Environment

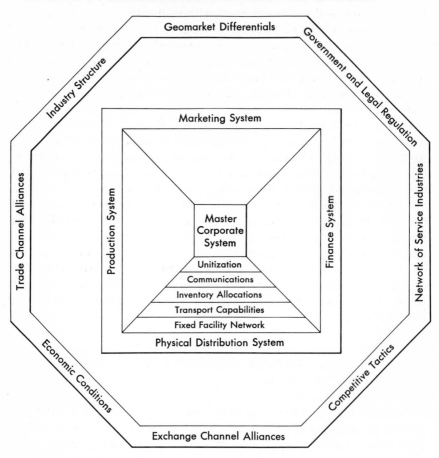

five primary activities of physical distribution must be in balance, so must the four significant parts of the master system function as a totality.

External to the four elements contained in a firm's master system are environmental forces that limit flexibility of corporate design. In total, environmental forces form the ecology of the firm. These forces are (1) industry structure, (2) geomarket differentials, (3) network of service industries, (4) exchange channel alliances, (5) government and legal, (6) economic conditions, (7) trade channel alliances, and (8) competitive tactics.

In total strategy, the firm is viewed as an integrated activity structured to function as a profit-generating enterprise within and adjusting to environmental constraints. Over a given planning period, environmental constraint remains relatively constant. The firm and competitors adjust corporate programs in an effort to obtain greater individual shares of the market for the particular product assortment offered. To the degree that any given firm gains favor in the eyes and behavior of buyers, that firm enjoys a differential advantage over competitors. Such advantage may be rapidly eliminated by competitors, or it may be retained over a substantial period of time. To the degree that a differential advantage prevails, the recipient firm gains lasting distinctiveness and long-run profitable growth.

The complexities of total corporate activity only gain importance to the degree that a firm is able to culminate all effort into profitable transactions. For any given firm to enjoy a continuous series of profitable transactions requires the efficient integration of all corporate resources toward the accomplishment of transactions. Thus, if a firm is to survive, all corporate systems — marketing, production, finance, and physical distribution — must function as a totality aimed at generation of a stream of profitable transactions. Each system of the corporation or any of its activity centers viewed in isolation has no justification. Only to the degree that any given part contributes to total corporate effort and the degree to which that total corporate effort results in profitable transactions, does a given part, or even the total corporate effort, gain economic justification.

Viewing business activity as a total system of goal-directed action has become commonplace. Equally common is the acceptance of an overall corporate marketing orientation as an underlying philosophy of management. This viewpoint of a market orientation is not designed to place marketing on a pedestal, but rather to underscore the importance of markets in corporate planning. Transactions take place in the marketplace. Likewise, transactions are essential to survival. Therefore, all corporate action must be geared to the transaction.

Within the firm the physical distribution system is central to completion of the transaction. Those firms with maximum physical distribution efficiency gain an advantage in terms of cost and service that is difficult to duplicate. Thus, those firms who have balanced their network of facilities, transport capacity, inventory allocations, communications, and unitization with the financial, marketing, and production systems of the corporation stand ahead of competition with respect to long-range differential advantage.

This balance of activity centers within the physical distribution system and of the physical distribution system to the remaining systems of the firm must be subject to constant adjustment. In the long run, underlying quicksands of economic and institutional changes may render the existing system inadequate as well as uneconomical. This inadequacy may result in increased costs or a loss of competitive advantage to rival firms.

Defining the Physical Distribution Mission

The physical distribution mission of the firm is to develop a system that meets the stated corporate customer service policy at the lowest possible dollar expenditure. Development of a satisfactory program requires two levels of adjustment: (1) integration of the logistical system with other corporate systems, and (2) development of total cost balance between logistical system activity centers. Both levels of adjustment constitute trade-offs.

MASTER SYSTEM INTEGRATION

As stated earlier the basic financial, production, marketing, and physical distribution systems of a firm must be integrated into a single effort. The physical distribution system is primarily concerned with support of the production and marketing systems. At the corporate level, the critical question centers around the expected level of support the physical distribution system will provide.

The question of corporate physical distribution support involves two factors: (1) delivery service performance level, and (2) cost expenditure. In terms of total performance level, it is necessary to consider both required performance time and consistency of performance. With respect to cost expenditure, the problem centers around the dollar requirement related to alternate levels of total performance.

The problem at the corporate level is to establish between performance and cost a balance that will result in the desired return on investment for the firm. This balance reflects the corporate physical distribution policy and becomes the managerial parameter for guiding logistical system design.

PHYSICAL DISTRIBUTION PERFORMANCE

With respect to total performance, almost any level of physical distribution service is possible if a firm is willing to pay the price. For example, a full-line inventory can be situated in close geographical proximity to all major customers. A fleet of trucks can be held in a constant state of delivery readiness. To facilitate communications, a hot line can be installed between the customer's facility and the supplier firm's distribution warehouse. Under this hypothetical situation, it is conceivable that a customer's order could be delivered within a matter of minutes. Although such a service situation might constitute a sales manager's dream, such extreme physical distribution performance is not practical or needed to support the marketing and production systems.

Physical distribution performance is, in final analysis, a question of priority and penalty. If a specific raw material is not available when required by the production system, it may necessitate a plant shutdown with the resultant costs and the ultimate loss of sales. The penalty of such a failure is great, and therefore the priority placed upon performance will be high. In contrast, a two-day delay in delivery of a product to a grocery chain store warehouse may cause little more than a delivery scheduling problem. Therefore, within limited ranges, the priority placed upon performance in this second situation will not be as severe, because the penalty for failure is not as drastic.

As noted above, total performance is measured with respect to time and consistency. The time measure is concerned with the total elapsed time from the placement of the customer order or commitment to the delivery of the material or inventory in satisfactory condition. Naturally, a firm desires the fastest possible delivery program. However, a fast delivery cycle is of little real value, unless it is consistently met in actual practice. It does very little good for a firm to promise second-day delivery, if in actual performance it can only achieve such standards a small percentage of the time.

Performance standards should be established on a selective basis. Some products are more critical than others as a result of their importance to the user. Some customers are more important to a firm as a result of their total purchases and related profitability. The stated level of delivery performance should be realistic and adjusted to the task at hand.

In general, firms tend to be overly optimistic in stating performance standards. Inferior or substandard performance to an unrealistic service policy often will cause greater operating and customer problems than had the firm stated less ambitious goals. The quality of consistency is of greater value than pure speed to a firm on the receiving end of a physical distribution pipeline.

PHYSICAL DISTRIBUTION COST

It is currently in vogue to talk about profit centers within the modern corporation. The physical distribution system should be considered a cost center and like all other expenses of a firm every effort must be made to hold expenditures to a minimum. Physical distribution costs have a direct relationship to a firm's selected service policy. The qualities of fast and consistent performance both have related costs. The higher each of these aspects of total performance, the greater will be the logistical system cost.

A significant planning problem stems from the fact that logistical cost and increased performance have a nonproportional relationship. A firm that supports a service standard of overnight delivery at 95 percent consistency may confront nearly double the physical distribution cost of one that develops a program of second-morning delivery at 90 percent consistency. The same firm committed to a delivery policy of overnight service at greater than 95 percent consistency could easily dissipate profits by attempting to provide performance not needed, expected, or even wanted by customers.

TOTAL COST ANALYSIS

The concept of total cost has gained wide usage in perfecting the integration of activity areas into an integrated system. Total cost is a measure of all expenditures required to accomplish the service performance policies outlined for a physical distribution system. Between the activity centers there exists an economic relationship capable of improving the total cost of the system. Thus, it makes little difference how much is spent for any given activity in the system as long as the total cost of all activities is at the practical minimum for the required level of performance. Taking advantage of this economic trade-off between activity centers is the main attribute of systems analysis.

The classical example of total system cost is the air freight illustration. Although air freight is one of the fastest methods of intercity transfer, it is also one of the highest cost on a ton-mile basis. However, when trade-offs are taken into consideration, it may be possible to reduce the inventory investment, the number of distribution warehouses, and even the amount of material handling in the total system. The net result of a total cost evaluation might be that the resultant savings in these other activity centers may more than offset the higher air freight transfer cost. Thus, the trade-offs between activity centers might render the air system the lowest total cost method of physical distribution.

This trade-off principle also works in the opposite direction when conditions are such that distribution warehouses and increased inventory investment will result in the lowest total cost. The significant feature is that once the performance standards are established, a wide variety of arrangements of activity centers must be tested to determine the total least cost system.

PHYSICAL DISTRIBUTION SYSTEM BALANCE

The typical firm will find that the best overall balance between physical distribution performance and cost is one that constitutes reasonable performance levels and realistic cost expenditures. Very seldom will either the lowest possible cost or the highest service performance system constitute the best corporate logistical system. Most firms can be expected to select a reasonable balance between cost and performance.

Significant advances have been made in the development of tools to aid management in the measurement of cost-performance trade-offs. A sound decision concerning desired performance can be formulated only if it is possible to estimate expenditures for alternate levels of system performance. Likewise, alternate levels of physical distribution performance are meaningless unless properly integrated into marketing, production, and finance.

Typical Physical Distribution Systems

The many aspects of physical distribution system development render the design of a program a very complex assignment. In addition to the development of a system having an acceptable balance of performance and cost, management must always keep in mind that change will require constant adjustment of the system. Thus, flexibility represents an important part of any system design. When one considers the wide variety of individual distribution systems operated by firms servicing widely diverse markets, it might seem astonishing that any design similarity exists from one situation to the next. However, all systems have two items in common. First, they are designed to encourage maximum product flow. Second, the systems must be designed within the existing technological development of the five primary physical distribution activity areas. A brief illustration is developed below to stress the concept of maximum flow desirable in a physical distribution system. The last part of this section contains some typical system arrangements.

PRODUCT FLOW PRINCIPLE APPLIED TO AN INDUSTRY

The petroleum industry in the distribution of gasoline for automotive consumption represents an ideal illustration of product flow. This industry is primarily composed of a number of scattered well sites, a system of collection and storage of crude petroleum, a main trunk pipeline, a refining facility, wholesale and retail outlets, and finally the ultimate consumer.

The design of the entire system connecting the origin of movement to ultimate destination must stress constant availability of refined petroleum at the retail level. Given this performance level, the best design is that which results in the lowest total cost.

The first step is to design subsystems for crude oil collections and gasoline deliveries. First, looking at the collection end of this system, wells will be located in a certain pattern within the producing territory. Given these existing patterns, the wells are then grouped into a series of self-contained producing units. Those wells that can be grouped into densely clustered, self-contained units ordinarily are connected together into a gathering system for that particular group. This gathering system usually is based on pipeline transport so long as the production from the individual well and its group has sufficient volume to justify the investment. The diameter of pipes is determined by the volume of crude oil expected from the well.

After the groups have been connected according to the above principles, they may be interconnected. Then, the total volume of crude oil tapped from all wells reaches the terminal delivery point (engineering design) of the main pipeline at minimum cost (economic design). Again, volume is critical in this decision. Finally, although pipeline collection is engineeringly feasible for the isolated low-producing wells, volumes seldom warrant pipeline investment from an economic point of view. Consequently, tank trucks may be used to gather the crude oil.

In moving the manufactured gasoline from the refinery to the local gasoline station, the principle of grouping local outlets again applies. Delivery systems are then designed to meet market requirements at each of these outlets. Because of the relatively low volumes sold at each retail outlet, and because market factors are more important in determining locations of stations, the employment of a pipeline system is not ordinarily justified for this distribution level. Rather, product pipelines connecting the refinery to the major markets are constructed in conjunction with storage depots at each of these points. Trucks deliver the gasoline from the depot to each individual station.

The selection of particular components of the distribution system depends upon the size of volume flow. Low volume flow requires a system with low fixed cost but high variable cost (trucks). High volume flow requires a system with high fixed cost but low variable cost (pipe). Generally, the greater the volume, the greater is the possibility of spreading the fixed expense over a large output.

The pipeline illustration is analogous to any physical distribution problem. To clarify, in Chart 5–2 a pair of parallel diagrams shows the relationship of the pipeline system to a general marketing and distribution system. The physical product flows for both systems illustrate certain nodal points. These points are either concentration (*C*) or break-bulk (*B*) points.

In Chart 5–2, all movements to the point of entering the major intercity trunk line essentially result from regrouping and combining shipments into larger lots. Transportation is required between any two nodal points, but the feasible engineering alternatives may well vary because of differences in physical distribution problems between any two nodes.

Each nodal point beyond the manufacturing level is a break-bulk point. The total production of the plant is regrouped to serve more efficiently particular market segments with total demand less than annual plant production.

For each consolidation or break-bulk point, particular, specialized marketing institutions exist. These institutions are indicated in the chart by representative types. Although long and detailed listings of such institutions could be made, the relevant ones depend on the industry being studied. Particular stress is on institutions performing exchange functions. At any point, incoming movements differ from outgoing movements in volume and in size of shipment.

When cast in this framework, the physical distribution portion of marketing takes on a new competitive complexion. Assuming erratic consumer demand, new developments in transportation, changing relative importance of markets, and a continual revolution in technology and products, effective marketing

CHART 5-2 Crude Oil and Gasoline Physical Distribution System Compared to a General Marketing Physical Distribution System

CRUDE OIL AND GASOLINE SYSTEM

Raw Materials	Raw Materials Processing	Intercity Transport	Manufac-turing	Warehouse and Storage	Wholesale	Retail	Consumers
C	C	C	C	B	B	B	
Distribution of Well Sites 2" Pipe	Storage and Collection Depot of Crude Oil	Pipeline	Refinery	Refinery and Storage	Field Gasoline	Gas Station	

GENERAL MARKETING SYSTEM

Pattern of Raw Materials and Supplies Locations	Raw Materials Market	Truck, Rail, Air, Water, Pipe	Plant	Plant Storage	Warehouse Wholesaler	Retail Outlet	
C	C	C	C	B	B	B	

KEY:

⊙ = Raw Materials Resources   C = Consolidating Function
● = Customer Unit   B = Break-Bulk Function

6" Pipe

6"–10" Pipe

10"–30"

6"–10" Pipe

Transport

119

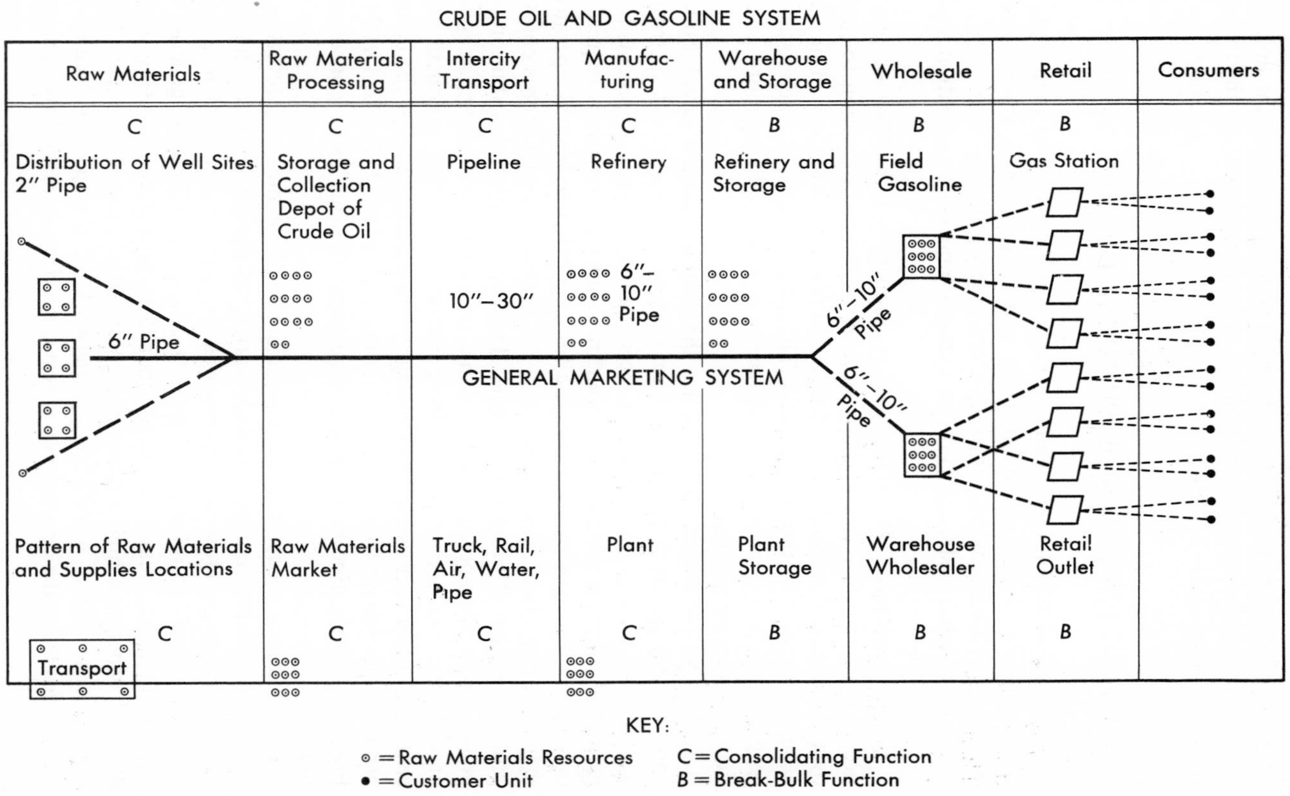

requires continual assessment and revision of physical distribution alternatives. The assumed fixity of distribution channels now becomes dangerously erroneous for a firm to follow. Although few industries have the flow potential found in petroleum distribution, all attempt to encourage the maximum flow possible in system design.

COMMON PATTERNS OF PHYSICAL DISTRIBUTION

The limit of technology available in the performance of major physical distribution activities results in some common patterns among systems. Three basic patterns stand out as the most widely utilized designs for product flow: (1) echelon systems, (2) direct systems, and (3) combination systems.

Echelon Systems.   The term *echelon* implies that the flow of products proceeds through a series of steps as it moves from production to point of ownership transfer. Such steps consist of the accumulation of inventory groupings in distribution warehouses. Thus, the essential characteristic of an echelon system is that inventory allocations exist at one or more points in the product flow pipeline.

Two common echelon patterns are the establishment of break-bulk and consolidation points in the distribution system. The break-bulk distribution warehouse exists for the purpose of receiving large volume shipments from a variety of different suppliers for assortment into combinations required for individual customers or retailers. The food distribution centers operated by major grocery chains such as Kroger, A&P, and Colonial Stores constitute prime examples of break-bulk points. The consolidation distribution warehouse is normally operated by a firm that produces a product line at a variety of different production plants. By consolidation of all products at one central point, it is possible to ship large volumes consisting of the complete product line. Major food processing firms such as H. J. Heinz, Del Monte Foods, or Hunt Foods are prime examples of firms using consolidation points.

Distribution systems that employ facility echelons normally revert to this pattern in order to combine a wide variety of products into a single large volume shipment. However, inventories are also held in field locations in order to provide rapid delivery given a customer order. The general trend appears to place greater emphasis upon distribution warehousing in order to enjoy benefits of high volume and complete product assortment distribution. When volume is sufficient, a network of strategically located field inventories offers the best balance of service performance and cost economies.

Direct Shipments.   In contrast to echelon systems are those systems that operate direct from one or a limited number of central inventory accumulations. These firms find that their particular marketing systems can best be supported by holding a central inventory from which customer orders are filled. Direct systems often utilize high-speed transport in order to overcome the extensive geographical separation from customers. Examples of direct shipments are found in the mail order and electronics industries.

In contrast to echelon systems, direct systems normally result when high-value, low-volume products are marketed. Such products encourage the centralization of inventories in order to reduce total investment.

Combination Systems.   The most common distribution systems are those that combine the principles of the echelon and direct distribution systems. As noted earlier, selectivity is encouraged in the design of a physical distribution system. Some products may be held in distribution warehouses whereas others are distributed directly.

For example, one firm supplies consumer replacement parts to the automobile after-market. Their distribution system is designed to echelon inventories at various distances from prime markets. The slower the part turnover, the more centralized is the inventory. The slowest moving parts are held at one central location, which directly supplies the entire world.

In contrast, a second firm, which supplies industrial replacement parts, follows a completely opposite distribution policy. In order to rapidly meet unexpected demands, this firm inventories sufficient quantities of all slow movers at each distribution warehouse. In contrast to the first firm, fast- and medium-turnover products are supplied on a regular basis direct to customers from plants and central supply centers.

This differential in policy is easily explained, when one examines the market each firm serves and the degree of product differential each enjoys. The first firm faces extensive competition on replacement parts on new models. However, as the original product ages this competition decreases, making this firm the only supplier. The second firm, on the other hand, sells a product, which has very little style deterioration and a high degree of competitive substitutability. In this firm's market, a supplier is measured by purchasing agents with respect to how fast unexpected production breakdowns can be remedied.

Each firm faces a different marketing problem, and each follows a different pattern of combined physical distribution with respect to finished product inventories. In general, each firm must study its own situation to develop the physical distribution pattern which will best satisfy its customer service requirement at the lowest total cost.

Summary

Each firm confronts a particular series of requirements and limitations in the development of a physical distribution system. To compete effectively in the market place, a physical distribution support system must be developed capable of providing the desired level of customer service performance at the lowest possible total cost. Design of such a system is a complex process, which requires an integration of all activity centers involved in physical distribution. In Part II attention is directed to a detailed review of the physical distribution activity areas.

Discussion Questions

1. Why does classical economic study often ignore the possibility of location advantages and transportation cost differentials? Why cannot a businessman follow this same approach?

2. What factors are of primary importance in the establishment of a firm's transportation capability?

3. How is forecasting related to inventory control?

4. What savings may come about because of an improved distribution communication system?

5. What is the physical distribution mission of the firm?

6. What does the term *total cost analysis* refer to? Why has this approach not been implemented in more businesses up to this

7. What is the difference between break-bulk and consolidating function? How are they alike?

PART II Distribution

Activity Centers

CHAPTER 6 Transportation—

Institutional and Regulatory Framework

TRANSPORTATION accounts for $62.6 billion of total physical distribution cost. About 90 percent of the total transportation cost for intercity freight movement is accounted for by business and government expenditures on rail and motor carrier transport. The relative size of the $62.6 billion expenditure is easily seen by comparison with the Gross National Product (GNP), which is the total of all goods and services produced in the United States in a single year. At present, GNP is approximately $700 billion. Thus, the transportation bill of the United States equals about 9 percent of the GNP.

The relationship of transportation cost to total distribution cost varies by industry. In industries with very highly valued commodities, such as cameras, automobiles, jewelry, electronics, radio, television, and many others, transportation cost accounts for only a small percentage of the total cost of the final product. In other industries, such as coal, iron ore, sand, gravel, basic chemicals, fertilizers, and many others, transportation cost accounts for a significant percentage of total cost of the final product.

Percentage variations of transportation cost to total cost of final product range from less than 1 to more than 30 percent. The main impact of these ratios relates to the major emphasis upon transportation cost control by industry. In the basic high transportation cost industries, physical distribution frequently takes the orientation of strong control of transportation costs. In the high-value industries, emphasis in physical distribution control is more apt to center on other areas of integrated management.

The purpose of this chapter is to introduce the subject of transportation. An experienced traffic manager may elect to bypass the initial sections of the chapter. Emphasis is placed upon a managerial discussion of transport institutional and regulatory framework as they relate to physical distribution system design.

The initial section of the chapter deals with transport supply. Attention is then directed to transportation rate regulation. The following section discusses special forms of transport pricing based upon cost, market, and production influences. Next, attention is directed to the terms of sale and the importance of volume control. The following two sections deal with transport cost and service characteristics. Specific aspects of Traffic Management are developed in Appendix 6A.

The final section of the chapter presents a development of unitization. In Chapter 5, unitization was introduced as one of the five major activity centers of an integrated physical distribution system. The subject matter of unitization is developed in this chapter because of its close relationship to transportation. Treatment here also serves the purpose of once again illustrating the interrelation of all physical distribution activity centers.

Transport Supply

A vast array of transportation alternatives is available for firms to utilize in physical distribution system design. Transport supply can be studied from a number of different approaches. In this summary, four types or groupings of supply are singled out for discussion: (1) legal forms of transport, (2) modes of transport, (3) special transport, and (4) coordinated transport.

LEGAL FORMS OF TRANSPORT

Four legal forms of transport currently exist: (1) common, (2) contract, (3) private, and (4) exempt. The basis for legal groupings is one of regulation. To various degrees, each type of carrier is subject to federal and state regulations. Common and contract carriers are considered for-hire carriers. Because of the basic nature of their operations, they are subject to the most direct regulation by state and federal governments. Private carriers cannot legally operate as for-hire transport carriers. Exempt carriers do operate on a for-hire basis, but the restricted nature of their operation limits the need for a high degree of direct regulation. Private and exempt carriers are regulated by their need to comply to basic law, licensing, weight, and safety provisions of various governmental bodies. Many firms utilize all four types of legal carriers in the day-to-day operation of their physical distribution system.

Common Carriers.   Most regulated for-hire carriers are classified as common carriers. A common carrier is any transportation firm that offers transport service to all shippers on a fee basis. They accept a basic responsibility to transport specified goods at any time between authorized locations without discrimination as to rate or service among shippers.

To conduct business as a common carrier, a firm must apply to and receive from the appropriate regulatory agency a "certificate of convenience and necessity." This certificate is authorization to conduct business as a common carrier. To obtain the certificate, the carrier must demonstrate an economic need for the proposed service.

Certificates are of two types: (1) specialized commodities such as petroleum and household goods, or (2) general commodities. The certificate of operating authority indicates the geographical area the carrier may service and specifies if the service will be on a regular or irregular route basis. In return for operating authority, the common carrier assumes full responsibility for safe delivery of shipments.

Although the above discussion provides a basic review of legal characteristics of common carriers, it does not provide a "feel" for the basic importance of common carrier transport in the United States. Not all common carriers are alike in either service or range of commodities transported. A great many specialists function within the category of common carrier. These specialists may service only specific key cities or may perform a type of service limited in use to a few shippers. However, whatever service they render must be offered to all potential shippers without discrimination. It would be a rare firm that did not utilize the services of a common carrier on a regular basis either in raw material collection or in finished goods distribution. As such, the network of common carriers servicing industry and government represents the backbone of the United States' transport system.

Contract Carriers. Contract carriers are those who (1) service a limited number of shippers (the number not being clearly defined), (2) carry a restricted number of commodities, and (3) serve a limited number of geographic points.

The name *contract carrier* is derived from the agreement between the shipper and the carrier to engage in a continuing relationship. Contracts between shippers and the transportation company are normally for a minimum of six months. Contract carriers must obtain a permit from the Interstate Commerce Commission (ICC) if they wish to engage in transport between states. These permits are less specific than the certificate given to common carriers; however, they do specify routes to be utilized and commodities to be transported.

In terms of a firm's distribution system design, the main attributes of contract carriers are that (1) transport costs on shipments are entirely variable through the avoidance of fixed investment by the shipper, and (2) a close relationship between shipper and carrier is developed that results in more personalized service than is available from common carriers.

Private Carriers. Private carriage consists of (1) control over drivers and equipment by the shipper; (2) bona fide ownership of the commodity shipped, that is, it is related to the primary business of the shipper; (3) ownership or lease of transport equipment.

Exempt Carriers. Many carriers are exempt from direct regulation. The basis of exemption varies, depending upon circumstances. The three most common bases for exemption are (1) geographic area, (2) specific commodities, and (3) associations.

Exempt Areas. Certain geographic areas may be exempt from regulation. Interstate Commerce Regulation has defined areas around the periphery of certain cities as constituting exempt zones. Within these zones or areas anyone may perform transport services without price regulation restraints.

Exempt Commodities. In some cases, commodities may move via any legal form of transportation without pricing regulation. Foremost among these are agricultural products, a list of which is maintained by the ICC. Exempt commodities often move at prices from 10 to 25 percent lower than by regulated forms, especially common carriers, depending on tradition in specific geographical areas.

Exempt Association. The law provides for certain exemptions based upon the nature of the shipper associations. Foremost among these are agricultural cooperatives, which may carry virtually any commodity either on its own account or on that of its members. Another important form of exempt associations is the shippers' cooperative, which usually consists of a grouping of like shippers, joining for the purpose of reducing their transport costs. Among industries using shippers' cooperatives are (1) candy manufacturers, (2) retail stores, and (3) machine parts manufacturers. The benefit of a shipper cooperative is its ability to aggregate numerous small shipments into larger, more economical shipments.

MODES OF TRANSPORTATION

Five basic modes of transportation are available for use in physical distribution system design. The term *mode* is used to differentiate between the methods by which goods or commodities are physically transported. The basic modes are (1) rail, (2) motor carrier, (3) water, (4) pipeline, and (5) air.

Traffic Shares by Modes. Traffic shares for the major modes of transportation may be measured in terms of tons or ton miles. A comparison of these two measures is shown in Table 6–1.

Certain modal characteristics are illustrated by the statistics shown in Table 6–1. Basically, the motor carrier industry finds its niche in the transport

TABLE 6–1* COMPARISON OF TONS AND TON MILES MOVED BY VARIOUS TRANSPORT MODES — 1963.

Transport Mode	Tons	Ton Miles
	%	%
Rail	32.8	36.4
Truck (Common Carrier)	25.9	14.2
Truck (Private)	16.2	4.6
Air	—	0.1
Water	24.5	44.0
Other	0.5	0.6
Unknown	0.1	0.1
	100.0	100.0

*SOURCE: 1963 Census of Transportation, Commodity Transportation Survey, Part 1, Commodity Groups (U. S. Government), pp. 5–25.

market carrying products for short distances, as indicated by the 42 percent share of tonnage, but only 19 percent of the ton miles. Rail and water, on the other hand, account for smaller proportions of tonnage to their ton-mile generation. This suggests that they inherently perform transportation services for the long-haul market.

In addition to classifying gross movement by mode, a classification by product type sheds light on the proportion of freight moving by carrier group. Table 6–2 shows the relationship.

Some generalized observations may be made from the data. A specific industry's affinity for a particular mode depends upon (1) the relationship of transport cost to the final sales price, (2) the degree of competition among modes, (3) the marketing and production patterns in the industry, and (4) the aggregate tonnage offered to each mode.

Relationship of Transport Cost to Final Sales Price. Generally, the most inexpensive form of transportation is water. The relative average transport prices for each mode are shown in Table 6–3.

Referring to product type with affinity for low-cost transport, a rather pronounced characteristic for low-value products shows up for rail and water as compared with truck and air. Moving across industry groups, it seems that the value of products increased from water → rail → motor carrier → air.

Taking a basic commodity, such as fertilizer selling at $50 per ton on a bulk basis, moving from rail transport at $.01 per ton mile to truck transport at $.05 per ton mile will have a dramatic effect upon selling price. For this reason, low-cost transportation is essential if broad market penetration is to be achieved. Conversely, at $.10 a ton mile for air freight, transportation

TABLE 6–2*   ORIENTATION OF SELECTED COMMODITIES BY MODE (TON MILES) — 1963

A. **Rail-Oriented Products**	Percent by Rail
Cereal preparations	97.3
Canned meat	88.5
Animal byproducts (inedible)	87.7
Iron, steel scrap, and tailings	86.7
Metal, scrap wastes, and tailings	83.5
Lumber and dimension stock	81.6
Cigarettes	72.6
Canned specialties	72.3
Food and kindred products	66.1

B. **Motor-Carrier-Oriented Products**	Percent by Motor
Gloves and mittens	98.1
Envelopes, except stationery	96.2
Show and trophy cases	92.4
Architectural and ornamental metal work	85.9
Bedspreads and bed sets	85.1
Nonferrous metal castings	84.3
Special dies and tools, die sets, jigs, and fixtures	83.0
Rubber belts and belting	80.8
Specialty cleaning and sanitation preparations	78.6

C. **Water-Oriented Products**	Percent by Water
Distillate fuel oil	98.4
Residual fuel oil	95.3
Products of petroleum refining	94.2
Petroleum and coal products	93.0

D. **Air-Oriented Products**	Percent by Air
Computing and accounting machines	25.0
Calculating and accounting machines	8.3
Special dies and tools, die sets, jigs, and fixtures	6.6
Millinery — caps and hats	5.8
Parts and attachments for pumps	3.9
Miscellaneous apparel	3.8
Hardware and saw blades	2.7
Nonferrous metal	2.3
Rubber belts and belting	2.1
Women's handbags and purses	2.1
Heat exchangers and steam condensers	1.8

*SOURCE: Same as Table 6–1.

expense as a percent of selling price will probably be insignificant. The ratio of transport price to final selling price of products will affect demand elasticity through its impact upon geographic market penetration.

Degree of Competition.   For certain types of commodities, transport competition may be very low. For example, a bulk commodity, such as coal,

TABLE 6–3 RELATIVE TRANSPORT COST PER TON MILE[1]

Water	$.006
Rail	.01
Motor carrier	.04
Air	.10

[1]Assumed average costs.

enjoys a limited range of alternatives for any significant volumes, i.e., either rail or water. A large range of manufactured products does enjoy considerable flexibility in terms of mode choice. Within certain product groups, it is not at all improbable that the entire range of transport alternatives is available. Final selection will depend not only upon price but also upon the peripheral characteristics of different modes, such as schedule frequency, size of shipment permitted, transit times, packaging required, and others with a bearing upon mode selection.

Marketing and Production Characteristics. Where numerous producing points exist, local markets are generated around each location. Given proximity of markets and production points, transport choices tend to be restricted largely to motor carriers, which are the primary short-haul transportation agency.

Conversely, if production points are restricted but consuming areas are numerous and scattered, a mix of transport use to fit each market condition will arise. Although a major producing area for fruit products is in California, its markets are widely scattered. As a consequence, all modes will tend to be used, depending upon marketing requirements for each designated area. Similarly, in the same industry, seasonal production for local distribution, for example, fresh fruits and vegetables, will enjoy limited choice of alternatives, usually truck.

Aggregate Tonnage. Where tonnage tenders are large, choice is frequently restricted to rail or water (and also pipeline, which is not specifically discussed here). Trainload offerings of 6,000 tons or more compete directly with barge loadings in the same tonnage range.

Small package offerings of limited weight largely dictate truck or air. Tonnage offerings may vary considerably with the level of distribution. For example, trainloads of grocery products from a single production area may result in rail-water transport. Beyond the terminal point, however, small shipments to stores require smaller offerings, dictating use of truck or other small-shipment-suited mode.

SPECIAL TRANSPORT

In addition to the basic modes of transportation already discussed, a group of supplemental support agencies exists to complete the range of necessary transport supply. In some cases, these largely specialized services own transport equipment, and in others, they rely heavily upon the use of other carriers.[1]

United States Post Office — Parcel Post. Parcel post provides service on small shipments to all points in the United States. Many people do not realize the large use that parcel post enjoys, not only in the mail-order segment, but also in the parts supply of major manufacturers. Companies such as Ford and General Motors are as important customers for parcel post as are Montgomery Ward and Sears, Roebuck and Co.

Prices are on a weight-distance basis, with distance determined by the zone in which a specific destination lies from a specific origin. In some cases where volumes are large, the post office may establish an operating unit on the premises of the customer. In effect, this becomes a private post office for the shipper. The benefit to the shipper is that he need not deliver parcels for shipment but takes them directly from factory or warehouse to the postal station for mailing.

The new ZIP Code System has resulted in substantial service improvement and cost reduction.[2] ZIP Code is designed to reduce parcel handling and thereby improve service and economy of operation. The ZIP Code is a five-digit number, the first three of which identify the sectional center, of which there are about 500. The last two digits identify the specific post office to which the parcel is addressed. Each sectional center has a number of associated post offices for which it serves as a master post office in that area.

By coding all customers, through addition of their ZIP Code number, many possibilities for distribution or marketing become possible. As one example, consider the problem of distributing shrubs and plants by mail. Without a ZIP Code System, cumbersome methods must be employed to assure delivery at planting time. With each customer on a ZIP number, each market area can be classified as to planting times and shipments made on schedule. This is presently being done by a number of growers in the mail-order market. In parts distribution, at least one firm employs ZIP Codes as a method of traffic analysis. By measuring the quantity of shipments into an area, routing and consolidation potentials can be more readily identified. In addition to regular parcel post, air parcel post provides the same basic distribution coverage but at higher service levels and greater cost.

[1]For a more detailed discussion of special or ancillary transportation agencies see Charles A. Taff, *Management of Traffic and Physical Distribution* (Homewood, Ill.: Richard D. Irwin Inc., 1964).

[2]See Fred Belen, "Zip Codes — Bonus for Business," *Business Topics*, Spring 1967, pp. 19–25; and Martin Baier, "Zip Code — New Tool for Marketing," *Harvard Business Review*, Jan.–Feb., 1967, pp. 136–140.

Air Express.   Air express is a primarily high-cost service usually reserved for expedited shipments. Express shipments are picked up at origin and delivered at destination. Shipments receive priority after mail but before regular air freight on aircraft space availability.

United Parcel Service.   United Parcel Service (UPS) provides a service directly competitive with parcel post but on a more limited geographic scale. UPS operates in three territories: the East, Midwest, and Far West. Not all states are covered in these areas nor are all towns.

Prices charged compare favorably for select shipment sizes with REA Express and parcel post. One distinct advantage of UPS over parcel post is a regular pickup and delivery provided at a small weekly charge.

REA Express.   REA Express provides a combined rail and motor carrier capability for small package distribution. In recent times, REA has introduced new types of rate structures useful in certain types of distribution problems. Although regular point-to-point rates exist for a wide range of products, distribution rates from specified production points to rather broad geographic areas are available for larger quantity shipments. REA Express competes to a considerable degree with parcel post and UPS, but also provides service similar to that of the trucking industry.

Freight Forwarders.   Freight forwarders, as the name implies, collect small shipments from a number of shippers, consolidate them for large shipment economy, and program distribution to required markets. A freight forwarder operates as a transportation middleman whose operating margin comes from the low-volume rates he pays to rail or truck companies and the higher, less-than-volume prices he charges the shipper. His advantage is that he provides single carrier responsibility for the shipper and, in effect, acts as a purchasing agent to arrange the best combination of required pickup, line-haul, and delivery services.

Shippers' Cooperatives.   Shippers' cooperatives are similar to freight forwarders. They act in unison to increase the quantity of freight offered to the carrier, thus, more easily achieving low-cost volume rates.

Ordinarily, a related group of shippers establishes a cooperative. An office is set up which then (1) collects all orders from members, (2) designates a local pickup carrier (usually exempt) to bring all goods ordered to a freight terminal (usually rail), (3) arranges for the transportation from origin city to designation city, (4) arranges for delivery in the destination city (usually exempt transportation), and (5) pays all bills to carriers involved. Each shipper then pays on a pro rata basis based upon the percentage weight of his shipment to the total.

COORDINATED TRANSPORT

In addition to single mode transportation, multiple modes may be used to good advantage. Multiple mode movements characteristically combine the major advantages of two or more modes. Attempts at coordinated systems trace back to the early 1920's, but it was not until the 1950's that combination movements gained widespread usage.

Some examples of multiple mode transport are (1) trailer-on-flat-car (TOFC)[3], (2) ship-rail, (3) ship-truck, and (4) air-truck. The purpose of multiple mode selection is to generate greater economies or service capabilities than either mode can provide alone. Thus, TOFC takes account of the higher line-haul costs of moving a trailer over road as compared with moving the same trailer over the rails. Although truck trailers over road may incur a vehicle mile cost of $.39, the same trailer moved on a rail flatcar may incur costs of $.20 a trailer mile. This results from greater line-haul economies of rail transportation. Terminal functions and delivery, of course, can hardly be performed by a railroad in many-commodity movements. For this reason, where wide distribution within an area is required, truck trailers best perform the function. The combination of facilities usually results in lower costs to shippers and carriers.[4]

Transportation Rate Regulation

A primary classification of transportation types as discussed earlier relates to their legal forms. Thus, legal classification forms a useful basis for formation and regulation of rates.

COMMON CARRIER RATES

The common carrier is the most universally known legal form of transportation, accounting for the vast majority of intercity movements. As noted earlier, common carriers receive from a federal or state agency a certificate

[3]Piggyback plans fall into five major categories:

Plan I: Common carrier trucker provides the trailer and bills the customer.

Plan II: Railroads provide trailers and also perform pickup and delivery.

Plan III: Shippers on freight forwarder provide the trailer. The railroad provides only the line-haul between two designated points. Shipper on freight forwarder performs pickup and delivery. A flat charge is made regardless of contents (example, $200 per container).

Plan IV: Similar to Plan III, except railroad charges, a flat fee per car loaded on empty.

Plan V: Railroad and trucker participate in the same tariff. They may solicit traffic for the through-haul.

[4]For an expanded discussion see M. J. Roberts and Associates, "Intermodal Freight Transportation Coordination: Problems and Potential" (Pittsburgh, 1966).

TABLE 6–4   AGENCIES REGULATING PRICES AND SERVICES FOR DIFFERENT MODES OF TRANSPORTATION

Mode of Transportation	Two or More States	Within a Single State
Motor carrier Rail Pipeline Freight forwarder REA Express Inland and coastal waterways Bus	Interstate Commerce Commission (ICC)	Various State Commissions
Airlines	Civil Aeronautics Board (CAB)	Various State Commissions
Ocean transport	Federal Marine Board (FMB)	None

of convenience and necessity, by which they demonstrate an economic need for the services to be provided. In return, common carriers are subject to the scrutiny of public regulatory bodies (Federal or State Commissions) to assure a fair and impartial treatment to all shippers, localities, and products.

Table 6–4 lists the agencies that control the granting of certificates and regulation of prices and services for each of the various modes indicated.

Rate Regulation. Common carriers are regulated as to rates that they may charge. In interstate movement, the appropriate federal agency in Table 6–4 has jurisdiction. In intrastate movements, it is the appropriate state commission that has jurisdiction.

Rate Setting. A common misconception about interstate rate regulation is a general belief that the various commissions set each and every rate. On the contrary, well over 90 percent of all rates charged by common carriers are published similar to the way that Sears, Roebuck and Co. publishes its catalog of prices. The major difference is that Sears is subject to antitrust laws, the Clayton Act, and the Robinson-Patman Act. On the other hand, common carriers are exempt from both of the above acts by the Reed-Bulwinkle Act of 1948. Substituting for the Robinson-Patman Act and the Clayton Act are the Federal and State Commissions.

A common carrier may publish any rate desired, subject only to the approval or disapproval of the appropriate regulatory commission if some injured party objects or if the commission wishes to review on its own authority. The usual steps in setting a specific rate are as follows:

1. A specific shipper and a specific common carrier jointly agree upon a rate for a given commodity between a specified group of origins and destinations.

2. Legal opinion is sought as to the legality of the rate in question. If affirmative, then:
3. The carrier, not the shipper, proposes the change to a common carrier rate committee. The committee may approve or disapprove the application at this point.
4. (a) If the committee disapproves the rate, further negotiations step through the rate committee, but the carrier may publish rates on his own initiative.
   (b) If the committee approves, the rate is published. The carrier publishes the rate on his own authority, or the group of interested carriers publishes the rate in a tariff which applies to all.
5. Published rate then may be challenged by another carrier or by the shipper who feels that economic injury may result from the rate.
6. (a) If the rate is withdrawn, all further action stops.
   (b) If the rate is not withdrawn, it is subject to a formal hearing before the appropriate commission.
7. If the rate is denied by the commission, the shipper and/or the carrier may petition to the appropriate court for relief.
8. If the rate is approved, it is published, and all further procedures stop.

Chart 6–1 provides a flow diagram of steps involved in rate setting.

From the preceding discussion and diagram, it seems apparent that common carrier transportation strongly reflects legal, economic, and public policy issues. For a firm to be without an effective traffic manager can result in serious shortcomings in the entire physical distribution system.

One further note on rate proceedings is in order. Most texts on this subject emphasize the *positive* aspects of rate proceedings; that is, how to get a rate approved. However, because of the administrative and legal framework within which rate making takes place, the *negative* aspects of rate making are equally important. A change in a specified rate will, ordinarily, favor one shipper or carrier and adversely affect another. The adversely affected party has all the above machinery available to *prevent* a rate from being published. This strategy is frequently employed by shippers and carriers faced with economic injury due to a proposed rate change.

Types of Rates.   The basic types of common carrier regulated rates are (1) class, (2) commodity, and (3) exception.

Class Rates.   Class rates are based upon the average cost of carriers and, usually but not always, are the highest rates that a shipper pays. Any shipper who uses these rates exclusively probably is paying an excessive amount for transportation. As in the case of most cost-based rates, class rates are primarily a function of weight and distance. The lower the shipment weight, the higher is the cost per unit; the higher the shipment weight, the lower is the cost per unit.

CHART 6–1   Flow Diagram for Rate Proposals

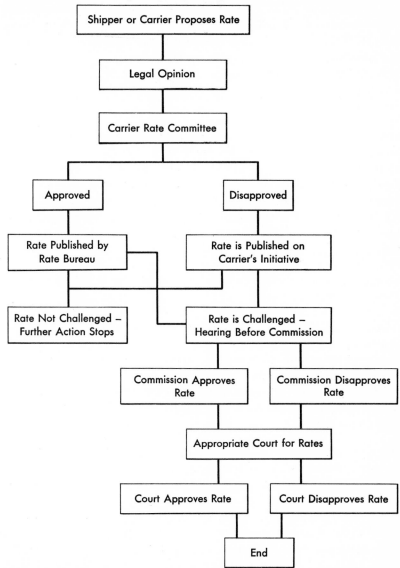

Class rates fall into two weight categories: volume or less than volume. In the case of trucks, the term is TL (truckload) and LTL (less than truck-load), and for rail it is CL (carload) and LCL (less than carload).

When a class rate is used, it is important' to use the correct classification of the product.[5] The classification is simply an organized grouping of com-

[5]The correct term for a given commodity classification is *rating*. See Appendix 6A for a detailed discussion.

TABLE 6–5 SAMPLE CLASS RATE SCALES TL AND LTL VOLUMES

Commodity	Rate per 100 pounds (cwt.)		
	LTL	TL	TL min. wt.
Auto Spring Assembly:			
Set up loose in packages	$2.00	$1.25	10,000
Knocked down (disassembled)	.85	.45	10,000

modities into a few classes of products with like transportation and marketing characteristics. Legally, both the shipper and the carrier are jointly and separately required to use the correct classification for a product. Lower rates apply to commodities when they have a lower classification or are shipped in larger volumes. Table 6–5 shows a typical range of prices that may exist on a single commodity, depending upon its classification and its shipment weight:

The conclusions that can be drawn are:

(1) Ship 5,000 pounds set up loose: rate applicable is $2 per cwt. Total charges are $100.
(2) Ship 10,000 pounds set up loose: rate applicable is $1.25 per cwt. Total charges are $125. Shipping twice the amount results in only 25 percent increase in costs.
(3) Ship 5,000 pounds disassembled: applicable rate is 85 cents per cwt. Total charges are $42.50.
(4) Ship 10,000 pounds disassembled: applicable rate is 45 cents per cwt. Total charges are $45.00. Shipping twice the amount results in virtually the same cost.

Exceptions and Commodity Rates. Two other types of basic rates exist within the common carrier structure: exception rates and commodity rates.[6]

Exception rates are based upon some exceptional circumstance surrounding the movement of a particular commodity. Shipping steel sheets on a flatbed trailer requires different equipment than shipping general freight in a regular trailer. Because the equipment required is less expensive, charging the regular class rate would be unfair to the shipper. For this reason, an exception is made to the classification so that the class rate shifts, in this case, downward. If the class rate were originally $2, then the exception rate would be less than $2. However, if the equipment cost were higher, say for a refrigerated truck, the exception rate would be higher than the class rate. An exception rate supersedes a class rate and may be higher or lower than the class rate.

[6]Technically, an exception rate occurs as a result of changing the classification of a product to one it would not normally carry.

The commodity rate is based upon the volume of movements of a specific commodity between specific points. For example, auto parts may move in heavy volumes between Detroit and assembly location in Newark. Because the loads are heavier on the average than for the volumes on class rates, the commodity rate should be lower than the class rate. Assume, for example, if the average weight of auto parts under a class rate were 15,000 pounds, and the average weight shipped between Detroit and Newark would be 30,000 pounds, the commodity rate should be about one-half the applicable class rate.

CONTRACT CARRIER RATES

A contract carrier is one who serves only one or a small number of shippers. Auto manufacturers use contract carriers in moving finished autos from assembly plants to dealers. Contract carriers are not subject to as stringent regulations as common carriers. They do, however, need to file with the ICC or State Commission the actual rates they charge.

The biggest advantage of contract carriers is their low cost. Low costs are generated because of better scheduling of truck fleets. In the case of a common carrier, scheduling is more difficult, because they serve numerous customers, whereas contract carriers specialize for only a few.

Gerber Foods in Fremont, Michigan, uses a contract carrier between Fremont and Chicago. Empty baby food jars are moved from Chicago to Fremont, and the filled jars are moved to Chicago in the same truck. This results in much higher loads and lower costs. Where the rate by common carrier may be $1 per cwt, via contract carrier it may be 75 cents or less per cwt. Wherever balanced loads exist in two directions from the same origins to the same destinations, contract carriage represents an attractive alternative.

PRIVATE TRANSPORT

The last important legal type of transportation is a private fleet. The legal definition of private trucking is that the shipper is the bona fide owner of the goods. The private trucking operator may not, therefore, legally accept freight from just anyone, because he would then be acting as a common carrier. Penalties may be leveled against private truckers acting as common carriers.

The main difference between a contract carrier and a private carrier is the amount of investment made by the shipper and his degree of managerial control. In the case of a contract carrier, the contract operator buys trucks and trailers. In a private fleet, the operators buy or lease the trucks and trailers.

The decision to go to a private fleet should be based upon return on investment or improved physical distribution service. Any firm requires a certain return on capital when undertaking an investment. The basic calculation for the Return On Investment (ROI) is

$$\text{ROI} = \frac{\text{Revenue} - \text{Cost}}{\text{Investment}}$$

In the above relationship, the revenue is the amount that would have been paid to common carriers if they had been used. The cost is based upon capital expense plus operating costs for a private fleet. In all cases, a conservative estimate of cost is required if errors in private fleet decisions are to be avoided. For example, the drivers' wages account should be set at Teamster Union levels in anticipation of unionization of the private fleet drivers.

Transportation Pricing and Related Services

Transportation pricing depends, as does all other pricing, on consideration of cost and demand schedules.[7] As indicated in the preceding sections, the total environment of regulation, production, marketing, and competition will influence pricing patterns in transportation. Present conditions in this context vary enormously from those upon which traditional transport policy originally arose. Originally, pricing patterns prevailed within the context of monopoly; that is, for all practical purposes, the only alternative was rail.

Under present conditions, numerous alternatives exist by mode and type, resulting in a wide range of transport choices, each with its unique cost and demand patterns. Under these conditions, competition rather than monopoly largely dictates pricing structures. Although this fact introduces pricing flexibility, it equally creates complexity. For this reason, a rather sophisticated knowledge of transportation cost and demand patterns is essential to proper transport selection.

OTHER FORMS OF RATES

In addition to the basic legal grouping of class, commodity, and exceptions rates, a grouping by objectives of a rate can be made. Rather than present a technical discussion of each objective, they are grouped below by their major economic purposes with sample types discussed.

Cost-Oriented Rates.   Cost-oriented rates are designed to assure recovery of some specified cost associated with providing transportation services. This

---

[7]Costs are dealt with in detail in Chapter 7. In this section the economic and environmental circumstances surrounding pricing decisions are discussed.

family of rates generally follows weight and distance forms. Pricing structures of a weight-distance type generally are specified on a point-to-point basis. The great advantage of such rates is their uniformity, which permits rather accurate estimates of transport costs if weight and distance are known. Uniformity, in turn, permits expression of transportation cost as a mathematical function, eliminating the need for excessive checking of individual rates between paired points.

Incentive loadings as a part of cost-oriented rates relate to the economies of equipment utilization. In essence, transportation costs primarily reflect the expense of moving a box from one point to another. Therefore, the nearer the load to full capacity, the lower is the cost per weight unit shipped. Incentive rates, recognizing this basic economic fact, induce the shipper to increase shipping weight in return for what amounts to a quantity discount for larger shipments. For example, if the basic rate on a specific shipment were $.80 per cwt, a 30,000-pound shipment would cost $240. However, for any amount above 30,000 pounds, the rate might be only $.60 per cwt. Therefore, the greater the amount shipped, the lower is the price per cwt for the entire shipment. In recent times, cost-oriented rates have received considerable impetus, resulting more from competitive factors, perhaps, than from economic theory.

Market-Oriented Rates and Services.   A group of rates are aimed toward achievement of marketing goals. Included in this group are (1) diversion and reconsignment priviliges, (2) blanket or area rates, (3) freight-all-kinds rates (FAK rates), and (4) stop-in-transit to load and unload.

Diversion and Reconsignment Privileges.   Diversion and reconsignment provide an important privilege where tight scheduling exists or marketing prices of products show volatile and geographically variable characteristics. Although not strictly a rate in the ordinary sense, a small charge for this privilege does place it in the pricing area. As an example, consider the problem of marketing fresh vegetables from California to New York. This particular market closely approximates perfect competition over a broad range with numerous buyers and sellers. Imperfections in market intelligence create price disparities for the same product in different locations, resulting from maladjustments of local supply and demand conditions. With different market prices, marketing vacuums based upon price differentiations come into existence, and rewards for quickly filling these vacuums benefit those in a position to do so. Diversion now enters as a way of accomplishing that result. If a carload of lettuce is moving from California routed to New York, it may be directed to a selected number of points where market opportunities appear highest on the anticipated delivery date. Thus, instead of a two-week forecast, necessary without a diversion privilege, markets may be watched closely, shortening necessary forecasts to as little as one day. Simultaneously with a diversion, a reconsignment may be necessary to accommodate the fact that a different broker or agent may take delivery.

Blanket Rates. Blanket rates provide another example of primarily market-oriented rates. In this family of rates, relatively large areas are blanketed with a single rate for delivery to all points. As an example, California oranges face serious competition from Florida sources simply because of adverse location of California with reference to eastern markets. In such a case, a blanket rate may cover a wide geographic area in the eastern part of the United States. The resultant averaging of costs to nearer locations, say Kansas City with farther areas such as Pittsburgh, enables greater overall market penetration.

FAK Rates. FAK means *Freight All Kinds.* Obviously, a rate applies to a specific commodity or a small range of commodities. In FAK rates, the mix of freight is unrestricted. This is an important advantage, because different commodities may be transported in one shipment without detailed listings, ratings, and rate determination. Without this type of rate, the shipper would either (1) ship each commodity as a small volume at high level rates, thus increasing transport costs; (2) ship full loads of single commodities, reducing his transport costs, but increasing his inventory levels; or (3) ship through a freight forwarder or other freight consolidating group or agency.

Stop-in-Transit to Load or Unload. This type of service associated with a rate proves particularly useful when two or more customers, each ordering small quantities, are located in the same direction from the point of origin. For example, if Customer A orders 10,000 pounds of steel and Customer B orders 20,000 pounds, both orders may be combined into one shipment. The first customer receives his order, and the carrier continues to the second customer. Although the charges generally exceed those for a single shipment of 30,000 pounds, they will total less than if two separate shipments had been made.

Production-Oriented Rates and Services.   Outstanding among production-oriented rates and service offerings of transport companies is a specialized privilege associated with the production process. In this case, a firm may ship a steel blank, which it intends to process further into a finished gear. Upon completion of the process, the finished gear then moves to a manufacturing location. Without a processing-in-transit privilege, the transportation price would consist of one short haul of the steel blank plus an additional short haul for the gear. With the in-transit privilege, it is assumed that the finished gear moves from the origin of the steel blank to the point where it entered the final product. This arrangement usually results in lower overall transport costs.

Privileges of this sort seem destined to play a decreasing role in transport for the future. As a result, certain industries, which historically have relied upon such privileges, face serious production and marketing adjustments. Outstanding among these industries are the flour and milling group. As transport prices perceptively move toward a cost-oriented distance-weight scale, milling locations based upon historical accident face economic adversity. It appears possible that with carefully scheduled changes in transport pricing, historically important flour and milling centers located in presently uneconomic locations will give way to more rationally located structures geared more closely to economic performance.

Volume Control — Terms of Sale FOB

"When Does Title Pass?"[8] — This question entails economic as well as legal reasoning. A critical dimension of its economic significance relates to Freight On Board (FOB) terms. Selection of the proper FOB terms closely relates to bargaining potentials in achieving transport pricing objectives. As in any bargaining transaction, the weight of economic power bends final results in favor of the party with the greater bargaining strength.

FOB terms conditioning the sales transaction provide opportunity for leverage in the same fashion as mass purchasing power of any group currying favor to its economic cause. Nowhere in corporate enterprise does the principle of mass purchasing power gain greater and unchallenged supremacy than that of finance. Although corporate structures may permit considerable managerial leeway to profit-centered operating units, rarely do corporate officers permit each profit-centered unit to seek its own source of capital in the external money markets. The principle underlying this posture clearly lies in the economic fact that large blocks of security offerings in the money market usually result in lower overall capital costs through risk averaging.

Rarely do corporate managements recognize the importance of the same bargaining principle in other functional areas under their general policy control, with the possible exception of materials purchasing. Among the stepchildren of corporate inattention in this regard stands foremost the transportation function, and its implementation lies in the more prosaic and legalistic framework of title transfer.

FOB terms provide the key to domination or abandonment of the economic conditions surrounding title transfer. The first important consideration surrounding FOB terms revolves around managerial policy with reference to amassing tonnage to influence transport purchase terms. If a firm chooses to abandon its purchasing power in the transport arena, it sells FOB origin and buys FOB destination. If it wishes to capitalize upon its transport purchasing power, on the other hand, it will buy FOB origin and sell FOB destination.

The ultimate economic choice in this dichotomy depends upon the relative strengths of buyer and seller in the transport markets and not the product

[8]Thomas Bugan, *When Does Title Pass?* (Dubuque, Iowa: W. C. Brown & Company, 1951), provides a more detailed discussion.

markets. The ultimate strategic choice may well depend upon other considerations, such as trade practice, sources of supply, or reliability performance factors, rippling out in ever-descending importance from the central vortex of management policy and objectives. The channel captain, for marketing reasons, may indeed exist as a different business personality than the channel captain in the transportation sense.[9]

As a general rule, the largest aggregation of purchasing power in any transactional relationship weighs heavily in the determination of final contract terms. This basic principle applies to purchasing of transportation, as well as to products and other sources. In the product markets, specific firms may enjoy control over distribution alternatives due to product advertising, promotion, and control, but simultaneously may lack sufficient image to influence the transportation markets of which they are a part. This is one of the major reasons for the separation of exchange and transportation channels as developed in Chapter 3.

Nontransportation Costs vs. Direct Transportation Costs

Too frequently, the decision to select a specific transport alternative is based upon comparison of direct transportation costs. In the crudest case, a simple rate comparison is made, and selection is based upon lowest published rate. Thus, if a rail rate were $5 per cwt and a truck rate $6 per cwt, the choice would be rail.

Standard management practices of comparing performance through accounting and budgetary procedures frequently force a knowledgeable traffic manager to make selections solely upon the basis of these simple rate comparisons. These standards of performance usually consist of percentage ratios or cost per unit. If a traffic purchase decision is based upon these managerially-determined standards, pressure unavoidably arises to select the lowest direct cost alternative. However, the lowest direct cost alternative almost invariably results in inflated costs in other cost centers of distribution (called here the nontransport costs associated with a specific transport alternative).

In Chart 6–2, direct transport costs for rail are only 90 cents, whereas for truck they are $1. Shifting from truck to rail transportation would seem to be a rational purchase decision, because it results in a $.10 direct cost reduction. However, rail shipments may move at 80,000 pounds and truck at 40,000. In that case, certain nontransportation costs will rise — among them are material handling, inventory, and storage. It certainly appears that larger storage requirements, more expensive material handling costs, and higher inventories result from the larger shipment quantities necessitated by rail shipments. These are shown in the chart as 40 cents per cwt for rail-associated nontransport costs and 20 cents per cwt for truck. Thus, when

[9]See Chapter 3, page 43.

CHART 6–2*   Direct Transport Costs and Nontransport Costs in
Transport Purchase Decisions (Cost/cwt)

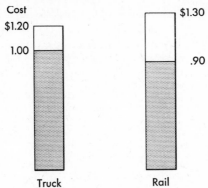

*Based upon unpublished paper by R. L. Banks and Associates, Washington, D.C.

the nontransport costs are included in the purchase decision, it results in a complete reversal of the decision favoring truck over rail, even though truck shows the higher direct costs.[10]

The remarkable fact about the above phenomenon is that all related cost centers can show improved efficiency based upon a unit cost reduction if the wrong transport choice is made. As will be discussed in detail in Chapter 11, each physical distribution cost center usually experiences certain fixed costs and other costs that are variable with volume. Thus, if rail shipments of 80,000 pounds were used instead of 40,000-pound truck movements, volume moving through a warehouse would be larger. The consequence of this is that warehouse unit costs will be lower for rail than for motor carriers. However, total costs may rise for the entire system. An example may demonstrate the point.

The traffic manager frequently need not take into account nontransport costs in making his selection. However, he must be able to provide relative carrier pricing information, cost information on noncommon carrier alternatives, and nontransport costs closely related to transportation. Foremost among these nontransport cost components are those which affect inventory levels (transit times and average loads per shipment), loading and unloading costs, and paperwork costs for a range of feasible alternatives.

Unitization

The general study of physical distribution management is involved with a number of subject matters that do not represent major functional activity

[10]For a more extended discussion of this principle, see John R. Meyer, *et al.*, *Economics of Competition in the Transport Industries* (Cambridge, Mass.: Harvard University Press, 1959), Appendix D; and Charles W. King, "How Total Costs Affect Ratemaking," *Distribution Age*, December 1965, p. 25.

**TABLE 6–6 UNIT AND TOTAL COST COMPARISON —
RAIL VS. TRUCK**

	Direct Cost (cwt)	Volume (cwt)	Warehouse Fixed Cost Annual Basis	Warehouse Variable Cost (cwt)	Warehouse			Total Direct and Warehouse Unit Cost (cwt)
					Fixed Unit Cost (cwt)	Variable Unit Cost (cwt)	Total Unit Cost (cwt)	
Truck	$1.00	400	$200	$.10	$.50	$.10	$.60	$1.60
Rail	.90	800	$300	.10	.38	.10	.48	1.38

Total Cost*	Rail	Truck
Transportation	$720	$800
Warehouse fixed costs	300	200
Warehouse variable cost	8	8
Total	$1,028	1,008

*Based upon 80,000 pounds on 1 rail trip and 2 truck trips.

centers in the same sense as transportation, inventory control, communications, and distribution warehousing. These additional areas of concern could be considered as supplemental to the major activity centers and therefore are treated in a less comprehensive manner. However, because they require a great deal of managerial control and substantial expenditures, a comprehensive treatment of physical distribution should not exclude coverage of the more significant supplemental activity centers.

In this treatment, one major group of these supplemental activity centers has been incorporated under the title *Unitization*. These specific areas of treatment influencing the physical distribution function are the factors of packaging, containerization, and material handling. Each of these three areas of managerial concern transcends the major functional areas of a physical distribution system. For example, material handling is essential for efficient distribution warehousing as well as transportation. The very essence of material handling is related to the physical transfer of inventory. Furthermore, material handling interrelates the packaging and containerization functions. Thus, unitization is best viewed as occurring throughout the total physical distribution system. The degree of unitization required in any given system is a function of the geographic configuration of distribution warehouses and the overall policy regarding final product delivery service to customers.

The logic of combining packaging, containerization, and material handling is twofold. First, from a physical distribution viewpoint the three are interrelated in terms of handling the basic product under consideration. The industrial package serves as a master carton in grouping products to facilitate their movement through the system. The container, which may be a single industrial package or a grouping of industrial packages, reduces the number of individual packages that require handling for any given transfer. Finally, the act of moving the individual industrial package or the container is the process of material handling.

The second aspect of our logic in combining packaging, containerization, and material handling under the label *unitization* is to stress the omnibus interrelationship of these supplemental functions to all other activities of the total physical distribution system. These individual subjects cannot be treated solely in the context of distribution warehousing or transportation, for this approach would fail to stress the intra-intercompany impact of unitization decisions.

The following treatment considers two basic factors that influence unitization decisions: (1) product characteristics, and (2) basic package. The product and the basic package are prime determinants in all decisions related to material handling and containerization.

PRODUCT CHARACTERISTICS

The product affects unitization with respect to specific product characteristics. These characteristics are (1) design, (2) fragility, (3) form, and (4) pilferage.

Design.   Product design affects the package and, in turn, unitization by its unique configuration of width, height, and length. These unique configurations may not achieve maximum cube utilization or minimum handling requirements. To achieve maximum cube utilization, the optimal configuration for a product would be where the product design satisfied a perfectly cubical package. This package in conforming to the product's design will use a minimal amount of cubic space by increasing the package's density per cube of space. Also material handling costs will usually be reduced.

Many manufacturers use the principle of maximum cube utilization when they ship their products "knocked down" (disassembled) or "nested" (one inside the other). This allows them to achieve a lower physical distribution cost per unit, because more products are able to fill a given cubic area such as a railroad car, truck van, or warehouse. For example, bicycles are seldom assembled at the manufacturing location. Rather, they are assembled in the marketplace to considerably reduce the cube moving through the distribution system.

Fragility.   Fragility relates to the damage probabilities a product will encounter as it moves through the distribution system. Each time a product is handled and all the time a product is in transit, susceptibility to damage is present in varying degrees. To reduce damage losses in the system, products may need considerable protective packaging to protect from the physical hazards of vibration, puncture, impact, and compression. Also, products may need to be unitized in some manner thereby reducing the probabilities of damage conditioned by the number of material handling functions.

To design a proper system to protect the fragile product, the total environment of the physical distribution system the product passes through must be considered. When all the physical and environment hazards are identified and the extent to which they occur is determined, proper adjustments can be made in the product and its relationship with unitization. In no instance should a proper protection system be based upon inconclusive laboratory tests or physical and environmental factors.

Form.   Form relates to the configuration of the product as well as to its physical characteristics. Often form considerations may be dictated by manufacturing and marketing considerations. When such is the case, a distribution analyst should still be able to provide valuable guidance in new product forms. If possible, marketing, production, and physical distribution should form an intracompany communication network to advise one another on how new product forms will affect each function. Physical distribution's gain in each instance is unitization for better physical distribution economies.

In many instances, marketing, production, and physical distribution have assisted one another in maintaining the product's basic form while simultaneously altering the outer protective package in order to realize physical distribution economies. One example may illustrate this point:

Not too many years ago, paint manufacturers produced a wide range of colors for inventory. The inventory levels depended upon the manufacturer's product line. The longer the line, the more paint tied up in inventory. As you can analyze, physical distribution costs were increasing for the manufacturer.

To reduce costs, the paint manufacturers altered the product form. Instead of sending gallon and quart cases of individual paints, they went through a unitization process. This resulted in the manufacturer making a few basic colors that were shipped to the dealers in 55-gallon drums. The manufacturer also produced a wide range of pigments. Then, in the retail outlet, pigments were mixed with the basic colors to achieve an unlimited spectrum of colors.

This whole process stimulated by a change in outer protective packaging reduced distribution diseconomies and increased customer service levels.

Pilferage.   Pilferage is a problem inherent with certain types of products of high value and small size. Cigarettes, jewelry, watches, and appliances generally experience high pilferage rates. With large consolidated product groupings, carry-off ease diminishes. Attendant with consolidation, product identity tends to become more obscure as the shipper reduces to a minimum the amount of product information on the protective packaging. Thus unitization serves as preventive pilferage insurance, and the result is always a rather substantial reduction in risk insurance for the shipper and the handler.

BASIC PACKAGE

The basic package is a unit of a product or quantity of items uniformly processed, wrapped, and sealed in a container for storage and/or shipment. The package should be analyzed from the viewpoint of (1) motivation, (2) product protection, and (3) accessibility.

Motivation. Motivation relates primarily to the design of the package for sales and marketing functions and frequently operates at odds with the physical distribution demands for packaging. Here a distinction must be made between consumer packaging and industrial packaging. Consumer packaging incorporates motivational techniques of (1) color, (2) design, (3) size (billboard effect), and (4) styling, to promote the product's sale. Furthermore, the consumer package needs protective packaging while in storage and transit. Industrial packaging, on the other hand, provides protection in the distribution process. It, in most instances, does not act as a motivational instrument.

Because a consumer package needs the added protection of an industrial package during periods of storage and transportation, the motivational role of consumer packages can affect the industrial package design. These motivational factors determine the outer configuration of the industrial package resulting in extreme variations. For example, a cereal company may select a box with a reduced width and increased height to maximize the facing dimensions of the package. This policy then maximizes the display area provided each cereal at the expense of the grocer's available shelf space. This policy may also cause diseconomies within the physical distribution system by inefficient use of available cube and by increased handling expenses.

From a total strategy viewpoint, trade-offs may appear between uneconomical package design for the physical distribution system and increased opportunities for substantial sales generation. As long as the increased sales outweigh the increased costs attributable to the uneconomical package, no objection should be raised to the distribution diseconomies. When the balance swings in the opposite direction, steps must be taken to improve the package's design as a motivational tool and as a component of the distribution system.

Of greater interest to the distribution analyst are the three remaining aspects of the package: (1) product protection, (2) form, and (3) economy of materials.

Product Protection. Product protection requires tailoring the inside consumer package and the outside industrial container to withstand the environmental hazards of heat, cold, water, water vapor, and pressure plus the physical hazards of vibration, impact, puncture, and compression. Ordinarily the protective cycle begins at the end of the production line and

TABLE 6–7 BALANCING PACKAGING COSTS AGAINST LOSS AND DAMAGE EXPENSES*   (Based on 10 mm containers)

Packaging Material [1]	Cost Per Unit [2]	Total Packaging Costs [3]	Incremental Packaging Costs [4]	Damage Cost [5]	Incremental Damage Savings [6]	Net Gain or Loss [7]
Flat cardboard $\frac{1}{16}''$	$.01	100,000	—	500,000	—	—
$\frac{1}{8}''$ fluted corrugated	.02	200,000	100,000	300,000	200,000	+100,000
$\frac{3}{16}''$ fluted corrugated	.03	300,000	100,000	150,000	150,000	+ 50,000
$\frac{1}{4}''$ fluted corrugated	.04	400,000	100,000	50,000	100,000	—
$\frac{3}{8}''$ double-fluted triple-wall	.05	500,000	100,000	45,000	5,000	−95,000

*Table 6–7 does not reflect the added costs of transportation and space requirements due to heavier and/or bulkier packaging. In a complete analysis of cost trade-offs, the weight and bulk of different packaging and packing materials must be considered.

progresses through material handling, warehousing and transportation functions as established by the manufacturer, wholesaler, and retailer.

Essentially product protection principles for packaging designs result from applying technical analysis to various package configurations and computing the increase in damage savings against the increase in packaging costs. Given an assortment of packaging materials the marginal costs of additional protection can be readily measured.

The marginal analysis method of determining the required configuration of packaging materials serves as only a first approximation. It is highly unlikely, except for a zero-defect program, such as in the space program, that absolute protection will be required. In most commercial and industrial situations, damage may be permitted to some tolerable limit such as 5 per cent or as demonstrated in Table 6–7.

In Table 6–7, various materials have been tested for their effects upon product protection. Each material has an associated total packaging cost (column 3) and a total damage cost (column 5). From columns 3 and 5, incremental packaging costs and damage savings can be calculated. The crucial column is the one that measures net gain or loss for each material (column 7). Column 7 simply compares the incremental packaging costs and the incremental damage savings.

To find the most economical packaging material, the distribution analyst should find the point where incremental packaging costs are equal to the incremental damage savings. In this particular example, $\frac{1}{4}$ inch fluted, corrugated board appears to provide maximum savings. If $\frac{3}{8}$ inch double-fluted, triple-wall were used, incremental damage savings would for all practical purposes, reach zero ($45,000). However, to reach this point of near perfect protection, incremental packaging costs of $100,000 would result in incremental damage savings of $5,000 or a net cost of $95,000. Similar charts have been prepared by most manufacturers based upon the sensitivity of their product and the damage cost as based upon their distribution history.

The measurement of damage prevention effectiveness is somewhat more difficult than marginal analysis. Standard methods of determining damage prevention effectiveness include (1) laboratory tests conducted under controlled conditions in which various levels of damage prevention effectiveness can be determined, and (2) test shipments based upon statistical inferences over a stated sample period. Although laboratory testing is generally more efficient, the use of common carrier in transportation often requires test shipments even if laboratory test results show wide protective efficiency margins. Further difficulties with lab testing are the extreme variability in the customer's material handling systems and attempting to simulate all physical and environmental hazards may be near impossible. However, much can be done to refine packaging knowledge given certain distribution information.

In line with the above discussion, a general rule is to design a package for the most violent exposure you know your product will be subject to anywhere in the system. Then pare down the cost to the damage rates you will tolerate.

Accessibility.   The accessibility of a package has both marketing and distribution related applicability. To the average consumer, the accessibility of the consumer package should allow convenience of movement and easy removal of the product. However, in certain marketing environments and for certain products, convenience of movement and easy removal must be hindered to reduce pilferage. One method used to prevent pilferage is to increase the size of the package considerably beyond basic requirements. In so doing, the increased package size reduces the convenience of movement and also increases the checkout cashier's ability to detect shop lifters. In addition, thick poly packs formed over the product may be employed so ease of access is reduced. Packaging therefore may become an effective agent in preventing pilferage.

In industrial situations, the accessibility of the package should allow for ease of movement throughout the system. For purposes of production efficiency and when order picking is required, fast accessibility is desired. However, when the package is in transit or in permanent storage, easy accessibility must be reduced to prevent pilferage and damage.

Summary

As illustrated in this chapter, the transportation industries provide a wide array of services, each designed for a solution of specific physical distribution problems. Analysis of transportation requires an expert's knowledge and, therefore, dictates administrative and technical strength in the traffic management function.

The function of the traffic manager in a distribution program is not only to provide expertise in day-to-day administration, but also to cast cost and service characteristics of alternatives into an appropriate form suited to distribution study requirements. The role of the traffic manager is developed in Appendix 6A. Due to ever-changing price relationships and service capabilities, constant monitoring of the transport market becomes essential to maintenance of good performance for the physical distribution system as a whole.

Application of unit-load principles in a physical distribution system can result in substantial economies. Although the engineering and economic aspects usually receive the attention of specialists, it should not be overlooked that more than mere engineering and cost analysis is involved. When properly fitted into a distribution system, unit loads can also play a major role in effective marketing of a product.

Not only do unit loads lead to lower costs, but they also can have an effect upon sales generation. Too often an engineering approach focuses upon the cost of only a single link in the total distribution chain.

Discussion Questions

1. What is transit inventory?

2. What is the difference between common carriers, contract carriers, exempt carriers, and private carriers?

3. If the rate on cans from Boise, Idaho to Portland, Oregon was quoted by a common carrier as being $1.37/cwt for commodity shipments and a contract carrier filed a rate of $1.50/cwt for the same haul, would a shipper in Boise be wiser to use the common carrier?

4. If a firm shipping auto batteries from Chicago to Detroit with its own trucks was asked to ship zinc on its return trip by its customer to another Chicago-based firm for $.23/cwt, would this be a good way for it to reduce its total distribution costs? If they were asked to ship grapes at $.97/cwt, would this be an equally acceptable means of reducing total costs?

5. What does FAK mean? Would it be of more importance to a novelty producer or to a steel mill? Why?

6. Why would a firm buy materials FOB origin and sell finished products FOB origin?

7. What are exempt products? What types of producers and carriers are usually involved with exempt products?

8. The ICC requires that common carriers collect outstanding bills within a specific period of time. What is the reasoning behind this regulation?

9. Define transportation's position in the total physical distribution network. What are the other components of the physical distribution network?

10. Evaluate the role of transportation costs in the computer industry versus the steel industry. How do transportation costs relate to total physical distribution planning? Should the physical distribution manager consider transportation costs of sole importance in physical distribution decisions? If not, what other factors need to be considered?

11. Describe the technical modes of transportation supply. What types of goods are moved in each mode? Does the transport distance have any effect on the mode selected?

12. How do the legal forms and the technical modes differ? How are they the same?

13. The value of the product in-transit determines the mode. Explain.

14. How is a rate developed? What are positive aspects of a rate proceeding? What are the negative aspects?

Appendix 6A
TRAFFIC MANAGEMENT AND PHYSICAL DISTRIBUTION

Historically, the largest single block of responsibilities in physical distribution have rested with the traffic department of the firm. With the advent of the physical distribution concept, responsibilities for exacting traffic management have increased substantially. In the past, it was not at all unusual for the traffic manager to be strictly responsible for his major function — transportation purchasing. However, in the new context, his duties will frequently encompass packaging, materials handling, inventory management, warehousing, and other areas of physical distribution.

Regardless of his exact scope of authority, under the physical distribution concept, the traffic manager will become more involved with other corporate activities such as marketing, production, and finance. The recent awareness to total physical distribution systems has created confusion regarding the proper role of traffic management. In general, physical distribution is much broader in concept and function than transportation. Thus, transportation management is but one aspect of overall physical distribution management. However, it is one of the most important aspects of total physical distribution control.

The advent of integrated physical distribution has increased the need for exacting transportation management. A system in total cannot function adequately unless the management of transport is effectively and efficiently performed and integrated to corporate efforts in all other areas. Thus, it appears safe to conclude that the demand for professional traffic management is at an all-time high. As long as physical distribution constitutes a major area of corporate effort, traffic management will be a vital ingredient of the total effort.

The purpose of this appendix is to develop the role of traffic management in a physical distribution organization. Because total books are devoted to this subject, the content of this appendix falls considerably short of a detailed professional development of the field of traffic management.[1] The appendix aims to provide the nonprofessional reader with a basic familiarization of the specialized field of traffic management.

The major functional responsibilities of a traffic department can be grouped into two areas: (1) administration and (2) research. Each area of responsibility is reviewed below.

Traffic Administration

The administration responsibility of the traffic department consists of day-to-day control of freight movement. In cases where all movements are by for-hire carriers, this daily responsibility consists of purchasing services and movement control. If a firm operates private transport equipment, the traffic department is responsible for administration and scheduling of equipment. In both cases it is the objective of traffic management to provide a transport service that meets requirements of the physical distribution system. These system requirements relate to speed of service, size of order to be shipped, and assignment of the specific plant or warehouse to make the shipment. For any given period, the operating standards for transport are given and must be met if the firm is to achieve its desired physical distribution goals. However, the research responsibility of traffic management, discussed in the next section, outlines the way in which the transport sector of the firm can and should take an active role in setting physical distribution standards.

The administration of transportation consists of (1) freight classification, (2) obtaining lowest rate for a given movement consistent with service requirements, (3) equipment scheduling, (4) documenting, (5) tracing and expediting, (6) auditing, and (7) claims.

FREIGHT CLASSIFICATION

All products normally transported are grouped together into uniform classifications. The purpose of the classification is to take into consideration characteristics of a product or a commodity that will influence cost of handling or transport. Products with a similarity are grouped into a given

---

[1] For a complete treatment of traffic management see Charles A. Taff, *Management of Traffic and Physical Distribution* (Homewood, Ill.: Richard D. Irwin, Inc., 1964).

class, thereby reducing the wide range of possible ratings to a manageable size. The particular class that a given product or commodity receives is called its rating. A products rating is not the price that must be paid to have a product transported. The rating is a products classification placement. The actual price that must be paid is called the freight rate. As will be explained below, the rate is found from price lists called tariffs. Thus, a products rating is used to determine the actual freight rate.

Motor carriers and rail carriers each have independent classification systems. The basic motor carrier system is the "National Motor Freight Classification," and rail classifications are published in the "Uniform Freight Classification." The motor classification has 23 classes of freight; the rail system has 31. In local or regional areas, individual groups of carriers may publish additional classification listings.

Classification of individual products is based on a relative percentage index of 100. Class 100 is considered the normal class with other classes running as high as 500 and as low as 35 in the National Motor Freight System. Each product is assigned an item number for listing purposes and then a class rating. As a general rule, the higher a class rating, the higher is the transport cost of a product. Thus, a product classified as 400 would be four times more expensive to transport than a product rated as class 100. Products are also assigned classifications based upon the quantity shipped at an individual time. Thus, less-than-carload (LCL) or truckload (LTL) shipments of identical products will have higher ratings than carload (CL) or truckload (TL) shipments.

To illustrate take item 70660 from the National Motor Freight Classification No. A-7. Item 70660 is described as "Carpet or Rug Cushions, Cushioning or Lining, sponge rubber, in wrapped rolls." Item 70660 falls into the general product grouping 70500 "Floor Coverings or Related Articles." For LTL shipments, item 70660 has a $77\frac{1}{2}$ rating, whereas in TL shipments it is assigned class 45 providing a minimum shipment of 30.2 hundred weight (cwt) is shipped. Many products will also be assigned different ratings based upon packaging. Thus, sponge rubber cushions may have a different rating when shipped loose, in bails, or in boxes than when shipped in wrapped rolls. Thus, a number of different classifications may apply to the same product depending upon where it is being shipped, the size of the shipment, the transport mode being used, and the packaging of the product.

One of the major responsibilities of the traffic department is to obtain the best possible rating for all products shipped by the firm. Although there are differences in rail and motor classifications, each are guided by classification rules. These rules are similar; however, the rail rules are more comprehensive and detailed than those for motor freight classification. It is essential that members of a traffic department have a comprehensive understanding of classification rules. These general rules handle all normal situations and specific rules are available as exceptions to the general rules.

It is possible to have a product reclassified by making written application to the appropriate classification board. These boards review proposals for change or additions with respect to minimum weights, commodity descriptions, packaging requirements, and general rules and regulations. All changes other than corrections in classification require public hearings prior to publication. Other interested parties are thereby provided an opportunity to be heard prior to acceptance or rejection of the proposal. After the proposal is accepted or rejected, methods of appeal are provided.

Thus, an alert traffic department must take an active role in classification. Many dollars can be saved by finding the correct classification for a product or by recommending a change in packaging or quantity shipped that will reduce the rating of a firm's product.

FREIGHT RATES

The main body of Chapter 6 contained a description of basic transportation rates and rate regulation. For any given shipment it is the responsibility of the traffic department to obtain the lowest possible rate consistent with service requirements. Determination of transport cost by method of movement — rail, air, motor, pipeline, parcel post, United Parcel, REA Express, freight forwarders, *et al.* — is found by reference to tariffs. In this connection, it is important that the traffic department have adequate access to current tariffs. The most important information resource available to the traffic department is its tariff library. Many tariffs exist and relevant ones must be kept up-to-date for all changes and modifications.

As indicated several times throughout this text, the lowest possible cost for transportation alone may not be the lowest total cost of distribution. Thus, the traffic department must seek the lowest rate consistent with service standards. For example, if two-day delivery is required, the traffic department seeks to select the method of transport that will meet this standard at the lowest possible cost or freight bill.

EQUIPMENT SCHEDULING

In cases where private transportation equipment is used one major responsibility of the traffic department is scheduling. This responsibility also exists when common carriers are utilized. One of the largest bottlenecks in physical distribution can occur by the building-up of carrier equipment waiting to be loaded or unloaded at a shipper's dock.

Railroads and motor carriers each have special charges for equipment delay beyond normal times allowed in the tariffs. Motor carriers specify times based upon individual situations and when these times are exceeded detention charges are made. Railroads normally allow 48 hours for unloading with time in excess charged as demurrage.

As a general rule, demurrage and detention should be held to a minimum, because they represent a penalty charge which increases the total cost of distribution. However, in special cases, it may be desirable to pay delay penalties in order to reduce other expenses. For example, demurrage charges may represent a favorable trade-off if overtime can be reduced. Each situation must be evaluated on the merits of the alternatives. The objective is to eliminate special service charges unless they reduce other costs of physical distribution.

DOCUMENTATION

Several basic documents are involved in transportation management. Two of the most important are the bill of lading and the freight bill.

Bill of Lading.   The bill of lading is the basic document in the purchase of transport services. It serves as a receipt for goods shipped through the description of commodities and quantities as detailed on the document. For this reason, accurate description and count is essential. In case of loss, damage, or delay, the bill of lading provides necessary evidence for damage claims resulting from inferior carrier performance.

The bill of lading specifies the terms and conditions under which the carrier liability is extensive and includes all possible causes of loss or damage except those defined as acts of God. It is important that these terms and conditions be clearly understood so that appropriate actions may be taken in the event of nonperformance or inferior performance.

Variations in bills of lading exist. In addition to the uniform bill of lading, others commonly used are order notify, export, livestock, and government. It is important to select the correct bill of lading for a specific shipment.

An order notified or negotiable bill of lading is a credit instrument. It provides that delivery shall not be made unless the original bill of lading is surrendered to the carrier. The usual procedure is for the seller to send the order notified bill of lading to a third party, usually a bank or credit institution. Upon payment of the invoice value of the goods, the credit institution releases the bill of lading to the buyer. The buyer then presents it to the common carrier who in turn releases the goods.

An export bill of lading permits the use of export rates which are sometimes lower than normal domestic rates. Thus, when a shipment is being moved domestically for export, savings in transport can sometimes be enjoyed. An export bill of lading also permits greater time at the port for transfer of freight from a rail car to ship. In many cases the export bill also eliminates the need for special broker services at the port facility.

Government bills of lading may be used when the product is owned by the United States Government. A government bill of lading allows the use of "Section 22" rates, which are normally lower than regular rates. Under Section 22 of the Interstate Commerce Act, when goods are shipped on government account, rates may be based on bids by carriers resulting in more competitive rate structures.

The named individual or buyer on a bill of lading is the only bona fide recipient of goods. A carrier is responsible for proper delivery according to instructions contained in the document. In effect, title is transferred with accomplishment of delivery.

Freight Bill. The freight bill represents a carrier's method of charging for transportation services performed. The freight bill is derived from information contained on the bill of lading. It may be either prepaid or collect. A prepaid bill means that transport cost must be paid for prior to the transportation performance, whereas a collect shipment shifts payment responsibility to the buyer.

Freight bill payment periods vary. Motor carriers must bill shippers within seven days of delivery and the shipper must pay the carrier within an additional seven days after receipt of the bill. In the case of rail, 96 hours are allowed for carloads and 120 hours for LCL shipments. Unless credit arrangements have been made with carriers, collect shipments are payable upon delivery.

A great deal of transportation administration is involved in preparation of bills of lading and freight bills. Several firms and carriers are jointly working to reduce this administrative burden. Some firms elect to pay at the time of creating the bill of lading, thereby combining the two documents into one. Such arrangements are based upon financial analysis of the relative benefits of advanced payment to reduce paperwork costs. Many attempts are also underway to produce all documents in the required number of copies simultaneously. This has become more practical with the advent of computer facilities to aid in document preparation.

TRACING AND EXPEDITING

One of the largest areas of transportation management is the responsibility of tracing and expediting. Shipments committed to the vast transportation network of the United States are bound from time to time to go astray or get delayed in route. Most large carriers maintain a tracing department to aid shippers in locating a shipment. The tracing action must be initiated by the shipper's traffic department. Once initiated, it is the carrier's responsibility to provide the desired information.

Under conditions of exacting product movement control, the shipper may desire to expedite a given shipment in order to overcome some unexpected change of events. Under these conditions the shipper is often provided a "pro" number, which corresponds to the carrier's waybill and vehicle number. Identification of the shipment's pro number allows rapid location at points of destination terminal and transfer terminals.

AUDITING

Auditing of freight bills is another important function of the traffic department. Due to the complexities involved in finding the correct rate, the probability of an error in rate determination is higher in purchasing transportation than in most other purchasing decisions. Given the fact that transportation costs in the United States exceed 60 billion dollars, a one-percent error in calculating a rate will result in a 600-million-dollar potential loss to either carriers or shippers.

The freight audit is of two types: (1) preaudit and (2) post audit. A preaudit determines the proper rate and charges prior to payment of a freight bill. A postaudit makes the same determination after payment. Either or both types of audits may be employed.

Auditing may be either (1) external or (2) internal. If external, specialized freight auditing companies are used whose personnel are usually assigned to specific commodity groupings, and this generally is more efficient than internal personnel. Payment for an external audit is usually based upon the revenues reclaimed through inadvertent overcharges in the original payment. It is crucial that a highly ethical firm be employed for this purpose, because valuable marketing and customer information is contained in the freight bill, which, if not held confidential, may adversely affect corporate activities.

A combination of internal and external auditing is frequently employed. The division of this activity in such cases is based upon the freight bill. Thus, for a bill of $600 a 10-percent error results in a $60 recovery, but for a $50 bill a 10-percent error results in only a $5 recovery. Bills with the larger recovery potential may be processed internally, whereas the ones with the lower recovery potential may be handled by an external auditing firm.

External versus internal auditing may also be affected by the size of the firm and the degree of rate computerization. Large traffic departments are in a position to have specialized clerks for auditing purposes. Firms on computerized systems of freight payment can build in appropriate applicable rates on a large majority of points and weights. In that case, automatic checks on proper payment can be made by computer programs designed for that purpose.[2]

[2]For a more complete discussion of freight auditing see J. S. Traunig, *Thumb Your Way to Profits* (New York: Carlton Press, 1967).

CLAIM ADMINISTRATION

The transport carrier is a specialized middleman who agrees to perform a specified service for an agreed-upon fee. When these services or fees do not meet the predetermined standards, shippers can make claims for restoration. Naturally, carriers and shippers desire to prevent as many claims as possible. The advent of a claim situation indicates that the planned physical distribution of a product has broken down and corrective action is in order. Most claims can be settled between the carrier and shipper without resort to some higher authority. However, when necessary the framework for third party settlement is detailed.

In general, claims break down into two categories: (1) loss and damage, and (2) overcharge-undercharge. Loss and damage claims represent a shipper's demand for carrier payment of partial or total financial loss resulting from improper fulfillment of the transport agreement. Charge claims result from variance in actual charges from those published in tariffs.

A specialized body of rules apply to the proper procedure for claim filing and the responsibility of parties involved. A discussion of this detail is beyond the intent of this brief appendix. From the viewpoint of physical distribution management, two factors regarding claim administration are of primary importance. First, detailed attention should be given claim administration because such recoveries will only be realized by aggressive shipper programs. Second, the advent of a large volume of claims indicates that carriers selected are not performing their specified service obligation with desired consistency. Regardless of the dollars recovered by claim administration, the breakdown in physical distribution performance from loss and damage claims constitutes a deficiency to the shipper firm in the eyes of customers.

SUMMARY — TRAFFIC ADMINISTRATION

The seven administrative responsibilities of traffic management developed above could be expanded in substantial detail. In total, they break down to selection of carriers who can perform the desired service and areas of shipper follow-up required. Emphasis has been placed upon the purchasing of transport services rather than administration of private or contract fleets. Depending upon the transport mix used by a specific firm, the responsibilities of traffic management could very well encompass duties concerning common, contract, and private transport.

Traffic Research

Beyond traffic administration, the traffic department has a basic research responsibility with respect to the transport area and to the overall physical distribution system. Almost all traffic managers are able to perform the administrative responsibilities of transportation adequately. To be sure, some are far superior to others in day-to-day administration. However, most all get the job accomplished. The true distinction of professionalism among traffic managers comes in their capabilities in the area here called traffic research.

Traffic research is divided into two areas of responsibility. The first represents activities to improve the cost of transportation services and/or the quality of service received. The second constitutes activities aimed at improving the total distribution effort of the firm. Each is discussed in turn.

TRANSPORT SERVICES RESEARCH

Traffic managers should always be on the lookout for information to improve carrier service or obtain lower freight rates for a given quality of service. This means that an aggressive program of performance measurement and rate negotiation should represent a continuing function of transportation research.

Carrier performance measurement is perhaps one of the most void areas of traffic research. Information is normally accumulated regarding the number of claims required with individual carriers as well as tracing requirements. However, in addition, shippers should make an effort to measure how well carriers meet stated service obligations. Such obligations concern (1) equipment availability, (2) tracing efficiency, (3) expedite capability, and (4) transit consistency.

Among these four measures of performance, the one most difficult to obtain reliable information about is transit consistency. In Chapter 8 the subject of inventory control is developed. One vital aspect of control systems is the lead-time required to obtain replenishment. Regardless of how fast a supplier is able to ship, if the transport carrier provides inconsistent delivery, problems in inventory control will result. Likewise, sales can be lost and production lines shut down if carriers fail to meet their service obligation. As a general statement, the smaller a given shipment, the greater the service variance between consecutive shipments. Thus, while a truckload or carload shipment may regularly meet published schedules, the same efficiency may not be enjoyed in LTL or LCL shipments. Some carriers are superior to others and the task is to determine which among the many available is most consistent.

One shipper that purchases from a number of suppliers for delivery to several different warehouses obtains this information as follows. When suppliers ship, they are required to record date and other critical information on a postcard. When the order arrives at the firm's warehouse, it is so noted on the daily data transmitter to the central purchasing headquarters. Both dates are retained in a computer file by individual carriers along with a statement of expected performance. The variation between actual and expected performance is determined by a simple computer routine and the average actual performance is calculated and updated on a regular basis. At specified intervals, the performance record of each carrier is printed in report form and forwarded for traffic management review.

The above-mentioned consistency report coupled with statistics on equipment availability, tracing, and expediting performances provide valuable information for evaluation of carriers. Unless this type of information is collected on a routine basis, it is difficult to be specific or take corrective action about erratic carrier performance.

Another vital area of transport research is the matter of negotiation. Such negotiations are of two types: (1) formal and (2) informal. In formal negotiations, shippers must take active participation in proceedings before regulatory boards. Such proceedings may be aimed at achieving improvements in rates, ratings, or service provisions of a specific tariff or they may be aimed at preventing undue price increases or service detailments proposed by carriers. Informal negotiations consist of direct relationships between shippers and carriers. Despite the fact that transportation is a highly regulated industry, a great deal of latitude does exist between carriers and shippers. The effectiveness of both formal and informal negotiation will depend upon the shipper's ability to support proposals with accurate and complete information. Such information can only be collected by a well-administered research and analysis program.

Thus, one very important area of transport research deals with constant review of carrier performance and continuous examination of beneficial changes in existing classifications and tariffs.

DISTRIBUTION SYSTEM RESEARCH

For any given operating period, traffic management is expected to meet the specified service requirements within the stated transportation budget. However, it is also a responsibility of traffic management to look for ways in which transportation can be effectively used to reduce total physical distribution costs. For example, a slight change in packaging may open the door for negotiation of a lower classification rating for a product. Although packaging costs may increase by a slight amount, this added expense may be offset by a substantial reduction in transportation cost. It seems safe to assume that unless such proposals evolve from the traffic department, they will go undetected in the average firm.

As indicated earlier, transportation is the highest single cost area in most physical distribution systems. Because of this cost and the dependence of the physical distribution system on an effective transport capability, the traffic department must play an active role in future planning.

Summary

In this brief appendix the responsibilities of traffic management in physical distribution have been developed. A basic differential was made between duties of an administrative nature as those related to research and development. Perhaps the greatest demands of professional traffic management relate to the areas of research and development. It is in the area of transport services and basic system research that the skills of the traffic management group are vitally needed. Many potential benefits of integrated logistical effort are first recognized and then accomplished by aggressive and innovative traffic management.

CHAPTER 7 Transportation Costing

TO determine proper transportation alternatives in distribution system design, accurate costing of transportation by modes (rail, air, motor, water, and pipeline) and legal types (common, contract, private, leased, and exempt) is essential.

The transportation analyst faces a myriad of possible combinations of transportation useful for his needs. The purpose of this chapter is to present the basic methods employed in costing. As compared with other cost centers in physical distribution, transportation provides a unique set of circumstances because of its regulated characteristics. Economic regulation by the Federal and State Commissions, and other regulatory agencies provides a convenient benchmark of published methods available for the use of the transportation analyst. From the benchmark of publicly provided common carrier costs, alternative choices of both legal types and modes become relatively straightforward.

Transportation Costing Categories

Transportation costing is complicated by the fact that the plant, in large part, is mobile. In industrial costing, plant loads can be predetermined easier than in transportation costing. For this reason, greater reliance upon statistical cost estimates is made in transportation.

Besides the problems associated with costing for different modes (in effect, different plants), the problem remains of costing of different legal types (common, contract, private, leased, and exempt). In this chapter, attention is focused upon common carrier costing, because it provides the benchmark from which comparisons for other legal alternatives can be made.

The costing method selected is that of the ICC.[1] The economic categories of common motor carrier costs are fully allocated costs, joint costs, common costs, and out-of-pocket costs.

Fully allocated costs include all costs associated with performing the service, including a normal profit contribution. *Joint costs* consist of a single pool of costs which result in the production of two or more services. For example, if two or more different commodities are hauled in a single trailer, the costs are joint to all commodities and must be apportioned to each in some reasonable way. *Common costs* are similar to joint costs, because the problem of assignability is found in both. Common costs do not relate directly to the production of a service. Examples are the president's salary and other administrative expenses. *Out-of-pocket costs* are costs which are directly assignable to performing a service and which are the bare minimum necessary to continue the operation in the long run. Long-run out-of-pocket costs provide the rational lower limit to which prices may fall. The determination of out-of-pocket cost is now discussed.

THE COST CENTERS[2]

Common motor carrier regulation is based upon recognized ICC standard accounting systems and has four identifiable direct cost centers: line-haul costs, terminal costs, pickup and delivery costs, and billing and collecting costs.

Line-haul costs are defined as the movement over the road, either from one terminal to another or, in some cases, from a shipper's location to the destination. *Terminal costs* are defined as the handling and reworking of freight to match origins and destinations of outgoing and incoming freight. *Pickup and delivery costs* are defined as the function of picking up and delivering freight within a specified terminal area. *Billing and collecting costs* are those related to paperwork costs for each shipment.

The Service Unit. Each cost center is measured in terms of its relevant service unit. A service unit is the appropriate variable assigned to a specific cost center. The relevant service units for each cost center are shown in Table 7–1. This concept is exactly the same as that used in general accounting in cost allocation. The accountant also must find some method of allocating indirect costs such as rent. In the case of rent, a variable must be introduced (service unit), which reasonably allocates this share of work. Floor space

[1]*Explanation of the Development of Motor Carrier Costs with Statements as to Their Meaning and Significance*, ICC Statement No. 4–59, Washington, D. C., August, 1959. For rail costing see *A Short Guide to Railroad Cost*, A.A.R., Washington, D. C., 1963.

[2]The cost centers described may vary from mode to mode. For example, rail transportation will include such things as switching, yard expense, and others which strictly do not appear in motor transportation.

TABLE 7–1* OUT-OF-POCKET EXPENSES, SERVICE UNITS, AND COMPUTATION OF OUT-OF-POCKET UNIT COSTS FOR THE COST STUDY CARRIERS.

| | Total Out-of-Pocket Expenses | Service Units | | Out-of-Pocket Costs per Service Unit |
| | | Number of Service Units | Name of Service Unit | |
Item (1)	(2)	(3)	(4)	(5)
LINE-HAUL COSTS:				
1. Mileage cost	$ 43,000,000	307,143,000	Vehicle miles	$0.14
2. Hourly cost	52,224,000	10,200,000	Vehicle hours	5.12
3. Total cost	95,224,000	307,174,000	Vehicle miles	0.31
4. Total cost	95,224,000	68,010,204,000	Cwt. miles	0.0014
PICKUP AND DELIVERY COSTS:				
5. Mileage cost	$ 6,750,000	32,143,000	Vehicle miles	$0.21
6. Hourly cost	27,000,000	6,750,000	Vehicle hours	4.00
7. Total cost	33,750,000	6,750,000	Vehicle hours	5.00
8. Total cost	33,750,000	198,529,000	Cwt. rec.	0.17
TERMINAL PLATFORM COSTS:				
9. Total cost	$ 23,000,000	109,524,000	Cwt. platformed	$0.21
BILLING AND COLLECTING COSTS:				
10. Total Cost	$ 5,026,000	6,980,500	Shipments billed	$0.72
TOTAL OUT-OF-POCKET COST:				
11. Total dollars spent (Item Nos. 4, 8, 9, 10)	$157,000,000			

*SOURCE: These data and accompanying text are based upon ICC data, but are smoothed for ease of exposition. See *Highway Form A, Schedule A*, Sheet 6–1961, Statement No. 4–55, ICC, Washington, D. C., from which some of these data were taken.

related to a specific operation, revenue generated from a future proportion of direct labor, or other variables may be employed for this purpose.

Line-Haul Costs. The service units for line-haul costs are vehicle hours and vehicle miles, because some costs in the line-haul category vary with time (e.g., drivers' wages), and others vary with distance (e.g., fuel).

The relevant costs and service units for line-haul are the total costs (both distance and time costs) expressed in a cost-per-vehicle mile. In Table 7–1, the out-of-pocket cost per vehicle mile is $.31. This figure provides a measure of the required revenues to cover the cost of the line-haul. For example, if a truck trailer moves a distance of 100 miles, the revenue recovery factor for the line-haul portion is $31.00.

CHART 7–1   Key Cost and Linear Regression — Line Haul

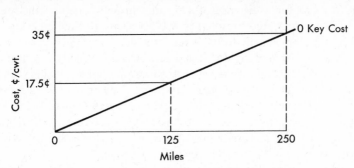

However, cost recovery depends upon the amount of product moving in the vehicle. For this reason, the service unit of cost per cwt mile is constructed. Now it is possible to construct an out-of-pocket cost scale for any distance and any weight, but the cost of $.0014 per cwt mile applies only to a specific load factor for an average commodity. In the study upon which these costs were based, the load factor was 231 cwt, which means that the average amount in a truck during a test study period weighed out to this amount.

The last piece of information required to construct a cost scale for all types of commodities for all possible distances is the average length of haul. In the study period, the average length of haul was 250 miles.

The Key Cost — Line Haul. It is now possible to develop the key cost from which all the other costs are determined. The key cost is found by multiplying the cost per cwt mile by the average length of haul. In this case, the key cost is

$$\$.0014/\text{cwt mile} \times 250 \text{ miles} = \$.35/\text{cwt}.$$

The key cost must be interpreted with some care. It is the cost per cwt for carrying the average type of product for the average length of haul. The measure of the average type of product is necessary, because it is desirable to assign costs to a range of products actually carried. Although numerous characteristics of a product may be used to determine its transport characteristics, the most important one is density, because it determines the amount of weight that may be carried in a vehicle. The optimum density factor is that one which fully utilizes both cube and weight limits of the vehicle.

Graphic Cost Scales. It is now possible to plot a range of cost scales, all of which are measured from the key cost just determined.

Given the slope of the cost lines for the average type of traffic, the cost for any mileage bracket can be measured. Remember that this applies only to the observed load factor of 231 cwt.

The first observable and measurable variable of cost relates to distance. If the distance is known, the cost can be calculated either by graphic means or by multiplying the cost per cwt mile by the given distance. For example, the cost per cwt for a distance of 125 miles (exactly one-half the average length of haul from study results) is $.175, exactly one-half the key cost. Of course, this applies only to the given load factor of 231 cwt.

Cost Recovery Factor.   It was stated earlier that the carrier must attempt to recover at least his out-of-pocket costs to assure a sound pricing structure. From Table 7–1, the necessary recovery factor for line-haul costs is $.0014 per cwt mile. It then follows that at the average length of haul of 250 miles, the required revenue to cover the cost is $80.85 (250 miles $\times$ 231 cwt $\times$ $.0014/cwt mile). If the carrier sets his key price equal to his key cost, his revenue generation is $80.85 ($.35/cwt $\times$ 231 cwt).

For a haul of 125 miles (exactly one-half of the average length of haul), the cost recovery factor is $40.42, which is exactly the result of multiplying $.0014/cwt mile by 125 miles by 231 cwt.

Cost Variations by Weight.   Thus far, it has been shown that the line-haul costs, by ICC formulas, are strictly linear with distance, and that a cost per cwt scale can be constructed to recover out-of-pocket line-haul costs for any distance if the load factor is held constant.

By the same token, changes in load factor will affect cost scales. Recalling that the purpose of a cost scale is to recover the total line-haul cost for any distance, doubling the load factor to 462(2 $\times$ 231 cwt) will result in a cost per cwt mile of exactly one-half the key cost or $.0007/cwt mile. Multiplying the new load factor times the new cost and key distance (250 miles) results in a revenue recovery factor of $80.85, initially the same as the revenue recovery resulting from the application of the key cost to its average load factor and average length of haul.

It is now possible to construct the line-haul out-of-pocket cost for any distance and any weight. The simplest way to understand the basic economics involved is to consider it to be similar to ordinary factory accounting. The cost that must be charged to cover a lathe operation is determined by dividing the lathe costs by the output. Similarly, the line-haul costs are analogous to a truck trailer, and its unit cost depends upon how far it travels and the amount of weight it carries. A table developed for various load factors is shown in Table 7–2.

Note that Table 7–2 refers to round-trip load factor. This is an example of one of the joint cost allocation problems in transportation. Because a truck usually goes from an origin to a destination and back, line-haul costs are generated in both directions. The usual way of allocating these costs is to calculate a round-trip load factor. Thus, if 30,000 pounds are shipped in one direction, and 10,000 in the other, the round-trip load factor is 20,000 (40,000 $\div$ 2). The approximate line-haul cost per cwt is then found under the 20,000-pound load factor (or 200 cwt), and in Table 7–2 is $.1575 per cwt mile.

TABLE 7–2* OUT-OF-POCKET LINE-HAUL COSTS FOR VARIOUS
ROUND-TRIP LOADS (Based upon a cost of $.31499/vehicle mile)

Average Round-trip Load (pounds)	Cost in Cents per cwt mile	Average Round-trip Load (pounds)	Cost in Cents per cwt mile
10,000	$.3150	26,000	$.1212
11,000	.2864	27,000	.1167
12,000	.2625	28,000	.1125
13,000	.2423	29,000	.1086
14,000	.2250	30,000	.1050
15,000	.2100	31,000	.1016
16,000	.1969	32,000	.0984
17,000	.1853	33,000	.0955
18,000	.1750	34,000	.0926
19,000	.1658	35,000	.0900
20,000	.1575	36,000	.0875
21,000	.1500	37,000	.0851
22,000	.1432	38,000	.0829
23,000	.1370	39,000	.0808
24,000	.1312	40,000	.0787
25,000	.1260	41,000	.0768

One-way costs are the same as round-trip costs when the load in each direction is the same. When the loads in each direction are different, the average of the outbound load plus the inbound load must be computed to select the proper cost.

For example, if the outbound load is 30,000 pounds and the inbound load is 10,000, the average round-trip load is 20,000 pounds. The out-of-pocket line-haul cost per cwt. mile is $.1575. For 300-mile actual haul, the out-of-pocket line-haul cost is $.473/100 pounds (300 miles × $.1575/cwt. mile).

*SOURCE: Previous data were based upon approximations. Data here are from *Cost of Transporting Freight by Class I and Class II Motor Common Carriers of General Commodities — Middlewest Region*, 1965, ICC Statement No. 4–67, Washington, D. C., April, 1967.

Pickup and Delivery Costs. As with line-haul costs, pickup and delivery costs have service units associated with time (drivers' wages) and distance (fuel). These costs are first collected from the books of account. The amount of cwt delivered in that specific pickup and delivery area is then collected from shipment records. Dividing the total pickup and delivery costs by the total cwt gives a cost per cwt. This cost was determined to be $.17/cwt.

It is now necessary to know only the number of cwt picked up and delivered in a specific shipment to calculate its share of pickup and delivery cost. For example, if the shipment weight is 260 cwt, the pickup and delivery costs are $44.20 ($.17/cwt × 260 cwt). In fact, Table 7–3, column 3, shows that the $.17/cwt for pickup and delivery cost is based upon an average of 240 cwt picked up and delivered.

TABLE 7–3*   OUT-OF-POCKET TERMINAL COSTS AT ORIGIN AND
DESTINATION AND AT INTERCHANGE POINTS FOR SHIPMENTS
WEIGHING 10,000 POUNDS OR MORE   (Costs in cents per hundredweight)

	Origin and Destination Terminal Costs Pickup and Delivery			
Weight of Shipment (pounds) [1]	Total Terminal Costs[1] [2]	Total P & D [3]	Platform Handling Costs [4]	Billing and Collecting Costs [5]
10,000	40.7	25.4	14.6	.7
11,000	37.6	24.7	12.2	.7
12,000	34.6	24.1	9.9	.6
13,000	31.9	23.5	7.8	.6
14,000	29.1	22.9	5.7	.5
15,000	27.3	22.3	4.5	.5
16,000	25.8	21.6	3.8	.4
17,000	24.8	21.1	3.3	.4
18,000	23.7	20.4	2.9	.4
19,000	22.9	19.9	2.6	.4
20,000	22.1	19.3	2.4	.4
21,000	21.2	18.7	2.2	.3
22,000	20.6	18.2	2.1	.3
23,000	19.8	17.6	1.9	.3
24,000	19.1	17.1	1.7	.3
25,000	18.4	16.5	1.6	.3
26,000	17.9	16.0	1.6	.3
27,000	17.3	15.5	1.5	.3
28,000	16.8	15.0	1.5	.3
29,000	16.1	14.5	1.4	.2
30,000	15.5	13.9	1.4	.2
31,000	15.1	13.5	1.4	.2
32,000	14.5	13.0	1.3	.2
33,000	14.1	12.6	1.3	.2
34,000	13.8	12.3	1.3	.2
35,000	13.7	12.2	1.3	.2
36,000	13.5	12.0	1.3	.2
37,000	13.3	11.8	1.3	.2
38,000	13.2	11.7	1.3	.2
39,000	13.1	11.6	1.3	.2
40,000 & over	12.0	10.6	1.3	.2

[1]Columns 3 + 4 + 5.

*SOURCE: Same as Table 7–2.

Again, as in line-haul costs, pickup and delivery costs are based upon
averages. It seems reasonable that for any specific weight category, a certain
percentage of shipments will not go through a regular pickup and delivery
operation, but rather will move directly from shipper to receiver. Table 7–3
shows these adjustments in column 3. In effect, for the weight category of

10,000 pounds (or 100 cwt), the $.254 per cwt cost implies that about 37 percent more of that shipment weight moves through a regular pickup and delivery operation, as compared with a shipment weight of 26,000 pounds (260 cwt). For the weight category 39,000 pounds, on the other hand, the $.116 cents per cwt cost implies that only about 25 percent less in that weight category goes through a regular pickup and delivery operation than for 26,000 pounds. In either case, the costs are charged to each shipment weight category so that, on the average, the pickup and delivery costs are recovered.

Terminal Platform Costs. Terminal costs are determined in much the same fashion as pickup and delivery costs. The total terminal costs are divided by total hundredweight platformed to calculate a cost per cwt.

Again, this cost is an average and must be adjusted for each shipment weight category. Once again refer to Table 7–3. Platform handling costs are higher per cwt for a 10,000-pound shipment ($.146/cwt) than for a 30,000-pound shipment ($.014/cwt). These variations of platform costs result from different proportions of each shipment weight moving across the terminal platform for consolidation and reshipment.

Billing and Collecting Costs. Billing and collecting costs consist of these expenses associated with paperwork connected with each shipment. They are found simply by dividing all paperwork cost by the number of shipments. Thus, this cost center is based upon shipments, and in its cost/cwt expression declines rapidly with increasing shipping weight.

Summary of ICC Cost Methods. By the ICC method of cost analysis, four cost centers account for all out-of-pocket costs. These are (1) line-haul, (2) pickup and delivery, (3) terminal platform, and (4) billing and collecting. The objectives in analyzing each center is to find the appropriate variable influencing costs. The two major variables are weight and distance. The reason for the dominance of these variables is that eventually a structure reflecting the cost of moving different shipment weights at different distances must be constructed if a price schedule covering all geographic points and all shipment weights is to be constructed.

In the next section, some significant variations from purely weight and distance considerations are described.

OTHER MODIFICATIONS OF COSTS

In the previous section, the basic out-of-pocket cost structure for the four major cost centers (line-haul, pickup and delivery, terminal platforms, and billing and collecting) was discussed. Some modifications of these costs have already been indicated in the discussion of cost centers. In the following sections a few additional modifications are developed.

Time-Related Costs. Because some costs are time related (vehicle hours, for example), variations around the average time to perform a function may cause significant variances in specific cost characteristics. In the line-haul portion, for example, the implied over-the-road speed of a truck-trailer combination is 33.9 miles, rounded to 34 miles, per hour at a vehicle-mile cost of $.31 (actual study average). If the possible speed for a particular shipment pattern is 45 miles per hour, the time related costs drop and result in a vehicle-mile cost of $.27. The second major category of time-related costs is in pickup and delivery. The $.17/cwt noted earlier is based upon an average of time- and distance-related costs.

However, there may be wide variations around this average. For example, if two shipments of the same weight are offered, with one containing more pieces than the other, the one with the greater number of pieces will require more time. The ICC method includes pieces only by implication, and these are hidden in the average cost per cwt. Similarly, one shipper or receiver may have poor loading dock facilities, which require more time to enter than one with efficient facilities. Finally, one specific area — downtown retail stores, for example — may have significantly higher traffic density patterns that slow average speeds and, thus, raise time-related costs.

Implications of Time Cost Variances to Regulation. Studies usually result in average cost structures that in time provide rather important evidence on the desirability of a particular price. If system averages are used to justify particular pricing structures, wide variations in profitability of specific moves will occur.

As described above, the study results on line-haul costs showed a cost per vehicle mile of $.31. If the distance of a specific move is 100 miles, the revenue recovery factor is $31 (100 × $.31). If, in reality, the cost per vehicle mile is $.27, the revenue recovery factor for a 100-mile trip is $27(100 × $.27). The difference between the two figures, then, represents a significantly higher contribution to profit for the faster road speed run. In the first case, at a total cost of $31 for the trip, if the road speed were actually 34 miles per hour, the contribution to profit (CTP) would be zero. However, in the second case, if road speeds were actually 45 miles per hour, the CTP would be $4($31 − $27). Conversely, if, on a specific trip, road speeds were below average, the carrier would experience a negative CTP. The same arguments hold true for time-related costs in pickup and delivery.

Implications of Time Cost Variations to Carriers. Individual carriers may attempt to alter their operations to achieve performances better than the averages indicated for time-related costs through formula costing based upon gross averages. For example, by selecting equipment specifically to achieve higher-than-average speeds in both line-haul and pickup and delivery, the carrier's actual cost will be below these indicated by formula costing. In that event, his costs are lower than the averages, and his CTP is higher. Recent trends toward terminal locations at the periphery of large cities rather than in the centers particularly will effect higher average speeds through the entire system, thus reducing costs below system averages.

Besides changing operations to reduce time-related costs below study averages, the carrier also may elect to establish a policy of *traffic selectivity*. This term means that the carrier attempts to select that traffic which results in lower-than-study-average costs to him. Although the legality of such practices is moot, nonetheless, they are practiced. By engaging in traffic selectivity, the carrier may be debasing his common carrier status.

Implications of Time Cost Variances to Shippers. From the shipper's point of view, time cost variances loom most important in the options other than common carriage that are available to him. For example, if by establishing a private fleet, the shipper can increase speed over study averages, his costs will be reduced. More of this will be discussed later in the material on private transportation in Appendix 7A.

The other important effect of time variances, from the shipper's point of view, relates to price adjustments as reflected by his unique characteristics. For example, if a shipper establishes a shipping point adjacent to an expressway and a receiving point similarly situated, he may find justification for reduced prices due to better-than-average road speeds. Although some doubt exists as to the possibilities of this approach, within the regulatory framework, when combined with private fleet options, the arguments sometimes prove persuasive to carriers.

Other Sources of Cost Variances. *Distance.* Routings by common carriers result from managerial discretion and regulatory restrictions. Because a carrier tends to serve a group of shippers, he will tend to establish routings for a number of shippers in a specific area. Individual shippers, however, may have access to more direct routings than those determined by carrier management. To this extent carrier costs will reflect the higher mileages of circuitous routings. By the same token, regulatory restrictions frequently require circuitous routing due to restrictions contained in the operating authority of the common carrier. For this reason, costs may be excessive for shippers who could utilize a more direct route due to their locations and shipping destinations.

Piece-Related Costs. Because study costs are based upon averages, they reflect an average number of pieces per shipment. Wide variations in piece count can exist for the same shipment weight. These variations occur whenever handling takes place, i.e., in terminal platform and pickup and delivery. Shippers who follow patterns of low piece count (containerization program, for example) will actually show lower costs than study results.

Density Factors. Density refers to the weight per cubic foot of the product shipped. Density factors affect handling costs through larger bulk and greater handling difficulty. They also affect line-haul costs through cube utilization; that is, the lighter the commodity, the less product that can be loaded.

However, density factors affect cube only when the product is so light that cube is filled before the weight limit of the vehicle is reached. If a trailer, for example, has 3,000 feet of cube and a load limit of 30,000 pounds is established, any product of 10 pounds per cubic foot or more has no density effect upon costs. But, if a product weighs less than 10 pounds per cubic foot, the load limit will not be reached and, consequently, an adjustment of cost to reflect the density factor must be made. For example, if the product weighs only 6 pounds per cubic foot, the maximum weight that can be loaded is 15,000 pounds. Because the revenue recovery factor is fixed for any distance, the costs must be increased to reflect proper revenue recovery factors.

CONSTRUCTING OUT-OF-POCKET COST SCALES

With the information presented above, it is possible to construct an out-of-pocket cost scale for any type of product for any distance. The scales presented below are strictly average costs without the adjustments mentioned in the example preceding material.

To review, the example out-of-pocket cost centers are:

1. Line-haul: $.31/vehicle mile.
2. Billing and collecting: $.72/shipment.
3. Terminal platform: $.21/cwt.
4. Pickup and delivery: $.17/cwt.

Given one shipment with a weight of 10,000 pounds, moving 100 miles, the cost is:

1. Line-haul: 31¢ × 100	$31.00
2. Billing and collecting: 72¢ × 1	.72
3. Terminal platform: 14.6¢ × 100³	14.60
4. Pickup and delivery: 25.4¢ × 100³	25.40
5. Total	$71.72

To find the cost per cwt, divide $71.72 by 100 cwt or $.7172, rounded to $.72. By this method, an out-of-pocket cost scale for all weights and all distances can be calculated. An example of the orderliness of such scales is shown in Table 7–4.

From these progressions, a simple statement of costs for each weight category and each mileage block may be made. The generalized formula is:

$$y = a + bx$$

where: y = out-of-pocket costs
  a = a measure of cost nonvariable with distance
  b = the rate of cost progression with miles
  x = miles

[3]See Table 7–3.

A completed table of such costs for various weights and differing distances, up to 600 miles, is found in Table 7–4.

TABLE 7–4*   OUT-OF-POCKET COST SCALES FOR SHIPMENTS BY WEIGHT BRACKETS AND BY DISTANCE — MIDDLEWEST REGION (Cost in Cents per/cwt)

Miles Rate-Making (1)	Weight Bracket			
	100 Pounds (2)	5000–9,999 Pounds (3)	10,000–19,999 Pounds (4)	40,000 Pounds or Over (5)
10	349	63	29	12
20	354	67	32	14
30	360	70	35	16
40	366	74	38	18
50	370	76	40	19
60	376	79	43	21
70	381	83	46	23
80	385	85	48	24
90	391	89	51	26
100	394	90	52	27
120	404	95	56	30
140	414	101	62	34
160	422	105	65	36
180	431	110	70	39
200	439	113	72	41
220	448	119	76	44
240	458	124	81	47
260	467	130	86	51
280	477	135	90	54
300	484	138	92	56
320	493	143	97	59
340	503	148	101	62
360	512	153	106	65
380	519	156	108	68
400	528	161	113	71
420	538	167	117	74
440	547	172	121	77
460	556	177	126	80
480	564	180	129	83
500	573	186	133	86
520	583	191	137	89
540	592	196	142	92
560	601	201	146	95
580	610	205	150	98
600	619	210	154	101

*SOURCE: Same as Table 7–2. Columns 2, 3, 4, and 5 are weighted averages of single line and interline movement.

Note the dramatic effect of increased weight upon out-of-pocket costs. For 100 pounds at 10 miles, out-of-pocket cost per cwt is $3.49, whereas for 40,000 pounds, it falls to $.12 per cwt. In these scales, all cost centers are included.

Relationship of Long-Run Out-of-Pocket Costs to Transport Prices. It was stated earlier that long-run out-of-pocket costs form the economic floor below which prices may not rationally fall. However, if all prices were set at out-of-pocket cost levels, not only would fully distributed costs not be covered, but also no allowance for a rate of return would be made. A price set to long-run out-of-pocket costs has application only upon traffic where excess capacity exists. In this context, a carrier may set prices to long-run out-of-pocket costs only when no other rational alternative exists. The two conditions that bring about a desirability for out-of-pocket levels of prices are (1) competition from other modes (rail vs. truck) or legal (common vs. private) types of carriers, or (2) when market prices of products seem unable to absorb other than an out-of-pocket cost based price, and this is reflected in lower desired price levels for transport.

FULLY DISTRIBUTED COST

Fully distributed costs are found by adding a percentage to each out-of-pocket cost to cover common costs that do not vary with traffic. These would consist of officers' salaries and the like.

It is important to realize that common costs will vary a great deal between individual common carriers. Such variation exists between modes as well as between carriers within a single mode. From the viewpoint of the individual carrier, common costs will vary depending upon managerial goals with respect to return-on-investment and profitability. The problem is further complicated by the fact that common costs will show marked variation from one year to the next depending upon the operational success the individual enterprise enjoys. Nevertheless, certain assumptions seem to hold concerning the average common costs of carriers for purposes of ICC formulations.

In the ICC formulation, common costs are found to be about 10 percent of fully distributed costs but vary by geographic region. Thus, if a specific out-of-pocket cost is $.90/cwt, fully allocated cost will be adjusted so that the constant costs are 10 percent and out-of-pocket costs are 90 percent of fully distributed costs. This can be done by the formula:

$$y = .90x$$
$$x = \frac{y}{.90}$$
$$x = \frac{.90}{.90}$$
$$x = 100¢$$

where:

$$y = \text{out-of-pocket cost}$$
$$x = \text{fully distributed cost}$$

The fully distributed cost at average length of haul and average load factors for the average commodity is $1.00/cwt.

PROFIT ALLOWANCE

The final adjustment for costing is a profit allowance. In the case of common motor carriers, profit allowance is made through the operating ratio. From standard accounting practice, the operating ratio is defined as the operating cost divided by operating revenue. If the operating ratio is 100, no profits are generated. Thus, for profitable operations, the overall operating ratio of a carrier must be less than 100. (For other modes, the rate of return plays a more relevant role than the operating ratio in pricing.) The distinction between use of either measure relates to proportion of fixed capital used in the enterprise. (The larger the fixed investment, the more likely the rate of return will be employed as a guide to pricing.)

Assume for purposes of illustration that an operating ratio of .95 is desired. Then to determine fully distributed cost plus a profit allowance of 5 percent, the 95 percent operating ratio is applied to the $1.00/cwt fully distributed cost:

$$y = .95x$$
$$x = \frac{y}{.95}$$
$$x = \frac{100}{.95}$$
$$x = \$1.053$$

where:

$$y = \text{fully distributed cost}$$
$$x = \text{fully distributed cost}$$
$$\text{plus profit}$$

The $1.053 then represents the fully distributed cost plus profit for the average length of haul and average load factor of the average commodity.

RELATIONSHIP OF COSTING TO PRICING

The costing principles outlined above show the benchmark from which prices are made. In addition to the various cost concepts described above, the market characteristics of transport supply and demand for transportation finally result in a price recommendation submitted for regulated approval.

Given the factors of cost analysis, demand, and competition, three pricing possibilities may result: (1) pricing at out-of-pocket cost levels; (2) pricing at full-cost levels, including a profit allowance; and (3) pricing at above-full-cost levels.

Pricing Structure in Common Carrier Transportation. As stated in Chapter 6, three dominant price types exist in common carrier service: (1) class rate, (2) commodity rates, and (3) exception rates.

Class rate is generally the highest price paid. It covers relatively small shipments for many shippers among many shipping points. It is a point-to-point price based upon weight and distance, covering a geographic unit which is more or less homogeneous, as well as homogeneous products within each class. These are generally fully distributed rates plus a profit allowance.

Commodity rates relate to specific commodities and are point-to-point rates. Competitive factors play a more dominant role in determining specific commodity rates, and they may vary from out-of-pocket levels to some upper limit based upon demand and market competition.

Exception rates technically are simply shifts to a higher or lower class rating. It is an area, or point-to-point, rate based upon weight and distance as is a class rate. The rationale is that either (1) carriers face higher or lower costs for a specific commodity because of some special circumstance surrounding the movement of the product, or (2) volumes vary significantly upward or downward in a special area as compared with the more general movement within a general area.

Each of the above rate structures can be analyzed within the costing principles discussed in this chapter. For illustrative purposes only, the line-haul portion of full truckload shipments will be singled out to indicate the different cost concepts applied to each rate category.

Recall the key cost (out-of-pocket) is \$.35/cwt at 250 miles. This figure is based upon an average grouping of commodities (class of commodities). The first correction requires adjustment of the out-of-pocket cost to fully distributed cost. Adjusting the key cost to reflect full cost is done in the following manner:

$$y = .90x$$

$$x = \frac{y}{.90}$$

$$x = \frac{.35}{.90}$$

$$x = \$.3888$$

where: y = out-of-pocket costs
x = fully distributed cost
.90 = out-of-pocket cost rate as a constant

CHART 7–2   Line-Haul Costs as a Function of Distance

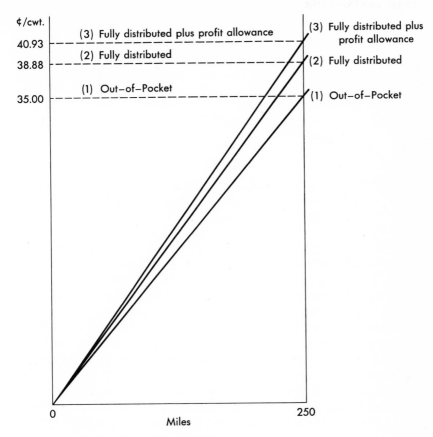

Average length of haul – 250 miles
Average load factor – 231 cwt.

This number ($.3888/cwt) is the fully distributed cost at average length of haul ($\bar{x}$) and average load factors for the average commodity. Connecting this point with the origin then represents the fully allocated cost under the conditions stated for all mileages.

With the same formula, the fully allocated costs are adjusted to reflect a profit allowance. This is done through the operating ratio in the following manner for an operating ratio of .95:

$$y = .95x$$

$$x = \frac{y}{.95}$$

$$x = \frac{\$.3888}{.95}$$

$$x = \$.4093$$

CHART 7–3   Cost Distribution to Different Classes of Traffic Fully Distributed Plus Profit

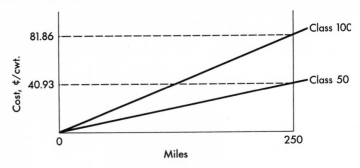

where: y = fully distributed cost
                  x = fully distributed cost plus profit
                  .95 = fully distributed cost factor

Again, connecting this point ($.4093/cwt) and extending to the origin provides a fully distributed cost plus profit, which then becomes the class rate for the average group of commodities under study, for the line-haul portion only. The extrapolated lines provide a convenient way for developing rates for varying distances.

Cost of Class-Rated Traffic.   Now it is possible to adjust the scales for various classes of traffic (groups of commodities with similar characteristics). To do this, Chart 7–2 is reproduced with only the fully allocated cost plus profit shown.

Now, suppose an index number is assigned to the class of traffic for which the cost factor has just been developed. If that number is 50 (based upon a scale of 100), the class rate scale for any specific grouping depends upon the index number assigned to it. It is assumed that the cost of any class of traffic is proportional to its index number (classification).

Thus, if the study traffic mix is class 50, then for class 100 traffic, it is exactly twice that of class 50 or $.8186/cwt. By this method, any cost for any class of traffic can be calculated, and a whole nest of cost curves can be constructed.

However, an infinite number of cost curves covering all possible gradations of classes will prove too cumbersome when posted in a pricing scale. For this reason, the number of permitted classes of traffic is limited — ranging from about class 30 to class 400, depending upon the specific area or group of carriers involved.

Weight Adjustment to Class-Rated Traffic.   Starting again with the key cost, it is possible to make adjustments for class-rated traffic (line-haul) for any weight category. The basic chart is reproduced as Chart 7–4.

Remember that the basic principle involved in establishing prices is to make a revenue recovery equal to the cost, which in this case is fully distributed and includes a profit allowance.

CHART 7–4 **Weight Adjustment for Class-Rated Traffic Fully Distributed Plus Profit**

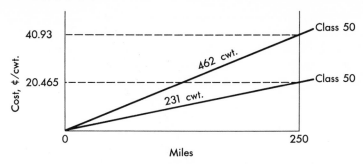

Suppose that a specific shipment at class 50 has twice the average load factor (462 cwt). In that case, the rate of this weight category of class 50 traffic must be one-half the key cost, or $.20465. The proof of this follows:

$$\$.4093/\text{cwt} \times 231 \text{ cwt} = \$94.55, \text{ and}$$
$$\$.20465/\text{cwt} \times 462 \text{ cwt} = \$94.55$$

The revenue recovery factor is exactly the same in both cases.

By observing the difference in classification, cost by class can be determined from the key cost. By observing the differences in weight within a class, cost by weight categories can similarly be determined. Again, to reduce the complexity of published price schedules, only a limited number of weight categories is used. If the load is reduced in a specific class 50 shipment to 231 cwt, its cost per cwt rises to $.4093/cwt. (See Chart 7–4.)

Adjustments for Commodity Rates. Commodity rates as discussed earlier are point-to-point and also apply only to specifically named commodities. Because of competition among markets and transportation alternatives, setting rates at out-of-pocket cost levels may be necessary. By finding the floor to which rates may legally fall (out-of-pocket costs), a bargaining base is established. However, it is necessary also to develop full-cost and full-cost-plus-profit return to investigate a range of alternative pricing structures.

For commodity rates, the most important variable to interpret is the average load. Again, the basic chart for study average costs for out-of-pocket, fully allocated, and fully allocated plus profit is shown in Chart 7–5.

To review once more, the preceding costs are based upon (1) average length of haul of 250 miles, (2) average load factor of 231 cwt, and (3) an average class of traffic.

Of all traffic characteristics, the most important one is density, because it pretty much determines maximum loading weights. As commodity rates are usually based upon full truckload shipments, this is an important consideration.

By doubling load factor, in effect assuring the carrier of an average load of 462 cwt over some period of time, a new set of out-of-pocket, fully allo-

CHART 7–5   Class and Commodity Cost Scales (Line-Haul)

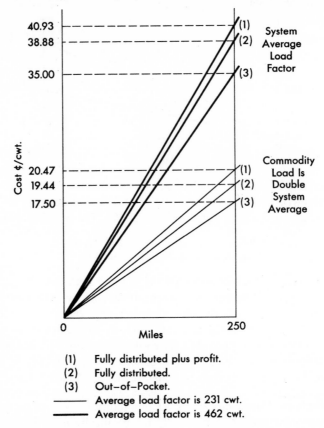

(1)   Fully distributed plus profit.
(2)   Fully distributed.
(3)   Out–of–Pocket.
──────   Average load factor is 231 cwt.
━━━━━   Average load factor is 462 cwt.

cated, and fully allocated plus profit cost schedules can be constructed. These costs will all be exactly one-half of those originally constructed and are shown by broken lines in Chart 7–5.

This new set of costs means that rates at out-of-pocket cost levels should not exceed $.175/cwt, and on the high side they should not exceed $.2047/cwt. Whether this commodity shipper and carrier can agree upon a final rate depends upon competitive and market factors.

An Application.   It may be useful at this point to consider the application of carrier costing techniques in physical distribution analysis. Note first the basic underlying orderliness of cost structure. The same is not true of prices eventually charged by carriers for service performed, because the marketing, demand, and competition elements tend to shift prices either upward or downward from those indicated by cost analysis. The transportation analysis of a study must, therefore, consider prices and costs simultaneously to assess the impact of changing transportation patterns in varying physical distribution systems design.

Consider a limited problem of placing a warehouse to serve a specific market.[4] Cost components that may change because of transport charges include (1) materials handling, (2) storage, (3) inventory, and (4) packaging.

Basic assumptions are that (1) average annual movement of a single commodity is 100,000 cwt, (2) distance from plant to warehouse is fixed at 1,000 miles, (3) shipment weight by truck is 40,000 (400 cwt) pounds, and (4) shipment weight by rail is 100,000 pounds (1000 cwt). These assumptions now permit an analysis of truck and rail costs, the only two transport alternatives considered, so that a minimum and maximum rate by each alternative is found.

The first step in the analysis, therefore, requires that an out-of-pocket cost scale for both rail and motor carrier is found for the given distance and given weights. The analysis shows that rail out-of-pocket costs for the 1,000 mile haul are $.50 per cwt, and truck out-of-pocket costs for the same distance are $.60 per cwt. The first conclusion, therefore, is to ship by rail, because it shows the lowest direct cost. On an annual basis, rail cost would come to $50,000 ($.50 × 100,000 cwt), whereas motor carrier costs would be $60,000 ($.60 × 100,000 cwt). The annual savings are $10,000 by choosing the lower cost form of transportation. From a budgetary point of view, these savings must be extended over the anticipated life of any capital commitment required. Thus, if the life of the proposed warehouse were ten years, savings over its lifetime would be $100,000 ($10,000 × 10 years).

Some adjustments to rates may be required because so far only the base out-of-pocket costs have been considered. This can be done by increasing the rate to fully distributed costs plus profit. The profitability of the rate to the carrier can also be measured through changes in the load factor. Thus, under existing assumptions, the carrier will be moving in one direction full and the other empty. If an offering of freight can be made to the carrier on the backhaul, the load factor will increase and so will the profitability. For purposes of discussion assume that the carrier receives a 50 percent backhaul; that is, one-half the time it will be moving fully loaded from the warehouse area to the plant. The result is that for the trucker, costs drop to $.50 per cwt due to higher load factors and for the railroad they drop to $.45 per cwt. Therefore, if the rates proposed are based upon recovery of out-of-pocket costs, the trucker receives a contribution to overhead and profit of $.10 per cwt, and the railroad receives $.05 per cwt. This process is called rate justification, which is based upon revenue contributions above out-of-pocket costs.

Table 7–5 shows the results of adding nontransport expenses as part of the cost for each alternative.

Under the above conditions, even on a total cost basis, rail is cheaper than truck. Cost differences show up in each nontransport cost category for

[4]Material on the section is based upon a paper presented by George G. Smith before the National Council of Physical Distribution Management, Tarrytown, N. Y., October 20, 1965.

TABLE 7–5   COMPARISON OF DIRECT TRANSPORT EXPENSES AND
NONTRANSPORT EXPENSES — RAIL VS. MOTOR CARRIER
(Annual Rate)

	Rail	Motor Carrier
1. Direct transport costs	$50,000	$60,000
2. Capital cost of a warehouse	5,000	4,000
3. Packaging costs (Truck in drums, rail in bulk)	—	2,000
4. Materials handling costs	2,000	3,000
5. Inventory costs	2,000	1,000
6. Total costs	59,000	70,000
7. Difference — $11,000		

the following reasons: (1) capital cost for rail exceeds that of motor carrier because of the larger loads required (100,000 pounds vs. 50,000 pounds), (2) packaging costs are higher by truck because drums are required, (3) materials handling costs are lower for rail because of bulk terminal operations, and (4) inventory costs are higher for rail because of larger shipments and larger inventory cycles.

The major difference between rail and motor carrier lies in the transportation rates. If the motor carrier wished to participate in their traffic, it must reduce costs by $11,000. This can be done by (1) reducing the rate or (2) reducing some or all of the nontransport cost categories. Cost analysis of transportation, therefore, permits a proper economic assessment of required rates to perform a transport service on an economic and competitive basis.

Summary

Cost studies provide the distribution analyst with a powerful weapon to reduce shipping expense. With keen competition among modes, cost studies can, and frequently do, lead to proper identification of the amount of price reduction required to share in potential traffic of shippers. However, this analysis must include consideration of nontransport costs. In Appendix 7A selected methods of transport cost analysis, which provide variations, are presented.

Discussion Questions

1. What is *optimum density*?

2. Why is a key cost a necessity in accurately determining what rate a carrier will charge?

3. What would be some of the costs involved under the heading "Terminal Platform Costs"?

4. Would the averaging method used by the ICC on determining rates prove to be of more benefit to the shipper or the carrier?

5. What effect does density have on determining the rates that a carrier will set for (a) a cereal manufacturer, (b) a steel fabricator, (c) a diamond merchant?

6. What is the cost per hundredweight for a carrier to ship a 12,050-lb consignment 342 miles if (a) Line-haul cost = $.37/cwt mile, (b) Billing and collecting = $1.02/shipment, (c) Terminal platform costs = $.17/cwt, (d) Pickup and delivery = $.19/cwt?

7. Assuming that a carrier had operating revenues of $973,427 and operating costs of $859,437, what is its operating ratio?

8. Differentiate fully allocated costs, joint costs, common costs, and out-of-pocket costs.

9. What are the cost centers associated with the transportation function? Define each. How are cost centers and service units related?

10. The XYZ Cartage Company is negotiating freight rates with the ABC Corporation. ABC ships 35,000 pounds of freight each day. Of this, 10 percent moves through the terminal and platform functions. Also, 10 percent of volume utilizes the pickup and delivery facilities. All freight moves 200 miles.

To assist XYZ Cartage Company in their negotiations calculate on a per cwt basis, out-of-pocket costs, fully distributed costs, and fully distributed cost plus a profit allowance using the following data: (a) Line-haul = $.09/cwt mile, (b) Billing and collecting = $1.25/shipment, (c) Terminal and platform = $.20/cwt, (d) Pickup and delivery = $.17/cwt.

11. When should a carrier consider pricing at out-of-pocket cost? At fully distributed costs? At fully distributed costs plus a profit allowance and higher? What happens if pricing occurs below out-of-pocket costs?

12. Describe the unit train principle. Where are the economies generated to make the unit train profitable for the railroad and transport purchaser?

Appendix 7A
ADDITIONAL TRANSPORTATION COSTING

Chapter 7 covered the basic principles of transportation costing particularly in the common carrier area. In this appendix, focus is centered on three variations of transportation costing: unit trains, private transportation, and leasing. Other alternatives exist, but those three illustrate a central theme indicating variations possible to minimize transportation cost.

Unit Trains

A recent example of the application of transportation costing is the innovation of unit trains. Generally, a unit train moves a single commodity in a single train from one origin to one destination. The general cost centers for a regular train movement are terminal, yard, switching and line-haul, and billing and collecting. In a unit train, terminal costs drop substantially, because only a single commodity is loaded and unloaded. In addition, yard and switching costs virtually disappear, because the train moves as a unit.

A measure of the impact of unit trains is dramatically demonstrated by possible cost reduction for bulk commodities. It frequently occurs that transportation prices will drop by at least one-third when unit trains move products as compared with single car rates.

Although unit trains have, up to this point in time, been applied only in bulk commodities such as coal and grain, it appears that the application of the same principle will be used for general commodities in the near future.

ESTIMATION OF TRANSPORTATION COSTS FOR UNIT TRAINS

One basic assumption used in developing unit train out-of-pocket cost estimates is that the company moving freight will cover the capital expense of the locomotives and cars. The railroad out-of-pocket costs will refer only to those costs the railroad would incur by moving a unit train over its roads. The freight rate will be viewed as the out-of-pocket cost plus some "fair" excess of the final rate over out-of-pocket cost, if ownership of equipment and responsibility of upkeep lie with the railroad. The cost estimates are valid on an incremental basis if the equipment is used specifically for the unit train move.

Equipment costs refer to all incremental expenses incurred in the purchase and upkeep of unit train equipment. Railroad out-of-pocket costs will refer to train crew costs, fuel and oil costs, incremental maintenance of way costs, and an allowance for railroad overhead. If additional out-of-pocket costs are incurred for such items as car delivery and yard switching, these costs should be included. The cost categories discussed in this section are the major items, and the final rate estimate should provide a reasonably accurate reflection of cost.

Basic assumptions underlying unit train cost analysis include (1) named origin and destination points and the actual rail miles between them, (2) estimation of annual tonnage to be moved, and (3) statement of cost function in each railroad cost center as a function of trainload volumes.

Table 7A–1 averages unit train costs for different sized trains over a fixed distance.

TABLE 7A–1   ESTIMATED UNIT TRAIN COSTS FOR DIFFERENT VOLUMES

| Annual Costs | Trainload Tonnages (tons/train) | | |
	5,000 tons	10,000 tons	20,000 tons
Operating Expenses	$1,000,000	$1,200,000	$1,400,000
Equipment Expenses	500,000	600,000	1,400,000
Total	1,500,000	1,800,000	2,800,000
Annual maximum tonnage (at full capacity)	400,000 T.	800,000 T.	1,000,000 T.
Cost per ton	$3.75	$2.25	$2.80

The key figure in the table is the cost per ton. Note that of the three options given, the most economical trainload cost is associated with a 10,000-ton train moving 800,000 tons of product at a unit cost of $2.25. This number, however, represents only the out-of-pocket costs to the railroad. A rate is constructed from this base cost by adding a dollar amount per ton, which will cover the interest costs, overhead, and profit allowance. The specific rate will depend upon bargaining processes between shipper and carrier.

The above illustration is based upon a chemical firm, which presently pays from $11 to $13 a ton to reach markets from existing sources of supply. The difference between $2.25 (or whatever rate is finally agreed upon) and $11 to $13 does not constitute all savings to the shipper. Due to larger shipment size (20,000 tons/train), holding facilities at both ends of the route must be constructed. In addition, expensive terminal equipment is usually required to load and unload.

One final note on unit trains, the high cost per ton at low volumes (10,000 tons) results from high fixed costs spread over that small volume. On the other hand, the high cost per ton associated with high volumes (30,000 tons) is due to slower road speeds and greater time consumed in loading and unloading.

Private Transportation

Of increasing significance in the transport mix of physical distribution systems is the possibility of using private transportation. Private transportation is defined as the movement of a product by the bona fide owner who controls both the vehicle and the driver. In some cases, private transportation is employed illegally, though, by outside contracts. For example, a flour wholesaler may deliver to a bakery and pick up a load of sugar on his own account, which he has previously agreed to sell to a food processor. This use of private transportation is illegal.

Private transportation is more often a financial decision rather than a purely transportation decision; that is, rate of return considerations on invested capital in truck or other equipment must be included in the analysis. Private trucks may be leased or owned. Both are illustrated below.

COST CATEGORIES

The first step in making a private truck fleet analysis is to consider the relevant cost categories to include.[1] A comprehensive set of truck cost accounts is shown below:

Direct Costs.

Drivers' expenses:

1. Drivers' wages
2. Helpers' wages
3. Other driver expense (exclude meals, tolls, lodging, fines)
4. Workmen's compensation taxes and insurance
5. Social Security Tax
6. Fringe benefits:
   (a) Health insurance and hospitalization
   (b) Vacation and holiday pay

Operating costs:

1. Fuel, oil, and grease (including filters)
2. Tires and tubes
3. Tire repair and recaps
4. Vehicle repairs and parts (private shop)
5. Repairs done outside of private shop (including parts and labor)
6. Road services
7. Protective services (fuel for heaters or refrigeration units, icing, and so forth)
8. Washing
9. Painting
10. Antifreeze and tire chains

Overhead:

Depreciation (including carrying charges, if any):

1. Straight trucks, excluding tires
2. Tractors, excluding tires
3. Trailers, excluding tires

[1]See ICC Highway Form B from Statement No. 4–66 Washington, D. C., February, 1966. These are based upon common carriers and must be adjusted for private fleet operators. Also for rail-leasing options, see Rail Form A. The costs in this section are based upon "Analyzing Private and Leased Truck Costs," by Edward W. Smykay, *Handling and Shipping*, Cleveland, Ohio, June, 1966, pp. 65–66.

4. Refrigeration units
5. Garage and shop
6. Garage and shop equipment (include replacement of lost and broken tools)

Insurance, taxes, licenses:

1. Comprehensive insurance on vehicles
2. Collision insurance
3. Public liability and property damage
4. Cargo insurance
5. Insurance on garage and equipment (fire, theft)
6. Personal Property Taxes (city, state, county)
   (a) Garage
   (b) Trucks and trailers
7. License tags and inspections
8. Registration fees
9. State use taxes (on gas, other fuels, and oil)

Interest on investment:

1. Straight trucks, excluding tires
2. Tractors, excluding tires
3. Trailers, excluding tires
4. Refrigeration units
5. Garage and shop
6. Garage and shop equipment (include replacement of lost and broken tools)

Indirect Costs.

Salaries (other than drivers' and helpers'):

1. Supervision (garage and shop)
2. Garage and shop employees
3. Traffic and transportation management (include executive time spent in general administration of trucking operations)
4. Office salaries and wages
5. Workmen's Compensation Taxes and Insurance
6. Social Security Tax
7. Fringe benefits:
   (a) Health insurance and hospitalization
   (b) Vacation and holiday pay
   (c) Bonus

Utilities, supplies, and so forth:

1. Heat, light, water
2. Telephone

3. Office space costs or rental
4. Office equipment and supplies
5. Rent (garage and shop, if not private)
6. Garage supplies (work uniforms, laundry)
7. Special equipment (tarpaulins, heaters, fire extinguishers)
8. Sign work
9. Other

TRAFFIC FLOWS

The second relevant type of information required for analysis is the flow of traffic. These data can be obtained from available records, such as bills of lading, freight bills, shipping notices, and sales records.

Once traffic flows are determined, they can be superimposed upon truck costs to calculate precisely when private trucking best fits the total transport requirements. Private transportation may be justified on either cost or service consideration. In the following analysis, however, exclusive attention is devoted to costs.

COMMON CARRIER RATES

The last piece of information required is common carrier rates. By comparing common carrier rates with private truck costs, private carriage can be fit into the transport scheme at precisely those points where it shows greater economy than does the use of common carriers.[2]

Privately Owned Trucking as Example.   Table 7A–2 shows a representative set of costs based upon a statistical accounting system and expected traffic generation. This table is based upon complete ownership and operation of both tractor and trailer. The relevant output for decisions is the cost per cwt found in the last row of data. Note especially that in this illustration interest on capital is charged at 6 percent (item 4). In a real case, the rate of interest charged should properly constitute at least the average rate of the return on the assets of the company as a whole, or preferably opportunity cost, both of which will likely be higher than 6 percent.

Also, as indicated in the heading of each round trip, the number of operating hours are required to measure accurately time-related costs, especially labor.

[2]*Ibid.*

TABLE 7A–2 REPRESENTATIVE PRIVATE TRUCKING COSTS FOR SELECTED ROUND TRIPS

Details of Operation — Tractor and Trailer	8 hrs 25 miles		8 hrs 100 miles		10 hrs 200 miles		12 hrs 300 miles		16 hrs 400 miles		16 + 4 hrs 500 miles		16 + 8 hrs 600 miles	
(1) Number of trips per day	1		1		1		1		1		1		1	
(2) Mileage per year	7,150		28,600		57,200		85,800		114,400		114,400		102,740	
(3) Payload per year	$11,440,000		11,440,000		11,440,000		11,440,000		11,440,000		11,440,000		11,440,000	
(4) Interest on investment at 6%	$ 835.21	12.0	$ 835.21	3.0	$ 835.21	1.5	$ 835.21	1.0	$ 835.21	.7	$ 835.21	.7	$ 835.21	.8
(5) License	497.20	7.0	497.20	1.7	497.20	.9	497.20	.6	497.20	.4	497.20	.4	497.20	.5
(6) Federal highway use tax	198.00	3.0	198.00	.7	198.00	.3	198.00	.2	198.00	.1	198.00	.2	198.00	.2
(7) Insurance	608.29	8.0	608.29	2.1	608.29	1.0	608.29	.7	608.29	.5	608.29	.5	608.29	.6
(8) Cost of fuel	306.43	4.3	1,225.71	4.3	2,435.82	4.3	3,677.11	4.3	4,902.85	4.3	4,919.20	4.3	4,427.28	4.3
(9) Tire cost	257.40	3.6	1,029.60	3.6	2,059.20	3.6	3,088.80	3.6	4,118.40	3.6	4,118.40	3.6	3,706.56	3.6
(10) Chains, binders and tarps	114.40	1.6	457.60	1.6	915.20	1.6	1,372.80	1.6	1,808.40	1.6	1,808.40	1.6	1,647.36	1.6
(11) Maintenance and repairs	286.00	4.0	1,144.00	4.0	2,288.00	4.0	3,432.00	4.0	4,576.00	4.0	4,576.00	4.0	4,118.40	4.0
(12) Tolls and layovers	214.50	3.0	858.00	3.0	1,716.00	3.0	2,574.00	3.0	3,432.00	3.0	3,432.00	3.0	3,088.80	3.0
(13) Depreciation based on 6 years	2,982.87	40.0	2,982.87	10.0	2,982.87	.7	2,982.87	.3	2,982.87	.2	2,982.87	.3	2,982.87	.3
(14) State excise tax	550.00	8.0	550.00	1.9	550.00	1.0	550.00	.6	550.00	.5	550.00	.5	550.00	.5
(15) Drivers' wages and fringe benefits	8,676.80	121.0	8,676.80	30.0	12,701.70	22.0	15,378.00	18.0	22,079.20	19.0	19,681.20	17.0	18,766.00	18.0
(16) TOTAL	$15,527.10	215.5	$19,063.28	65.9	$27,787.49	43.9	$35,194.28	37.9	$46,588.42	37.9	$44,206.77	36.1	$41,425.97	37.4
(17) Cost per mile × round trip	$ 59.12		72.49		96.80		125.40		167.20		198.00		244.20	
(18) Cost per trip + the weight	$ .14/cwt.		.17/cwt.		.24/cwt.		.31/cwt.		.41/cwt.		.39/cwt.		.36/cwt.	

191

TABLE 7A–3 REPRESENTATIVE LEASED TRUCKING COSTS FOR SELECTED ROUND TRIPS

Details of Operation — Tractor and Trailer	8 hrs 25 miles		8 hrs 100 miles		10 hrs 200 miles		12 hrs 300 miles		16 hrs 400 miles		16 + 4 hrs 500 miles		16 + 8 hrs 600 miles	
							Round Trip							
(1) Number of trips per day	1		1		1		1		1		1		1	
(2) Mileage per year	7,150		28,600		57,200		85,800		114,400		114,400		102,740	
(3) Payload per year	$11,440,000		11,440,000		11,440,000		11,440,000		11,440,000		11,440,000		11,440,000	
(4) Operating cost based on miles per year	$7,150.00		$28,600.00		$57,200.00		$85,800.00		$114,400.00		$114,400.00		$100,740.00	
(5) Cost of fuel	$ 296.45	4.3	$ 1,229.80	4.3	$ 2,451.24	4.3	$ 3,689.40	4.3	$ 4,919.20	4.3	$ 4,919.20	4.3	$ 4,418.37	4.3
(6) Chains, binders and tarps	114.40	1.6	457.60	1.6	905.85	1.6	1,372.80	1.6	1,830.40	1.6	1,830.40	1.6	1,647.36	1.6
(7) Greasing, oil change, washing	715.00	1.0	2,860.00	1.0	5,720.00	1.0	8,580.00	1.0	11,440.00	1.0	11,440.00	1.0	10,274.00	1.0
(8) Tolls and layovers	214.50	3.0	858.00	3.0	1,716.00	3.0	2,574.00	3.0	3,432.00	3.0	3,432.00	3.0	3,088.80	3.0
(9) SUB-TOTAL	$ 1,340.35	9.9	$ 5,405.40	9.9	$10,793.09	9.9	$16,216.20	9.9	$21,621.60	9.9	$21,621.60	9.9	$19,428.53	9.9
(10) Rental charge at $165 per week	$ 8,580.00	120.0	$ 8,580.00	30.0	$ 8,580.00	15.0	$ 8,580.00	10.0	$ 8,580.00	8.0	$ 8,580.00	8.0	$ 8,580.00	8.0
(11) Mileage charge at $.12 per mile	858.00	12.0	3,432.00	12.0	6,864.00	12.0	10,296.00	12.0	13,728.00	12.0	13,728.00	12.0	12,328.80	12.0
(12) Drivers' wages and fringe benefits	8,676.80	121.0	8,676.80	30.0	12,701.83	22.0	15,378.00	18.0	22,079.20	19.0	19,681.20	17.0	18,766.00	18.0
(13) TOTAL	$19,455.15	262.9	$26,094.20	81.9	$38,938.92	58.9	$50,470.20	49.9	$66,008.80	48.9	$63,610.80	46.9	$59,103.33	47.9
(14) Cost per mile × round trip	$ 72.05		90.20		125.40		165.00		215.60		258.50		316.80	
(15) Cost per trip + the weight	$ .17/cwt.		.22/cwt.		.34/cwt.		.44/cwt.		.58/cwt.		.56/cwt.		.52/cwt.	

192

LEASING OPTIONS

Table 7A–3 shows private fleet costs based upon leasing options. Note that the investment account drops out and is substituted for by leasing costs. The table shows costs for a specific type of lease, and these costs will vary, depending upon the lease agreement.

Again, in this table, the main output is the cost per cwt in line 15.

COST COMPARISONS

Table 7A–4 shows rates for owned and leased equipment options and associated costs per cwt for different round trips and varying load factors.

In the table, wholly owned, wholly leased, and combined leased and owned costs per cwt are shown. In addition, costs per cwt by common carrier in two different geographic areas are shown.

Comparing the wholly owned option and common carriers in Zone A and B shows that they are lower for all mileage brackets at 40,000 pounds.

For leased operators, the Zone A common carrier is lower in cost for all mileage brackets at 40,000 pounds. For Zone B, costs are lower for the leasing option for all round-trip mileages below 350 miles.

When load factors drop, costs rise. Thus, with a 20,000-pound load factor, costs rise substantially for the owned and leased combination and even more so when load factors drop to 10,000 pounds.

TABLE 7A–4 SAMPLE TRUCKING COSTS — IN CENTS PER HUNDREDWEIGHT

Weight and Carrier	Round Trip						
	25 miles	100 miles	200 miles	300 miles	400 miles	500 miles	600 miles
40,000# Owned Equipment	.14	.17	.24	.31	.41	.39	.36
40,000# Leased Equipment	.17	.22	.34	.44	.58	.56	.52
40,000# 50% Owned and 50% Leased	.16	.20	.29	.38	.50	.48	.44
20,000# Owned and Leased	.23	.27	.39	.51	.66	.78	.96
10,000# Owned and Leased	.30	.36	.52	.68	.88	1.04	1.28
40,000# Zone A Common Carriers	.15	.20	.26	.30	.35	.38	.44
40,000# Zone B Common Carriers	.22	.22	.30	.40	.47	.53	.59

CHAPTER 8 Inventory Allocations

ON an annual average, corporate assets committed to inventory in the United States approximate $300 billion. Basic categories of inventory break the total into (1) raw materials, (2) goods in process, and (3) finished products. Physical distribution management primarily focuses attention upon raw material stocks and finished products, and to a lesser degree on goods in process.

Inventory, from a financial point of view, requires a proper balance between procurement, sales, and production. A variety of ratios describe these relationships. Most important from a physical distribution point of view is the firm's average inventory commitment. This commitment is composed of stocks to satisfy average requirements and safety stocks to cover unexpected demand variations.

From a physical distribution perspective, inventory relates primarily to the creation of time and place utility as opposed to form utility resulting from the manufacturing and product design processes. The discussion of inventory in this chapter will focus around inventory commitments related to physical distribution management. The ordinary financial and accounting orientations, although alluded to, will not receive extensive treatment.

Cost of Carrying Inventory

Inventory carrying costs do not appear exclusively as a separate financial book entry, but consist also of implicit economic costs. For this reason, inventory carrying costs should be viewed in the same fashion as a prospective investment decision in machinery, equipment, or other fixed assets.

When an investment decision on fixed assets is contemplated, a flow of funds over the expected life of the asset is measured against the flow of fixed and operating costs over the same period. This method permits an

194

CHART 8–1 Proposal-Evaluation Chart

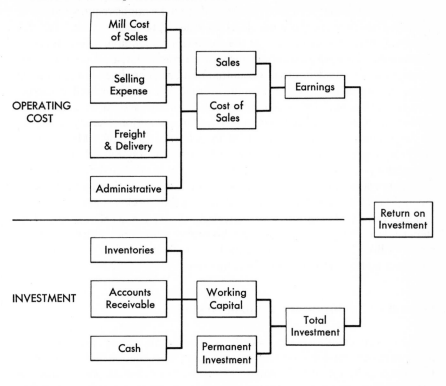

assessment of the anticipated rate of return, which provides an economic basis for a decision. Assigning a required rate of return is crucial to any proper capital resource allocation. This principle is demonstrated in Chart 8–1.

For the same persuasive reasons, a required rate of interest expressing carrying costs of inventory is crucial to proper resource allocation in the inventory sector. The carrying cost of inventory, however, consists of more than the cost of capital. The full cost includes obsolescence, loss and damage, shrinkage, and other elements of risk and cost associated with carrying inventory. If the total of these costs is low, high levels of inventory result, and conversely, if they are high, low inventory levels prevail. At least one reference suggests a 25 percent inventory cost associated with average inventory value.[1]

Although the above inventory costs are used in determining order quantities, to be discussed later in this chapter, other costs also influence inventory investment decisions. Primary among these costs, and not generally treated

[1]B. W. Puder, "Containerization: One Shipper's Problems, Solutions, Needs," *Management of the Physical Distribution Function*, American Management Association (New York, 1960), p. 108.

in many firms, are additional costs associated with the geography of inventory.[2] It is a fact that increased numbers of stock locations require additional inventory to support the same level of sales. The basic reason for this increased inventory investment is the expansion of required safety stocks as the number of inventory locations increases. From a statistical point of view, if total sales are divided into a substantial number of confined limited market ·areas, the standard deviation around average sales in each limited market increases. This requires added safety stock for the system as a whole. A mathematical function that generalizes required additional safety stock can be formulated and will be described in detail later. These added costs of inventory must be considered in physical distribution systems design.

Inventory costs are also important in physical distribution through product proliferation. A basic thesis of modern marketing is market segmentation. One important method of segmenting markets revolves around product design alternatives to fit precisely a given market segment. This step leads directly to increased stock-keeping units and added inventory costs.[3] Suffice it to say here that both base stocks and safety stocks must be increased as the number of products increases.

Objectives of Inventory Control Systems

The objectives of inventory systems revolve around a managerially agreed upon customer service level and measurement of related achievement costs. Economic order quantity formulas (EOQ) exist to calculate precise ordering practices regarding how much to order to minimize inventory cost. Other techniques are available to determine when to order. Both techniques are predicated upon a managerial policy concerning desired customer service levels.

The vexing problem in balancing inventory costs and service levels revolves around the difficulty of measuring the impact of an out-of-stock condition. A stockout, reflects immediate lost sales, which may or may not be measurable, and potential loss of a permanent customer. The full impact of a lost sale is directly related to the service policies of competitors. A customer who is denied by one supplier and serviced by a competitor may become a customer again only through the use of substantial sales and promotional effort.

Wide ranges of physical distribution systems design can accommodate a specific service objective. For example, two-day delivery can be achieved with numerous stock locations situated close to customers. Alternatively,

[2]See especially Richard A. Lewis, "Business Logistics Information and Accounting Systems for Marketing Analysis," unpublished DBA thesis, Michigan State University (East Lansing, 1964), p. 154, where geographic costs, including inventory are shown to account for about 68 percent of all distribution and marketing costs.

[3]John F. Magee, *Physical Distribution Systems* (New York, McGraw-Hill Book Company, 1967), pp. 25–29.

TABLE 8–1   ABC ANALYSIS

Item	Sales in Dollars		Percent of Total Dollars	Percent of Items	Item Category
1	20,000 ⎫	38,000	56	20	A
2	18,000 ⎭				
3	8,000 ⎫				
4	6,000 ⎪	23,000	34	40	B
5	5,000 ⎪				
6	4,000 ⎭				
7	3,000 ⎫				
8	2,500 ⎪	7,000	10	40	C
9	1,000 ⎪				
10	500 ⎭				
	$68,000				

the same objective may be achieved by a single stock location tied to electronic order processing and premium transportation. Inventory costs will vary widely between disparate system designs.

One objective of distribution analysis is to measure inventory cost differences as systems designs change. Although many paths lead to the same service results, each path bears a unique cost. The remaining sections of this chapter develop techniques to trace inventory cost changes over a wide variety of systems designs and provide the basis for development of unit control systems treated in Appendix 8A.

ABC Analysis

The basis of all unit control systems is the development of selective measures among products in the inventory mix. One of the oldest and most reliable approaches to selective measurement is ABC analysis. In ABC analysis, a rank array of items by sales activity is developed. Thus, the first item in the rank array accounts for the largest percentage of total sales, and so on throughout the entire product line. ABC analysis merely provides a quick way to identify those items where potential payoffs appear greatest from applying tighter inventory controls. That is to say, a 10 percent cost reduction or a 10 percent service improvement will show greater payoffs in an item ranked number one, as compared with the next item in the list, and so on.

Usually, ABC analysis provides insights into relative importance of products, but only in terms of sales dollars generated, and by no other criteria. A typical pattern of ABC analysis is shown in Table 8–1.

The A items, here defined as the top 20 percent, account for a total of $38,000 in sales, or about 56 percent of all sales activity. The B items account for 40 percent of the items and about 34 percent of the sales. Finally, the C items account for 40 percent of the items and about 10 percent of total sales. Items with high activity rates (A) should command greater attention from the inventory control system than those with lower rates (B and C).

ABC, CRITICAL VALUE ANALYSIS

As indicated previously, the raw sales dollars of an item determine its rank order of importance in an inventory control system. However, certain items low in sales volume may require greater attention because of their critical role in the total market offerings of a firm. For example, in the auto, an ignition replacement set may fall into the C category, based upon ABC analysis. From its position in the array, the ignition set deserves less attention than a right rear fender falling into the A category.

When the mission of the two replacement parts is evaluated, however, the ignition set is more crucial to the operation of a car then a right rear fender. Therefore, by ABC analysis, the ranking favors the right rear fender, although through critical value analysis, the ignition set receives higher priority. Astute competitors cognizant of this principle may properly hold to higher service levels for ignition sets and capture disparative amounts of the after market. Some method of combining traditional ABC and critical value analysis is required for effective control. Control may be accomplished by establishing a weighted set of values based upon the critical nature of the product involved and the ABC classifications. A selected set of combined values and their development is as follows:

Critical value:
1. Must be immediately available to maintain operation of machine.
2. Critical to continued operation but can be delayed for not more than seven days.
3. Not critical to continued operation, may be delayed by more than seven days.

The numbers 1, 2, 3 now represent a critical value scale. In the same way, a numerical value for each item can be set up by simply accepting the number of the item into the rank array. In this way, a combined scale of relative importance by two criteria can be developed. Table 8–2 provides an illustration.[4]

[4]The material in the section draws upon "Prime 100$_R$, Physical Distribution Management, The Total System Route to New Profits, (New York: American Management Association, Inc., 1967). Tables 8-II, 8-VIII, 8IX, 8X, 8XIV and 8XV are reproduced with the permission of A.M.A. The particular source is in programmed instruction format and contains more detail than presented in this chapter. It is used as a business training aid and as a supplement in university courses.

TABLE 8-2   ABC, CRITICAL VALUE ANALYSIS

Rank Array	Critical Value 1	2	3	Total Value (Rank Array Times Critical Value)
1			X	3
2	X			2
3		X		6
4			X	12
5	X			5
6		X		12
7			X	21
8	X			8
9		X		18
10	X			10

Although the method of critical value analysis has been accepted widely by the military, it is not yet in vogue among the nonmilitary. Perhaps the main reason for this fact is that the ranking by critical numerical values is easier to accomplish in the military than in the civilian economy.

In Table 8-1, item 1 is most important, but with critical value analysis, it drops to second place in total value. Critical values may also be employed for assigning weights to markets and customers. Rapidly expanding or highly profitable markets may receive greater attention from the perspective of inventory policy than slowly growing or unprofitable markets. The make or buy decision is an example of this strategy. Similarly, large or rapidly growing customers may receive more attention in stock availability than small or stagnant customers.

Time Dimensions of Inventory — Order Cycles

The inventory planning period is typically referred to as the order cycle. By normal accounting practices, it is impossible to identify costs associated with alternative order cycles, thus special analysis is required. Accounting reports generally carry the inventory only as expenses related to sales over a time period (in the P & L) or an amount fixed at a specified time (Balance Sheet). In both statements, true time dimensions, measured by flows, do not appear nor are total costs of inventory appraised.

Consider a firm with sales of $365,000,000. The average required daily inventory is $1,000,000 (365 mm ÷ 365 days). Under these conditions, the longer the time span between raw material delivery and finished product sales, the greater are the required inventories. If the time required for all processes to occur is 30 days, the average inventory in the system is at least $30,000,000. If this time dimension is shortened to only ten days, required

TABLE 8–3   EFFECT OF COMMUNICATIONS, ORDER PROCESSING, AND TRANSPORTATION TIMES UPON INVENTORY LEVELS   (Assumption: Daily sales equal 200 units)

	System 1		System 2	
	Time (days)	Inventory (Units)	Time (days)	Inventory (Units)
Communications	5	1,000	$\frac{1}{2}$	100
Order Processing	5	1,000	$\frac{1}{2}$	100
Transportation	10	2,000	1	200
Totals	20	4,000	2	400

inventory drops to $10,000,000, a savings of $20,000,000 in inventory investment, and about $5,000,000 in annual carrying costs appears (based upon a 25 percent carrying charge as stated earlier).

THE ORDER CYCLE

The total order cycle represents elapsed time from order placement to merchandise receipt and consists of (1) communications, (2) order processing, and (3) transportation. These three elements constitute lead time in a unit control system. Order cycle may change as a result of modifications in communications, order processing, and/or method of transportation. The faster the method of (1) communications, (2) order processing, and (3) transportation, the lower total inventory investment will be in the distribution system, and conversely. The impact of different order cycles on inventory is illustrated in Table 8–3.

The implications in Table 8–3 are that (1) with shortened lead times, inventory investment drops by 3,600 units, and (2) operating expenses, through reduced carrying costs and lower storage requirements, also drop. These reductions may, or may not be, offset by increased costs elsewhere in the physical distribution system.

ORDER CYCLES AND FORECASTING REQUIREMENTS

Order cycles are crucial to scientific inventory control, because they set the time limits on stock replenishment. Generally, the longer the order cycle, the greater must be the care exercised in determining proper inventory levels to serve future anticipated market demand. Because the objective of inventory control systems is to serve market demands appropriately over future time periods, forecasting becomes an essential requirement for setting levels properly.

In the other direction as the order cycle approaches zero, forecasting diminishes in importance as a factor in setting inventory levels. As an example, if lead time is 30 days, the possibility exists that out-of-stock can occur any time during that period. If a stockout occurs on the 15th day because of unexpectedly high demand, that condition will prevail under normal stock replenishment rules for the next 15th-day period, because that is the amount of time remaining until the current order cycle has been completed.

On the other hand, if the stock replenishment cycle is one day, stock may be replaced as each working day progresses, thus diminishing risk. This condition reduces the need for a highly sophisticated unit forecasting system. However, it increases the need for exacting communications, order process- ing, and transportation.

Some firms have experimented with *zero-response* inventory systems. By this concept, no attempt is made to forecast demand. Rather, a highly responsive information system linked to rapid communications and cycled deliveries is constructed to replace inventory rapidly as it diminishes. As an example, consider the demand for an electric drill in a local hardware store. If the demand pattern is such that on any single day none or one is sold, and if the probability of a demand occurring during lead time approaches zero, a zero response system on that item can be set up, eliminating completely the need for a sophisticated forecast. If the sale should occur on Monday and no further sales occurred before the next delivery date, say Thursday, that item would be placed on a demand order, which merely means that each time the item disappears from inventory, a new order is immediately placed for the next delivery schedule. Various applications and techniques of inventory control exist, but the basic principle described above applies to all. Examples of unit control systems are developed in Appendix 8A. Attention is now directed to the basic method of determining how much to buy, the economic order quantity (EOQ).

Economic Order Quantities

Determination of the traditional Economic Order Quantity requires a balancing of two costs: (1) ordering and (2) carrying. Ordering costs are a function of the expense of placing a single order multiplied by the frequency of orders. Therefore, the smaller the quantity ordered, the greater are the annual number of orders and the greater are the total ordering costs. Carrying costs depend upon the level of average inventories. The fewer the annual orders, the larger is the average inventory, and, consequently, the higher is the holding cost. Ordering costs, therefore, move in a direction opposite to holding costs as a function of the number of orders placed.

COMPONENTS OF EOQ

The components of EOQ consist of (1) holding cost expressed on the basis of cents per unit, (2) order costs, and (3) annual usage rate.

Holding cost is calculated by measuring all costs associated with holding stock. These would include two major categories of costs: (1) interest charge on money, and (2) the risk and physical costs of storage. If the interest cost is 10 percent and the risk and physical costs of storage are 15 percent, the total carrying costs are 25 percent. Any disagreements on carrying costs usually relate to the proper interest rates to charge on the use of money. These may include (1) opportunity costs, (2) average return on investment, (3) target return on investment, and (4) cost of debt money. The specific interest cost theory selected will affect EOQ. In the above list, the highest interest rate is associated with opportunity costs, i.e., the cost of foregone investment opportunities, and the lowest rate is associated with debt-carrying charges.

Order costs include all costs associated with placing an order. These costs will vary considerably, depending upon the nature of the order processing system. For regular and frequent reorders on standard commodities, order costs will tend toward the low side, whereas for specialized orders requiring considerable specification, they will tend toward the high side.

Annual usage rate forms the last component of the basic EOQ formulation. Usage rates provide information on total requirements over the year.

For these categories of required costs, it is necessary to undertake special studies to establish costs, because many of them will not be recorded in the books of account. Usage rates may be determined from sales records. This is especially true of the interest-carrying costs that are imputed and not book costs.

EOQ TABULAR METHOD

In the tabular method of demonstrating EOQ principles, all costs are expressed on a dollar basis for varying order quantities and frequencies. Table 8–4 illustrates the relevant costs for five different order quantities.[5]

Assumptions in Table 8–4 are (1) carrying costs equal $.25 per unit or 25 percent of average inventory, assuming unit costs of the product are $1; (2) order cost equals $20 per order; (3) average inventory equals one-half of order quantity; (4) total sales equal 5,200 units per year.

In Table 8–4, average inventory declines with order frequency (line 2). Average inventory is defined as one-half of the original order quantity. The carrying costs (line 3) are $.25 per unit and, thus, are proportional to average

---

[5]This illustration follows the one found in Edward H. Bowman and Robert B. Fetter, *Analysis for Production Management*, (Homewood, Ill.: Richard D. Irwin, Inc., 1961), p. 269.

TABLE 8–4   TABULAR METHOD FOR FORMULATING EOQ

	Number of Orders				
	1	2	5	10	20
(1) Size of order (Units)	5,200	2,600	1,040	520	260
(2) Average Inventory (Units)	2,600	1,300	520	260	130
(3) Carrying costs	$ 670	325	130	65	32.50
(4) Order costs	$ 20	40	100	200	400.00
(5) Total cost	$ 690	365	230	265	432.50

inventory, increasing as average inventory increases. Order costs rise with order frequency and are found by multiplying the cost of a single order ($20, line 4) by the number of orders. Because order costs and carrying costs act inversely to each other, one order frequency and order quantity will occur which will minimize both costs. In Table 8–4, the lowest total cost is found at five orders per year or $230.

However, from the tabular method, it is not certain whether the actual minimum has been found, because only a discrete set of order frequencies exists. To test finally whether the true optimum order frequency and quantity have been found, it is necessary to use either a graphic or mathematical expression of EOQ, which will define the precise order quantity and frequency associated with lowest cost.

CHART 8–2   Graphic Method of Applying EOQ

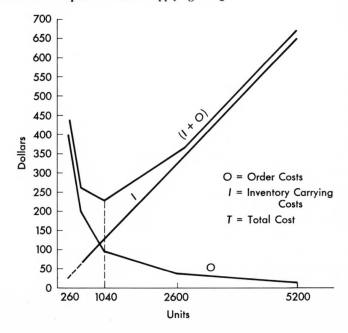

GRAPHIC EXPRESSIONS OF EOQ

It is possible to express order, holding, and total costs graphically and to approximate a solution by this means. In Chart 8–2, the relationship of the two cost functions (I, O) is shown.

By assuming both costs, a total cost curve is derived. The minimum total cost curve shows that the optimum order size is about 920 units. The graphic method, although somewhat more accurate than the tabular, still is a cumbersome way of actually employing EOQ.

MATHEMATICAL EXPRESSION OF EOQ

EOQ's may also be expressed mathematically.[6]

The basic components of EOQ formulas, remember, are holding and order costs. Specifically, they include:

$$a = \text{ordering costs (per order)}$$
$$s = \text{annual sales rate}$$
$$i = \text{interest costs per unit per year}$$

The above elements then are combined into the formula:

$$EOQ = \sqrt{\frac{2\,as}{i}}$$

Given the information from the above examples, values for each element are designated:

$$a = \$20$$
$$s = 5{,}200 \text{ units}$$
$$i = \$.25 \text{ per unit}$$

Combining these into the formula results in:

$$EOQ = \sqrt{\frac{2\,as}{i}}$$

$$EOQ = \sqrt{\frac{2(20)(5200)}{.25}}$$

$$EOQ = \sqrt{\frac{208{,}000}{.25}}$$

$$EOQ = \sqrt{832{,}000}$$

$$EOQ = 912 \text{ units}$$

The result is an EOQ of 912 units ordered about five times per year.

[6]See *Ibid.*, pp. 272–276, for mathematical deviations. See also W. E. Welch, *Tested Scientific Inventory Control* (Greenwich, Conn.: Management Publishing Corporation, 1956), p. 73.

CHARACTERISTICS OF EOQ

EOQ's are affected by the values put into them. As interest rates rise, EOQ's fall. As usage rates and annual sales increase, EOQ's rise. It, therefore, is necessary to calculate with reasonable accuracy each component entering the formula.

However, complete accuracy is not absolutely essential. For example, if interest rates employed in the above formula resulted in a unit carrying cost of $.20 per unit instead of $.25, EOQ would change to only 1,019 units. Thus, a 20 percent change in carrying costs results only in about a 10-percent change in EOQ. Other elements will act in almost the same way as interest costs.

MODIFICATIONS OF EOQ

The first significant modification in the use of EOQ's is the fact that sales volumes vary over time. Thus, the relevant usage rate is the one over appropriate lead times. If, for example, lead time is one month, and sales occur once in that month, EOQ will be one order for all sales to cover expected sales over lead time. If these sales reach 5,200 units for the next lead-time period, all 5,200 will be ordered at one time.

The two basic methods of allowing sales variations to enter inventory systems are (1) fixed order quantity and (2) fixed order time. In a fixed order quantity system, time between orders is permitted to vary while the economic order quantity is held constant. In a fixed order time system, quantity ordered is permitted to vary, while the interval between orders is fixed. Under the fixed order time approach, EOQ does not determine order quantity, but rather, order quantity is determined by forecast sales over the next lead-time period. Both systems have merit, and the selection of a specific one depends upon the operating circumstances faced by a firm in its distribution patterns.

For example, a grocery chain may wish to schedule its truck fleet to minimize transportation costs. This may result in a fixed schedule for store delivery with each store specified as to its delivery dates. In this case, each store will order on a fixed time schedule but will vary its order quantities for each item.

The same grocery chain may utilize a fixed order quantity and permit time between orders to vary at its warehouse level. Because no severe fleet scheduling problems exist, the need for balancing transport savings against order and holding costs is not nearly so persuasive. Secondly, at the warehouse level, large quantities will ordinarily be ordered, permitting some relaxation in the degree of unit ordering control so necessary to retail level. Variations in store level demand for a product is likely to be much greater than variations of the same product at warehouse levels, accounting in part for the different approaches at the two levels of distribution.

CHART 8–3   Graphic Comparison of Fixed Order Quantity and Fixed Order Cycle

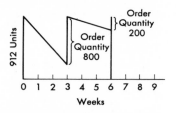

In Chart 8–3A and B, the order quantity needed to start the cycle is 912, as determined by the EOQ. In a fixed order quantity system (Chart 8-3A), the quantity always represents the amount ordered. In Chart 8–3B, the beginning inventory is 912. All subsequent orders are placed every three weeks in such a way as to replenish inventory to 912 units on hand for the next sales period.

Purchase Discounts.   Another variant in EOQ revolves around purchase discounts. Discounts enter the formula through landed cost of the product and related carrying costs. They may be of the usual quantity allowances or may be realized as lower transport cost due to larger shipment volume. Thus, if a commodity is valued on a landed cost basis (laid down at point of use), the actual landed cost is not only a function of price discounts on the product, but also transportation cost on the volume shipped. In both cases, a comparison is made of the total costs with and without the discount, and the lowest cost option is selected.

Safety Stocks.   One last adjustment is necessary before EOQ's result in an operating tool for managerial control, and that is an allowance for safety stocks. The discussion of EOQ immediately preceding this section results in determining base stock requirements. Base stocks consist of that amount of inventory required to service the average level of demand. Safety stocks are additive to base stocks and provide a cushion of additional inventory to cover demand variations above average levels.

The actual level of safety stocks depends upon a statistical determination of demand variations and integration of a management customer service policy. Because base stocks provide sufficient inventory to cover average demand, it follows that a stockout condition will occur 50 percent of the time if inventories are set only to this level. That is to say, 50 percent of the time a customer's complete order cannot be entirely filled. It seems appropriate, therefore, that additional stocks be placed in inventory to bring the level up to some predetermined standard.

Customer Service Levels Under Conditions of Uncertainty.   If it is assumed that demand is constant at 700 units per week, with total annual demand of

TABLE 8–5 FREQUENCY DISTRIBUTION BASED UPON VARYING DEMAND BY WEEKS

Demand in Units	Frequency (f)	Total Demand by weeks (Units)	d	fd	fd^2
100	1	100	−6	−6	36
200	2	400	−5	−10	50
300	3	900	−4	−12	48
400	4	1,600	−3	−12	36
500	5	2,500	−2	−10	20
600	6	3,600	−1	−6	6
700	10	7,000	0	0	0
800	6	4,800	+1	+6	6
900	5	4,500	+2	+10	20
1,000	4	4,000	+3	+12	36
1,100	3	3,300	+4	+12	48
1,200	2	2,400	+5	+10	50
1,300	1	1,300	+6	+6	36
Totals	52	36,400	0	0	392

36,400 units per year on the basis of a 21-day lead time, the result is an average inventory of 1,050 units. Under such regular and completely certain conditions, there really is no serious problem of inventory control.

However in the real world it is improbable that such a stable demand condition will prevail. In fact, demand is likely to be erratic, irregular, cyclical, and seasonal. Table 8–5 indicates a more probable type of demand schedule for an annual period.

Table 8–5, indicates that the average demand is 700 units. Average demand may be found by dividing total annual demand by the number of weeks. To review, this is 36,400 ÷ 52 = 700 units. However, inspection of the demand by weeks shows wide variation from a low of 100 units for one week of the year to a high of 1,300 units in another single week. Assume that the variation of weekly demand is known from historical records, but it is not known exactly what the demand will be in any given week. It would seem, therefore, that reliance on the inventory cycle developed earlier would result in substantial out-of-stock conditions about one-half of the time. For any week when demand exceeds 700 units, out-of-stock situations would occur with resultant lost sales. However, methods may be applied to this situation which will show to what levels inventory must be held to achieve any desired level of customer service. The method employed is statistical probability theory.

Probability Theory and Applications. As the name suggests, probability theory is based on the determination of a probable occurrence out of a large number of occurrences. Because a coin has two sides, it seems that the chances of a head occurring on any one toss is one in two. For two coins, the

CHART 8–4   Normal Probability Distribution of College Test Scores

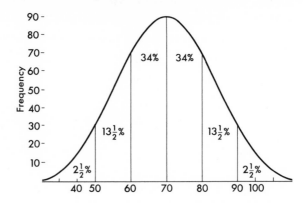

possible combination of heads and tails on four tosses are two heads occurring once in four tries, a head and tail occurring twice in four tries, and two tails once in four tries. Any number of coins may be included, and the probabilities of any combination of heads and tails may be mathematically determined. In a large number of possibilities, the different occurrences take the form of a bell-shaped curve. This is hypothetically indicated in Chart 8–4.

The largest number of occurrences in Chart 8–4 is at grade 70. The 60–80 area indicates the spread of the grades to one standard deviation. The standard deviation is a measure of dispersion, which states that, within the limits of plus or minus one standard deviation, approximately 69 percent of all occurrences will be found. Because the average grade of 70 is also the midpoint in this case, 34 percent will fall between scores of 60 and 70, and an additional 34 percent of all grades will be between the test scores of 60 and 80. For two standard deviations, about 95 percent of all scores will be found. That is $70 \pm 20 = 50$ to 90. Finally, for the standard deviations, 99 percent of all scores will fall within the limits of 70 ± 30, or 40 to 100 on the test scores.

In Table 8–5, the average of the weekly demand is 700 units. By calculating the standard deviation (SD), it is possible to determine the probabilities of weekly demand exceeding any particular level. The formula for the standard deviation by the short method is:

$$SD = I \sqrt{\frac{\sum f d^2}{N}}$$

where: SD = standard deviation
                N = number of occurrences
                I = size of the class interval
                f = frequency in each class
                d = deviation of the class from the average

TABLE 8–6 BASE STOCK, AVERAGE STOCK, AND SAFETY STOCK AT 84 PERCENT, 95 PERCENT, AND 99 PERCENT CUSTOMER SERVICE LEVELS.

		Safety Stock
Base Stock	700	
Average Stock at 84%	975	275
Average Stock at 95%	1,250	550
Average Stock at 99%	1,525	825

From the data presented in Table 8–5, the standard deviation becomes:

$$SD = 100\sqrt{\frac{392}{52}}$$
$$SD = 100\sqrt{7.54}$$
$$SD = 100 \times 2.75$$
$$SD = 275 \text{ units}$$

This means that by increasing the average inventory from 700 units to 975 units, about 84 percent of all demands will be satisfied. Note that because the average inventory of 700 units is already sufficient to cover 50 percent of all demands, which are less than 700 units, it is necessary to consider only those weekly demands that are greater than 700. In other words, by increasing inventory to 975 units, 275 additional units are sold. The customers ordering these units previously either were not served at all or had to wait for the shipment to arrive before they could be served. To cover 95 percent of all customer demands, average inventory must be increased by an additional 275 units to a total of 1,250 units. Finally, if 99 percent of all customer demands are to be satisfied, average inventory must increase to a total of 1,525 units. These results are summarized in Table 8–6.

Additional stocks required to achieve the desired service levels above are, in reality, safety stocks. These safety stocks result in increasing the average level of inventory as indicated. The unit data may now be readily converted to cost data by simply assuming a cost per unit at the warehouse. It shall be assumed, for purposes of illustration, that the cost will be $1,000 per unit. The average inventory investment then takes the schedule shown in Table 8–7. Assuming the costs of carrying inventory to be 25 percent, it is possible to determine the cost of carrying different levels of inventory. By calculating the gain in sales, it is also possible to measure the added gross revenues derived from carrying any additional amounts of inventory. These data are combined in Table 8–7 for customer service levels of 80, 90, and 99 percent.

Column I shows varying service levels. Column II indicates the number of standard deviations necessary to reach the desired service level. For 80-percent service levels, it is necessary to add .8 standard deviation to the basic level of inventory. This is (.8)275 or 220 units. Average inventory is

TABLE 8-7 INVENTORY INVESTMENT AND ADDED SALES AT 50 PERCENT, 80 PERCENT, 90 PERCENT AND 99 PERCENT LEVELS OF CUSTOMER SERVICE

I	II	III	IV	V	VI	VII	VIII	IX	X
Percent Level of Service	S.D.	Average Inv. ($)	Added Inv. Over Base Stock ($)	Incremental Inv. for Each Successive Stage ($)	Added Inv. Cost at 25%	Total Sales Each Level	Added Sales Each Level	Added Profit at 1% Margin	Net Gain or Loss
50	0	700,000	0	0	0	18,200,000	0	0	0
80	.84	931,000	231,000	231,000	57,750	29,120,000	10,920,000	109,200	51,450
90	1.28	1,042,000	342,000	111,000	27,750	32,760,000	3,640,000	36,400	8,650
92	1.41	1,088,000	388,000	46,000	12,500	33,488,000	728,000	7,280	−5,220
94	1.54	1,124,000	424,000	34,000	8,500	34,216,000	828,000	8,280	−220
95	1.65	1,154,000	454,000	30,000	7,500	34,580,000	364,000	3,640	−3,860
96	1.75	1,182,000	482,000	28,000	7,000	34,944,000	364,000	3,640	−3,360
97	1.88	1,217,000	517,000	29,000	7,250	35,308,000	364,000	3,640	−3,610
98	2.05	1,264,000	564,000	47,000	11,750	35,672,000	364,000	3,640	−8,110
99	2.33	1,340,000	640,000	76,000	19,000	36,036,000	364,000	3,640	−15,360

CHART 8–5   Graphic Presentation of Customer Service Level

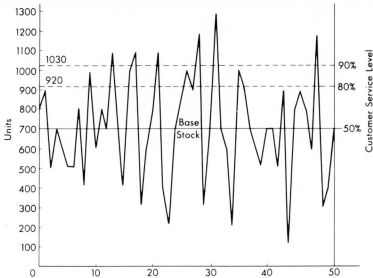

thus raised from $700,000 to $920,000 as shown in column III. Column IV shows the added inventory level associated with each successive service level. Column V shows the additional dollars of investment necessary as a result of each successive improvement in service levels. Column VI shows the added cost of inventory of 25 percent. Column VII indicates the total sales associated with each service improvement. It is found simply by multiplying the service level percentage by the total annual sales. Column VIII shows the additional sales associated with each improvement in service levels. Column IX shows the added gross profit associated with each increase in sales. Finally, column X shows the added net profit associated with each level of customer service.

As indicated above, service levels may be increased to 90 percent customer satisfaction. At this level, added net profits are still positive. Construction of a complete scale of added service levels, added costs, added gross profits, and added net profits will indicate exactly which level of customer satisfaction will yield highest total profits.

Graphic Presentation of Customer Service. The process of increasing levels of customer satisfaction may also be shown by graphic means. Chart 8–5 represents the weekly demand. The heavy line shows the base stock required to serve the market which is characterized by the given demand schedule. The base stock is 700 units. The dotted lines indicate the average inventory necessary to achieve the indicated service level. The additional satisfied customers may be found by measuring the added area between any two adjacent service levels inside the line indicating weekly demand.

The areas outside the boundaries established at each service level indicate the proportion of customers who will go unsatisfied.

TABLE 8–8   COSTS FOR VARIOUS STOCKOUT CONSEQUENCES

Back order	$ 5.00
Lost sale	25.00
Lost customer	1,000.00

Economic Setting of Safety Stocks.   The economic basis for setting of safety stocks is estimates of incremental costs associated with carrying additional inventory and the resulting incremental revenues from increased sales. Incremental costs and revenues associated with a stockout consist of three possible events:

1. A back order.
2. A lost sale.
3. A lost customer.

The cost of each event then becomes:

1. The cost of a back order.
2. The revenue loss from a lost sale.
3. The revenue loss due to a lost customer.

Costs or revenue losses must be assigned to each of these events. Cost calculations may be relatively simple: for example, the cost of placing a back order. However, some of the calculations may be extremely difficult, bordering upon sheer guesswork: for example, revenue loss due to a lost customer. For purposes of illustration, the costs in Table 8–8 are assigned arbitrarily.

Next determine the probability of each event. Probability assignments may be based upon historical records to some extent, but admittedly, judgment must play a role because the data, by their nature, will be incomplete. For example, if an item is not back ordered, no substantive method can be developed to determine that the customer was lost. Table 8–8 is expanded in Table 8–9 to include associated probabilities.

The next step in the analysis is to determine the probability distribution of demand. An assumed partial distribution is shown in Table 8–10. Only a partial table is shown, because we are interested only in the demand variations that exceed basic stock and indicate the need for safety stock additions.

TABLE 8–9   EVENTS, COSTS, AND PROBABILITIES ASSOCIATED WITH A STOCKOUT

Event	Cost	Probability	Product Loss
Back order	$ 5.00	.75	$ 3.75
Lost sale	25.00	.24	6.00
Lost customer	1,000.00	.01	10.00
		1.00	$19.75

TABLE 8–10 PARTIAL DEMAND DISTRIBUTION

I. Number of Units Sold in 1 Month	II. Inventory Carrying Costs Added	III. Number of Orders Filled	IV. Stockout Costs Saved
			(Col. III × $19.75)
300–349	$125.00	20	$395.00
350–399	125.00	15	296.25
400–449	125.00	10	197.50
450–499	125.00	8	158.00
500–549	125.00	5	98.75
550–599	125.00	2	39.50

In Table 8–10, the added inventory costs with each increment of 50 units is shown as $125 per each increment. The stockout-costs-saved column (IV) really is a measure of the added revenue generally associated with each inventory increment. The stockout-costs-saved column is found by multiplying $19.75 times the number of additional orders filled. Equilibrium occurs at that point where the added inventory costs just equal the stockout costs saved. This point occurs somewhere between monthly demands of 450 to 499 and 500 to 549. By selecting the inventory increment associated with the demand levels of 450 to 499, we are certain of not overstocking with resultant excessive costs. The result of this example is that only seven stockouts occur. If the total number of orders were 100, then a stockout ratio of 7 percent would be experienced.

Average Inventory. Average inventory is equal to one-half of base stock plus all safety stocks. Thus, if base stock is equal to 100 units over a specified lead time, average inventory would equal 50 units or one-half of base stock. Safety stocks represent the number of units needed above the base stock level. In Table 8–10, 53 units of safety stock are required to reach optimum inventory level.

Because safety stocks are permanently included in the inventory, they are included for their entire amount. Thus, the mathematical relationship is expressed:

$$\text{Average Inventory} = \frac{\text{Base Stock}}{2} + \text{Safety Stock}$$

MANAGERIAL MODIFICATIONS OF EOQ

Numerous reasons might exist for modifying average inventory as determined for EOQ and safety stock requirements. For example, for competitive reasons, a firm may wish to raise its inventory to near 100 percent in-stock position. This is especially characteristic of consumer products with high brand identification and industrial products critical to manufacturing operations.

In some cases, the firms may choose to keep a lower inventory than indicated. This could be due to lack of competitive alternatives to the customer (the monopoly case) or by conditioning the customer to anticipate stockouts. A retail store operating both a mail order and a regular retail operation might choose to understock in its regular operations and induce the customer to order by catalog. Trading stamp companies traditionally use the conditioning device by indicating in their catalogs that certain items may have to be ordered specially. In both cases, inventory reductions occur in one level of the physical distribution system, permitting better control and lower inventories in the more economically efficient level.

FORECASTING

The key to adequate inventory control depends upon short-term forecasts of demand for the appropriate sales period. Specifically, a short-term forecast for each inventory item over the lead time is necessary if inventories are to be sufficient to provide the proper customer service level.

In forecasting, past demand is analyzed to estimate what future demand requirements will be. Basically, the future is predicted by averaging past demand data. This gives a smoothing effect, which filters out the random fluctuations in demand. However, in some forecasting techniques, demand data from the past receive more weight than the more current demand data.

Many forecasting techniques are available to predict future demand requirements. Two such methods are trend analysis and exponential smoothing. Exponential smoothing differs from other forecasting techniques, because it provides a heavier weighting of demand in later periods than in earlier periods. Meanwhile, trend analysis and other techniques such as moving average make little or no allowance for weighting different demand periods. Table 8–11 illustrates the use of exponential smoothing and trend analysis.

In utilizing exponential smoothing, the new demand forecast is the old forecast plus a fraction of the difference between the new observation and the old forecast. This difference is discounted by the smoothing factor. In Table 8–11, two smoothing constants — .05 and .35 — are illustrated.

Exponential smoothing forecasts the number of units required to maintain proper inventory levels. As depicted in Table 8–11, the smaller smoothing constant (.05) creates a relatively slower and smaller change, with a change in demand. Meanwhile, for the larger smoothing constant (.35), a faster and larger change is observed. Thus, by utilizing a larger smoothing constant, reduced safety stocks are maintained while providing the established customer service levels.

TABLE 8–11   COMPARISON OF EXPONENTIAL SMOOTHING AND TREND ANALYSIS

| | | EXPONENTIAL SMOOTHING | | | | | |
| | | .05 Smoothing Constant | | .35 Smoothing Constant | | TREND ANALYSIS | |
Sales Period	Actual Demand	Expected Demand	Difference	Expected Demand	Difference	Expected Demand	Difference
1	254	254.00	0	254.00	0	280.410	26.410
2	270	254.80	15.20	259.60	10.40	281.623	11.623
3	320	258.06	41.94	280.74	39.26	282.836	37.164
4	272	258.757	13.243	277.681	5.681	284.049	12.049
5	222	256.919	24.919	258.193	26.193	285.262	63.262
6	306	259.373	46.627	274.925	31.075	286.475	19.525
7	342	263.505	78.495	298.401	43.599	287.688	54.312
8	338	267.229	70.771	312.261	25.739	288.901	49.099
9	297	268.718	28.282	306.920	9.920	290.114	6.886
10	300	270.282	29.718	304.498	4.498	291.327	8.673
11	281	270.818	10.182	296.274	15.274	292.540	11.540
12	243	269.427	26.427	277.628	34.628	293.753	50.753
			$E_1 = 385.804$		$E_2 = 246.267$		$E_3 = 351.296$

Trend analysis previously mentioned does not allocate different weights to the value of the information in respect to time periods. Its efficiency depends upon the amount of the average error. In Table 8–11, the data has an average error of .22. This is found by comparing the expected demand against the actual demand. The sum of the differences between actual and expected demand should be some number less than one as shown in this particular case. This gives the average error. However, one must remember that trend analysis does not weight the time periods differently.

So far, two types of forecasting and examples have been presented to illustrate exponential smoothing and trend analysis. Possibly now the question, "Which method is best?" arises. To find the best method, the differences between actual and expected demand are summed, disregarding signs. The lowest sum of all the methods illustrated then gives the best forecast. In this instance, E_2 is the lowest sum. Thus, the smoothing constant of .35 gives the best forecast by minimizing the total error. This then minimizes the safety stock requirements necessary to provide the desired customer service level.

INTEGRATION OF BASE STOCK, SAFETY STOCK, AND ORDER CYCLE TIMES

It is now possible to integrate base stock, safety stock, and order cycles to develop their interrelationships and effects. Charts 8–6 and 8–7 illustrate these relationships:

CHART 8–6   Inventory Cycle with 21-Day Lead Time (Fixed Order Quantity)

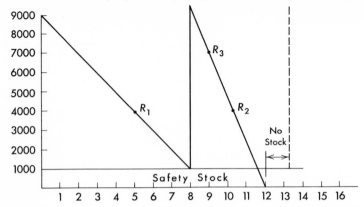

CHART 8–7   Inventory Cycle with 14-Day Lead Time (Fixed Order Quantity)

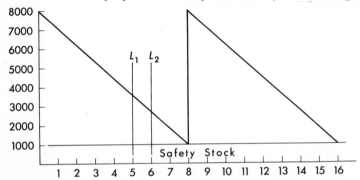

1. Annual sales	52,000 units
2. Average sales	1,000 per week
3. Transit time	14 days
4. Order processing time	7 days
5. Total lead time (14 + 7)	21 days
6. Reorder point (3 weeks' supply)	3,000 units
7. Rail carload shipment	4,000 units
8. Beginning order (3 weeks' demand)	3,000 units
9. Safety stock	1,000 units
10. Maximum inventory (beginning order plus safety stock)	4,000 units
11. EOQ	8,000 units

In Chart 8–6, lead time is shown as 21 days and consists of (1) order processing and (2) transit time. The only term thus far not defined is *review time*. The review period is the interval during which inventory status is reviewed and purchase decisions are made.

In the beginning cycle, the initial EOQ order of 8,000 units plus safety stock of 1000 units is forecast to be sufficient to satisfy the average rate of sales over the next 8-week period. During the first seven days of operation, inventories are periodically reviewed and a commitment made as to order placement. Assuming that the actual sales rate is equal to the forecast, an order is placed at the end of the fifth week to replenish stock in anticipation of the next sales period. It is crucial at this point to review stock position closely, because lead time of 21 days has occurred. Because seven days are required for order processing and 14 days for transportation for a total of 21 days, a delivery of 8,000 units will be made exactly when present stocks are depleted. The order quantity is determined by EOQ methods discussed earlier. Therefore, an order is placed to assure an adequate amount of stock on hand for the next sales period. In cycle one, because forecast and actual demand are equal, no safety stock is withdrawn.

In the next sales cycle, a rapid shift in demand occurs, and the sales rate increases to about 2300 units per week (8,000 units sold in 3.5 weeks). By holding to a reorder point of 4,000 units (R_1 and R_2 in Chart 8–6) an out-of-stock condition will occur. If 4,000 units are on hand at R_2 (including safety stock of 1,000), at a sales rate of 2,300, only a little less than two weeks of start are on hand to support that sales rate. Because lead time is three weeks, an out-of-stock condition will occur at the end of the twelfth week and remain for about two weeks during which back orders must be placed.

However, if a good forecasting system exists and rectifies the changing sales trend as it occurs, the reorder point required to assure no stockouts is at R_3 where stock on hand is just sufficient to cover sales during lead time.

A second alternative, and one usually employed in solving problems of this type, is to complement the basic ordering pattern with a back-up expediting system. Thus, if the reorder point is set at 4,000 units, an out-of-stock condition may be alleviated by speeding up the order cycle, the transportation, or both.

Now consider an order cycle time of 14 days with order processing and transit time reduced to two and five days, respectively. All other conditions remain the same (see Chart 8–7).

Note that safety stocks are reduced because of quicker reorder time, and lower levels of service are required because of that reason. The difference in lead times is measured by L_1 and L_2 in Chart 8–7.

Base stocks remain the same, because they are based upon EOQ requirements. Both cycles are compared and their average inventories are measured in Table 8–12.

Thus, the time dimension of inventory does influence the amount of average inventory in the system. The shorter the cycle time, the lower is the safety stock requirement. Trade-offs in inventory can now be measured in terms of the entire physical distribution mix. However, detailed treatment of the trade-off concept is reserved for another chapter.

Distribution Planning Aspects of Inventory

In physical distribution planning, one additional feature of inventory, not ordinarily found in discussions of the subject, is the geographic impact upon

TABLE 8–12 COMPARISON OF BASE STOCK AND
SAFETY STOCK REQUIREMENTS WITH
VARYING LEAD TIMES

21-day Cycle (units)		14-day Cycle (units)
8,000	EOQ	8,000
4,000	Average Base Stock	4,000
1,000	Safety Stock	500
5,000	Average Inventory	4,500

required inventories. EOQ's and similar analysis primarily provide operating and control systems for a fixed system and generally provide little for use in planning alternative systems designs. Although inventory levels vary with customer service, ordering costs, holding costs, and the like, they also vary significantly with geographical configurations of physical distribution systems, the number of stock locations, and their size.

Considering the impact of inventory in its geographic sense, changes required can be measured in base stock and safety stock as the number of stock locations increases from one to two.

BASE STOCK

Because base stock is defined as the amount of inventory necessary to serve the *average* level of demand, changes in system configuration will have virtually no effect upon base stocks.[7] Taking the demand pattern in Table 8–13 this principle can be demonstrated.

From the table, base stock requirements for the total market are 53. If two warehouses were used to serve the market, average inventory would still require 53 for the total market. Only small fractional differences would account for any variations, and, therefore, would be minimal.

SAFETY STOCK

Safety stock requirements vary with demand fluctuations. Table 8–14 shows a set of demands and forecasts, which indicate safety stock requirements and penalties due to out-of-stock conditions.

For the total market, assuming a 100-percent instock factor (no stockouts), 12 additional units must be stocked for each of the ten weekly periods to have sufficient inventory to cover peak demand. Therefore, total stock requirements for one week are 53 units to meet average demand, and 12 additional

[7]It is assumed here that cycle times are held constant.

TABLE 8–13   CHANGES IN BASE STOCK
AS A FUNCTION OF THE NUMBER OF
STOCK LOCATIONS

	Week	Demand		
		Total Market	Market 1	Market 2
	1	50	40	10
	2	55	5	50
	3	65	45	20
	4	60	20	40
	5	55	35	20
	6	45	10	35
	7	50	40	10
	8	40	10	30
	9	45	35	10
	10	65	10	55
Total	10	530	250	280
Base stock Requirements		53	25	28

TABLE 8–14   INVENTORY REQUIREMENTS
FROM ONE STOCK LOCATION

	Week	Total Market Demand	Forecast	Stock-outs
	1	50	53	0
	2	55	53	2
	3	65	53	12
	4	60	53	7
	5	55	53	2
	6	45	53	0
	7	50	53	0
	8	40	53	0
	9	45	53	0
	10	65	53	12
Total	10	530	N.A.	N.A.
Average		53	N.A.	12

N.A. — Not applicable.

units for safety stock, or a total inventory requirement of 65. Twelve units
of safety stock must be maintained each week, because demand fluctuations
are unpredictable as to time and occurrence. Average inventory per week
will be calculated as $\frac{1}{2}$ of 53 + 12 or 38.5 units.

TABLE 8–15   INVENTORY REQUIREMENTS FROM TWO STOCK LOCATIONS

		Location I			Location II	
Week	Demand	Forecast	Stockouts	Demand	Forecast	Stockouts
1	40	25	15	10	28	0
2	5	25	0	50	28	22
3	45	25	15	20	28	0
4	20	25	0	40	28	12
5	35	25	10	20	28	0
6	10	25	0	35	28	7
7	40	25	15	10	28	0
8	10	25	0	30	28	2
9	35	25	10	10	28	0
10	10	25	0	55	28	27
Total 10	250	N.A.	N.A.	280	N.A.	N.A.
Average	25	N.A.	15	28	N.A.	27

N.A. — Not applicable.

Table 8–15 now shows a distribution of the same demands, assuming that two warehouses are used for logistical support.

In Table 8–15, again base stocks remain static at 53 (28 + 25). However, stockouts increase in market 1 to 15 (from 12) and to 27 (from 12) in market II. Table 8–16 summarizes total inventory requirements needed to assure a 100-percent instock function in the two-warehouse system.

TABLE 8–16   STOCK REQUIRED FOR TWO LOCATIONS

	Base Stocks	Safety Stock	Total Stock	Average Stock
Market I	25	15	40	27.5
Market II	28	27	55	41.0
Total	53	42	95	68.5

Recalling that a one-location system required a total inventory of 65 units, a two-location system raises this to 95 units, or about a 50-percent increase. The more meaningful measure (average inventory) for a two-point system compared with a one-point system rises from 38.5 units to 68.5 units, or a virtual doubling of average inventory. Of course, the data show that *all* of the increased requirements arise from additional inventories required in the safety stock category.

Generalized Model of Inventory Requirements as a Function of the Number of Stock Locations.   It is possible to generalize the relationship of stock requirements to the number of locations. Because base stocks do not enter the calculations in any meaningful way, due to their static nature, safety

CHART 8–8   Stock Requirements in Relation to Number of Stock Locations

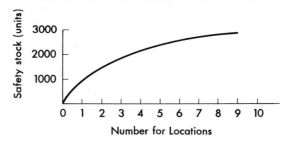

stocks (SS) exclusively account for the increases. Chart 8–8 develops a generalized illustration of the relation of safety stock and the number of stock locations. In actual cases, safety stock increases at a decreasing rate as the number of stock locations increases. This general relationship is mathematically expressed as:

$$SS_n = \frac{SS_1(n)}{\sqrt{n}}$$

where:

SS_n = safety stock for n locations
n = number of locations
SS_1 = safety stock for one location

Assuming the following values:

$$SS_1 = 1,000 \text{ units}$$
$$n = 100$$

then:

$$SS_n = \frac{1,000(100)}{\sqrt{100}}$$
$$SS_n = 10,000 \text{ units}$$

Therefore, increasing the number of locations from 1 to 100 will tend to increase safety stock from 1,000 units to 10,000 units, or a 100-percent increase. In actual cases, it is necessary to calculate required safety stock for each location due to individual market sales variations.

Referring back to the curve in Chart 8–8, the impact of safety stocks with reference to the number of locations appears greater when the numbers of warehouses under consideration is small. Thus, the greatest impact upon safety stock requirements will appear when moving from one location to two. Much lesser increases are involved as the number of stock locations increases.

Summary

Inventory control is regarded as a key element in efficient planning. Without a physical distribution orientation, management planning tends to omit the geographic and time-related questions of inventory. Too often, inventory control is viewed as an operational control tool and not as a business-planning device.

Through the perspective of physical distribution, inventory planning supplements control in its traditional sense. Through this method, the impact of changing systems of doing business can be measured in terms of their inventory impact.

As shall be demonstrated later, inventory planning in physical distribution plays a key role in systems designs through its impact upon geographical and time dimensions.

Discussion Questions

1. How does the "make-or-buy" decision relate to inventory control?

2. Are accounting records useful in determining inventory levels? How?

3. What are the elements of lead time?

4. What is the purpose of maintaining safety stocks?

5. How could a firm condition its customers to expect stockouts with their resultant delay in delivery and to still maintain their business?

6. Why might a firm choose to use exponential smoothing rather than regular trend methods in helping to establish its sales forecasts?

7.

Demand in Units	Frequency
50	3
75	4
100	9
125	18
150	9
175	4
200	3

Given the above data, what is average demand and what safety stock is needed to be sure that 95 percent of all customer demands are met?

8. Describe ABC Analysis, Critical Value Analysis, and ABC Critical Value Analysis. Which method would you select? Why?

9. How is inventory reduced? Why? Demonstrate the affect of order-cycle time on inventory levels?

10. What is EOQ? How is it important to inventory management? Where do the "trade-offs" occur in inventory management?

11. Distinguish between a fixed order quantity and fixed order time inventory system.

12. Calculate the EOQ for the following data: (a) Ordering costs are $25, (b) Annual sales are 10,500 units, (c) Interest cost per unit is $.30. Find the EOQ if order costs increase to $30. Find the EOQ if annual sales increase to 12,000 units. Find the EOQ if interest costs are reduced to $.10.

13. Do purchase discounts and transportation costs affect the calculation of EOQ? How?

14. In the DEF Corporation, the costs associated with various stockout consequences are as follows: Back Order: $10, Lost Sale: $30, Lost Customer: $1000.
The probabilities associated with these situations are 80, 19, and 1%, respectively. In the following chart, DEF Corporation has made some calculations to determine the inventory level. Find the product loss and the proper inventory level.

Number of Units Sold in One Month	Inventory Carrying Costs Added	Number of Orders Filled	Stockout Costs Saved
400–449	125	10	
450–499	125	8	
500–549	125	5	
550–599	125	2	
600–649	125	1	
650–699	125	0	

Describe those factors affecting proper inventory control.

Appendix 8A
UNIT INVENTORY CONTROL SYSTEM

Unit inventory control, as a technique separate from dollar inventory, was developed to provide information on the physical characteristics of merchandise (e.g., size, weight, number, and color). It performs this function by controlling inventory levels with respect to minimizing out-of-stock situations and by minimizing the amount of capital tied up in inventory. Either out-of-stock or excessive inventory situations can lead to unnecessary expenses for a firm from the standpoint of lost sales and good will or poor utilization of invested capital.

As a management tool, unit inventory control shows merchandise turnover, purchase requirements, and the amount of stock on hand at any time without taking a physical inventory. Inventory status reports can be generated on demand or periodically in most systems.

There are four major reasons for limited usage of unit control systems:

1. Many executives believe that the costs of setting it up and maintaining it exceed the benefits that are received from the information it supplies.

2. Because of a failure to decide exactly what is the primary purpose of the system, necessary data may not be generated but a large amount of superfluous reports can be produced.
3. Smaller operations on many instances believe that it is too large, complicated, and expensive for them to utilize.
4. For some enterprises, there is no question that it is too complicated and expensive; it requires a period of time for set-up that may be considered too long; it requires precise record keeping if it is to function correctly so that it provides the information it is designed to; and for sales organizations that sell a large variety of low-priced items it may be unfeasible — examples would include hardware wholesalers, variety stores, and notions departments (this has been reduced to a large extent by EDP applications that will be discussed later in this paper).

EDP GENERAL

Data processing systems can be separated into two major categories: listed, or library, programs and unlisted programs. Library programs are those which have been developed in such a way that they provide control over an individual problem, such as inventory control, bookkeeping, payroll, purchasing, or other area, and can be applied in the majority of situations where problems arise in these regions of activity.

Unlisted programs are those designed specifically for a particular problem in an individual business firm. These programs can be so extensive as to cover the entire operations of a system, or limited to a point where they handle only a small segment. With either type of program, unit inventory control systems have procedures for the regular processing of transactions and for the comparison of stock status with objectives set by management. Optimum inventory levels are calculated for each item in stock, a process that considers a large number of variables — desired level of customer service, past demands on inventory, past forecast error, lead times, discount structures, lot sizes, and others — that it would be impossible to do this without the speed and accuracy provided by a computer. Normally included in the process of setting unit control is the simulation of demand data and periodic management review of policy implications.

Computer programs are intended to optimize the amount of capital invested in inventories, to achieve a high level of customer service, and to review inventory and place purchase orders at the correct time. Some programs are part of other systems or include as part of their own system other procedures that provide for billing, payroll, and so forth.

For the remainder of this discussion, three programs of the listed, or library type, are examined. These are IBM's IMPACT, designed for both retail and wholesale operations; NCR's REACT, concerned primarily with retail operations; and, Honeywell's PROFIT, which is aligned toward the distribution phases of business. These three systems are representative of this type of data-processing aid which is available today to aid in unit control.

Impact — International Business Machines Corporation. To assist wholesale and retail operations in obtaining more positive control over inventory, IBM has developed IMPACT — Inventory Management And Control Techniques — a standardized approach to the inventory problem. Essentially it allows management to select the policies best suited to its objectives, and it optimizes inventory investment to produce a scientifically balanced inventory. The performance of the firm is measured against standards derived from management's policies and the level of service and the investment on inventory are continuously monitored.

There are four basic steps on the implementation and running of an IMPACT system. In order, these are simulation, forecasting, the setting of decision rules, and control subsystems.

Simulation, with its normally attendant advantages and disadvantages, is concerned with finding the answers to the following types of questions:

What level of investment is necessary to provide a given level of service?
What level of service can be achieved, given a specific level of inventory investment?
How frequently should stock be reviewed?
What is the best ordering strategy?
What will be the result of a reduction on lead time?

The second step on the procedure, forecasting, uses mathematical functions that describe patterns of demand with probability. IMPACT uses six basic demand patterns — constant, seasonal, trend, trend-seasonal, low volume, and "lumpy-demand" — with adaptive smoothing of past data applied to obtain its forecast.

Decision rules are concerned with the two basic questions of inventory control — when to order and how much to order. The system uses probability with statistical procedures in the determination of the order rules. Considerations that are included on the when-to-order question are lead time, the number of days between inventory review, forecast sales per unit of time, forecast error, and the desired level of customer service. The how-much-to order decision rule is based on whether merchandise is staple, fashion, or end-of season; for staple merchandise the decision rule is of the order-up-to-level type where the computer calculates the order quantity needed plus the amount of stock on hand to bring inventory up to a specified level.

The control subsystems implement management policies in performing traditional functions of inventory control. Included in these are total department control and reporting, the maintenance of complete and up-to-date data in inventory, and the preparation of purchase orders. In addition, IMPACT makes report generation easier, monitors departmental performance, provides comprehensive error detection, and has a provision for feedback to forecasting that includes the capture of data from multiple sources.

Profit — Honeywell, Incorporated. PROFIT — Programmed Reviewing, Ordering and Forecasting Inventory Techniques — is Honeywell's entry in programmed inventory control. It is one part of their management information and control system, which also includes order-processing applications and accounting procedures.

PROFIT handles the routine activities such as reviewing inventory records, determining when to reorder, and automatically producing purchase orders to relieve the buyer of these activities and to provide him with more and better information for decisions that require his judgment and experience. The program also uses joint replenishment techniques, determines economic order quantities, schedules inbound freight, and balances purchasing and inventory carrying costs to achieve the best total cost for the inventory function.

Management sets the desired customer service level, and PROFIT provides the optimum inventory to support this level. The system uses exponential smoothing (exponentially weighted moving average of past demands) in setting up its forecasts and maintains safety stock proportional to the level of expected forecast error. The variables that are considered in this ordering and scheduling function include past demand, buying costs, inventory carrying costs, lead times, item and vendor discounts, CL and LCL requirements, vendor minimums and maximums, single or joint item ordering, warehouse and storage costs, shelf life, and package size.

There are four steps to implementing PROFIT: initialization, simulation, installation, and production operation. Initialization consists of the processing of various data to determine what forecast model to use, the parameters for use on simulation, and the initial values for inventory control. In the simulation state, the program uses simulation techniques to discover the effects of various buying policies on inventory levels and costs to determine the "best" levels for various products. The installation stage refers to the installation of automatic data-processing equipment. The production operation phase is the one where the user begins to gain information and assistance from PROFIT. It generates new sales forecasts, calculates order points, allocates orders, reports on customer service levels, provides automatic stock status reports and exceptions, and prints purchase orders.

React — The National Cash Register Company.[1] REACT — Register Enforced Automated Control Technique — has been developed for retail operations that use a check-out system of operation. It provides information on a number of business functions including sales recording, inventory levels, management reports, accounts payable, payroll, and accounts receivable.

REACT was designed to provide an automated system for inventory replenishment of basic stock items. It also provides status reports, on mer-

[1]A flow diagram of the REACT system is presented in Chart 9–4, p. 234.

chandise that is not directly under unit control. The computer system prints purchase orders to bring inventory up to predetermined levels with consideration being given to a number of variables including order pack, lead time, discounts, economic order quantities, and shipping costs.

The first step in REACT is the classification of merchandise within each department to provide the base for securing account information and reports. Classifications, when established, are numbered, and a color and size code is prepared. These numbers are then used as the basis of product identification on all purchase orders and other documents, including inputs to data-processing programs.

With a proper classification system established, the buyer notes the number assignment as to size, category, type, and any other details important to each item of merchandise. Purchase orders can then be sent to the accounts payable department for vendor numbering and, along with the coded classifications, all information is recorded on an alpha-numeric bookkeeping machine equipped with punched paper tape for input into the data-processing system. With all the necessary information on each item permanently stored in the processing system, it is always available for fully automatic reports of any type desired. When merchandise arrives at either store or distribution center, it is simply tagged and marked to show the department, price, item number, color, and size.

NCR offers two language mediums in its automated merchandise reporting, both of which are developed by the register at the point of sale. The first is a punched paper tape, designed for use as the direct input for the computer. The second medium is also used directly as input for the computer, but it can also be read visually and is called optical tape.

CHAPTER 9 Information Flows and

Physical Distribution Communications

THE design and control of information flows is one of the most critical responsibilities of physical distribution management.[1] The quality and speed of information within the logistics system facilitates integration of all physical distribution activity centers of the firm. On the negative side, a poor communications network, which allows order bottlenecks or information errors to go undetected, can create havoc on the balance required for an effective physical distribution system. Such errors or bottlenecks tend to amplify and distort stock-out problems, production schedules, and inventory accumulation patterns.

Further, it is axiomatic that the more sophisticated the physical distribution system the more vulnerable it is to any internal or external communication malfunction. Take for example, a zero-response inventory system where an order is placed after the item is sold for delivery the next morning. In such a system there is no safety stock at the retail level. The shoe retailer, for example, stocks one pair of men's brown wing tips in size 11D. When this pair of shoes is sold, an order for another pair is placed. The retailer is out of stock of this particular size and style until his replacement order is filled from the replenishment point. In such a system the lag between sale (impulse) and order fulfillment (response) must be of short time duration or prolonged out-of-stock will exist at the retail level. In this type of inventory system, the only way to insure rapid response is through an efficient communications network. Companies that use zero-response type of inventory systems frequently rely on high-speed store-to-distribution center communi-

[1]Philip H. Thurston, "Who Should Control Information System?," *Harvard Business Review*, November-December, 1962.

cations. If there is a communications breakdown either through a mechanical failure, transmission error, or bottleneck, the results can be serious, because delay increases the probability of an out-of-stock at the retail store and possible amplification of these problems throughout the supplier channel.

Increasing information technology, on the one hand, and management's recognition of information potential, on the other, has given impetus to a corporate philosophy of total information systems. An information system may be defined as "An integrated corporate intelligence system designed to permit management by exception, based on timely information, randomly available, and guided by rigorously determined relationships and decision rules."[2]

Hence, when discussing a logistics information requirement it should be recognized that typically it is part of a total information system. One author identified three major elements of a typical management information system: (1) logistics or physical distribution information system, (2) financial information system, and (3) personnel information system.[3] He stated further that each of these major elements can be broken down further into subsystems. In the case of the physical distribution information system such subsystems might include procurement, a raw material inventory control, production scheduling and control, finished goods inventory control, and order processing.[4] Additional views of management information systems are demonstrated by Singer's newly reorganized system (Chart 9–1) and the E. F. MacDonald Stamp Company (Chart 9–2).

The purpose of this chapter is twofold. First, it relates information requirements and the process of communication information to objectives of physical distribution management. Second, it presents a framework for analyzing and implementing a logistics information system.

SOME GENERAL CONSIDERATIONS AFFECTING LOGISTICS INFORMATION SYSTEMS DESIGN

Each communications network is designed and functions to serve a particular need of an individual firm. However, certain considerations to some degree influence the functioning of all communications systems. They are (1) system compatibility and balance, (2) systems complexity, (3) separation of physical flow and information flow, and (4) external versus internal information flows.

[2] Roger Christian, "The Total Systems Concept," from a speech delivered before the 14th Annual International Systems Meeting, October, 1961, p. 8.

[3] John Dearden, "How to Organize Information Systems," *Harvard Business Review*, March–April, 1965, pp. 65–73.

[4] John Dearden, *Computers in Business Management* (Chicago: Dow Jones-Irwin, Inc., 1966), p. 122.

CHART 9–1   Singer's Management Information System

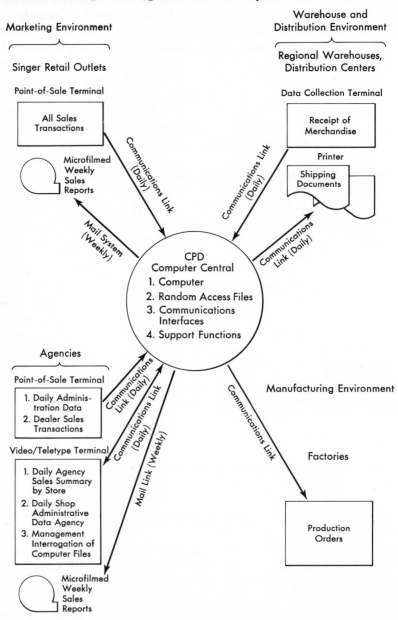

SOURCE: *Sales Management*, May 1, 1967, p. 33.

System Compatibility and Balance.   The communications network of the firm must be balanced with the other components of the physical distribution system. This is true for all links in the communications network as well as between communications and other activity centers such as transportation

CHART 9–2   Total Information System — E. F. MacDonald Stamp Company

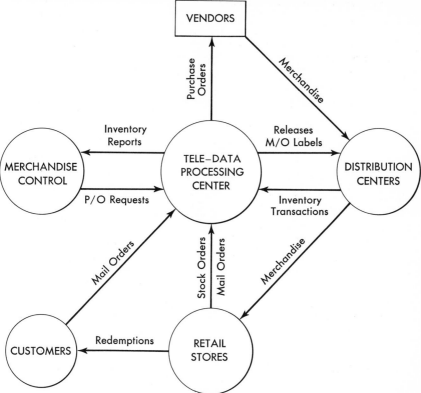

SOURCE: Donald J. Bowersox, "Total Information Systems in Logistics," *Transportation and Distribution Management* (October 1964), p. 23

and distribution warehousing. A logistical information system cannot realize its full potential as a management tool unless it is balanced and compatible with the system.

For example, there is marginal value in arranging for customer orders to be relayed from a sales office by direct communication if there is a two-day bottleneck in key punching a customer order for computer input. Similarly, in the zero-response example noted earlier, the costs of store-to-distribution-center direct communication hookup are probably not justified unless coordinated with other activity centers in the physical distribution system.

System Complexity.   The communcations network grows almost geometrically in complexity as new elements are added to the system. Where one retailer is communicating with one customer and one manufacturer-supplier, the system is fairly simple. If the system includes different products, distinct classifications of customers and multiple suppliers, the communications problem becomes more complicated.

CHART 9-3 Product, Parts, Service and Communications Flow for a Large Manufacturer of Household Appliances

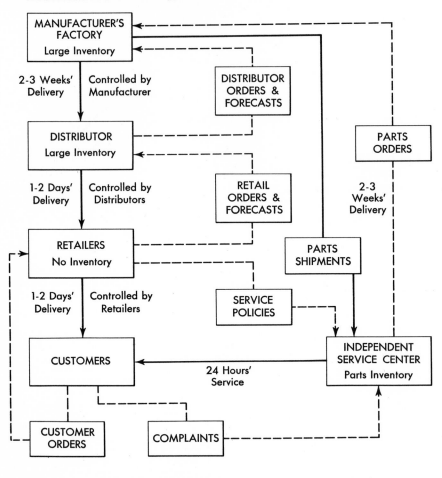

─────────── Products, Parts, or Service Flow
─ ─ ─ ─ ─ ─ Lines of Communication

An added dimension of complexity can be found in the split control of the physical distribution channel. It is much easier to structure information flows in a channel where a firm owns or controls all channel elements. In the Singer and MacDonald examples, management can require reports on a regular basis since all channel members are under direct control. The opposite situation is illustrated in Chart 9-3. In the case of the appliance company the distributors are independent businessmen and cannot be forced to remit information regarding sales, inventories, or any other physical distribution related information. In the case where the channel is not integrated or controlled from one source, it is necessary to educate all channel members on the mutual value of efficient information flows.

Separation of Physical and Information Flow. There is usually a substantial difference between the physical channel for a product and the information channel. In Chart 9–3 the flow of products, parts, service, and communications are graphically presented. Note carefully that this exhibit is a simplified version of the actual physical distribution system. In addition to the segment presented, the firm has a substantial private brand business with a split channel of distribution, which results in an even more complex communications. Chart 9–3 also does not include the relationship to production or to over 300 major vendors of transportation, raw materials, subassemblies, and supplies. If the full range of flows noted above were graphically illustrated, it would require a separate systems manual, which the company has developed to depict these complex relations.

However, for purposes of illustrating the divergence between channels of communications and channels of product, parts and service flow, the chart is descriptive. First, there is a clear split between the communications channel and the physical distribution channel of the product. Second, there is an equally apparent split in the control of the channel. That is, no segment of the channel controls all of the communication or all of the physical movement function. A third factor is the variable time lags, which are controlled by different members in the channel. These factors are more or less typical of most businesses and dramatically illustrate the role of information and communications in physical distribution management.

External vs. Internal Information Flows. A distinction is often made between internal and external flows in an information system. External flows are those that are either directed from an external source to the firm (customer order) or from the firm to an external point (shipping instructions to a carrier). Internal flows are those that begin and terminate within the company (requisition to purchasing or warehouse shipment notice). Although the internal-external division of information flows provides a good perspective for understanding the role of communications, an analysis of information flows by principal linkage is more helpful in systems analysis.[5]

The physical distribution information system has essentially four links in the achievement of communications' objectives. The first link consists of inbound communication in the form of customer orders. The second link in the system is integration of this information with other corporate activities affected by customer order. The third link is the command function, which directs order fulfillment. The fourth link is the control phase wherein management establishes and monitors feed-back to insure desired system performance.

In Chart 9–4 a graphic flow chart of National Cash Registers' Register Enforced Automated Control Technique (REACT) is illustrated. Although

---

[5]For a descriptive and complete development of this concept see William Lazer and Eugene J. Kelley, *Managerial Marketing: Perspectives and Viewpoints*, 3rd ed. (Chicago: R. D. Irwin, Inc., 1967), pp. 526–532.

CHART 9–4   National Cash Register's REACT System
COMPUTER INPUT SYSTEM

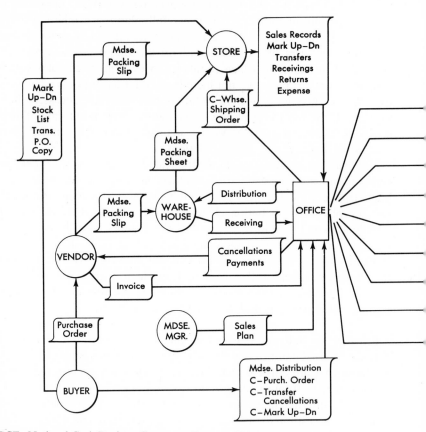

SOURCE: National Cash Register Company, Dayton, Ohio.

originally designed to illustrate a retail inventory management system, Chart 9–4 illustrates the type of linkages that could be analyzed in developing an effective system of information flow. By utilizing this type of analysis, it is also possible to detect bottlenecks in the system where delays are caused and where corrective action should be implemented.

THE ROLE OF COMMUNICATIONS IN PHYSICAL DISTRIBUTION MANAGEMENT

The communications network generally speaking has the same role as the other activity centers of the physical distribution system. All exist in integrated performance to balance customer service and distribution cost. However, the

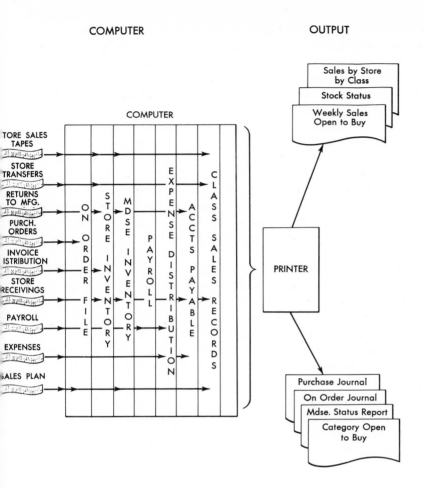

method by which a communications network achieves these objectives is somewhat different from the other physical distribution activity centers.

In addition to the general functions of the physical distribution system, the communication system has three managerial functions: (1) order processing, (2) systems control and monitoring, and (3) internal communications.

Order Processing. The information system should provide for effective and efficient order processing. A managerially designated maximum of speed and a minimum of error are objectives of the order processing procedure.

Any increase in order processing speed generally results in reduced inventories throughout the system. The effect of a decrease in order processing cycle results in a decrease in reaction time to a customer order and consequently a lowering of systems safety stocks. In general, if a supplier can reduce order processing time from ten days to five days, he can also reduce lead time inventories. In this respect, there is a cost trade-off between increased communications cost (for example, teleprocessing) and decreased inventories.

However, as safety stocks are reduced and the system is brought into more delicate balance, it becomes more vulnerable to any communication or information malfunction.

A number of methods can be used to detect errors in order transmission and insure accuracy of data. Mechanical detection devices will make consistency checks in the transmission of data.[6] A computer can be programmed to provide review by exception of any orders which exceed certain established ranges in quantity or cost. The computer can also be programmed to check cost extension, product codes, and other order details. In general, it could be stated that the more times a piece of information is handled, the greater is the chance of error in transmission. This is particularly true where manual transmission of information occurs.

In summary, the following are three principles of order processing. First, time span for order processing should be as consistent as possible, considering the risks of systems malfunction and consequent stock-out problems. Second, order processing transmission should be as direct as possible with a minimum of changes in order form and transmission relays. Third, wherever possible, customer orders should be transmitted by mechanical rather than by manual means to assure a minimum of human error in transmission.

System Control and Monitoring.   The systems control and evaluation function of the physical distribution information system may be subdivided into two subtasks. The first task is a command function, and the second is a monitoring function.

After a customer's order has been processed and order documentation completed, including inventory allocation, credit check, and any information storage, the system must prepare shipping directions. The shipment order can be both internal and external. Internal nonlogistical communications are discussed below. Within the physical distribution system appropriate instructions must be directed to distribution centers and common carriers (external) in order to insure proper order fulfillment. This command function can either be performed automatically through an integrated data processing system, wherein inventories are automatically updated and shipping instructions prepared and released, or it can be done manually either through verbal or written instructions.

The monitoring function is an extremely important aspect of the physical distribution information system and physical distribution management re-

---

[6]E. Jerome McCarthy and J. A. McCarthy, *Integrated Data Processing Systems* (New York: John Wiley & Sons, Inc., 1966).

sponsibility. If the physical distribution information system is used as a monitoring device, management must establish specific systems objectives insuring feedback. Feedback is the return of information for management review, regarding all distribution activities which require monitoring. These activities always relate to some aspect of customer service or cost of system performance. It is one thing to state a customer service level of two-day delivery for 95 percent of the orders and another to make certain that this target level has been achieved. A multiplant or multiproduct supplier will typically not review each individual delivery to each customer but rather design a review on an exceptions basis. Standards might be established to allow plus or minus one-day delivery deviation from programmed customer service levels. The only items reviewed are those that exceed the upper or lower limits of this range.

A similar type of review procedure can be designed to evaluate, on a continuous basis, vendors, transportation suppliers, back orders, and damaged merchandise. Exception reports from physical distribution monitoring can also be transmitted to other functional areas of the firm. For example, a listing of warehouse shipments expressed as turnover rates over time might be of interest to purchasing or marketing in evaluating suppliers or customers.

Another principal advantage of physical distribution systems monitoring is its usefulness in identifying developing trends. Shifts in color preferences and sizes, and shifts in regional demand and competitive actions can also be identified by closely observing movement within the physical distribution system. By proper reviewing and evaluating this information and relaying it to decision points within the firm, a more accurate reaction to unanticipated or uncontrollable factors in the marketplace can result. It provides the firm with a flexible management tool with which informed adjustments can be made to the total marketing program of the firm.

One important end result of physical distribution system monitoring is what might be termed *production leveling*. Both timely communication and a systems monitoring design that facilitates management review of emerging trends contribute to better production and distribution scheduling. The net effect of systems monitoring in this case is to reduce amplification and distortion in the system.

An illustration is presented of amplification in Chart 9–5. The chart graphically illustrates the interrelationship between sales, stocks at various distribution levels, and production output. Some assumptions on time lags and functional relationships in the system are made, and the simulated impacts of different variables in the system are presented. In Chart 9–5 the assumption is made that a sales increase of 10 percent occurs in January. This in turn peaks out as a 16 percent increase in distributors' orders from retailers.

The entire chart indicates the importance of time lags in amplifying inventory and production requirements of the firm. It should be noted that

CHART 9–5 Response of a Simulated Production-Distribution System to a Sudden 10 Percent Increase in Sales at the Retail Level.

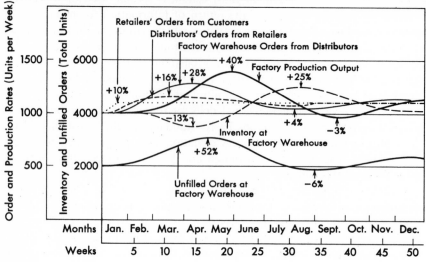

SOURCE: Jay W. Forrester, "Industrial Dynamics," *Harvard Business Review*, July-August, 1958, p. 43.

basically the same type of process, but reversed, would occur if sales dropped 10 percent in early January.

For purposes of this discussion, Chart 9–5 illustrates the vital role of timely communications between production, distribution, and marketing. If the marketing department develops a program that will result in a 10-percent increase in sales, it is important to assure physical distribution support of the program. Any anticipated shift in sales that is not carefully coordinated with production and distribution could result in lost sales due to stockouts or higher costs due to overtime and expedited shipments. Careful monitoring of the physical distribution system can reduce these amplifications through rapid relay of customer orders into adjusted production schedules.

Internal Communications. The third function of the physical distribution information system is to insure a timely and accurate flow of information to functional areas outside of physical distribution. Depending on the company, useful information can be transferred to most of the functional areas in the typical firm by a physical distribution information system. For example, purchasing should be notified when raw material requirements drop below reorder points. In some companies, this can be done automatically through computer review of raw material inventory and automatic computer printout purchase orders. In addition, production scheduling can be linked directly to customer orders and warehouse shipments. Accurate transmission of data allows for production leveling and a more orderly overall production process.

In addition to these key areas, the physical distribution information system can provide useful data to marketing, sales, and finance. Marketing and sales can receive sales analysis data as noted above, as well as immediate order status and market evaluation data. As noted in Chapter 4, it is most often desirable to tie a physical distribution information system into a georeference information base. Finance and accounting are very much concerned with anticipated accounts receivable, as well as investment commitments in raw material inventory and finished goods inventory.

In summary, the physical distribution system has an impact on many other functions within the business organization. A design must be developed which will insure adequate two-way communication — between physical distribution and other functional areas of the firm.

Planning and Implementing a Data Communications System[7]

When a firm accepts the philosophy of information management, it is faced with the problem of designing a data communications system. The data communications system is the actual physical method by which information is transmitted. The design of a data communications system is a never-ending management task. Alterations in information inputs and communications technology must be constantly reviewed in order to maintain the most effective communications system for the individual firm.

Chart 9–6 shows a schematic diagram of the steps involved in building a data communications system. Each of these steps is discussed in brief detail.

IDENTIFY AND DEFINE PROBLEM AND DESCRIBE OBJECTIVES

The establishment of a data communications system for physical distribution management may have a wide variety of objectives, which in many cases overlap with other objectives of the firm. The primary objective of a physical distribution system is to provide the best customer service level at the lowest possible total cost. Both the overall information system and the data communications can facilitate the physical distribution function in the following ways.

First, this may be done by shortening the order processing time through elimination of time delays in the system. This in turn leads to a reduction in inventory holding costs with no sacrifice in customer service levels. Second,

---

[7]This section draws heavily on Edgar G. Gentle, Jr., ed., *Data Communications in Business: An Introduction*, published for the American Telephone and Telegraph Company by Publishers Service Company, New York, 1965.

**CHART 9–6   A Summary of the Steps Involved in Planning a Data
Communications System**

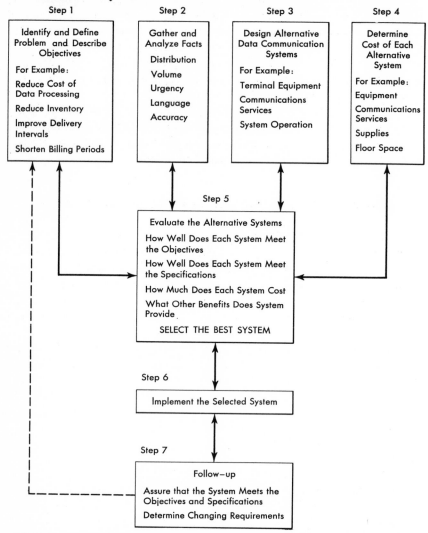

SOURCE: Gentle, Edgar G., Jr., *Data Communications in Business*, American Telephone
and Telegraph Company, New York, 1965, p. 79. Copyright © 1965 by the American
Telephone and Telegraph Co.

by improving customer service level management can immediately identify
any deviation from standards of customer service and take corrective action;
third, it may improve distribution planning by having available timely, accurate, and reliable information for short-run and long-range planning purposes; fourth, it may improve customer relations through facilitating rapid
and reliable communications flow on matters of mutual interest. Finally,
it may improve the profit position of the company by reducing accounts

receivable, by production leveling, and generally by providing rapid and reliable information required by other departments of the firm.

Generally speaking, the emergence of a managed information and communication system often results from a problem that has occurred in the business. Such problems as order errors, delayed shipments, noncompetitive service levels, and excessive back order can cause management to re-evaluate its information handling procedures. When the analyst has determined the probable cause of the problem and has defined his objectives, he can then proceed to the next step in building a data communications system.

GATHER AND ANALYZE THE DATA

Information to be moved within a system has five basic characteristics: (1) structure of information flow, (2) volume, (3) urgency, (4) language, and (5) accuracy. Before a data communications system can be designed, each of these characteristics must be analyzed in depth.

Structure of Information Flow.   The sources of information input and the structure of information flow must be identified as it currently exists in the company. For example, sales orders can be generated directly from customer, from manufacturer's salesmen, from distributors, and so forth. Sales orders could be generated by salesmen within the district and accumulated at district level and again at regional level before transmission to the home office. It is often helpful to construct a chart that illustrates the two-way flow of communications.

In Chart 9–7,[8] the physical distribution information flow for a relatively small company is illustrated. From the chart, it can be noted that the company has a centralized information system with most of the information flowing out of the headquarters office. Regardless of the degree of complexity, almost all communications systems can be broken down into one or more of four basic patterns: (1) one point to one other point, (2) one point to many other points, (3) many points to one point, and (4) many points to many other points.

A "one-point-to-one-point" pattern is the most basic communications pattern. The flow of information could be in one direction only, in both directions alternatively or in both simultaneously. The first alternative is termed *one-way;* the second, *half-duplex;* and the third, *duplex* in communications technology.

---

[8]The chart is designed to depict a two-way flow of communications between spatially separated points. There is communication of the nature described in this section within each of the areas. For example, communications patterns exist within the headquarters office.

"Communications," *Modern Materials Handling,* January, 1967, p. 49–53.

Marshall McLuhan and John McLaughlin, *Information Technology and Survival of the Firm* (Chicago: Dow Jones-Irwin, Inc., 1966).

CHART 9–7   Information Flow Format for a Small Company

From \ To	Headquarters	Factory	Factory Warehouse	Field Distribution Center	Sales Office A	Sales Office B
Headquarters		Order & Production Schedules	Shipment Releases	Shipment Directions	Administrative Messages	Administrative Messages
Factory	Production Reports		Shipment Notices	Shipment Notices		
Factory Warehouse	Stock Status	Shipment Receipt		Order Status	Order Status	Order Status
Field Distribution Center	Orders		Shipment Receipt		Order & Shipment Status	Order & Shipment Status
Sales Office A	Orders			Inquiry on Orders		
Sales Office B	Orders			Inquiry on Orders		

The "one point to many other points" is a communications pattern where one central location will transmit information to many other points. For example, a physical distribution system where all data processing is centralized would likely have this pattern of communication. A situation where the centralized source initiates the message to outlying points is also an example of this type of communication system.

The third type of communication flow, "many points to one point," is probably best typified by an inquiry system to a centralized data source where calls are initiated outside the system.

The fourth and most complex communication pattern is the "many-point to-many-point" system. In this system, every point in the system can communicate with every other point in the system. However, as a practical consideration, most of these systems have switching centers, which allow for temporary connections rather than permanent connections between points in the system. Many companies have more than one system in operation to suit the particular needs of a division or department.

Volume of Information.   The volume of information transmitted in a system has a direct impact on ultimate systems design. The analyst must design a system with the capacity to handle adequate loads but without expensive excess capacity.

The volume of information within the current communications system must be analyzed if a more effective system is to be designed. This usually involves drawing a scientifically selected sample of actual messages at all points within the system. The sample should be drawn so as to eliminate any bias in message sending or receiving patterns. After the sample is selected, the following information should be collected from each sampled message: (1) origin and destination; (2) length, including all additional characters (for example, spaces) necessary to send message; (3) filing time or time originator wanted to send the message; and (4) charges and other information relevant to the individual firm.

Urgency of Information. If it is critical that information be transmitted at a certain rate and at a certain time, the system must be built to accommodate this requirement. However, it is usually the volume of information rather than the urgency of information which is the prime determinant of communications system design. Priority messages are normally best accommodated on an exceptions basis.

Language of the Information. The term *language* is used in two different ways in communications. First, it is used to describe the physical form of the information. For example, the physical form could be handwritten, magnetic tape, microfilm, punched paper tape, and so on. The second use of the word language refers to the code used to record the information. Usually, if the message is in different media such as punched cards and punched paper tape, the code language used will also be different.

When an analyst begins to design a communication system, he must pay careful attention to language compatibility within the system. Although it is possible to convert data, for example, punched paper tape to cards, this adds both time and cost to the system.

Accuracy of the Information. In a communications system, errors can occur in either the terminal equipment or the transmission line. Such errors are usually rare and easy to detect.

Equipment errors are normally detected by verification procedures. On the other hand, human errors are more difficult to detect, because they normally occur in a random manner.

In designing a communications system, every effort should be made to insure the accuracy of information. However, there exists a trade-off between the cost of error detection and the expense of an error. It is possible to increase accuracy by (1) moving as close to the source of information generation as possible; (2) decreasing the number of times information must be converted or handled; and (3) taking as much human input as possible out of the system.

DESIGN ALTERNATIVE DATA COMMUNICATIONS SYSTEMS

After the preceding analysis has been completed, alternative data communications systems should be designed. This is generally done by drawing up a sketch of different communications configurations, which meet the required specifications of the system. These charts should show the points of message origin and destination, the communication link between the points and the form of the information at various points in the system.

Using the statistics on volume and flow, it is possible to determine some of the specific equipment which will match the characteristics of information flow.

DETERMINE THE COSTS OF EACH ALTERNATIVE SYSTEM

Usually, five major cost elements must be measured in each data communications system. These expense centers are (1) personnel expense, (2) supplies, (3) space costs, (4) communication channel costs, and (5) equipment costs. The two largest cost items are generally the equipment and channel costs.

The various costs should be reduced to some common denominator for purposes of comparison. A monthly estimated cost is the common denominator often used, because most lease charges are quoted on a monthly basis.

On the basis of this survey, the average daily volume, message size, transmission time, and peak volume patterns can be calculated. A great deal of sampling and classification is required in such a survey.

EVALUATE ALTERNATIVE SYSTEMS

The alternative systems are evaluated in terms of relative costs and benefits. This analysis should be a thorough one, because factors other than direct cost must be analyzed. For example, the future anticipated needs of the company must be taken into account in selecting a system flexible enough to accommodate expansion.

IMPLEMENT THE SELECTED SYSTEM

Prior to actual implementation, a careful plan of the sequence of implementation should be developed. Employees who operate the system should have adequate time for training and becoming familiar with the equipment. Some time for "debugging" equipment, especially in a complex system, should be built into the implementation plan. If the system is large, it may be well to consider a gradual phasing in of the equipment over a period of time.

Depending on the complexity of the system and the critical nature of the data, it is often a good idea to arrange for temporary backup to the system. If any unusual "bugs" should develop in the new system, the backup system could be used until the problem can be identified and corrected.

FOLLOW-UP

After implementation of the system, it is a management responsibility to follow up and insure that the proposed system satisfies the objectives and meets the specifications. Careful attention should be devoted to unanticipated bottlenecks that develop in the system.

As a company's needs change, its requirements for a data communications system will also change. It is a continuing management responsibility to review and evaluate the data communications system. In re-evaluating an operating system, the same type of analysis described in step 1 and step 2 should be performed. If this analysis indicates any significant change in pattern, the remaining part of the analysis should be completed.

Summary

The communications network is the vital link that integrates information flows into total physical distribution planning and control. New information handling technology along with an increased awareness and acceptance of the concept of total information systems has led to a more scientific approach for physical distribution information control.

In addition to providing improved customer service and cost reductions, a communications system can monitor the performance of a physical distribution system. In this respect, the system can be designed to monitor any deviations in customer service levels, in vendor and carrier performance, and in developing trends or patterns in the marketplace. Thus, the communications network becomes a positive management tool in controlling and evaluating on a continuous basis, the overall physical distribution program.

Discussion Questions

1. What is the difference between physical flow and communication systems? What criteria are used to evaluate a physical movement system? A communications system?

2. What is *management by exception*?

3. Should a firm set up a separate system to facilitate the flow of information for managers of physical distribution?

4. In detecting trends, would a firm be able to detect them more quickly if it owned its own retail outlets or if it went through the traditional middlemen? Why?

5. Why is volume rather than urgency normally the prime determinant of communications system design?

6. How could an improvement of the communication system lead to a reduction in accounts receivable for a firm?

7. Would a sales manager have any objections to the use of the sales force as part of the distribution communications system?

CHAPTER 10 Distribution

Warehousing

A DISTRIBUTION warehouse is a specialized fixed facility included in the design of a physical distribution system to accomplish a specific objective. That objective is to provide the desired level of customer order delivery at the lowest total cost. Unless utilization of a distribution warehouse meets this objective, there exists no justification for operation of such a facility.

It is important to fully understand what type of a facility qualifies as a distribution warehouse.[1] The distribution warehouse exists as a physical facility used to complete the process of product line adjustment in the exchange channel.[2] Primary emphasis is placed upon product flow in contrast to storage. Volume shipments are concentrated from supply points at the distribution warehouse in order to realize maximum economies of transportation. Upon arrival, bulk shipments are sorted and grouped into specific assortments for selected wholesale or retail dispersement. The specific mission of a given distribution warehouse determines the range of product assortment handled and the degree of storage performed.

In this chapter, the concept of distribution warehousing is developed in detail with primary development upon historical development and marketing requirements. Next, attention is directed to the geographical positioning of warehouses in the overall distribution system. Location strategy is directly related to the degree of differentiation in product line assortment. The final sections of the chapter are concerned with an elaboration of distribution

---

[1] The name *distribution warehouse* is preferred by the authors. A term commonly used to describe the same type of facility in industrial circles is *distribution center*.

[2] See Chapter 3, p. 47, for a complete discussion of the adjustment process.

warehouse functions, planning, and establishment of operations. The overall objective of the chapter is to introduce the modern concept of distribution warehousing as a vital link in logistics planning.

The Concept of Distribution Warehousing

Product storage has traditionally been an important part of economic activity. In the early stages of American development, the economy was essentially one of individual households serving somewhat as self-sufficient economic units. Consumers performed the function of storage and accepted the attendant risks. For example, meats were stored in smokehouses, and underground storage such as food cellars protected perishable products.

As transportation facilities developed, specialized economic activity began to evolve. Product storage was shifted from the household to retailers, wholesalers, and manufacturers. Early marketing literature indicates the warehouse was initially introduced as a storage unit designed to help satisfy basic marketing processes.[3] Product storage was viewed as an ancillary function required to match supply with erratic demand. Thus, the warehouse was the location for product storage until demand became sufficient to support distribution. The creation of the time utility principle was used to justify this type of economic activity.[4] This tendency to consider storage as merely a required facilitating function generally resulted in criticism of efficiency with little appreciation of the broader distribution spectrum in which storage played a vital role. The warehouse served as a static unit in the product pipeline. The warehouse functions of order filling and reshipment were noted but given little emphasis. Internal management controls and maximum product turnover received little, if any, attention.

Literature of this early era correctly depicted the situation which existed. Firms attempting to effect distribution closure between the point of manufacturing and point of final consumption gave little attention to internal economies. The formation of a rudimentary logistics network was essential for the initial survival of the firm, but little emphasis was placed on qualitative aspects. Engineering efforts were centered on the major problem of this early era, namely, production.

The reported internal operation of early warehouses illustrates the general neglect of efficiency concepts. These warehouses received merchandise by car or truck, which was manually moved to the storage area. The merchandise was then hand-piled in stacks on the floor. When different products were stored in the same warehouse, merchandise was continually lost. Stock

---

[3]Hugh B. Killough, *The Economics of Marketing* (New York: Harper and Brothers, 1933), p. 101.

[4]Theodore N. Beckman and William R. Davidson, *Marketing* Eighth Edition. Copyright © 1967 The Ronald Press Company, New York.

rotation was poorly handled, and products often deteriorated. When orders were received from retailers, selection was made by hand-picking merchandise for placement on carts. These carts were then manually pushed to the shipping area, where the merchandise was reassembled and hand-packed on outbound trucks for delivery.

Because of cheap labor rates, manpower was freely utilized with little consideration of efficiency in space utilization, work methods, or material handling. To sum up, early warehouses despite their shortcomings were necessary to bridge the storage gap between marketing and production.

After World War II, managerial attention shifted toward increasing marketing efficiency. Progressive firms became market-oriented and devoted extensive resources to the determination and satisfaction of customer wants. Increased competition soon forced firms to operate and obtain adequate profits on constantly diminishing margins. Although emphasis continued to be placed upon improved selling techniques, competitive pressures forced attention on cost reduction. Aggressive firms began to critically appraise the distribution structure which had evolved, and gradually management devoted an increasing proportion of time to developing methods of physically serving markets.

General interest in the concept of developing distribution warehouses may be traced to (1) the logistic experience gained from wartime military operations; (2) the realization that strategic location of forward inventories has marketing implications far greater than those traditionally embodied in the warehouse storage concept; and (3) the postwar profit squeeze resulting in part from increasing physical distribution cost.

Management at the intermediate level of distribution was forced to justify the traditional warehouse in the product flow pipeline. Forecasting and production scheduling had improved, reducing the need for extensive inventories. Production processes had been perfected, eliminating long time delays during manufacturing. Seasonal production still demanded storage facilities, but the overall need for storage had been reduced. However, the basic character of the retail order supported the need for warehouse facilities. The retail store, faced with the necessity of stocking a variety of different products, could not gain the advantages of consolidated shipments. Cost of procurement in less-than-quantity shipments made direct ordering largely prohibitive. The need for distribution warehouses capable of satisfying the demand for rapid and economical inventory replenishment became increasingly important. At the wholesale level, the warehouse became a customizing unit for filling retail orders. Numerous alert firms developed integrated warehouse systems capable of providing increased retail service at reduced operating costs.

Improvements in distribution warehousing at the wholesale level soon were adopted by manufacturers selling directly to wholesalers. For manufacturers producing multiple products at many locations, distribution warehousing offered a method of reducing inventory, storage, and handling costs, while at the same time maximizing customer service. A basic stock of all products could be maintained at the warehouse, thereby reducing the need to fill orders at each plant. Utilizing consolidated shipments, products could be transported to the warehouse and then to the customer at lower total expense. Having all products grouped at one point also opened the door for mixed carloads to customers. The mixed carload gained marketing importance because it increased the appeal of manufacturers who could provide this extra service.

For the customer, mixed carloads had two distinct advantages. First, inventories could be reduced because the advantages of consolidation were combined with a number of products in place of only one. Second, slow turn-over products could be economically ordered in smaller quantities. As competition increased, the manufacturer who could provide a mixed carload on 24-hour demand gained a competitive advantage.

The distribution warehouse also offered economies to the manufacturer selling directly to retail outlets. For many firms, storage at the production point with relatively small-lot shipments direct to retailers had been the primary method of distribution. By decreasing costs, while at the same time increasing service, the distribution warehouse offered a way to more efficient distribution.

Distribution Warehouse Location Patterns

This evolution of marketing thought, coupled with the various economic justifications supporting distribution warehouses, helps explain the logic of such distribution points. The warehouse, viewed as a vital link in the dynamics of market logistics, renders service or cost advantages to a firm in a given market segment. The geographic location of a distribution warehouse is controlled by production locations and markets to be penetrated.

Distribution warehouses represent only a segment of a firm's total strategy for creating time and place utility. The dependence of distribution warehouse locations upon manufacturing and retail or customer locations must be visualized. From a total corporate viewpoint, retail or customer locations represent the final point of product distribution. Nested in the center of demand, the final outlet for a firm's product stands at the apex of the total marketing effort. Thus, the distribution center location is subordinated and perhaps only justified to the degree that it increases sales impact at the point of final product transfer.

Manufacturing or plant locations represent the originating point of the value creation process. Over the years, a relatively refined body of knowledge has emerged concerning the location of manufacturing facilities. Today, firms are capable of drawing upon analytical sophistication tempered by sound theory to guide the selection of plant locations offering maximum economic and competitive benefits.[5]

[5] For a review of plant location literature and procedure, see ending appendixes.

Logically, three types of distribution structures evolve when distribution warehouses are adopted. Under Hoover's plant location classification, these may be identified as being market-positioned, production-positioned, or intermediately-positioned.[6]

MARKET-POSITIONED DISTRIBUTION WAREHOUSES

A market-oriented distribution center serves the basic function of inventory replenishment to retail stores and merchandise delivery to consumers. The distribution center, located near ultimate product consumption, affords maximum transport consolidation economies from distant shipping points with relatively short product movements in local delivery. The geographic market area served from a market-oriented distribution center is dependent upon the required speed of inventory replenishment to customers, size of average order, and cost per ton of local delivery.

Market-oriented distribution centers may be retailer-, manufacturer-, independently-owned. The mission of the distribution center will vary, depending upon the ownership arrangement. Retailer-owned distribution centers are designed to serve as break-bulk points for various products purchased from different sources. Because the product line processed through retailer-owned distribution centers is extremely wide, the magnitude of demand for a given product need not be much of the warehouse's total volume.

The average retail store, whether large or small, does not have sufficient demand to order inventory in consolidated quantities directly from manufacturers. Retail product lines, manufactured or processed at widely scattered geographic points, are usually extensive. In order to obtain rapid inventory replenishment of this heterogeneous product line, the retailer normally requires the services of some form of distribution center.

The basic purpose of the distribution warehouse is to consolidate purchases from distant procurement points and replenish inventory to retail outlets. A distribution warehouse strategically located to provide a cost-and-service benefit to retail stores is best located near the outlets it serves. This allows maximum advantages of consolidated shipment with relatively short local delivery. Therefore, retail store location modifies distribution center location.

Good examples of market-oriented distribution warehouses are found in the food industry. The modern food warehouse is typically located near the point of highest sales concentration. At this location, local deliveries are held to a minimum average length of haul. Delivery times determine the proximity of the warehouse to the most distant retail outlet. The Kroger Company, for example, operates two distribution warehouses to serve the Michigan market. If two-day or overnight service were acceptable, one warehouse could satisfy

[6]Edgar M. Hoover, *Location of Economic Activity* (New York: McGraw-Hill Book Co., 1948), p. 35.

demand requirements. In the food industry, generally, maximum local delivery of approximately 150 miles is desirable.

This description of market-positioned distribution warehouses represents one location pattern. The basic point, their location close to the market served, rests upon the need to replenish customer inventory rapidly and the desire to achieve product distribution at lowest cost.

PRODUCTION-POSITIONED DISTRIBUTION WAREHOUSES

A production-oriented distribution warehouse is located close to production plants in order to act as a collection point for many products manufactured at different plants. The fundamental reason for production-oriented distribution warehouses is the manufacturer's desire for maximum service to customers. Quantities of products from each plant are shipped to the collection center from which customer orders are filled.

Upon order receipt, merchandise is shipped in the mixture necessary to satisfy customer requirements. Location strategically located to manufacturing plants allows such mixed carloads to move to customer locations at consolidated transport rates. Under carload conditions, a customized order may be shipped to a customer faster than smaller quantities, thereby allowing rapid replenishment and lower basic inventories. This mixed carload service stimulates purchase of products, which normally move under less-than-carload rates. Therefore, the advantage of a production-oriented distribution warehouse is the ability to furnish superior service for a total product assortment. To the degree that a manufacturer can offer all products in custom assortments at consolidated transportation rates, a competitive differential advantage may be obtained in customer service.

Several major food processing firms currently operate production-oriented distribution warehouses. Leading examples are Pillsbury, Green Giant, and H. J. Heinz Company. At Heinz, a satellite warehouse is located at selected production points. Qualities of all major products are shipped to each warehouse. For example, an order requiring primarily pickles is filled from a warehouse adjacent to the pickle-processing plant by adding other products required. A similar procedure is followed for other major products.

INTERMEDIATELY-POSITIONED DISTRIBUTION WAREHOUSES

Distribution warehouses located between customer locations and production locations are referred to as intermediately-positioned. Such warehouses, similar to those that are production-oriented, find economic justification on the basis of increased customer service.

Industrial location theory points out that plants producing a particular type of product often must locate near required raw materials.[7] For reasons of production economy, firms may be faced with geographically decentralized production plants. For purposes of marketing control, the firm may prefer to engage a convergent marketing program for their entire multiple-product line.[8]

Under conditions of joint marketing, a distribution warehouse may be located at an intermediate location and operated as a collection point for various products produced at decentralized locations. By grouping all products in the line, a firm can deliver mixed shipments. Mixed shipments allow customers to realize economies of consolidated transport and faster replenishment of all products normally purchased only in quantity lots. Besides gaining a competitive advantage by providing these additional services, the firm offering mixed shipments may combine slow-moving products with faster movers, and, thereby, offer the total product line at consolidated transportation rates.

Location Strategy and Product Differentiation

From the preceding discussion, it is clear that distribution warehouses enter a physical distribution system only when a degree of differential advantage results from their inclusion between manufacturing site and final product destination. Differential advantage gained by adding distribution warehouses culminates from achieving a distribution cost or service advantage in a given market segment.

The particular location strategy followed by a firm depends greatly upon the degree of product line differentiation prevailing in a particular industry.

LOCATION STRATEGY WITH NONDIFFERENTIATED PRODUCTS

In an industry characterized by nearly identical products, little consumer loyalty is commanded by individual firms. The industry demand curve is relatively elastic. Fundamentally, individual firms may attempt to differentiate their products by location dispersion. Under these conditions, Losch's hexagon and generalizations concerning location patterns are likely to be experienced.[9] The major firms in the industry seek plant locations in prime

[7]Melvin L. Greenhut, *Plant Location* (Chapel Hill: University of North Carolina Press, 1956), p. 113.

[8]Thomas A. Staudt, "Program for Product Diversification," *Harvard Business Review*, Vol. XXXII, No. 6 (November-December, 1954), p. 125.

[9]August Losch, *The Economics of Location* (New Haven: Yale University Press, 1954).

CHART 10–1   Market Extension by Use of a Distribution Warehouse

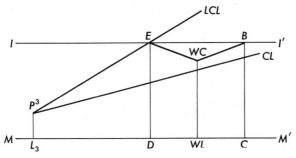

markets and at low-cost production points. Smaller high-cost firms normally find economic justification by selecting locations in marginal markets contained in space islands; these islands are created by the inability of major producers to place products at a competitive price. It is equally possible that major producers located in prime markets may utilize distribution warehouses to service marginal markets. By locating distribution warehouses in space islands, major producers may extend their effective market coverage. This type of market extension creates entry barriers to the location of high cost producers in space islands.[10]

Consolidating shipments is a basic economic principle underlying the utilization of distribution warehouses to extend market coverage to secondary areas. The major producer may initially sell FOB mill over his entire market area. Each customer is shipped products directly from the production point by some method of less-than-quantity shipment. The consolidation of product shipments to a distribution warehouse substantially reduces transportation expenses. Thus, the monopolist can move large quantities of his product into market areas, previously beyond his reach, at a total cost considerably below the consumer's price acceptance level. The savings must be sufficient to cover the cost of facility operation and inventory. Products may then be distributed FOB distribution center in all directions to a point where total product price reaches the level of consumer indifference.

Chart 10–1 contains an example of market expansion through a distribution warehouse.[11] The case of the spatial monopolist is illustrated in only one direction for the linear market. Under conditions of direct shipment, the monopolist can sell only as far into the market as point *D*. At the line *ED* the total cost of his product reaches the consumer-indifference price level. Beyond line *ED* the high-cost producer could exist in a marginal market. By placing a distribution center at some point in the market beyond *D*, the monopolist can consolidate shipments to the distribution warehouse at a landed cost below the consumer-indifference price level. Shipments are then

[10]For an expanded discussion, see Appendix E-2.
[11]Chart 10–1 is adapted from John H. Frederick, *Using Public Warehouses*, (Philadelphia: Chilton Company, 1957), p. 81.

returned toward the production point and farther into the market area until total price once more becomes prohibitive to the consumer. The total market expansion achieved by utilizing a distribution warehouse is expressed in the linear diagram by the area *DC*.

To generalize further, locating a number of such distribution warehouses around the total market area initially served by the spatial monopolist will produce again a system of Losch hexagons, and stability will exist. However, marginal markets are now served by distribution warehouses controlled by the major producer rather than by competitive high-cost producers. Thus, one function of distribution centers is to extend prime markets under conditions of nondifferentiated products.

LOCATION STRATEGY WITH
DIFFERENTIATED PRODUCTS

Distribution warehouses often are vital to the expansion of firms that sell differentiated products nationally. Because products offered by all firms are differentiated in the consumer's eyes, the neat theories of spatial monopoly break down. Each firm is forced to sell over a larger total market area in order to realize sales volumes sufficient for survival. These conditions probably will compel large producers to concentrate product plants where low production costs and much industry demand exist. This is necessary, because no individual submarket demands a firm's total production. From such concentrated locations, each firm may be characterized as playing a waiting game.[12] Each can meet the service capabilities of competitors, and all confront similar transportation costs. Under these conditions, the industry initially settles down to conventional tactics of nonprice competition in order to achieve differential advantage.

The dynamics of spatial competition enter the industry when differentiated products begin to gain acceptance in distant markets. The firm finds it desirable to decentralize physical facilities when sales volumes become sufficient in submarkets to justify distribution centers and, then, branch plants. The transportation principle justifying the use of distribution warehouses is the same as in geographically dispersed industries. When total demand in a given market segment becomes substantial enough to consolidate shipments, the resultant economies may justify a distribution warehouse. Thus, a second economic force leading to the use of distribution warehouses is the normal expansion of firms selling differentiated products nationally.

[12]Basically, this type of location strategy represents a game in which each player possesses perfect information concerning opponents' ex-post moves. Consequently, each player is content to maintain status quo until an allocation alternative offering a definite payoff is discovered. For a discussion of the logic of game theory in competition, see Martin Shubik, *Strategy and Market Structure* (New York: John Wiley & Sons, 1959), pp. 3–18.

Once a major producer obtains sufficient volumes to support a distribution warehouse in a market segment, the waiting game which earlier characterized such a concentrated industry is abandoned. In addition to transportation economies, firms that operate distribution warehouses also gain a service advantage in these market segments. These select firms then replenish consumer inventories more quickly than can major competitors. For customers this means faster special order handling and an overall reduction of basic inventories. Thus, the firm with distribution warehouses has one more method of gaining a differential advantage. The counter-strategy is for all major firms to neutralize this location advantage by developing a competitive system of distribution points when sufficient sales volumes are obtained.

Distribution Warehouse Functions

The distribution warehouse contains goods on the move. Because the operation is essentially a break-bulk and regrouping procedure, the objective is to efficiently move large quantities of products into the warehouse and customized orders of products out of the warehouse. A common and desirable practice is to have products arrive and depart from the warehouse during the same working day.

The functions performed in the warehouse may be grouped into movement and storage categories. In the distribution warehouse, movement is primarily emphasized with storage receiving secondary rank. Within these two broad categories, movement is divided into four subfunctions and storage into two subfunctions.

MOVEMENT FUNCTION

In the movement function, quantity shipments are reduced to customized retail orders. As noted above, movement consists of four basic subfunctions: (1) receiving, (2) transfer, (3) selection, and (4) shipping. The distribution manager should have a basic knowledge of each in order to properly understand internal warehouse operations.

Receiving. Merchandise normally arrives at the warehouse in carload and truckload quantities. The first movement function consists of unloading. In most warehouses, unloading is primarily manual. No mechanized methods have been developed that are adaptable to varying product characteristics. Generally, one or two men unload the shipment. If the product is small enough to hand-stock, pallets are used to construct a unit load so as to maximize movement efficiency. Larger merchandise may be unloaded directly from the car or truck for movement into the warehouse.

Transfer.   There are at least two, and possible three, transfer movements of merchandise. The merchandise is first moved into the warehouse and placed in a designated spot. The inbound movement is handled by fork-lift trucks when pallets are used and fork-lift truck or other mechanical traction in the case of larger products.

A second internal move may be required prior to order selection, depending upon the operating procedures of the warehouse. If merchandise is stored primarily upon pallets, some units may be moved from the receiving dock to a remote storage area. When these products are subsequently required for order selection, they will once more be moved by fork-lift trucks to a specialized selection area. When the merchandise is large or handled in full pallet loads, this second movement may be omitted.

In the final transfer, the specialized order is moved from the warehouse to the loading dock. The type of materials handling equipment best suited depends upon the nature of the product and the order selection procedure utilized. As noted above, if the product is large or if it composes full pallet loads, this movement may be accomplished with fork-lift trucks. If the product is small and consists of a large number of different items, the final transfer may be handled by a tractor and trailer or by a continuous-movement towline. In some special cases, conveyors have been employed.

Selection.   Order selection is the primary function of the distribution warehouse. At this point, movements are primarily aimed at regrouping products into customized orders. For a large number of small products, one part of the warehouse may be established as a selection area. Automatic data processing may be utilized to facilitate accuracy in billing. Order pickers then place all items billed on selection carts for transfer to the shipping area. A number of materials handling methods have been devised to facilitate this final transfer.

Shipping.   The shipping function consists of checking and loading orders for outbound movement. As in the case of receiving, in most systems shipments are normally manually handled. It has become increasingly popular to ship full pallet loads, as considerable time can be saved in loading. Some firms have experienced considerable savings; however, damage in transit normally increases. When delivery trucks are not company-owned, the additional problem of returning empty pallets may offset some of the savings. A checking operation is required when the merchandise is changing ownership as a result of shipment. Checking generally consists of item counts, but in some instances, an individual piece check for proper brand, size, and so on is necessary.

STORAGE FUNCTION

In addition to processing custom or special orders, the distribution warehouse performs all functions of the traditional storage warehouse. The basic subfunctions of storage are (1) temporary storage and (2) permanent storage.

Temporary Storage. As previously noted, primary emphasis is placed upon product flow in the distribution warehouse. Regardless of inventory turnover, all goods received must be stored for some time period. Providing storage for basic inventory replenishment is referred to as temporary storage. Temporary storage time will vary in different distribution systems, because temporary storage time is based upon the inventory replenishment cycle. Temporary storage must provide a sufficient quantity of goods to satisfy demand and adequate safety reserves. The exact amount of temporary storage required is dealt with in Chapters 5 and 10. However, this function must be satisfied in order to ensure adequate product flow.

Permanent Storage. Permanent storage, although somewhat misleading, refers only to storage in excess of inventory required for normal replenishment. In some special situations, storage may be needed for several months. The distribution manager should understand the reasons why permanent storage may be required. A constant effort should be made to encourage warehouse managers to minimize permanent storage and concentrate upon maximum product flow. There are five basic reasons for a modern distribution center to store goods in excess of normal replenishment requirements. Each of these reasons is considered a special case rather than normal operating procedure.

Seasonal Production. Regardless of advances in production scheduling, some products are seasonal because of growing periods. If the firm in question engages in this type of processing, extensive storage may be required during specific periods. Special storage warehouses or public warehouses may satisfy this requirement. Even if the firm does not engage in production but only in retail distribution, it may be necessary to purchase large quantities of seasonal products to assure a year-around supply. Canned tomato products are an example of merchandise often stored in a distribution warehouse.

Erratic Demand Requirements. When a product with an extreme demand fluctuation is handled, it may become necessary to carry additional supplies in order to satisfy heavy demand requirements. An example is air conditioners. Because air conditioners are expensive items, retailers prefer to carry small inventories. When a period of high temperatures begins, the manufacturer has a very limited time to distribute additional units. With such products, surplus supplies may be held at warehouses in anticipation of excessive heat waves. Past experience has proven it not unusual for a carload of air conditioners to chase a heat wave across the entire country without ever arriving for distribution at a geographic point experiencing maximum temperatures.

Conditioning. Some conditioning is required of a few products at the distribution warehouse. These products may be stored for a limited period of time in excess of temporary storage. The ripening of bananas is a case in point. Modern food distribution centers include ripening rooms to hold products until they reach peak quality.

Speculation. The distribution warehouse seldom stores goods for speculative purposes. The degree to which this activity takes place will depend upon the products handled. For example, it is not unusual to store grain for speculative reasons.

Realization of Special Discount. The wholesale distribution warehouse often requires space for the storage of products offered at special discount. The purchasing agent may be able to realize a substantial reduction during a specific period. Under such conditions the warehouse contains inventories additional to those required for normal replenishment. Manufacturers of fertilizer often attempt to shift the warehousing burden on their product by offering off season discounts.

Evaluation of Distribution Warehouse Requirements

Once a decision has been made to consider establishment of a distribution warehouse, it is necessary to determine size, product mix to be inventoried, and the specific customers to be serviced from the proposed facility.[13] Fundamental to these decisions is the connection of accurate information. The following discussion centers upon typical information requirements related to a market-oriented distribution warehouse. The basic considerations are applicable to other types of warehouse facilities and to any firm examining distribution warehouses regardless of their particular product flow. Required categories of specific information depend upon the individual firm.

MARKET CONSIDERATIONS

Of initial concern is a detailed analysis of product flows to the market area or customer grouping under consideration. Such market analysis does not require that the final location of the distribution warehouse be known. However, some estimate or general market area is required.

Estimating the General Market Area. The general market area of a warehouse may best be analyzed through existing records. In the absence of

[13]In general, customers to be serviced will be based upon comparative transportation costs and basic standards of management with respect to total order cycle time.

records, a market survey may be made. Assuming direct shipments are currently being made to the West Coast by a manufacturer located in Cleveland and existing records indicate to what points and in what volumes shipments are made, charting this data on a geographically referenced map of the West Coast will give the firm a general idea of the complexion of the market. In this case the intervening mountain ranges tend to separate this market from all others. Whenever such natural barriers are present, individual market areas may be more or less readily defined.

Further analysis indicates that shipments cluster around two points, Seattle and Lower California. The decison must then be made whether or not these clusters should be served from one or two warehouses. Analysis of current movements to each cluster indicates their respective volumes of shipment. The economies of consolidation measured against present costs will yield potential savings. These dollar savings may then be gauged against possible warehouse costs to judge whether further analysis is justified. Market areas are then assigned to each cluster on the basis of cost. The cost equalization point between the two areas is accepted as a rough determinant of the confines for individual study. This breaking point is a line drawn in such a way as to represent equal distribution costs via either warehouse.

Sales Forecast.   A forecast of expected sales for distribution outlets must be included in the analysis. Sole reliance upon historical records may result in gross errors in estimated costs under alternative systems.

Additional Market Information.   With an approximation of the market area, more precise data collection may begin. In addition to shipping points and annual tonnages, average size of shipment, average time in transit, mode of transportation currently used, current effective rates, and the number of special orders required to supplement the normal replenishment cycle may be included. On the basis of examination of these data as well as other pertinent information, management may readily identify the dimensions of the market under analysis. Utilizing the data collected concerning the market, specifications for the warehouse may be established in terms of annual tonnage, number of shipments, and number of points served.

PRODUCT CONSIDERATIONS

A second and independent area of quantitative analysis is a precise study of the products to be distributed through the proposed warehouse. This analysis provides information concerning the product mix which requires handling. The operation of a proposed warehouse is directly related to the character of the product mix. Each product should be analyzed in terms of annual sales, stability of demand, weight, bulk, and packaging. In addition, it is desirable to determine the total size, bulk, and weight of the average order processed through the warehouse. These data provide the necessary information for determining requirements of warehouse space, design and layout, materials handling equipment, operating procedures, and controls.

A firm distributing a wide variety of unrelated products faces an entirely different distribution problem than one handling a few specialized products. For example, a food distribution warehouse may handle 6,000 or more products each with different characteristics. In contrast, an appliance center may handle less than 50 products. The degree of complexity, therefore, depends upon the number and characteristics of the products distributed. Only by detailed analysis of products can management specifically determine what factors are relevant in developing the distribution warehouse. Analysis of these factors and the formulation of appropriate specifications provide the necessary guides for selecting among alternative handling systems. The character of the product line handled also helps establish which modes of intercity transportation can be utilized for product shipment.

SERVICE

Analysis of the service standards of the proposed system represents a critical area of analysis. As noted earlier, superior service may be a dominant factor in creating competitive advantage in a given market area. In addition, the degree of effectiveness attainable is directly related to the level of service rendered.

Before service levels in a proposed system are specified, a detailed analysis of current service in the market area should be undertaken. This analysis should include service rendered by the firm undertaking the study as well as that provided by major competitors.

In a firm employing a policy of direct shipment, service standards can be readily measured. Essentially, the problem is one of ascertaining time between order placement and shipment arrival. Basic statistical methods provide a simple and accurate method of estimating the necessary information. Invoices from each distribution point can be sampled and examined in order to determine time between the placing of the order and its final delivery.

Analysis of services provided by competitors is much more difficult to determine accurately. By simply plotting present points of production and warehousing on a map, capabilities of various competitors in serving particular markets may be determined. It is generally a safe procedure to estimate in transit times on the basis of the mode of transportation predominantly utilized for moving the product(s) under consideration. This time must then be adjusted to allow for order processing. One method of estimating the order processing time of competitors is to assume they enjoy an efficiency equal to that of your firm. This time should then be added to the in-transit time to arrive at an estimate of service rendered. By adding the order process time and the in-transit time, an estimate of service by the total time standard is achieved.

A closely related problem is stock availability at the retail outlet. Among products which have close substitutes, stock shortages mean lost sales and a possible dilution of market penetration. Although it is difficult to ascertain, management must approximate the current level of stock availability. A convenient system for quantifying this data is the use of a frequency index. On the basis of 100 customer calls, the percentage of individual demands that cannot be met may be measured by the current distribution system. Once this ratio has been determined, specifications for the proposed system can be established. These specifications should represent an optimum compromise between stock availability and its related costs.[14]

GENERAL CONSIDERATIONS

Depending upon the circumstances of the individual firm, several additional factors should be subjected to detailed analysis. Foremost are two areas generally neglected during analysis of warehouse feasibility: (1) expansion and (2) policies.

Expansion.   Future expansion introduces a series of factors often neglected when a firm is considering an immediate extension of its distribution facilities. Inclusion of a warehouse component into the distribution structure should be partially based upon estimated requirements for future operations. Well-managed firms often establish five-, ten-, and twenty-year expansion plans. This results in a continual assessment of distribution requirements as market conditions change in time.

Future plans calling for decentralization of newly constructed plants influence the location of a warehouse associated with existing plant. Likewise, a market-oriented distribution warehouse should be considered as one point in an expanding network of warehouses.[15] Future plans will greatly influence the size of structure and location selected. For example, if a firm intends to expand the warehouse operation at some future time, construction must be guided by special requirements. A site that offers room for expansion must be selected. Transportation facilities must be adequate to handle increased volumes without delay or excessive cost. Although such planning may lead to increased short-run costs, it will yield long-run economic benefits.

[14]See Chapter 8, p. 212.
[15]At best the location of any given distribution warehouse is secondary in importance with respect to the complete network of all facilities from which shipments can be made. For an expanded discussion, see Chapter 12, p. 316.

To ease expansion without seriously affecting normal operations, special construction must be considered. Food distribution centers are often designed and constructed to allow rapid expansion. Selected walls may be constructed of semipermanent materials to allow easy removal. Floor areas, designed to support heavy movements, are extended to these walls in a manner that facilitates expansion. Plans for future expansion also affect selection of automated processing systems.

The projection of long-range distribution needs is unquestionably a difficult and delicate assignment. Careful analysis of such factors as past growth, population shifts, coupled with management expansion plans, may afford a reasonable estimate of future needs. These projections should be given consideration when determining final specifications.

Policies.   Like expansion considerations, policies are seldom included in specifications. In actual operation, managerial preferences can become primary cost determinants. The newly proposed component must be designed as part of an integrated system. To ease communications and control, operating procedures must be consistent with the remaining distribution structure.

The following example illustrates improper consideration of the total structure when planning a distribution warehouse. Recently, a large firm developed a new distribution warehouse point. Product line analysis indicated that the most satisfactory method of internal materials handling would be via a conveyor system. A materials handling manufacturer designed an excellent system, which was subsequently installed in the warehouse. The system would have been sufficient if an earlier management decision to convert all operations to palletized unit loads had not been overlooked. Shortly after the distribution point was introduced into the system, all merchandise began arriving on pallets. The conveyor system, designed to easily handle the largest product case of the firm, was insufficient to handle full pallets. After a costly period of shipping in nonpallet loads to this single distribution center, the conveyor system was discontinued.

Additional policy questions influence location preferences, inventory control, and ordering procedures. For example, the basic decision to buy or rent is, in part, the product of management preference. When a new distribution center is established, newly hired personnel may require training in company operating procedures; industrial or materials handling systems may be analyzed by company staff or outside consultants; detailed consideration must be given in establishing operating specifications for the system.

After policies have been determined, quantitative analysis provides the information necessary to evaluate the economic feasibility of including a warehouse component in the distribution system. In addition, it provides the necessary information for establishing specifications to guide the implementation of the component. The point cannot be too strongly emphasized that

CHART 10–2   Total Warehouse Demand — One-Year Period

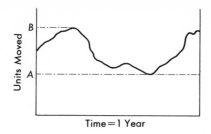

successful introduction of a warehouse may rest upon the ability of management to isolate prime cost determinants. Based strictly upon cost, warehouse inclusion requires sufficient sales volumes to render significant savings through the consolidation of shipments.

WAREHOUSE SIZE REQUIREMENTS AND UTILIZATION RATES

Estimation of warehouse size requirements must be made before a decision concerning investment is considered. The basic consideration in determination of size is the rate of expected future growth. Once long-term estimates are available, a maximum size warehouse can be calculated. However, commitment to the maximum size facility required at some time in the future will adversely affect unit costs of present operations by reducing the average volume of warehouse through-put over the planning period.

It is desirable, under these conditions, to break down expected throughput into (1) basic requirements to service the market during each period, and (2) the seasonal and cyclical variations in through-put. This analysis determines the minimum size facility that will yield the highest average warehouse utilization. If the original size of the warehouse is designed to meet only basic requirements, the unit cost of the facility will be at a minimum. An example of this approach is presented in Chart 10–2.

In Chart 10–2, the minimum size warehouse results in 100-percent utilization, and, therefore, lowest cost is determined by the firm demand (illustrated by line A). The maximum size warehouse necessary to assure product service from the warehouse will always be determined by peak secular demand (represented by line B). As demand increases with growth of the firm, both peak and firm demand may be increased. Chart 10–3 illustrates this phenomenon over a three-year period.

A tabular presentation of the above material may clarify the specific nature of the problem and its alternative solutions. The assumptions are (1) the warehouse space may be constructed for one dollar per square foot; (2) construction to meet peak demand requires three times the space as does

CHART 10–3   Total Warehouse Demand — Three-Year Period

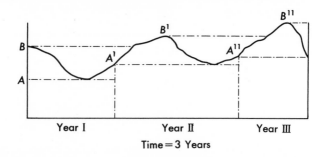

Time = 3 Years

construction to meet firm demand; and (3) utilization at peak demand is 50 percent.

Table 10–1 should be read as a composite for the three-year expected demand cycle. For Year I(1–1) the cost impact per pound on firm demand is $.02, whereas if the warehouse is constructed to service peak as well as firm demand, the cost is $.03 per pound, an increase of 50 percent in warehouse cost.

If a warehouse is constructed to accomodate firm demand for Year II(2–2), the cost per pound for the Year I firm demand rises to $.022 per pound, whereas for peak demand for Year I(2–1), the cost rises to $.033 per pound. Construction of a warehouse in Year I to accommodate firm and peak demand conditions for Year III(3–1) is $.024 per pound for firm demand and $.036 per pound for peak demand.

This generalized discussion of warehouse requirements suggests the type of information required to make proper decisions concerning such facilities. One such decision concerns selection between private and public warehouse facilities for a given area. If the decision is in favor of private facilities, it is necessary to select between new construction, existing construction, as well as purchase or lease arrangements.

The analysis of utilization presented above introduced several problems related to variation in through-put. These flow considerations are directly related to warehouse alternatives.

Warehouse Alternatives

In consideration of warehouse alternatives, four arrangements are available: (1) private owned; (2) private leased; (3) public; and (4) combinations of one through three, based upon seasonal variation in warehouse space requirements. As a broad grouping, warehouse facilities are normally classified as private or public.

A private distribution warehouse facility is one operated and managed by the firm who owns the merchandise handled through the facility. A public

TABLE 10-1   TOTAL WAREHOUSE DEMAND — THREE-YEAR PERIOD

Year	A Peak Demand in lbs.	B Firm Demand in lbs.	C Sq. Ft. Peak $1 sq. ft.	D Sq. Ft. Firm $1 sq. ft.	E Cost per lb. peak	F Cost per lb. firm
1–1	5,000,000	2,500,000	155,000	50,000	$.03	$.02
2–2	5,500,000	2,750,000	165,000	55,000	.03	.02
3–3	6,150,000	3,025,000	181,500	60,500	.03	.02
2–1					.033	.022
3–1					.036	.024
3–2					.033	.022

warehouse, in contrast to private, is operated by a professional warehouse-man to provide a range of services to a number of different firms on a fee basis.

PUBLIC WAREHOUSES

Public warehouses are widely used in modern distribution systems. About any combination of services desired can be arranged with the operator of a public warehouse. One classification of public warehouses has been developed based upon the range of specialized operations performed.[16] Public warehouses are classified as (1) general merchandise, (2) refrigerated, (3) special commodity, (4) bonded, (5) household goods and furniture, and (6) field warehouse.[17] As would be expected, many public warehouses offer combinations of the above operations.

In distribution warehouse consideration, emphasis is placed upon the use of public facilities to assist in development of product assortments. As such, the current treatment is more concerned with the distribution capabilities of public warehouses. The distribution public warehouse performs four specialized services: (1) stock-spotting, (2) complete line assortment, (3) break-bulk, and (4) intransit-mixing. Each of these specialized services is briefly reviewed.

Stock-Spotting.   Spot stock capabilities of public warehouses are most often used by manufacturers in their physical distribution systems. In addition, manufacturers with limited product lines are more prone to utilize this specific service. Rather than warehouse inventories in facilities near production plants, delivery time can be substantially reduced by pretrans-action movement to strategic cities. Thus, a consolidated carload of the firm's

[16]Frederick, op. cit.

[17]A complete review of the characteristics of each classified type is beyond the scope of present interest. For an updated review, see Charles A. Taff, *Management of Traffic and Physical Distribution* (Homewood, Ill.: Richard D. Irwin, 1964), pp. 527–530.

product line is "spot-stocked" in a public warehouse from which customer orders are filled upon receipt. Utilizing public warehouse facilities for spot-stocking allows inventories to be placed in a wide variety of markets adjacent to key customers.

Complete Line Assortment. A public warehouse used for complete line assorting may be employed by either a manufacturer, wholesaler, or retailer. In this case the public warehouse performs the complete range of functions outlined earlier in this chapter for distribution warehouses. Products are stocked in anticipation of customer orders, with customized assortments being grouped upon demand.

The differential between stock-spotting and complete line assortment is one of degree. A firm following a stock-spotting policy will normally have a narrower product line and will place stocks in a wider range of different markets than one using public warehouses for complete line assortment.

Break-Bulk. Break-bulk public warehouse service represents a form of assistance in a distribution system that does not involve any storage. Public warehouse concerns often operate local delivery equipment, which can be hired by firms distributing in the general market area. A manufacturer can combine orders of different customers located in the market area into one pooled shipment and send the entire combined shipment to a public ware-houseman. The public warehouse then separates the individual orders and performs a local delivery. Utilizing the services of a public warehouse in a break-bulk capacity allows the advantage of consolidated freight rates plus reduces the difficulty of controlling a number of individual small shipments to a given market.

Intransit Mixing. Intransit mixing is similar to break-bulk services; however, when product plants are geographically separated, overall trans-portation charges as well as overall warehouse requirements can be reduced by this special service. Intransit mixing may involve shipments to one or more consignees. Solid carloads or truckloads are shipped from production plants to the public warehouseman providing the mixing service. Each large shipment enjoys the lowest possible transportation rate. The loadings of each product are designated to be mixed for specific customers at the public warehouse.

Upon arrival at the public warehouse, the solid cars are unloaded and the proper customer requirements of each product assorted. Shipment is then made to each individual customer. This total process of intransit mixing is illustrated in Chart 10–4.

The economies of intransit mixing have been increased by the develop-ment of some special transportation tariffs.[18] These special tariffs are

[18]See Chapter 6, p. 142.

CHART 10–4   Public Warehouse Intransit Mixing

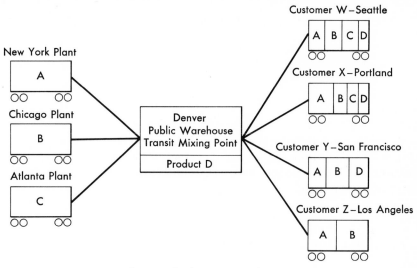

Products Involved – A, B, C, and D

modifications of basic storage intransit privileges. Products are shipped from production plants, mixed as well as combined with products currently stored at the public warehouse, and then transported to customers under a special tariff provision. Through freight rates are applied on the basis of each commodity rather than on a mixed or freight-all-kinds rating. This special provision has the net effect of reducing total freight charges.

It will be apparent that the specialized public warehouse services of breakbulk and intransit mixing have the net effect of reducing the amount of product storage required in product distribution. This objective is fully consistent with the total concept of distribution warehousing.

PRIVATE WAREHOUSES

A private warehouse may be either owned or leased. The decision of which best fits an individual firm's requirement is essentially one of financial planning. It is often not possible to find a warehouse facility for lease that will fit the requirements of a given firm. In general, it is easier to locate facilities suitable for storage than for distribution warehousing. If a considerable amount of material handling is planned for the distribution warehouse, a readily available building may not be conducive to efficient product flow.[19]

[19]An efficient warehouse should be designed around a material handling system in order to encourage maximum ease of product flow.

CHART 10–5   Combined Private and Public Warehouse Facilities

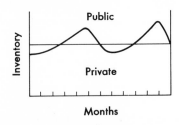

Recently, a number of real estate developers have built distribution warehouses for specific firms to their specifications on a leased basis. Such custom construction is available in many markets on a lease arrangement as short as five years in duration.

COMBINATION SYSTEMS

As would be expected, many firms utilize a combination of public and private distribution warehouses in product distribution. A private facility is used to cover basic requirements that are more or less constant the year around, whereas public facilities are used to handle peak requirements. Chart 10–5 illustrates the combined concept.

A public warehouseman normally charges on the basis of packages or hundredweight stored or handled by his facility. Such charges will normally exceed the cost of warehousing equivalent volumes in a distribution facility constructed to service basic demands. Public warehouse rates must be adjusted to different seasonal demands of a variety of customers. Full public warehouse space utilization through the cycle of annual activities of all customers appears remote. For this reason, the rate structure of a public warehouse used for only peak overflows will reflect lower efficiencies than can be experienced by construction of a private warehouse designed for stable demand.

As a planning rule, if a private warehouse is employed, it should be designed to be at capacity between 75 and 85 percent of the time. Thus, from 15 to 25 percent of the usable space is available to accommodate seasonal requirements. Public warehouses as a supplement should only be used to temporarily store requirements greater than the 15 to 25 percent internal expansion capacity. When such public warehouse supplements are utilized, it can be expected that additional product handlings and transfers will be required.

The above discussion is somewhat pessimistic regarding the resultant efficiencies from attempting to combine private and public warehouses to service a single market area or grouping of customers. However, this reluctance concerning joint utilization of private and public facilities in the same market should not be interpreted as a general rejection of combination systems. A firm may very well find that private distribution warehouses can be best used in specific markets, and public warehouses are used in other market situations. In physical distribution system design the objective is to locate whatever combination of the two types of distribution warehouses most economically meet customer service objectives.

In recent years the traditional role of public warehouses has dramatically changed in overall distribution. Many individual public warehousemen have formed associations that allow a firm to purchase their services in a number of different cities. The associations may even provide additional services such as inventory control, billing, and arrangement of transportation for local delivery. In addition to associations, some larger public warehouse firms are expanding their operations to a network of facilities located in key market areas. The indications are that these forms of multiple-point public warehouse networks under one management coordination will substantially increase in number and geographic coverage. It is equally expected that more firms will find the flexibility of using such networks a distinct advantage.

Location Techniques

Within the general market area to be serviced by a distribution warehouse, considerable latitude often exists in selection of a specific location. It is not uncommon for a single distribution warehouse to service customers or retail stores located throughout a several-state area. At least two general mathematical methods are available to aid the selection of a distribution warehouse location.

The first method involves formulations for averaging transport costs within a predetermined market area. The basic system of calculation is analytic geometry. Several alternate formulations, depending upon the specifics of the problem, have been developed and tested.[20] All solutions represent a weighted average of a given number of independent variables such as delivery locations, annual tonnage, and delivery time. The dependent variable is the distribution warehouse location.

The second method currently popular for solving location problems is linear programming. It is possible to determine the distribution warehouse location through a modified version of the transportation or distribution

---

[20]See "Warehouse Location Based on Trucking Costs," *Materials Handling Manual No. 1* (Boston: Boston Publishing Company, Inc., 1955), pp. E84–E86; Donald J. Bowersox, *Food Distribution Center Location Technique and Procedure.* Marketing and Transportation Paper No. 12 (East Lansing: Bureau of Business and Economic Research, Michigan State University, 1962), pp. 9–32; and C. G. Eneborg, "How to Plot the Ideal Location for a Warehouse," *Management Methods*, Vol. XIII (January, 1958), pp. 52–55.

model.[21] The simplest application requires the assumption of an array of possible locations, with the result of isolating the best location among the array. The general technique given an array of potential locations is to use controlled substitution for selecting that location which minimizes transport cost.

The techniques developed using analytic geometry have the advantage of simplicity. Location problems covering as many as 100 retail outlets can be solved without the aid of electronic data processing. No assumption covering the final distribution warehouse is required, because the mathematical process seeks the single best location within the search area. A deficiency of the analytic-geometrical approach is the difficulty of expanding the analysis beyond transport costs. Consequently, the application of this technique is limited to a single-location selection in which transport expense predominates.

The linear programming technique is well fitted to a problem in which only a limited number of sites are available upon which a facility can be constructed. When a distribution warehouse is being built to primarily service a single geographical market such as one city, only a few sites may offer the required space and transportation facilities. Linear programming can help select which site would be best suited for the distribution warehouse under consideration.

Appendix 10A provides a complete discussion of the mathematics of the analytic geometry approach to solving the location problem. The technique of linear programming is developed in Appendix 13A, which deals with the general family of quantitative techniques available to assist scheduling problems.

Distribution Warehouse Establishment

The process of establishing a warehouse component involves a series of decisions which, in total, mold the structure within which the distribution functions will be performed. The following discussion is management-oriented. Managers who have not previously experienced warehouse establishment often repeat the mistakes others have previously made. This brief review will provide a working background for such managers. In addition, it will indicate the type of information that will be expected from management by specialists called in to work on specific problems.

If a warehouse is economically justified, the problem of establishment receives primary attention. When planning a warehouse, management will

[21]Robert Dortman, Paul A. Samuelson, and Robert M. Solow, *Linear Programming and Economic Analysis* (New York: The Ronald Press Co., 1957); Nyles V. Reinfeld and William R. Vogel, *Mathematical Programming* (Englewood Cliffs, N.J.: Prentice-Hall, Inc., 1958).

find problems that cannot be separated; decisions made in one area will influence decisions concerning other areas. These interrelations must be recognized in order to develop an integrated warehouse system.

PLANNING THE DISTRIBUTION WAREHOUSE[22]

The first problems confronted are those directly related to planning the warehouse. The modern concept that a distribution warehouse is an enclosure for a material handling operation requires detailed analysis before the size, type, and shape of the enclosure are determined. Too often the building is designed and construction is well under way before the materials handling system is selected. A master plan of such related areas as materials handling, layout, space requirement, and design should be developed. In addition, a specific site for the warehouse must be selected. Construction decisions are the most rigid decisions related to implementation. They establish the character of the warehouse which, in turn, determines what degree of efficiency can be obtained in materials handling.

Site Selection.   Techniques of location analysis help in selection of a general area for warehouse location. Once this analysis is completed, a specific building site must be selected. Selection of a site for warehouse construction can normally be completed in all communities. Generally, three areas in a community may be considered for location: the transshipment zone, outlying areas served by motor truck only, and the central or downtown area. Selection of the site is based on the most economic satisfaction of the warehouse requirements.

In site selection, attention must be directed to cost analysis. Naturally, the direct cost of procurement is the primary governing factor. Normally, sites can be purchased at a cheaper price per square foot near the fringes of a metropolitan area than near the city center. A warehouse need not be located in major industrial areas. In city after city, one can observe warehouses among industrial plants, in industrial parks, and generally in areas zoned light or heavy industry. This is unnecessary, because most warehouses can legally operate under the restrictions placed upon commercial property. The supply of desirable industrial sites may be limited in a given community, and one who desires such a site can expect to pay premium prices.

In addition to procurement costs, such setup and operating expenses as obtaining rail sidings, utility hookups, taxes, insurance rates, and highway access require evaluation. These expenses vary between sites and may render

---

[22]The following discussion is oriented to problems encountered during construction of a distribution warehouse. In special situations, it may be possible to purchase or lease an existing structure. When such is the case, the problem becomes one of developing as effective a materials handling system as possible within limitations of the existing structure.

one site economically desirable over alternatives. For example, because of insurance rates, a food distribution firm recently rejected what otherwise appeared to be a totally satisfactory site. The parcel of land under consideration was located near the end of the water main. During most of the day, adequate water supplies were available to handle all operational requirements in addition to any emergency demands. The only possible water problem occurred during two short periods each day. From 6:30 A.M. to 8:30 A.M. and from 5:00 P.M. to 7:00 P.M., the demand for water along the line was so great that sufficient supplies were not available to handle emergencies. Because of this deficiency, abnormally high insurance rates were required for necessary protection, and the site was consequently rejected.

In addition to low costs, several other requirements must be satisfied before the site is purchased. The site must offer adequate room for expansion. It is a good practice to purchase or option land totaling three to five times the total footage of the proposed structure. The site should be serviced by rail capable of handling volumes considerably higher than those initially planned without excessive cost or delay. Highways to facilitate truck movements to and from the warehouse must be available. Utilities necessary for operating the warehouse must be available. The site must offer a type of soil capable of supporting the structure, and it must be sufficiently high to afford proper drainage. Additional requirements will be situationally necessary depending upon the type of structure to be constructed. In summary, the site finally selected must be preceded by extensive analysis.

Selection of Materials Handling System.   A materials handling system is one of the initial considerations. Movement of various types is the main function of a distribution warehouse. Consequently, the warehouse is viewed as a structure designed to facilitate maximum product flow.

Several materials handling systems are capable of satisfying required movements. Management should clearly understand the nature of the movement requirements in order to appreciate the reasons for selecting a specific system. The fact must always be kept in mind that handling, per se, adds no value to the product. Handling and rehandling give the appearance of a busy operation, but they also create a costly operation. The objective in selecting a given materials handling system is to accomplish necessary product movement with a minimum of handlings.

Basically, a materials handling system consists of movement and supporting equipment. Movement equipment includes devices designed to facilitate product flow. Some examples of movement equipment currently utilized in distribution warehouses are fork-lift trucks, various types of continuous movement tow-lines, tractors designed to pull one or more trailers, conveyors, and hand trucks. Each type of equipment is designed to do a specific job. Normally, more than one type of movement equipment is necessary in a total handling system.

The most common types of supporting equipment are pallets and skids. Pallets are recognized as one of the most efficient means of handling merchandise, which can be grouped into a unit load.[23] The pallet provides a platform for the unit load. Unit loads permit movement of large quantities of small products at one time. A unit load also permits a single handling of merchandise before it is necessary to break bulk for customized order selection.

Complete pallet loads can be vertically stacked without the use of racks. Similar advantages cannot be achieved with partial pallets. Consequently, partial pallets of products awaiting order selection may be placed in storage racks. The rack also helps to increase the number of products which can be placed in a limited selection area. Partial pallets of two or more different products can be placed upon different shelves of the rack. The advantages of vertical stacking are not lost when racks are utilized to support partial pallets because full pallets may be placed on top of the rack.

Three factors, which can vary extensively among warehouses, determine what type of equipment is best suited for a particular system: (1) the product handled, (2) the volume of movements, and (3) distance and dimension of movement. If products with varying characteristics are to be handled, the type of movement and supporting equipment will be considerably different than for standardized products. For example, in the former case, a fork-lift truck palletized system might be most satisfactory, whereas in the latter a conveyor might best satisfy the movement function. In the selection of a handling system, the weight, bulk, size, and shape of the product are determinants of the most efficient type of equipment. Likewise, the volume of movements plays an important role. Normally a continuous movement system, for example, a towline, is economically justified only if the equipment can be kept in motion with a high degree of utilization during the total working period. The distance and dimension of movement are also important in selecting basic movement equipment. Some types of equipment are designed for long movements, whereas other types are designed primarily for shorter hauls. Although a single-level warehouse is ideal, for various reasons a multiple-story warehouse may have to suffice. Under such a condition, special equipment will be required for vertical movements between floors as well as horizontal movements on each floor.

The distribution manager cannot hope to understand fully the details of each available system. It is not the purpose of this brief introduction to attempt a coverage of such details. Management should have an adequate understanding of the importance of materials handling. This requires a fundamental realization that materials handling represents the core of the distribution warehouse. Extreme caution should be employed in using check

[23]Unitization is defined as a number of products grouped together to facilitate movement. Such loads may be grouped on pallets, skids, or some form of container. For a more detailed discussion, see Chapter 6.

lists or so-called lists of principles concerning materials handling equipment as guides for evaluating proposed systems. Because of the vast amount of equipment available and the different characteristics of each movement problem, the selection of a materials handling system must remain a tailored operation.

Warehouse Layout.   The layout of a warehouse depends upon the proposed system of materials handling. Normally a materials handling system is designed with a specific layout in mind. Consequently, a layout and the materials handling system must be planned together. Layout basically consists of developing a floor plan that will facilitate product flow.

It is difficult to generalize because of the vast difference between layouts designed to fit specific needs. If pallets are utilized, the first step is to determine what size pallets may be employed. A multitude of different size pallets is available. When specialized products are handled, a nonstandard pallet may be desirable. Whenever possible, standardized pallets should be used because of the ease of lower expense procurement. The sizes most frequently utilized are 40 × 48 inch and 32 × 40 inch.[24] In general, the larger the pallet load, the lower is the cost of movement per pound or package over a given distance. One fork-lift truck operator can move a large load in the same time and with the same effort as is required to move a smaller load. The packages to be piled on the pallet and the related patterns which can be worked out will, to a certain extent, determine the size of pallet best suited to the operation.[25] Regardless of the size finally selected, management should adopt one size for the total operation.

The second step in planning a layout involves the positioning of pallets. There are only two possible methods: (1) ninety degree or square and (2) angle. Ninety-degree or square placement means that the pallet is positioned perpendicular to the aisle, and angle placement means that the pallet is placed at some angle. The angles employed range from ten degrees to 45 degrees with $26\frac{1}{2}$ degrees most common. Chart 10–6 shows the two methods of positioning. The square method was widely utilized in early warehouses because of layout ease. The angle method is rapidly gaining acceptance, because it renders a savings in operating efficiency. Aisle width can be reduced because the fork-lift truck can position a pallet in the angle placement system without making a full ninety-degree turn. This offsets any space lost due to angling. Operating efficiency is increased, because of the ease of placement resulting from the shorter turn required. The method of pallet placement utilized in a particular layout will depend upon the specific

[24]In reference to pallets, it is customary to name the dimension which is placed lengthwise of the forks in the lift truck first. Many pallets are designed with four-way entry; consequently, the two dimensions of the pallet can be used interchangeably.

[25]Several guides to pallet patterns have been developed to help in the selection of proper patterns. For one excellent guide to patterns for the 40″ × 48″ pallet, see *Pallet Patterns*, NAVSANDA Publication 269, Bureau of Supplies and Accounts, Washington 25, D.C.

CHART 10–6   Alternative Methods of Pallet Placement

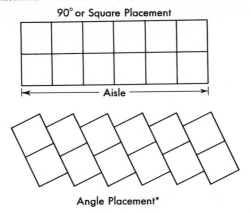

Angle Placement*

problems experienced.[26] Often the two methods can be combined to arrive at the most efficient overall layout.

Once all details have been isolated, the equipment selected must be integrated into a final layout. Normally the path of product flow will depend upon the materials handling system. To indicate the relationship between materials handling and layout, two systems and respective layouts are reviewed. The following illustrations represent only two of a multitude of potential layouts.

System A.   Layout A, Chart 10–7, represent a materials handling system with related layout utilizing fork-lift trucks for inbound and transfer movements and tractor-trailers for order selection. The products are assumed adaptable to a palletized operation. The layout is greatly simplified, because offices, special areas, and details are omitted.

The proposed floor plan in layout A is approximately square. The advocates of this particular system feel that a square structure provides the best plan for operating efficiency. As indicated earlier concerning utilization of some materials handling systems, products are clustered in a specific area of the warehouse for order selection. Such is the case in layout A. This area is labeled the selection area. The primary purpose of a small selection area is to minimize the distance order pickers must cover when selecting an order.

The selection area is normally supported by a storage area. When products are received by rail or truck, they are palletized and placed in the storage area. The selection area is then replenished from storage as required. When a compact selection area is utilized, products are placed in this area according to weight, bulk, and velocity characteristics in an attempt to minimize outbound movement problems.[27] Special orders are then accumulated by the

[26]For a detailed discussion, see Donald J. Bowersox, "Resolving the Pallet Layout Controversy," *Transportation and Distribution Management*, June, 1962, pp. 43–46.

[27]For a formulation to assist product space assignments see J. L. Heskett, "Cube-Pre-Order Index — A Key to Warehouse Stock Location," *Transportation and Distribution Management*, April, 1963, pp. 27–31.

CHART 10–7   Layout A

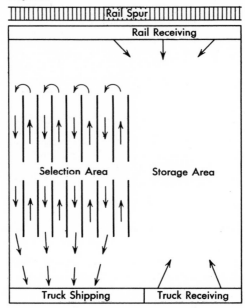

order selector moving a tractor and trailer through the selection area. The arrows in layout A indicate the general flow of product movements.

System B.   Layout B, Chart 10–8, represents a materials handling system with related layout utilizing fork-lift trucks for inbound and transfer movements and a continuous movement towline for order selection. Again, products are assumed adaptable to pallets, and once more the illustration is greatly simplified. The floor plan is a rectangular shape. In a system employing a continuous movement towline, the special selection area is omitted. Rather, selection is made directly from the storage.[28] Products are moved from rail and truck receiving into storage areas adjacent to the towline. The orders are then selected directly from storage and loaded onto four-wheel trucks, which are propelled by the towline. Merchandise is placed in the storage area to minimize inbound movement. Because the towline moves all products with the same degree of efficiency, the weight, bulk, and velocity concepts are not important for outbound movement. The arrows in layout B indicate major product movements. The line in the center of the layout illustrates the path of the towline.

Both layouts A and B have been greatly simplified, and, consequently, neither has been given detailed consideration. The main purpose of their inclusion is to indicate the relationship of materials handling systems and proposed layouts.

[28]With the minor exception that some products have bulk storage in the center of the warehouse. Such bulk or remote storage occurs when extra heavy stocks of a given product are procured.

CHART 10–8   Layout B

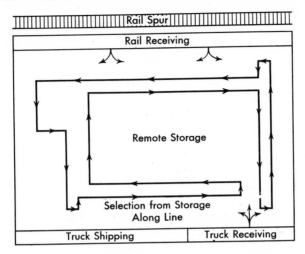

Precise Determination of Warehouse Space.   Several methods are currently used to determine the exact amount of required warehouse space.[29] Each starts with a sales forecast or some other projection of the total tonnage that will move through the warehouse during a given period. This tonnage is then used to develop base and safety stocks. Some require consideration of firm and peak utilization rates; others do not. The neglect of utilization rates can result in overbuilding with correspondingly increased costs. However, it is important to note that one of the major complaints of warehouse supervisors is the general underestimating of warehouse size by management. A good practice is to allow a ten percent safety factor to account for increased volume, new products, and so on.

A product line analysis, coupled with a sales forecast, provides the necessary information to determine specific space requirements. The first step is to convert the basic inventory requirements to pallet loads. The pallets can then be summed to arrive at the number of basic units to be placed in the warehouse. The second step is to arrive at the number of items to be placed along the selection line. This step is necessary whether a separate selection area or a selection line along a continuous movement system is to be employed. In the first case, the size of the area is relevant; in the second case, the length of the line is relevant. The third step is to determine the size of the reserve area. The depth and the height of stacks depend upon the nature of the merchandise and the average inventory of the items temporarily stored. The final step is to determine the amount of space required for offices, grouping areas, maintenance areas, and so on. The summation of the area satisfying each requirement considered in the four steps is the total space

[29]See Andrew J. Briggs, *Warehouse Operations Planning and Management* (New York: John Wiley and Sons, Inc., 1960).

CHART 10–9   Example of Correct and Incorrect Fire Door Placement

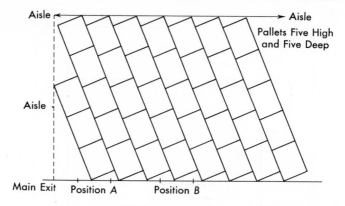

necessary for the warehouse. Space is best considered in terms of cubic rather than square footage. The objective is to obtain maximum cubic utilization.

Warehouse Design.   Designing a warehouse is a special area of planning usually contracted to the architect. Design and construction characteristics must not hinder product flow. Consequently, management must communicate to the architect the need for primary emphasis upon unrestricted movement. In order to properly design a warehouse, the architect will require specifications for the size of the structure, layout, and predetermined path of materials handling equipment. The materials handling specialist must work closely with the design specialist in order to develop an integrated system.

A number of small details directly related to efficiency are left to the architect. For example, doorway clearances must be carefully planned to ensure adequate widths and heights to accommodate materials handling equipment. If not correctly placed, a fire door can eliminate as many as 50 pallet positions. Assume a firm has selected a layout using angle placement of pallets, five deep and five high, along the outer wall of the warehouse. Note in Chart 10–9, if the door is placed in position A, three pallet positions, five high, are eliminated or, in total, 15 positions. If the door is placed in position B or at any other point along the wall, ten pallet positions, five high, are eliminated or, in total, 50 positions.

Other items that require careful consideration are the placement of overhead obstructions such as lights, steam pipes, sprinkler systems, and heating ducts. All of these items must be kept above the tiering height if 20 feet of vertical clearance is planned for the materials handling operation. The placement of supporting columns is also an important design consideration. Generally, a latitude of positioning is available depending upon which way the columns run with reference to the supporting walls of the structure. To ensure a minimum of restricted storage bays, it is of prime importance that the layout be planned in coordination with column placement.

The floor areas, which must be specially treated to ensure sufficient hardness, depend upon the predetermined path of the materials handling equipment. The choice of a square or rectangular design depends upon the characteristics of the selected materials handling system. The length and the width of receiving and shipping docks depend upon the volume of products handled, the systems of receiving and shipping employed, and the equipment used. The heights of the respective docks depend upon the height of trailer and railroad car bodies.

The above-noted items are but a few of the extensive reasons why the warehouse must be designed to facilitate product flow. Each item taken alone is small, but in total a number of improper decisions may greatly hinder product flow. The modern warehouse is founded on the efficient use of every cubic foot of space and available materials handling equipment. The structure is designed to stimulate this efficiency.

The Integrated Plan. Once management has selected a site and planned the size, layout, materials handling equipment, and design, construction may begin. It is generally a good idea to develop a small-scale model of the proposed structure. By utilizing a model and templates, a clear three-dimensional image of the proposed structure may be developed. A scale of $\frac{1}{4}$ inch equal to one foot will provide a good model. Such a model will help point out minor shortcomings of the proposed structure allowing modifications prior to costly construction.

INITIATING WAREHOUSE OPERATIONS

To begin operation, management must stock merchandise, hire personnel, develop work procedures, establish a method of billing and inventory control, and initiate a system of local delivery.

Stocking the Warehouse. The best procedure to follow when stocking a warehouse is to obtain the complete inventory prior to initiating distribution. The individual products to be distributed through the warehouse and the quantities of each in the basic inventory were determined when the warehouse was planned. The problem in stocking is to schedule the arrival of this merchandise in order to obtain an even flow into the warehouse. Upon arrival, merchandise must be rapidly transferred to a predetermined position in order to avoid congestion and excessive delays on the receiving docks. The time required to initially stock a warehouse depends upon the number and quantity of products to be handled. For a warehouse containing 4,000 or more products, it may take from 30 to 60 days to complete initial stocking.

In the storage area, products are assigned in full pallet loads to a predetermined area. Specific products that fall into a designated area can be placed at any point within the area. In the selection area, a coding system is normally used to identify products and positions. The coding system consists of a numerical classification and a slot position. The numerical classification is assigned upon product arrival and is retained as long as the product is held in inventory. This number may be coded to an automatic data processing installation to facilitate inventory control.

The assignment of slots refers to the floor position where merchandise is placed. A slot represents nothing more than a predetermined pallet position. Two methods of slot assignment are commonly used: (1) variable and (2) fixed. The variable slot system allows the product position to be changed each time a new shipment arrives in order to best utilize warehouse space. Under variable slot systems of placement, a given product may be in slot 1161 at one time and in slot 1831 the next.

Under the fixed slot placement system, a permanent position is assigned to each product placed in the selection area. The product retains this position as long as volume of movement maintains the same level. If volume increases or decreases, the product is reassigned. Fixed placement provides an advantage over variable slot placement, because it provides a method of immediately locating a product. Regardless of what slot system is employed, each inbound product should initially be assigned a location. Upon arrival, the merchandise should be identified by position number and transferred immediately to the selection or storage area.

Personnel Training.   Hiring and training personnel qualified to operate a distribution warehouse present a serious problem. Regardless of how good the proposed system is in theory, in practice it will be only as efficient as the operating personnel. Proper training is necessary in order to ensure optimum results from the system. The firm establishing a warehouse operation will undoubtedly have extensive experience in hiring desirable personnel; consequently, attention is directed to training.

Training personnel to operate a distribution warehouse is not a difficult assignment if properly executed. Normally, the full work force should start work a few days prior to merchandise arrival. People hired for specific jobs should be given extensive indoctrination in their jobs and the part their jobs play in the total system. Examination of the scale model and tours of the actual structure will rapidly familiarize the personnel with the system.

After a period of general indoctrination, each group of employees should be given extensive training in its specialized job. Personnel hired to operate a warehouse may be grouped in the following categories: administrators, supervisors, selectors, equipment operators, laborers, and miscellaneous workers, i.e., maintenance, salvage, and so on. These categories may be large or small depending upon the degree of management activities to be housed at the warehouse. For example, it is not uncommon for the regional or district office personnel to be headquartered in the warehouse structure.

When initial stocking begins, the work force obtains actual training in merchandise handling. Normally, the manufacturer supplying the basic materials handling equipment sends an instructor to help train equipment operators. Once the basic inventory is in stock, it is a good practice to spend some time running sample orders through the warehouse. For example, simulated orders can be selected and loaded into delivery trucks. The merchandise may then be treated as new arrivals and transferred back into stock.

Developing Work Procedures. The development of work procedures goes hand in hand with the training of warehouse personnel. The specialist who develops the materials handling system generally establishes a work procedure which ensures maximum utilization of the system. It is the responsibility of management to see that all personnel understand and use these suggested procedures.

In the average distribution warehouse, approximately 65 percent of the floor personnel are employed in some phase of order selection. Generally, modifications of two basic methods of order picking are employed in distribution warehouses: (1) individual selection and (2) area selection.

Under the individual system, one selector completes a total order. A number of trailers are placed behind the tractor and, at a designated time, normally when the order is half completed, the trailers are hauled to the shipping dock. This system is not widely utilized, the primary application being when a large number of small orders is being selected for shipment on the same truck. Under the more commonly used area selection system, each selector is assigned a certain portion of the warehouse. Under this system, many selectors handle one order. Because each man has a thorough knowledge of the selection area, no time is lost in hunting for items.

Specific procedures must also be established for receiving and shipping. Merchandise received must be checked in order to ensure inclusion in the inventory accounting system. If pallets are used, the merchandise must be stacked in patterns to ensure maximum load stability. For example, there are approximately 30 different patterns in which merchandise can be placed on a 40 × 48 inch pallet. Personnel working on receiving must be trained in which patterns to employ. Personnel working primarily in shipping must have a knowledge of loading procedures. In specific types of operations, primarily when merchandise changes ownership, items must be checked during loading.

Work procedures are not restricted to floor personnel. A definite procedure must be established for proper handling of inventory control records. Most firms employ some type of automatic data processing equipment. The purchasing or reordering of merchandise for the warehouse can cause a serious operational problem if proper procedures are lacking. Normally there is little cooperation between buyers and the warehouse personnel if the warehouse is operating below capacity. The buyer tends to purchase in the quantity that will afford the best price, and little attention is given to the problem of space utilization. Under such conditions, it will not be long until the warehouse is overstocked and demurrage charges begin to occur. The problem can be eliminated before it develops if the proper procedures are employed.

Buyers should be required to check with the warehouse manager before any abnormally large orders or new products are purchased. Some firms feel so strongly about this point that buyers are required to obtain a space allotment for all merchandise ordered. An equally serious problem is the quantity of cases ordered at a given time. The buyer should be required to order in pallet multiple quantities. For example, if a product is placed upon pallets in a pattern containing 50 cases, the buyer should order in multiples of 50. If an order is placed for 110 cases, upon arrival the cases will fill two pallets plus ten on a third pallet. The extra ten cases will require the same space as 50 and will require the same amount of movement effort.

The illustrations above indicate a few of the operational bottlenecks that can result from a lack of work procedures. Only if the system is offered standard inputs can an efficient operation be realized. It is a basic responsibility of the warehouse manager to assure that such standard procedures are developed.

Billing and Inventory Control. Most firms handling a large number of products with various turnover characteristics find it economical to employ some type of atuomatic data processing equipment to handle billing and inventory control. Under such a system, cards are normally punched for each case of merchandise received at the warehouse. When an order is received, the appropriate cards are pulled, and the order is printed, listing products in the order of warehouse placement. For example, if an area method of selection is employed, the order will be grouped by areas and printed in either numerical or slot order for the selector. Machine systems facilitate reordering, because warning cards may be placed in the inventory tubs to indicate reorder points. It is possible to rapidly make a card inventory of merchandise on hand at any given time. At selected times, the card inventory must be checked against a physical inventory in order to ensure continuous accuracy in receiving and shipping records. Management cannot be expected to understand the details of all available processing systems. Normally, a particular type of system is adaptable to an individual warehouse. The representatives of the various equipment companies will survey the problem and suggest a tailored system to meet the requirements of that particular warehouse.

Initiating and Programming Local Delivery. The final problem to be solved is a method of local delivery. Most shipments from market-oriented warehouses will be made to the retail outlet via motor truck. Three methods of local delivery are generally available: company fleet, common carrier, and leased carrier. Management must determine which is most economical for the specialized situation.

Common carrier is widely utilized when the shipments are varied in size, duration, and number. The common carrier offers the basic advantage of eliminating the problem of scheduling company-owned trucks in order to obtain maximum utilization. The leased carrier plan embodies the granting of a contract to a private carrier to handle all shipments. The main advantage of a leased carrier is the shifting of scheduling, maintenance, and load problems to a specialized operator. This plan is widely adopted because of these distinct advantages. For example, the A & P Company has a policy of utilizing leased carriers whenever possible. The company fleet has the main advantage of being adaptable to the requirements of the specific firm. When the operation requires extensive trucking facilities and trained personnel are available, the company fleet can offer a definite saving in distribution costs.

As noted above, when a company fleet is utilized, a problem is encountered in scheduling movements to ensure maximum utilization at minimum costs. Some aggressive firms have developed linear programming techniques to help solve this problem. The linear programming approach seeks minimum or maximum point of a function. Through the use of matrix algebra, the sequence of events resulting in the desired minimum or maximum are identified. In the case of programming local deliveries, the objective function to be minimized is the cost of distribution which, for example, may be expressed as a function of vehicle mileage.[30]

Organization

Generally a distribution warehouse is organized on a functional basis. The criteria used for developing individual departments are the similarity in work and ease of supervision. The chief benefit gained from using a functional organization structure is a high degree of specialization. The efficient operation of materials handling equipment is a highly specialized activity, which justifies the division of labor in order to develop the necessary operating skills. Two rules should be followed in the organizing of a warehouse operation: (1) definite lines of responsibility and authority should be developed for all functions performed, and (2) the span of control of supervisors should be held to a minimum.

Because of the flexible nature of a materials handling operation, it is imperative that each employee know the supervisor to whom he is directly responsible. A fork-lift truck operator may cover several miles during a

[30]For broader development of linear programming applications, see Appendix 13A.

CHART 10–10   Model Organization

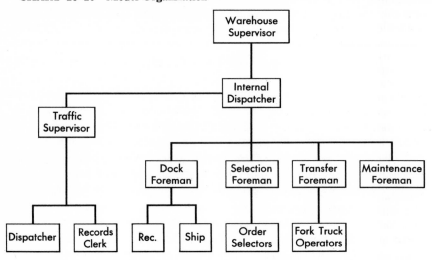

working day, encountering problems at different places within the warehouse. He will come into contact with a number of employees performing specialized activities. In order to control such a flexible operation, he must understand to whom he is responsible for work orders. Likewise, his immediate supervisor should have the direct responsibility of only a small number of men in order to facilitate rapid movement to various trouble spots.

No model organization may be suggested for all distribution warehouses. Each organization must be tailored to the particular operation. Thus, it is difficult to generalize on a "proper" or "one best" type of organization. For illustrative purposes, assume a warehouse handles a wide variety of products on palletized unit loads. Fork-lift trucks transfer unit loads from receiving to storage, and when necessary, to a clustered selection area. Tractors and trailers are utilized in a system of area selection for the combining or re-grouping of orders.

In this assumed case, how might the floor operation, organized on a functional basis, appear if placed on an organizational chart? Chart 10–10 expresses the general idea of functional organization. The chart is simplified, omitting administration and supporting organizations. The personnel concerned with each special movement function are grouped under one foreman directly responsible for supervising work related to that portion of materials handling. Each foreman reports to the internal dispatch supervisor who heads a small group of employees responsible for scheduling specific jobs for the various sections. However, each day a completely different schedule of work must be developed to process the wide variety of special orders. By concentrating upon their respective functions and becoming specialized in that particular type of movement, each section maintains the flexibility necessary to adapt to varying work loads.

Naturally the problem of communication is paramount in a materials handling operation. How does an order selector get a pallet load of a particular product when it runs out in the selection area? In most warehouses, communication is facilitated by the use of an intercommunications system originating from the internal dispatch office. Each fork-lift truck is assigned to a specific area of the warehouse floor. The dispatch clerk has a list of assignments for each fork-lift truck operator. When a selector needs a pallet load in a particular area, he calls dispatch on one of several phones located along the selection line. The dispatch clerk then calls the responsible truck operator with instructions to replace the product. Past experience has proven the functional organization is a highly efficient means for obtaining maximum product flow. Naturally the organization structure will vary depending upon which functions receive primary emphasis in a particular operation.

SAFETY AND MAINTENANCE

Accident prevention is a paramount problem in each area of the distribution warehouse. A well-balanced safety program should include constant examination of work procedures and equipment. The problem is to locate and correct unsafe conditions before they result in accidents. Accidents occur when workers become careless or when they are exposed to mechanical and/or physical hazards. Regardless of how often a fork-lift truck operator is warned against carrying overloads, some still attempt such short cuts when not properly supervised. The floors of a distribution warehouse may become a major source of accidents if not properly cleaned. Through normal operation, rubber and glass deposits collect along movement aisles. From time to time, broken cases will cause all types of products to seep onto the floor. If proper cleaning procedures are followed, the risk of accidents resulting from these hazards may be minimized.

A preventative maintenance program for materials handling equipment is necessary. Unlike production machines, movement equipment is not stationary. Consequently, it is easy to neglect proper maintenance. A preventative maintenance program requiring a periodic check of all handling equipment should be installed.

MEASURING WAREHOUSE EFFICIENCY

Maintaining warehouse efficiency requires the development of measurement techniques and standards for evaluation. There are several measures of warehouse efficiency currently in use in distribution warehouses. The two most popular measures are physical and dollar evaluations.

Physical Systems of Efficiency Measurement.   Physical systems of measurement consist of unit and weight evaluations. For example, a unit measure may be cases moved per man-hour or pallets per man-hour. Generally a tabulation is made of the number of units handled in each functional area of the warehouse, i.e., receiving, selection, and shipping. The physical unit system of measurement is also a convenient method for evaluating individual employees.

Weight systems normally employ a popular measure referred to as tons per man-hour (usually written TPMH). TPMH may be computed for the total warehouse or for individual functional areas. Normally the TPMH figure for the total warehouse is obtained by adding together the tons of merchandise received (TR) and shipped (TS) and then dividing the sum by the number of total direct handling hours. The formula is:

$$\text{TPMH} = \frac{\text{TR} + \text{TS}}{\text{Hours}}$$

In some special cases where the shipment is via common carrier, it is not necessary to include handling hours spent in loading. Normally the merchandise is delivered to the dock, and the private carrier assumes the responsibility for loading. When such is the case, the TPMH figure should be figured excluding loading hours. Such measures are normally referred to as TPMH less loading.

Dollar System of Efficiency Measurement.   The most widely used dollar measure is one expressing warehouse expense as a percentage of the cost of merchandise delivered to the warehouse during a given period. By weighting the relative dollar figures to a percentage figure, the problem is changing dollar values between time periods is partially omitted. The problem of different rates of change in prices and wages still exists, and the resultant figures should not be relied upon for period analysis. The dollar system is also inadequate for measuring efficiency between two warehouse systems during a given period because of regional cost differences.

MEASUREMENT STANDARDS

The selection of standards presents a delicate management problem. The standard is the primary reason for measuring various activities. The various measures result in figures that may be compared to standards, thereby determining whether specific functions or employees deviate substantially from the expected level of activity.

A performance standard can be set only after one has obtained a thorough knowledge of all particulars relating to the job. Extreme care should be taken in making warehouse comparisons on the basis of physical measures and related standards. Management should realize that there is no such thing as an absolute standard for measuring warehouse efficiency. Figures vary substantially between warehouses depending upon methods of calculation and the various details of operation. Each warehouse should be considered as a special operation, and specific standards should be established on the basis of the potential of that operation. Physical standards do offer a convenient means of making internal employee comparisons. For example, order selectors may be evaluated to point out which workers are exceptionally fast or slow. The results of such an evaluation may be compared with accuracy figures to determine which selectors require additional training and supervision.

Regardless of what system of standards is employed, if applied to evaluate various workers, it should represent a reasonable goal rather than a measure of optimum effort. Setting of standards is a difficult problem worthy of management attention. Only if measuring techniques are consistently applied and performance standards realistically developed will management have a true picture of warehouse efficiency.

Summary

The concept of distribution warehousing has made a dramatic change in the range of capabilities available for design of physical distribution systems. By utilizing the principles of distribution warehousing, customers can often be rendered better service at lower cost. When product storage is required, it can often be accomplished at strategic locations in the product flow pipeline. Unfortunately, not all markets can support a distribution warehouse operation. Therefore, the number of facilities, their location, and product mix carried in each is of primary concern in distribution system design.

Discussion Questions

1. Is storage the principle function of a physical distribution warehouse?

2. What is the difference between a market-positioned warehouse and a product-positioned warehouse? Is their reason for existence the same?

3. What is the difference in the strategies behind the use of nondifferentiated product warehouses and differentiated product warehouses?

4. Would damage in transit increase with full pallet loads? Why?

5. Under what conditions would a firm require permanent storage in a physical distribution warehouse?

6. What is the cost justification of a decision to locate a warehouse?

7. How important is the communication network to efficient warehouse management? Does the importance of warehouse communications vary by industry or product?

Appendix 10A
LOCATION TECHNIQUE

A number of methods, both mathematical and nonmathematical, can be used to locate distribution warehouses. Here, a algebraic method for solving the location problem is presented. By using this system, it is possible to calculate the ton-center, mile-center, ton-mile center and time-ton-mile center of the physical distribution service territory.[1]

Other methods such as linear programming, grid analysis, and heuristic applications can also be utilized in solving the distribution warehouse location problem. The cost and complexity of the technique should be matched to the difficulty of the problem. This appendix presents a method for a single facility location. Where it is necessary to locate multiple distribution warehouses in a total distribution network, other more complex techniques would be used. These techniques are discussed in Chapter 12.

A supermarket application of the algebraic solution is presented to demonstrate the technique. Although this industry is somewhat unique, the principles demonstrated have application over a wide range of consumer and industrial distribution situations. The input variables will change, because basic market configurations will vary widely by industry but the technique presented in this appendix remains the same.

Method

The mathematical technique employed evolves from an application of analytic geometry to the location problem.[2] The system is based upon Cartesian coordinates. By utilizing only the positive or northeast quadrant, the geographic market area under examination is simulated by establishing uniform mileage scales along the x and y axes. Given this system of orientation, it becomes possible to locate any point in the two-dimensional plane by identifying the relevant coordinates.

In a system of Cartesian coordinates, the horizontal, or east-west axis is traditionally labeled the x axis. The vertical, or north-south, axis is labeled the y axis. Together, these two axes differentiate four quadrants, which are customarily numbered as illustrated in Chart 10A–1.

Any given point in quadrant I can be identified with reference to the x and y coordinates. The y coordinate of a point is called its ordinate. The ordinate is found by measuring its distance from the x axis, parallel to the

---

[1]The Appendix is adapted from Donald J. Bowersox, *Food Distribution Center Location: Technique and Procedure*, Marketing and Transportation Paper No. 12 (East Lansing, Michigan: Bureau of Business and Economic Research, Michigan State University, 1962).

[2]The mathematical technique employed in this illustration is based upon "Warehouse Location Based on Trucking Cost," *Materials Handling Manual No. 1* (Boston: Boston Publishing Company, Inc., 1955), pp. E84–E86.

CHART 10A–1   Cartesian Coordinates

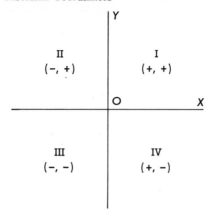

y axis. The x coordinate of a point is referred to as its abscissa. This is the distance from the vertical y axis, measured parallel to the x axis. Taken together, the abscissa and ordinate form the coordinates of a given point, the abscissa being given first. Chart 10A–2 illustrates the abscissa and ordinate of point A in the positive quadrant. In Chart 10A–2, the distance Ox_1 equals the abscissa of point A, and the distance Oy_1 equals the ordinate. Assuming the values of 40 miles for x_1 and 30 miles for y_1, the coordinates of point A would be read as A (40, 30).

By utilizing this basic system of orientation, it is possible to simulate the geographic market area in which the distribution warehouse is to be located. All retail stores are plotted in the Cartesian plane. Each store is identified by a subscript and placed in the simulated market with reference to its coordinates. In other words, retail stores are plotted with reference to their abscissa and ordinate, measured on a uniform mileage scale.

The algebraic method for solving the location problem identifies the co-ordinate position of the proposed distribution warehouse. The problem is essentially a weighted average of a given number of independent variables, with the dependent variable being the warehouse location. The algebraic process solves for the abscissa and ordinate of the warehouse. Consequently,

CHART 10A–2   Location of a Point in the Positive Plane of Cartesian Coordinates

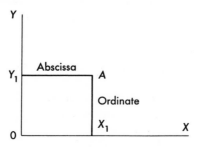

it is necessary to solve independently for the x and y coordinate locations of the warehouse. The formula expressing this calculation depends upon the independent variables, which are expressed in the location measure employed. Therefore, the exact formulations will be presented in the following section.

The Algebraic Solution

In the algebraic formulation the data utilized as basic measurement input represents independent variables. The resultant warehouse location is the dependent variable. The location problem is structured with identical service standards required from all potential distribution warehouse locations. Given this service standard, the location goal is to minimize physical distribution costs.

Generally, it is accepted that private carrier trucking costs are a function of time, weight, and distance. However, historically, when mathematical techniques were employed, not all of these cost factors were included as independent variables in the measurement device. Four measurement devices are available for analysis: (1) ton-center solution, (2) mile-center solution, (3) ton-mile center solution, and (4) time-ton-mile center solution. As the titles suggest, the first three contain combinations of only those variables related to weight and distance. The fourth measurement device includes both these, and an additional cost-influencing factor. The solution derived by utilizing this measure renders a superior location. By utilizing the Cartesian reference system and related algebraic formulations, the location problem is presented for each measurement device.

TON-CENTER SOLUTION

In the ton-center solution, the point located represents the center of gravity or center of movements in the market area. When obtaining a ton-center solution, the assumption is that the center of movements represents the least-cost location. However, accepting cost as a function of time, weight, and distance reveals the basic limitation of this measurement device — only weight is given consideration. Because the center-of-movements solution has been used, a computation of the ton-center location is completed for each model.

All outlets are plotted in the Cartesian plane and identified by subscripts. To express tonnage requirements to each supermarket, annual tonnage is reduced to standard trailer units. The standard trailer employed is a 36-foot semivan capable of handling 35,000 pounds of dry grocery merchandise. Once each supermarket location is determined and the total trailers to each are known, the warehouse location may be determined.

The location solution is found by adding the products of store location and trailer frequency for each supermarket from the x coordinate and dividing by the total number of trailers. The same process is repeated from the y coordinate. The result is a location in terms of x and y for the distribution center. The final location solution indicates the point that provides the balance of weight between stores for the given period. This basic algebraic procedure is followed for all mathematically derived location solutions with appropriate modifications necessary to handle the inclusion of different variables.

The algebraic formula for the ton-center computation is:

$$x = \frac{\sum\limits_{i=1}^{n} x_i F_i}{\sum\limits_{i=1}^{n} F_i} \qquad y = \frac{\sum\limits_{i=1}^{n} y_i F_i}{\sum\limits_{i=1}^{n} F_i}$$

where:

x, y = unknown coordinate values of the distribution warehouse
x_n, y_n = supermarket locations designated by appropriate subscript
F_n = annual tonnage to each supermarket expressed as standard trailers identified by appropriate subscript

MILE-CENTER SOLUTION

The mile-center solution isolates that geographical point which results in the least distance to all delivery points. The assumption underlying the solution is that delivery costs are a function of mileage. Therefore, if mileage is minimized, a least-cost location is determined. The basic deficiency in the mile-center solution is the omission of tonnage and time considerations.

Unlike the ton-center solution, the mile-center solution cannot be determined simply by solving for the weighted average along each coordinate. In order to find the mile-center, it is necessary to establish the distance of each store location from an original warehouse location, thereby obtaining a mileage value. This mileage value is determined by utilizing the general distance formula for finding the length of a straight line connecting two points. The exact procedure for this measurement is developed below.

Because the solution requires an initial x and y value for the distribution center, the final solution is found by a trial and error procedure. Starting with initial values for x and y, each time a computation is completed, new values are generated for the distribution warehouse in terms of x and y. The location problem is solved when the new values are equated to zero or within an acceptable tolerance of the last previous values. For example, if the initial values of x and y are 30 and 40, respectively, the location solution is obtained by utilizing these values to determine the new distribution warehouse coordinates. Assuming that the new values obtained are $x = 43$, the procedure has failed to set the new values equal to the original values. Thus, additional computation is required. For the second computation, the most recent values, $x = 36$ and $y = 43$, are employed. If the second computation results in the values of $x = 36$ and $y = 43$, the location solution equates to zero, and the problem is completed.

In all trial and error solutions, an acceptable tolerance of $\pm$ one mile is usually established for the x and y distribution warehouse coordinates. This means that all solutions are correct within a four-mile square area. If through the trial and error procedure a value for x and y within this tolerance is reached, the location is accepted as the center of the four-mile square area. This results in a maximum location error of one mile.

The algebraic formula for determining the mile-center solution is:

$$x = \frac{\sum\limits_{i=1}^{n} \dfrac{x_i}{d_i}}{\sum\limits_{i=1}^{n} \dfrac{1}{d_i}} \qquad y = \frac{\sum\limits_{i=1}^{n} \dfrac{y_i}{d_i}}{\sum\limits_{i=1}^{n} \dfrac{1}{d_i}}$$

where:

x, y = unknown coordinate values of the distribution center
x_n, y_n = supermarket locations designated by appropriate subscript
d_n = location until the trial and error procedure is completed

The value for d expressing the distance from a distribution center location can be determined from direct measurement on the coordinate plane or by utilization of the following distance:

$$d_n = \sqrt{(x_n - x)^2 + (y_n - y)^2}$$

where:

d_n = mileage distance between store and distribution warehouse designated by appropriate subscript
x, y = given coordinates of distribution warehouse
x_n, y_n = supermarket location designated by appropriate subscript

Because the value of d for all supermarkets changes each time a new set of distribution warehouse coordinates is determined, the distance formula is utilized in each step of the trial and error procedure.

TON-MILE CENTER SOLUTION

The ton-mile center solution combines the variables of weight and distance in selecting the distribution warehouse location. The assumption is that costs are a function of ton-miles. The ton-mile solution is superior to the mile-center solution, because it takes frequency of delivery to each store into consideration in selecting the location. It is superior to the simple ton-center solution since the impact of distance is taken into consideration. The solution once more calls for a trial and error procedure since d is included in the formulation.

The ton-mile formulation is:

$$x = \frac{\sum_{i=1}^{n} \frac{x_i F_i}{d_i}}{\sum_{i=1}^{n} \frac{F_i}{d_i}} \qquad y = \frac{\sum_{i=1}^{n} \frac{y_i F_i}{d_i}}{\sum_{i=1}^{n} \frac{F_i}{d_i}}$$

where:

x, y = unknown coordinate values of the distribution warehouse
x_n, y_n = supermarket locations designated by appropriate subscript
F_n = annual tonnage to each supermarket expressed as standard trailers identified by appropriate subscript
d_n = supermarket location differentiated in miles from the initial distribution warehouse location and sequentially from each new location until the trial and error procedure is completed

TIME-TON-MILE CENTER SOLUTION

The fourth location measurement device includes all cost-influencing variables. Because costs are a function of time, weight, and distance, the distribution warehouse location derived as a product of this device should represent a superior least-cost location. The procedure for selecting the time-ton-mile solution is trial and error, because both the time and distance factors are differentiated from a given distribution warehouse location.

The formulation is as follows:

$$x = \frac{\sum_{i=1}^{n} \frac{x_i F_i}{M_i}}{\sum_{i=1}^{n} \frac{F_i}{M_i}} \qquad y = \frac{\sum_{i=1}^{n} \frac{y_i F_i}{M_i}}{\sum_{i=1}^{n} \frac{F_i}{M_i}}$$

where:

x, y = unknown coordinate values of the distribution warehouse
x_n, y_n = supermarket locations designated by appropriate subscript
F_n = annual tonnage to each supermarket expressed as standard trailers identified by appropriate subscript
M_n = supermarket location differentiated in terms of miles per minute from the initial distribution warehouse location and sequentially from each new location until the trial and error procedure is completed

To arrive at a value for M_n, it is necessary to ascertain both the distance and time to all supermarkets from the given distribution center location. The distance value is determined by use of the basic distance formula. The time in minutes to each supermarket is found by calculating a time value from the coordinate plane. An estimate of delivery time must include number of miles, type of highway, and traffic. A general rule is that time per mile decreases as the number of miles per stop increases. In order to account for these basic factors influencing driving time, zones representing different attainable movement rates are constructed in the simulated market area. These zones consist of two basic types — rural and urban. Movement rates accounting for the influence of the above factors are adopted for each zone from a Department of Agriculture publication.[3] This publication represents a study of eight wholesale grocery firms' trucking operations. The purpose of the study was to develop methods for establishing time standards for dry grocery delivery in urban and rural areas. Two master estimation tables were developed which can be utilized for estimating delivery times between two points.

For use in a distribution warehouse location problem, the development of such estimating tables represents substantial savings in research cost. Utilizing these tables, the total time necessary to traverse the distance between a given distribution center location and a supermarket can be rapidly estimated. This eliminates expensive engineering time studies for each alternative distribution warehouse location. The time zones and respective movement rates are presented in Table 10A–1.

In this illustration, urban zones are defined as the geographic area of all cities with a population greater than 25,000. All other areas are considered

TABLE 10A–1*   TIME ESTIMATION TABLE

Urban Area		Rural Area	
Distance in Miles	Minutes per Mile	Distance in Miles	Minutes per Mile
Under 1	8.8	All Rural	2.2
1.0–1.5	7.0		
1.6–2.0	4.8		
2.1–3.0	4.0		
3.1–4.0	3.5		
Over 4.0	3.4		

Example: If a delivery trip consists of 16 urban miles and 38 rural miles total time would be 138 minutes (16 × 3.4)(38 × 2.2).

*Adapted from the Crossed and Kriesberg study, pp. 8–14.

[3]Charles Crossed and Martin Kriesberg, *Procedures for Evaluating Delivery Operations of Wholesale Food Distributors* Washington, D.C.: USDA, 1960.

rural. Given the values of distance and time through rural and urban zones, M_n is calculated in the following manner:

$$M_n = \frac{d_n}{t_n}$$

where:

M_n = attainable miles per minute to the appropriate supermarket
$d_n = \sqrt{(x_n - x)^2 + (y_n - y)^2}$
t_n = total time to store in minutes

PART III System Design

and Administration

CHAPTER 11 Total Cost Planning

THE objective of total cost planning is to (1) establish the level of costs by activity center, (2) state each cost in terms relevant to analytical requirements, and (3) measure trade-offs between and among the various activity centers. Trade-offs measure a cost reduction in one area against a cost increase in another. Thus, total cost analysis in the trade-off framework measures relative cost changes between activity centers, rather than absolute cost levels in any one specific area. In addition to total cost performance, service requirements in terms of customer delivery standards also provide added information influencing final system design.

The purpose of this chapter is to develop physical distribution cost functions for activity centers and to examine their interrelationship. The initial part of the chapter deals with the concept of trade-offs. Next, significant cost centers are identified and their characteristics examined. Three different techniques for measuring total system cost are developed to illustrate the interrelationship of activity centers. The final section deals with alternative distribution policies available to guide physical distribution system design.

Trade-Offs

Chart 11–1 illustrates trade-off combinations within a physical distribution framework.

TRADE-OFFS WITHIN AN ACTIVITY CENTER

First, trade-offs are possible within a single activity center. For example, in the transportation area, all possible alternatives are stated: rail, motor carrier, water, and any other relevant possibility.[1] The first level of trade-off

[1]For expansion of the trade-off concept see Robert Lekashman and John R. Stolle, "The Total Cost Approach to Distribution," *Business Horizons*, Winter 1965, vol. 8, No. 4, pp. 33–46.

CHART 11–1   Potential Trade-off Combinations Within a Physical Distribution System

	Transportation	Inventory	Unit Loads	Communications	Warehousing
Transportation	X				
Inventory		X			
Unit Loads			X		
Communications				X	
Warehousing					X

in the transport area revolves around mode selection. Given a mode, a second level of trade-off is possible within that mode; for example, a leased truck in comparison with a common carrier. The basic principle of trade-off within an activity area is that one alternative results in lowest total costs *without* affecting costs in other activity centers. In the same way as described above, trade-offs between each of the activity centers of physical distribution must be considered.

TRADE-OFFS BETWEEN ACTIVITY CENTERS

Of greater significance in physical distribution analysis is the trade-off between and among activity centers. Thus, the selection of a transport alternative may, and probably will, affect inventory, unit loads, communication requirements, and warehousing. Although trade-offs within a single activity center are identified with relative ease, their measurement between and among centers is more difficult. A high degree of activity center interaction is required if valid comparisons are to be made between different system designs discussed in the next chapter.

TRADE-OFFS BETWEEN CORPORATE ENTITIES — THE CONCEPT OF CONTINUOUS COSTING

Up to this point, the concept of total cost is framed within a single corporate entity. Under the concept of continuous costing, central focus is placed upon the entire chain of cost events from the original source of raw materials or parts supplies to the final consumption of the end product. As a theoretical matter, such costing ideas have been expressed in a number of places; but as a practical matter, the business application of continuous costing principles is limited by the interface between buyer and seller or between immediately adjacent exchange intermediaries. This interface de-

TABLE 11–1*   MOVEMENT OF GROCERY
PRODUCTS AT RETAIL LEVEL OF DISTRIBUTION

Rate of Sales Per Week	No. of Items	% of Total
Less than 1 case	3,753	89.5%
1 or 2 cases	244	5.8
3 to 5 cases	156	3.7
6 to 10 cases	33	0.8
Over 10 cases	9	0.2
Total	4,195	100.0%

*SOURCE: "The Dillon Study," *Progressive Grocer*, May, 1960, p. D–18.

pends upon the degree of compatibility of the physical distribution program of the buyer, coupled with the seller's receptivity.[2]

An example may demonstrate this point. From a materials handling point of view, it is generally more economical to increase size of units handled rather than decrease them. Industrial engineering principles suggest that economies can be generated to some upper limit of size. However, industrial engineering economies generally do not reflect the underlying environment within which economic transactions take place. Thus, although costs fall, these cost reductions do not necessarily result in improved profit performance. This is especially true at the distribution interfaces.

In the grocery trades, the traditional carton for sale of dry groceries contains 12, 24, or 48 units. It follows that generally, the 48-unit pack will have lower handling costs than either a 24- or 12-unit pack. Adherence to industrial engineering principles for lower costs suggests the 48-unit pack. However, sale activity of grocery products consistently shows that the vast majority move at the rate of one case lot per week or less. Turnover relationships are shown in Table 11–1.

The high peaking of sales in one-case lot per week is clearly illustrated in the table. In fact, nearly 90 percent of all grocery products move at the rate of one-case lot per week or less. This turnover relationship places the producer in a position to design unit packs to match more closely demand patterns. This may well result in higher handling costs all along the line, but also in higher profits for both seller and buyer. By focusing upon both demand requirements and supply conditions, a more viable physical distribution plan evolves than if based upon either demand (revenue) or supply (costs) alone.

The principle of interface may be demonstrated by focusing upon one specific product packed in 48-unit cases. Assume that demand is six units per week and the inventory cycle of the product is eight weeks ($8 \times 6 = 48$). The store's average inventory, therefore, is 24 units ($48 \div 2$). Suppose the

[2]See Chapter 3 for a detailed discussion of interfirm relationships.

manufacturer designed a new case with eight compartments, each holding six units. The eight compartments handled as a unit satisfy industrial engineering requirements, but package costs will increase. The 48-unit, eight-compartment pack may be shipped from processing plant to factory warehouse, then to the buyer's warehouse in order to achieve materials handling economies. However, at the buyer's warehouse, case lots are broken down into six-pack units if store demand indicates splitting is desirable. Other multiples of six may be shipped to any store with demand requirements for 12, 18, 24, 36, or 48 units.

However, consider a store that experiences a demand of six units per week. A six-unit pack (one-eighth of the master case) will result in matching inventory requirements more closely to demand. A store with this demand pattern and a six-unit delivery each week now experiences an inventory cycle of one week and an average weekly inventory of only three units.

Assigning a $4.80 per 48-case lot cost results in an average dollar inventory of 24 units or $2.40. In the second example, the average inventory is three units per week at $.10 per unit or $.30 inventory investment. Assigning a very conservative 10 percent carrying cost, the cost in the first example is $.24 annually, and in the second it is only $.03. The difference between $.24 and $.03 represents a saving, which can be shared between buyer and seller. In effect, any annual cost increase to the retailer of less than $.24 will still increase his profits. If added packaging costs are not greater than $.03 and absorbed by the retailer, profits will increase at the manufacturing level.

Identification of Cost Centers

The first requirement underlying total cost analysis is the identification of relevant cost centers. The cost centers relevant to total cost analysis are (1) transportation, (2) inventory, (3) unitizing, including packaging and materials handling, (4) communications, and (5) warehousing.

Individual cost centers may be more or less important, depending upon the particular situation of the firm. In high-volume transaction firms, order processing, picking, and packaging may have high relevance. In high-value commodities, the order cycle may be considered specifically as a cost center so as to keep transit inventories to a minimum. No specific list of relevant cost centers is sacred, and careful attention must be devoted to the identification of those relevant to the specific operating environments of the individual firm.

To illustrate the necessity of proper identification of relevant costs, consider the fact that great stress is almost always placed upon minimizing inventory levels and stock locations in inventory control literature. Yet, in some industries, exactly the opposite orientation is required. Bandages and chewing gum require maximum market exposure to maximize sales opportunities. Numerous stock locations and relatively high inventories are generally required for such firms. Thus, each firm must determine the cost centers relevant to its operations and market environment.

STATEMENT OF COST CENTERS

Once appropriate cost centers have been identified, the next crucial step is in defining their proper statement. Proper statement depends upon the analytical method selected to test alternative total cost solutions. Linear programming, simulation, and heuristics each require different cost statements, and each has different limitations, which restrict the alternative formulations available.[3]

FIXED AND VARIABLE COSTS

Cost functions may be expressed as fixed and variable. This is usually accomplished by going through the accounting classification system and separating fixed costs from variable costs. Even in one specific function, costs may shift from fixed to variable, depending upon the nature of ownership and control surrounding the purchase transaction. For example, an owned warehouse will have both fixed and variable costs, but a leased or public warehouse may have wholly variable costs. Once the costs have been properly identified and stated, it is possible to make total cost comparisons.

In the following sections, three techniques of total cost analysis are developed to illustrate the interrelationship of cost centers: (1) comparative statics — two alternatives; (2) comparative statics — more than two alternatives; and (3) multiple analysis.

COMPARATIVE STATICS — TWO ALTERNATIVES

In comparative statics, volumes moving through the distribution system are held constant and costs are calculated for alternative distribution system designs. The example selected is based upon a choice of either a rail-warehouse distribution system or direct distribution via air freight.[4] The cost centers in this example are (1) inventory, (2) warehousing, and (3) transportation. All other costs are omitted from the analysis to simplify the presentation. Although the example does not differentiate among market

[3]These techniques are developed in Chapter 12.
[4]For expanded treatment see *United Air Lines' Profit Analyzer* (Chicago: United Air Lines, 1961). For an early example of this same concept see Howard T. Lewis and James W. Culliton, *The Role of Air Freight in Physical Distribution* (Boston: Harvard University, 1956).

territories, in real cases a market territory must be defined. Thus, a California-to-New York air shipment may be feasible, and a New York-to-Chicago shipment may not be.

TABLE 11–2   EXAMPLE OF COMPARATIVE STATISTICS

	Rail-Warehouse	Air Direct
I. Inventory cycle costs		
A. Transit inventory (days)	10	2
B. Plant warehouse inventory (days)	5	1
C. Field warehouses (days)	30	0
Total days	45	3
Total days transit inventory saved	—	42
D. Annual inventory carrying cost		
1. Cost of capital	20%	20%
2. Obsolescence risk	5%	2%
3. Insurance (on value)	1%	1%
4. Taxes (on value)	2%	2%
Total	28%	25%
E. Assumed value of products eliminated from rail-warehouse system (days of inventory eliminated)	$5,000,000	

F. Annual inventory savings $\dfrac{(D)(i)(I)}{365}$ by air direct inventories

Where D = Days transit inventory saved
$\quad\quad i$ = Carrying cost of inventory
$\quad\quad I$ = Dollar reduction of inventory levels

$$\frac{42 \times .25 \times \$5,000,000}{365} = \qquad \$143,836$$

II. Savings in warehousing costs by air direct		
A. Rent (capital cost if owned)	$200,000	$150,000
B. Labor	$200,000	$100,000
C. Operating cost	$100,000	$ 50,000
Total	$500,000	$300,000
Savings		$200,000

III. Annual gross savings on freight (inventory and warehousing)		$343,836

IV. Transport cost comparison and savings by rail-warehouse distribution		
A. Freight charges	$350,000	$500,000
B. Local delivery charges	$100,000	$150,000
Total	$450,000	$650,000
Savings — surface transportation	$200,000	

V. Net savings, air direct vs. rail-warehouse ($343,836 − 200,000)		$143,836

**TABLE 11–3 COST CENTERS AND SAMPLE
RELATED VARIABLES**

1. Transportation	cwt miles
2. Inventory	average inventory
3. Unitizing	units handled
4. Communications	message units
5. Warehouse	throughput volume

In the preceding example, sales levels are held constant and a simple comparison is made of two alternative distribution methods. Although the air distribution system has substantially higher transport costs, savings in other cost areas (trade-offs) make air distribution the lowest total cost system.

COMPARATIVE STATICS —
MORE THAN TWO ALTERNATIVES

Typically, more than two alternatives exist in the development of a distribution system to service a specific market. However, it is cumbersome to isolate individual costs for all activity centers by the direct appraisal method used in the airline example. Therefore, when considering a number of alternatives, it is desirable to express costs as a function of a standard measurement unit. Table 11–3 illustrates cost centers and sample related variables for cost quantification.

The particular form of a cost function depends upon the environment and ownership relationship of the activity center.[5] In this case, certain assumptions are made to restrict the range of cost statements.

Transportation. By assuming exclusive use of common carriers, motor carrier costs have been developed from applicable rates and tariffs expressing each weight category, distance, and rate territory, as a regression. For example, the rate schedule for two different weight categories might be as shown in Table 11–4, and air freight scales as shown in Table 11–5.

In the same fashion, a complete set of costs are built up for all transport alternatives included in the study. Once cost studies have been formed, they are employed to determine the appropriate transport cost for any mileage and any weight bracket.

Inventory. Inventory costs in more than two alternatives are calculated on the basis of transit stocks required for each alternative plus safety stocks and base stocks. As shifts from one system to another occur, significant

[5]For an expanded development of costs related to distribution, see L. Gayle Rayburn, "Setting Standards for Distribution Costs," *Management Services*, March-April, 1967, pp. 42–52.

TABLE 11–4 MOTOR CARRIER RATE SCALE (¢/cwt)

Miles	100 lbs	10,000 lbs
10	324	33
20	327	35
30	330	36
40	333	38
50	336	40
60	339	42
70	343	44
80	345	46
90	349	48
100	351	50

TABLE 11–5 AIR FREIGHT RATE SCALES (¢/cwt)

Miles	100 lbs	10,000 lbs
200	650	600
250	664	609
300	678	618
350	692	628
400	707	637
450	721	645
500	734	654
550	748	663
600	762	672

time-related inventory changes will take place. To calculate these shifts, an estimate of transit time of alternative system designs is made. Thus, for a firm with $250,000,000 of sales, the daily sales rate is $1,000,000 based upon a 250-day working year. A reduction in transit times by one day will result in approximately $1,000,000 savings in transit stocks.

Changes in safety stocks are somewhat more difficult to measure, because they depend upon the complete order cycle and also upon demand variations. On short-order cycles, safety stocks may drop due to faster response time. As the number of stock locations increases, safety stocks may rise because of larger variations of demand in smaller market areas. Base stocks are the least sensitive to system variations, because they are defined as the amount of inventory necessary to serve the average level of demand.[6]

Unitization.   Unitization costs are affected by the degree of consolidation in a specific system. Direct shipments to customers ordinarily result in smallest consolidation, since order size is equal to shipment size. In systems with long lead times and a number of distribution warehouses, consolidation

[6]For a complete discussion of these relationships, see Chapter 8.

TABLE 11-6 SHIPMENT OF AUTO PARTS IN BOXCARS AND ON TRILEVEL CARS IN UNIT LOADS

Assumed distance	610 miles
Assumed weight	40,000 pounds
Rate per cwt pounds	$1.25
Distance transport cost	$500.00
Loading and unloading cost	$200.00
Packing and dunnage	$100.00
Total cost	$800.00
Assuming 4,000 pounds of parts equal 1 car, 40,000 pounds equal 10 finished cars:	
Number of cars shipped as parts	10
Total cost per vehicle	$ 80
Transport cost per vehicle	$ 50
Unit loading of finished cars at plant sent to market 610 miles distance:	
Transport costs	$549
12 autos per rail car	$ 45.75/unit
Loading costs at plant	$ 5.00/unit
Unloading cost at market	$ 2.00/unit
Total cost	$ 52.75/unit
Unit savings in unit shipment of finished cars	$ 27.25/unit

opportunities for unitization increase and economies are possible in materials handling.

In many discussions of total cost analysis, handling costs receive less attention than they deserve. It is not at all unusual to find that handling costs at the loading dock constitute a large percentage of the direct transport expense. Thus, in the auto parts field, handling costs on rail shipments may account for one-fifth or more of the transport bill. In the same industry, handling costs for automobiles on tri-level cars may be only $4 to $6 at origin and $2 to $3 at destination, a significant difference. These differences will seriously affect decisions regarding assembly plant locations. This impact of handling cost is illustrated in Table 11-6.

A comparison of the two cost structures shows it is cheaper to transport finished cars in complete units than equivalent parts at a distance of 610 miles. Including only transport costs in the comparison suggests economies in setting up assembly locations. However, including the loading and unloading costs with a high savings factor favoring the unitization of finished cars, the conclusion is reversed.

Communications. Communications may run the gamut of computer-electronic messages, WATS line, mail, data phone, or other types of devices. Communication costs generally increase as the degree of system sophistication increases. Highly sophisticated systems, although expensive in total dollars, may prove economic if the volume of transactions is high.

In complex distribution systems, a multiplicity of communications systems may be employed simultaneously. For orders between large volume points (New York, Chicago), a highly sophisticated electronic-computer-oriented system may be used. However, for very small demand generating points, mail may prove sufficient. It is imperative that goals and objectives of the system be clearly stated in designing required communication networks. Too frequently, distribution systems are designed for high performance levels (24-hour service), and unless the communication system chosen is compatible with that performance level, the whole system breaks down. Conversely, if a system is designed for low performance levels (two weeks' delivery), high performance communications networks are not required. Given a communication system, costs are variable with the number of transactions and the number of line items encompassed in each transaction.

In addition to the normally construed communication costs associated with order processing, other factors may be equally important. For example, because many railroads use computer systems to keep track of car locations, it is possible for a shipper to tie company data-processing equipment into railroad computers. This permits a daily report of car location status and expected delivery dates, as well as assisting in loading schedules for the available fleet.[7]

Communication is one of the more difficult cost centers to calculate, because the volume input messages are normally variable at each terminal point in the system. If a single plant warehouse is used to serve many scattered customers, direct message volume from each customer location will be small and costs of electronic-computer systems high. Conversely, when distribution points are relatively few in number—ten warehouses, for example—input messages per terminal point will be high and may justify electronic-computer-oriented systems.

Warehousing.   Warehousing costs are a function of throughput volume; that is, the volume moving through a warehouse facility over a time period. In measuring warehouse costs, it is first necessary to separate fixed and variable costs. This is done in Table 11–7.

From Table 11–7, fixed costs yield an approximation of costs associated with constructing a new warehouse. Variable costs reflect the impact of volume throughput.

If the above data represent an average warehouse operation, the fixed costs represent the amount of services necessary to construct and operate a specified size warehouse. The variable cost component measures cost as functions of volume. Thus, if the total throughput of an average warehouse is 1,000,000 cwt, the variable cost per cwt is $.679 per cwt. If throughput

---

[7]Eugene J. Landis, *TELSCAR: An Industrial Approach to Rail Transport Quality Control*, Proceedings: Railway Systems and Management Association Meeting, Chicago, Illinois, August, 1964.

TABLE 11-7 FIXED AND VARIABLE WAREHOUSE COSTS
(One-Year Sample)

Account	Fixed Costs	Variable Costs	Total Costs
1. Warehouse salaries	$ 60,000	$60,000	$120,000
2. Light, heat, water	1,100	100	1,200
3. Supplies	5,500	500	6,000
4. Rent (or depreciation, if owned)	12,000	—	12,000
5. Invoice	400	100	500
6. Taxes	5,000	1,000	6,000
7. Depreciation — equipment	600	—	600
8. Office salaries	20,000	4,000	24,000
9. Office supplies and miscellaneous	10,000	2,000	12,000
10. Communications	1,000	200	1,200
11. Travel	600	—	600
Total	$111,200	$67,900	$179,100

increases to 2,000,000 cwt, the variable cost component is still $.679 per cwt. but total variable costs increase.

Fixed costs change if warehouse size is varied. To solve this problem, fixed costs are divided into (1) those related to space, and (2) those related to personnel. For the space function, cubic feet of space per unit of product is first calculated. Given the cubic requirement per unit, added warehouse space then depends upon the peak volume moving through the system. Multiplying peak volume by cubic feet per unit of product results in estimated required warehousing space.

Fixed personnel costs measure the minimum number of supervisory personnel and labor required to perform the necessary tasks. Schedules are constructed for this purpose, depending upon (1) the number of shifts worked, and (2) size of labor force.

Total Cost Comparisons. The final step in comparing more than two system alternatives is the development of total cost comparisons.[8] A sample period, usually a year, is selected to generate sales data. Sales are then converted to average shipments and are processed through each of the cost functions to identify the cost for each activity center and for the combination of all centers.

For a 100-pound shipment moving ten miles, the cost is generated from the proper transport cost schedule (motor carrier, LTL, air freight, and so forth). A selection is made from all cost schedules to select the minimum cost alternative. The cost for the shipment is generated and stored for future accumulation of total costs. In the same way, costs are generated for the remaining cost centers.

[8]Locational variables are handled in more comprehensive analytical treatments discussed in Chapter 12.

TABLE 11–8   TOTAL COSTS AND NUMBER OF STOCK LOCATIONS (Sales = $400,000,000)

Costs	1	10	20	40	60
Transportation:					
Rail	$18,000,000	19,000,000	18,000,000	17,000,000	15,000,000
Motor Carrier	20,000,000	10,000,000	3,000,000	2,000,000	1,000,000
Air	100,000	20,000	10,000	0	0
Warehousing:					
Fixed	500,000	1,000,000	2,000,000	4,000,000	6,000,000
Variable	500,000	600,000	700,000	800,000	900,000
Communications:					
Mail	500,000	500,000	200,000	100,000	100,000
Telephone	500,000	500,000	500,000	400,000	400,000
Computer	0	0	1,000,000	1,200,000	1,400,000
Unit Loading:					
Packaging	800,000	600,000	500,000	500,000	500,000
Inventory Carrying Costs:					
Base stock	10,000,000	10,000,000	10,000,000	10,000,000	10,000,000
Safety stock	10,000,000	15,000,000	19,000,000	21,000,000	23,000,000
TOTAL COST	60,900,000	57,220,000	54,910,000	57,000,000	58,300,000

By this process, every customer and shipment is costed in such a way as to identify the total cost of each system under consideration. A sample cost schedule is shown in Table 11–8. This table shows the cost relationship of activity centers. Although data are assumed in the illustration, general cost characteristics are valid for most distribution studies. Among the five systems studied, the alternative having 20 stock locations resulted in the lowest total cost system.

MULTIPLE ANALYSIS

Multiple analysis permits the study of alternative systems under different assumptions concerning future volume requirements. The scope of physical distribution planning introduced by multiple analysis may be expanded to include any number of systems for specific markets and alternative volumes. The general rule is that alternatives must be arranged according to the level of fixed cost. These are ranked from the highest fixed cost system to the lowest. Any system with higher fixed cost and higher variable cost than the preceding alternatives will make it impossible to achieve a point of indifference. The reason for these points of indifference is the constantly diminishing variable cost slopes of successive alternatives. If, in comparing two alternatives, the slopes diverge from each other, no equilibrium is possible as volumes increase or decrease. This is the case when a system with both higher fixed costs and higher variable costs than any existing alternative is injected

TABLE 11-9 ASSUMED DATA FOR A MULTIPLE ANALYSIS PROBLEM

Alternative	Fixed Cost	Variable Cost per Ton
Air freight	$10,000	$1.00
Motor common carrier	20,000	.50
Direct rail	30,000	.25
Rail warehouse	40,000	.125
Branch plant	50,000	.0625

into the system. Therefore, alternatives of this type may readily be eliminated from further consideration.

To illustrate further, suppose that five alternative systems of physical distribution are under consideration in multiple analysis. These are arranged, starting with the lowest fixed cost to the highest, in Table 11–9. Following the rule above, the associated variable cost is lower with each successive alternative. Table 11–9 provides the necessary data to determine the system with lowest total cost at any volume level.

Again, the cost data are derived from the system of accounts within the firm and are classified as to fixity or variability according to management policy and economic circumstances. The various volumes of indifference, which cause a shift from one physical distribution system to another, are labeled x_1, x_2, x_3, and x_4. The formulas required to solve all indifference values are as follows:

$$x_1 = \frac{F_2 - F_1}{V_1 - V_2} = \frac{20,000 - 10,000}{1.00 - .50} = \frac{10,000}{.50} = 20,000 \text{ tons}$$

$$x_2 = \frac{F_3 - F_2}{V_2 - V_3} = \frac{30,000 - 20,000}{.50 - .25} = \frac{10,000}{.25} = 40,000 \text{ tons}$$

$$x_3 = \frac{F_4 - F_3}{V_3 - V_4} = \frac{40,000 - 30,000}{.25 - .125} = \frac{10,000}{.125} = 80,000 \text{ tons}$$

$$x_4 = \frac{F_5 - F_4}{V_4 - V_5} = \frac{50,000 - 40,000}{.125 - .0625} = \frac{10,000}{.0625} = 160,000 \text{ tons}$$

The proof of the validity of these calculated points of indifference is derived by simply showing total costs via each alternative at each value for x. For x_1, or 20,000 tons, the following is shown:

	F_1V_1	F_2V_2
Fixed cost	$10,000	$20,000
Variable cost	20,000	10,000
Total cost	$30,000	$30,000

The various points of indifference are indicated in Chart 11–2.

CHART 11–2   Least Cost Chart for a Number of Alternative Physical
Distribution Systems

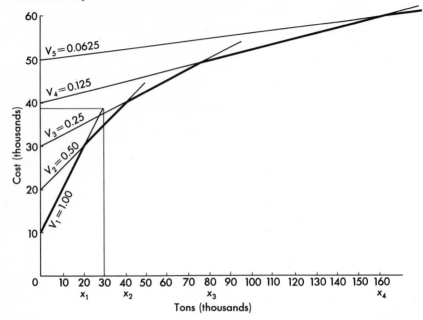

Chart 11–2 shows the limitations of the comparative method discussed earlier. Although the comparative statics will indicate the proper alternative to be selected at 1,000 tons, it is cumbersome to determine when a shift in the basic physical distribution system becomes imminent as a function of volume.

The origin of the lines on the vertical axis represents the levels of fixed cost determined for each alternative. They are derived from Table 11–9. The sloped lines, labeled V with appropriate subscripts, represent the variable costs under each system. The various points of indifference appear as intersections of the sloped lines. These intersections are labeled x_1, x_2, x_3 and x_4.

Under the comparative static approach, as was indicated earlier, a solution is reached for a unique problem. For example in Chart 11–2, if the volumes to the market under analysis were 10,000 tons, air freight would be indicated as the most economical form of physical distribution. But the volumes at which air freight may become an undesirable method are not known and cannot be discovered. It is conceivable, therefore, that when volumes or costs shift in a particular market, adherence to a limited model may lead to increased physical distribution expense. For example, if volumes increased to 30,000 tons and air freight were still employed, costs would be higher than necessary to serve the market. This is indicated in Chart 11–2 by the line rising vertically at 30,000 tons. The excess costs are then measured by the difference in total costs via air freight (V_1) and by motor carrier (V_2).

CHART 11–3   Total Cost Approach Converted to a Unit Cost Basis

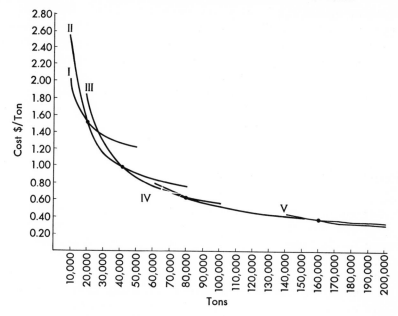

It appears to be about $5,000.

Because in the total cost approach cost functions are expressed continuously, it is possible to see at a glance which alternative is appropriate under varying volume conditions. To select the most economical form of physical distribution, it is necessary to find only the volume moving into the specific market being analyzed and move vertically from that point on the horizontal axis until the first cost curve has been reached. That point indicates the most economical physical distribution alternative. This can also be shown by starting as zero output and moving along the lowest cost curve. At each point of indifference a shift to the form with the next highest fixed cost level and next lowest variable cost level is indicated. This is shown in Chart 11–2 by the bold line.

EFFECT OF THE TOTAL COST APPROACH ON UNIT COSTS OF PHYSICAL DISTRIBUTION

The effect of moving along the lowest cost curves as volumes increase will tend to reduce the unit cost of physical distribution. Reference to Chart 11–3 shows that if the above rule is followed, the percentage change in volume exceeds the percentage change in cost, resulting in a constant reduction of unit expense. The unit cost curves for all of the above system are presented in Chart 11–3 to illustrate the point.

The curve labeled I indicates the lowest fixed cost alternative. Curve II indicates the next highest fixed cost alternative, and so forth. The lowest unit cost curve for volumes to 20,000 tons shows that the air freight system yields lowest unit cost. At that point, however, the next alternative system has identical unit costs. Beyond 20,000 tons, the air freight unit costs continue to fall, but the motor carrier system cost curve falls at a faster rate. This indicates that for volumes beyond 20,000 tons the better alternative, if cost is the sole standard, is motor carrier direct service. The curves continue, successively indicating each indifference volume.

Alternative Distribution Policies

Establishment of service and cost objectives constitutes a critical managerial policy preceding distribution system design. The system must be designed to meet service objectives and to stay within anticipated costs. Extreme care should be taken in the establishment of objectives. As a generalization, firms fall into the trap of being overly optimistic in the statement of service policies. The result is an excessively high commitment to customers, followed by erratic performance. This dichotomy results from a true appreciation of the cost of facilities and operations required to support high service commitments.

As indicated throughout this book, the objectives of individual departments responsible for physical distribution activities often stand in conflict. Therefore, formulation of system objectives cannot be left exclusively to department managers. Service policies must remain the responsibility of top management. Four basic strategies are available to guide managerial planning: (1) minimum total cost, (2) maximum customer service, (3) short-range profit maximization, and (4) maximum competitive advantage. Each basic strategy normally requires a different system design.

MINIMUM TOTAL COST POLICIES

Just as a physical map of a geographical area shows the elevations, depressions, and contours of land surface, an economic cost map illustrates differences in the cost of physical distribution activities between different areas. Generally, peak costs for labor and government services occur in large metropolitan areas. However, because of geographical demand cluster, total distribution costs resulting from reduced expenditures on transportation and inventory will be at a minimum at these metropolitan points. Lower total distribution costs result from the density of demand in these major markets.

At first approximation, a policy of least total cost distribution will seek to select a combination of facilities that will require lowest fixed and variable

CHART 11–4   Total Least-Cost Distribution System

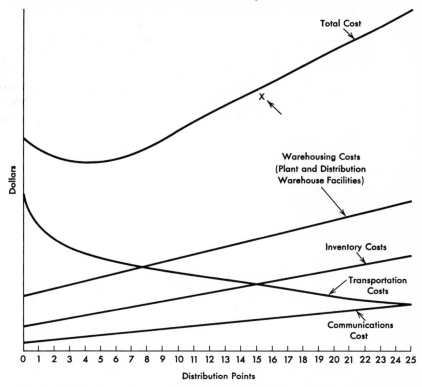

cost expenditures. Such a system will be designed purely for economies, with resultant customer service capabilities being a function of cost relationships among distribution activity centers.

In terms of activity center relationships, the point of total least cost is illustrated in Chart 11–4. In this particular example, the lowest total cost distribution system is one which utilizes five distribution warehouses. Although this least-cost combination is not the lowest cost point for any individual distribution activity area, it is the minimum point of overall system fixed and variable costs.

Under the conditions of least total cost, each customer is serviced on the basis of cost equalization between warehouse and plant locations included in the system. In a multiproduct situation, selection of service territories of each facility will depend upon the products stocked at each location and the degree of product mixing on individual customer orders. Because distribution costs have significant geographical differentials, the service area of any given facility will vary in size and configuration. Chart 11–5 provides an illustration of warehouse territory boundaries based upon an equalization line of total delivered cost. The irregularity of service territories results from distribution cost differentials in various directions out of the three distribution points illustrated.

**CHART 11–5   Determination of Distribution Territories
Three-Point, Least-Cost System**

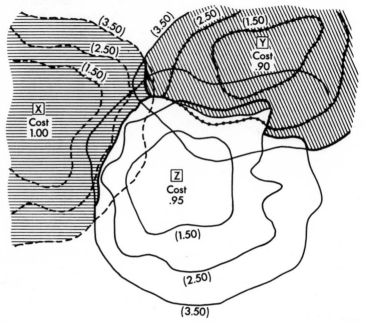

In Chart 11–5, the three distribution facilities are identified by the letters *X, Y,* and *Z.* The cost illustrated at each facility location represent the average order cost for all physical distribution costs not related to transportation. The differential of average order cost between facilities is reflective of geographical and individual system differentials.

Around each facility three total cost distribution lines are displayed at intervals of $1.50, $2.50, and $3.50. The value on the line represents the total cost of distribution to points located along the line. The area within a given line can be serviced at something less than the parameter cost displayed on the line. In actual practice, equal total cost distribution lines ($1.20 costs) would be constructed at smaller dollar intervals than the $1 range illustrated in Chart 11–5. The irregularity of the cost interval lines is reflective of the nonlinear characteristics of transportation rates.

The actual area serviced by each distribution facility is illustrated by the dark line. This territory boundary line represents the point of equal total cost distribution between two facilities. Along this line of equal costs, the firm is indifferent as to which facility services the specific customer involved.[9]

The student should be aware of two conditions contained in Chart 11–5. First, the illustration is based upon an average order, and thus, distribution costs are equated on the average. To the degree that order size varies from the average, alternate territory boundaries will be required. Second, an

[9]Bruce J. Riggs, "Sales, Production and Transportation Factors in Plant Location," *Transportation and Distribution Management,* October, 1961 p. 18.

element of time is included because transportation cost is calculated upon the basis of common carrier rates and costs occurred while inventories were in transit. Thus, the conclusion cannot be made that delivery times will be constant within territories nor to the point of equal total distribution cost between two service areas.

The fact that a least-cost physical distribution system is designed for maximum economy does not mean that customer service standards are omitted from managerial policy. The elapse time from customer order placement to product delivery in a least-cost system will be longer on the average than for other types of systems. However, customers located in the heart of the market will enjoy very high standards of service. Because the least-cost array will tend to favor areas of highest demand concentration, a substantial number of customers will enjoy fast order cycles. The customers who will suffer the greatest effect of longer order cycles will be those located at the point of equal distribution cost between two distribution facilities.

Regardless of the resultant delivery time, management will be in a position to make customer commitments concerning expected delivery. Such a statement might be expressed as follows:

Order cycle for area A will be 10 days from receipt of orders at our distribution facility. It is our policy to be able to fill 90 percent of all orders within the 10-day period.

The operational capability of the firm's physical distribution system is measured by the degree to which service standards to established areas is constantly met in practice.

MAXIMUM CUSTOMER SERVICE POLICIES

In actual situations, a maximum service strategy is rarely found. In essence, a system designed to provide maximum service would not attempt to deliver products faster than on a 24-hour cycle. Thus, the problem is to select the network of facilities that is capable of consistent 24-hour delivery.

Emphasis in maximum service shifts from cost to delivery time. Thus, a territory division is developed similar in appearance to the least-cost service areas illustrated in Chart 11–5. However, the cost lines are transformed into time or service lines. The limits of each facility service area are determined by the capability to provide overnight transportation. Similar to cost-oriented service areas, time-oriented areas will be irregular, because of transport route configurations.

The amount of total cost variation between least-cost and maximum service models will be substantial. To service the total United States market on an overnight basis would require from 30 to 40 distribution facilities or the use of very high-speed, high-cost transportation.

MAXIMUM PROFIT POLICIES

Objectives of maximum profit policies are those to which firms most commonly aspire in the design of physical distribution systems. At a theoretical level, the service area of each facility is determined by establishing a minimum allowable profit margin for customers located at varying distances from the facility. Because the distribution facility will be located in high volume markets, the greater the distance a customer is located from the service area center, the greater are the costs of distribution. This occurs, not only because of distance, but also as a result of lower customer density at the periphery of the service area. At the point where the costs of serving peripheral customers result in minimum allowable margins, further extensions of the service territory become unprofitable on a total cost delivered basis.

If the customer were offered better delivery service in terms of speed or frequency to complete an order, more of the product assortment might be purchased. Therefore, additional service is introduced to the point where marginal revenues equal marginal costs. At this point of equilibrium, no additional service is economically justified. The addition of service may or may not result from increasing the number of distribution warehouses. The service may best be provided by a supplemental system of direct physical distribution. The theoretical profit maximization position is easier to state than to accomplish in practice. However, the goal of equated marginal revenue and marginal cost represents a normative situation management should strive to approximate.

In the development of a highly profitable system, management is seeking a balance between service and cost. By referring to Chart 11–4, the balance will normally be found along the total cost curve to the right of the least cost point, but considerably short of the point marked X where total costs rise rapidly. Thus, as a first approximation, for the situation illustrated in Chart 11–4, the profit maximization system could be expected to fall between a network of five and 15 distribution points.

Table 11–10 presents a quantification of the service capabilities of the ten best networks of distribution points in comparison with a hypothetical customer configuration. The assumption is made that all systems are geared to a 95 percent probability of inventory availability upon receipt of a customer order. Although the actual service gains accruing will vary by each firm and every market situation, several principles are illustrated in Table 11–10 and Chart 11–4.

First, incremental delivery service is a diminishing function as distribution points are added to the overall network Although the addition of the sixth distribution point increases the percentage of 24-hour customers by 10 percent the addition of distribution facility number 15 adds only a 2 percent gain in the 24-hour service category. Second, high percentages of service are reached for those customers receiving longer service intervals substantially faster as distribution points are added. In terms of customers relegated to 48-hour

**TABLE 11–10   HYPOTHETICAL SERVICE
CAPABILITIES OF ALTERNATE DISTRIBUTION
POINT CONFIGURATIONS**

Number of Distribution Points	Percentage of Customers Serviced by Hour Intervals			
	24	36	48	60
5	25	37	60	80
6	35	47	78	87
7	42	67	85	90
8	47	73	88	91
9	52	78	90	92
10	57	80	90	92
11	61	82	91	92
12	64	84	91	93
13	67	85	92	93
14	70	86	92	93
15	72	87	92	94

service, the percentage increases by only 4 percent as distribution points eight through 15 are added. Finally, in reference to cost as illustrated in Chart 11–4, the incremental cost of each additional point is nearly linear but is increasing at an increasing rate in the relevant study range. Thus, each distribution point adds to the system costs more than the previous facility and adds less service capability than the previous facility.

The amount of dollar variation between each of the systems under consideration shows the additional total costs of reaching higher service levels. These dollar estimates provide an assessment of the value of added service against added cost. Given a schedule of these cost-service relationships, management is afforded considerable information to help in the establishment of service delivery standards.

MAXIMUM COMPETITIVE ADVANTAGE POLICIES

Under special situations, the most desirable physical distribution policy to guide system design may be the accomplishment of maximum competitive advantage. Although there are many cases where systems may be modified to gain competitive advantage, two are developed here to illustrate this range of policy considerations.

Core Market Considerations.   The first general case concerns modifications in system structure aimed at protecting major customers from competitive inroads. In the case of a firm that is able to provide 42 percent of the customers with 24-hour delivery at 95 percent inventory availability, management should be concerned with the welfare of major customers under this service policy.

To illustrate, assume that this firm is typical among those engaged in mass marketing and that 20 percent of their customers purchase 80 percent of their product output. Further, assume that 20 percent of the customers represent 75 delivery or terminal points to be serviced. Is this 20 percent of core customers included in the 42 percent of total customers receiving 24-hour delivery? Under conditions of equal customer geographical dispersion, the probability is about .5 that the array of 42 percent of total customers would include all of the significant 20 percent. In other words, we would expect that on the average approximately 40 to 45 of the core customers would get 24-hour service. However, because we know the system is biased toward location of distribution facilities at points of highest demand, we might assume that as many as 65 of our core customers would receive prime service.

By identification of core customers, it is an easy process to isolate the service received by each. Core customers are identified as critical terminal points and the frequency by delivery service interval is obtained by an interrogation process. Table 11–11 presents the results of a hypothetical interrogative process.

TABLE 11–11   CORE CUSTOMER INTERROGATIVE RESULTS

Total Core Customers	Number of Core Customers Serviced by Hour Intervals			
	24	36	48	60
75	53	16	4	2

The actual number of core customers receiving 24-hour delivery is 53. Thus, although 42 percent of all customers receive 24-hour service, 76 percent of the core customers receive prime consideration. In addition, the interrogative process points out that the remaining core customers receive varying degrees of service with two of these critical customers obtaining only 60-hour delivery.

Providing management is so disposed, this situation can be rectified by a restatement of objectives. The cost of a system providing 24-hour service to 90 percent of all customers can be isolated. Thus, management can equate the dollar-and-cents requirements of a core customer policy.

Several additional systems modifications may be evaluated similarly to the core customer illustration above. Management may wish to examine service provided to the most profitable customer. Evaluations can be made regarding customers or noncustomers having the greatest potential. In addition, a firm may wish to evaluate incremental cost of providing prime service to the core customers of major competitors. Although all such modifications may increase total cost and decrease short-range profits, the long-range gain may be a substantial improvement in competitive position.

Economically Justified High-Cost Distribution Facility. An additional application of design modification to capitalize on competitive activities is the case of the economically justified high-cost distribution facility. This situation is especially pertinent to a small business enterprise. Because of rigidities inherent in large firms, pricing policies are likely to be somewhat inflexible. Present antitrust legislation tends to reinforce these rigidities. The result is that large firms selling in broad geographical markets tend to disregard unique cost and demand conditions in localized markets or find it legally impossible to adjust marketing and logistical systems to accommodate these localized situations. This inflexibility creates opportunities for smaller and localized operations. Such opportunities may encourage management of these smaller firms to make significant modification in least-cost distribution policies.

Location of a small scale plant or distribution facility in a minor market some distance from major competitors results in a localized space island which is more or less insulated from competition. The logic of this special situation is developed under the general discussion of factors influencing distribution facility location.[10] At this time it is sufficient to point out that major firms follow one of two courses concerning these localized situations with respect to physical distribution design.

First, a major firm can elect to avoid these localized situations with respect to providing special service. This policy of concentrating on primary markets results in an opportunity for the higher cost, smaller firm. Second, major producers may introduce smaller scale distribution facilities or institute direct distribution systems in an effort to create a differential advantage in these local demand situations. Following the first policy will more or less result in a distribution system approaching a least-cost configuration. The second policy will require substantial system modification with resultant higher costs and lower short-range profits. It is interesting to note that firms who adjusted to the localized West Coast situation in the late 1930's find their market position very desirable today.

Summary

Total cost analysis provides a framework for analyzing physical distribution systems in (1) a limited two-choice alternative; (2) a more expanded consideration of several alternatives; and (3) multiple analysis, which permits alterations in volumes sold and provides a long-range planning tool to aid management in anticipating broad future configurations of system design.

Total cost analysis requires identification of cost centers and also must include an appropriate statement of each facility the analytical framework

[10]See appendixes at end of book discussing facility location factors and procedures.

selects for a specific study. By these methods, least-cost systems can be identified, permitting management to focus attention upon payoffs associated with design changes to meet (1) customer service requirements, (2) market condition, and (3) competitive practices. As you might expect, the complexity of physical distribution planning to service widely divergent markets may require more powerful analytical tools than those developed in this chapter. These are discussed in Chapter 12.

Discussion Questions

1. Why do most firms place importance on minimizing inventory levels and stock locations in their inventory control programs?

2. In what way do variable costs affect throughput of volume on warehouse operations?

3. What are the primary causes of geographic differentials in distribution costs?

4. Would customers prefer to have firms analyze their physical distribution systems with regard to least cost or a specified service level?

5. Why are handling costs often overlooked on the analysis of a physical distribution system? In what types of firms are handling costs most important?

6. What is meant by the term *interface*?

7. Why must management take a serious interest in the service level that will apply to its physical distribution system?

8. What is the concept of *continuous costing*? What is needed to make it applicable in a given situation?

9. In the future, what will physical distribution's position be in the activities of a large corporation? A small corporation? How will systems analyses affect physical distribution managers of the future?

10. What is total cost analysis? Why should the physical distribution manager consider using total cost analysis in physical distribution management?

11. What are trade-offs? Describe trade-offs and the effects within activity centers and trade-offs and effects between activity centers.

12. How does the intensity of market demand affect the physical distribution system? Total costs?

CHAPTER 12 Distribution

System Design

PHYSICAL distribution system performance is measured by two standards; (1) level of customer service capability and (2) total cost requirements. Whether or not a firm's management is aware of the fact, the combination of transportation, warehousing, inventory, and communications currently used constitutes a physical distribution system. The objective in system design is to bring the firm's logistical structure to the highest possible performance level. This development and related problems of implementation are basic responsibilities of physical distribution management.

The purpose of this chapter is the development of system design concepts. The initial section is concerned with some basic considerations in design. Next, integrative techniques available to assist in system design are developed. The last section presents a managerial guide to system design.

Basic Considerations

Prior to development of specific aspects of distribution system design, several basic managerial considerations are reviewed. These considerations include (1) nature of distribution facility commitments, (2) locational considerations, and (3) degree of system optimization.

NATURE OF DISTRIBUTION FACILITY COMMITMENTS

It is helpful in system design to visualize the entire physical distribution process as one concerned with manipulation and control of physical flow.

Such flow of physical property can be evaluated in terms of temporal or spatial relationships. The element of time relates to how long it takes to complete an order cycle. Systems can be designed to have very fast order cycles by either having a large number of distribution facilities or by using very high speed transportation. To enjoy the fastest potential of the above delivery structures a speedy system of order processing is also required. However, a firm may not elect to utilize the fastest order cycles available, because a variety of slower cycles exist. Most physical distribution systems will be designed to utilize a combination of different cycles. In general, the faster a system's response time to an order, the greater is the total cost of the system.

The spatial aspect of a distribution system relates to a network of facilities through which physical properties flow. The facility network includes the number, arrangement, and size of manufacturing plants and distribution warehouses. The point of final destination in a physical distribution flow is classified as a terminal location. Typical terminal locations are company-owned plants, distribution warehouses, retail stores, or customer locations. All distribution facilities exist for the purpose of bringing the desired assortment and quantity of materials and finished inventory as needed to the appropriate terminal facility.

For purposes of corporate planning it is useful to divide distribution facilities into classes: (1) fixed facilities and (2) support facilities. Fixed facilities relate to financial commitment and include those owned and operated by a firm. Maximum control exists over fixed facilities. However, to achieve this control it is necessary for the firm to invest fixed capital into the facility network. Support facilities represent those available for use at a specified fee. The duration of commitment in support facilities varies extensively. The cost of support capability is variable in nature, with the per unit cost being a function of volume and duration of time commitment. Although support facilities are controlled, the degree of control is less than that enjoyed in the case of fixed facilities.

To illustrate the relationship of fixed and support facilities take the case of a public- versus a company-owned distribution warehouse. At one extreme a firm may own a warehouse constructed with internal or borrowed capital. This investment makes the warehouse a fixed facility. It is common for such facilities to be amortized for periods as great as 25 years. At the other extreme, a firm may use a public warehouse for short periods to meet peak demand requirements. The public warehouse would be a support facility. Between these two extremes are various other alternatives. For example, a distribution warehouse can be built on a lease-back arrangement as short as five years and involving no fixed capital investment and contractual obligations. Likewise, a contract may be arranged with a public warehouseman for any reasonable time duration.

Attention to the division of facilities as fixed or support is of primary concern in system design. In cases of doubt concerning a firm's stability in an individual market, managerial preference may be for maximum flexibility. To achieve maximum flexibility, system facility design should concentrate on the use of support facilities. A physical distribution system utilizing a high degree of support facilities will normally have higher operating costs than one structured around a majority of fixed facilities. In addition, a support facility network is less controllable than one using fixed facilities. Thus, the trade-off is between maximum flexibility and reduced capital investment on the one hand, as compared to lower variable cost and greater control on the other. The balance of these alternatives will vary between firms and even between markets serviced by individual firms. In order to develop the most desirable distribution system, all relevant combinations of fixed and support facilities should be evaluated.

Among all possible combinations of fixed and support facilities there exists an arrangement that will be better for a given firm than all others. This superior arrangement will lead to the desired performance at minimum resource commitment. Finding this combination of fixed and support facilities has been referred to as the classical physical distribution problem.

LOCATIONAL CONSIDERATIONS

A firm should place primary attention on the locational arrangement of facilities, because they represent the structure for product flow. Although some degree of flexibility does exist between fixed and support facilities, commitments to a facility structure represent the most durable decisions in the physical distribution complex. Inventory, for example, may be modified up or down within a relatively short period of time. Common carrier transportation is even more flexible to the end that the degree of requirement is directly related to volume. Fixed facilities, in contrast, constitute a stable commitment over longer time periods. Thus, commitments to distribution facilities represent the primary point of concern in system design.

It is atypical to find a high degree of priority centered upon locational structure in treatments of system design. The more common approach is to assume facility locations. Attention is then directed to integration of transportation, inventory, and communications in an effort to determine the best combination of these variable factors. When locational networks are evaluated, the normal approach is to seek the best arrangement of distribution warehouses within a given group of potential locations.[1]

To be sure, limited integrative treatments often result in the addition or elimination of distribution warehouses and often the modification of a plant location. However, the entire process rests upon management judgment.

[1]For example see Alfred A. Kuehn and Michael J. Hamburger, "A Heuristic Program for Locating Warehouses," *Management Science*, July, 1963, pp. 643–66, or Harvey N. Shycon and Richard B. Maffei, "Simulation-Tool for Better Distribution," *Harvard Business Review*, November–December, 1960, pp. 65–75.

In no way does this limited approach to system modification provide assurance that the best possible network of facilities is selected to accommodate the task at hand.

The basic managerial justification for restricted facility analysis is based upon practicality. From a purely operational viewpoint no firm of any substantial size has the capacity nor could it justify the risk of simultaneously relocating all physical distribution facilities. In fact, as indicated earlier, many fixed facilities are frozen during a substantial period of time as a result of long-range contractural and financial commitments.

Objections to a limited approach are twofold. First, there exists a direct relationship between the number of distribution facilities and required expenditures for all other elements included in the system. For example, as illustrated in Chapter 8, safety stocks are directly related to number of distribution facilities. Similar relationships were demonstrated in the chapters dealing with transportation. Unless all aspects of an integrated network are fully examined in system design, it is difficult if not impossible to measure performance quality of the resultant structure. Second, unless the total system is studied no individual facility can be relocated, added, or deleted with complete assurance that it will complement the remainder of the system. Therefore, although it may appear expeditious and practical to eliminate complete facility location analysis from system design, such simplification may lead to costly mistakes.

DEGREE OF SYSTEM OPTIMIZATION

The above discussion implies that a firm should seek to establish an optimum distribution system design. The design of an optimal system is a noteworthy objective, but one that is never achieved. The tempo of business change coupled with an inability to consider all facilities and resource commitments variable results in considerable imperfection in the design process. Even if an optimum system could be conceived, it is doubtful that construction and overall implementation could be completed in sufficient time to enjoy the perfect arrangement. Thus, although the objective is to design the best possible system, seldom will the results achieve an optimum solution.

The high degree of change characteristic of business renders the task of physical distribution system design a continuing management responsibility. Complete system studies are not a common occurrence. Once completed, such studies serve as a guide to evaluation and modification of specific segments of existing facility structures. Changing patterns of customer demand, corporate objectives, technological developments, and competitive tactics will necessitate frequent modification to basic systems design. The single most important benefit of distribution system analysis is to provide a blueprint to guide modifications and adjustments as required. Over a period of time, sufficient change may occur so as to occasion a complete review of the basic design plan.

Design Integration Techniques

Several different techniques exist to aid management in the development of a system design. At a technical level, available techniques can be grouped as (1) optimizing and (2) less than optimizing. As noted earlier, problems of distribution system design seldom can be mastered to the level of optimum configuration. The fact that human involvement is a critical part of a physical distribution system limits the ability to achieve a fully closed design. However, a more limiting factor in design optimization is the inability to develop precise and accurate measures of operational interrelations within and between logistical activity centers. Therefore, all of the techniques explained in this section fall short of deductive optimizations.

By order of development the basic nature of simulation and modeling is first reviewed. Next, five integrative techniques are developed. In general, the discussion of integrative techniques moves from limited to more generalized approximations to optimum conditions.

SIMULATION

All techniques developed in this section are classified as simulations. Simulation is a process by which a model of a particular situation is developed and tested using facts from real world conditions. As one would expect, the range of simulations in terms of complexity and subject studied is unlimited.

In physical distribution system design, concern is with models containing various combinations of activity centers. The simulation process attempts to measure anticipated performance given a specified set of business conditions. With the exception of some very simple simulations, the complexity of the distribution system design process requires the use of computers to handle numerical computations.

MODELING

The central area of concern in development of distribution system simulations is the concept of modeling. The model represents a substitute for testing actual distribution system designs. By developing and testing a model it is possible to evaluate the impact of alternative policies prior to resource commitment.

Models are of two general types: (1) physical and (2) abstract.[2] The physical model is a replica of the object under study. The process of physical modeling is frequently used in construction. Most distribution managers use physical models when planning a new warehouse facility. Abstract models are more difficult to visualize. The abstract model uses symbols rather than physical devices to represent a system. The use of mathematical symbols to describe an abstract model is commonly found in physical distribution. However, it is possible to develop flow diagrams to illustrate some models tested in physical distribution system designs. For purposes of distribution system design it is also useful to classify models in terms of (1) static-dynamic characteristics and (2) stability.

Static-Dynamic Relationships.   A model is static if it deals with time periods on an exclusive basis. It is dynamic if the model attempts to deal with intertime period relationships. For example, a static simulation may study model performance over a 13-period operating year. As such, the static simulator will cover an extended time period. The process is static if each of the time periods is treated independently. The process becomes dynamic if each of the thirteen periods are linked on a recursion basis. Such linkage is accomplished by development of feedback mechanisms in the model design.

Feedback mechanisms refer to a range of system results considered as inputs for the next activity period. Given any demand period, the prevailing system model must have excess capacity, adequate capacity or be deficient to the task at hand. The optimum situation would be a system model that remained adequate to the desired performance over the entire study system. Under these ideal conditions, it would not matter if the model were structured as dynamic or static. However, adequate capability is never the case when system demand is engaged under the conditions of uncertainty which prevail in the real world. Thus, given any demand load, the system will normally be either abundant or deficient. Both situations result in performance penalties. A condition of excess capacity results in higher than necessary total costs. Excess penalties can be handled properly in both static and dynamic simulations. A deficient condition is more critical.

Deficiencies influence both cost and service performance. For example, demand for a specific products that is deficient at a primary service facility may (1) result in shipment from a secondary location at greater cost and possible reductions in customer service; (2) result in a backorder with related cost and service penalties; (3) result in an order cancellation with possible penalty of customer loss. Static models can only handle these events as independent occurrences related to the study periods under consideration. Dynamic models consider such feedback elements critical to performance

[2]For an extensive discussion of models see Jay W. Forrester, *Industrial Dynamics* (Cambridge, Mass.: The M.I.T. Press, 1961), pp. 47–59.

for future operations. Thus, dynamic models, although more complex, are more realistic approximations of real physical distribution problems.

Stability. Dynamic models are classified stable or unstable. A stable model will strive to maintain original condition as disturbing events occur. An unstable model tends to amplify disturbances because of lags and improper interruptions to the point where extensive demands are placed on the system.

Given a stable system, a disturbance, like a two-week out-of-stock on a fast-moving product, would be expected to result in temporary adjustments in stock levels to protect the desired level of inventory availability. However, unless demand stabilized at a higher level, the model would seek to reinstate the original condition. In any event, a stable model would retain the desired performance level with a minimum of oscillation. In contrast, an unstable system would be more apt to experience prolonged oscillation between excessive and deficient inventories.

The typical distribution manager may not view out-of-stock performance in terms of stability; however, the odds are high he has experienced instability at work. An unstable situation seldom improves until some external force intervenes. In consecutive periods, such external force may well be the controller when inventories peak and the sales manager at times of inventory drought. The development of stability in the physical distribution system can greatly reduce this conflict.

COMPARATIVE STATICS

The simulation technique of comparative statics was introduced in Chapter 11 for the purpose of illustrating total cost analysis. The comparative static approach to system design deals with two or a limited number of different system design alternatives at a specified level of physical distribution volume.

In comparative statics flow diagrams are charted for each system design under consideration.[3] Each flow diagram is a model of an alternative system. Next, estimates are made for each cost element included in distribution activity centers of each system. Cost estimates are based upon the required number of average size shipments needed to fulfill the volume requirements to the specific market under study. Finally, the selection of the best system is made by a comparison of total cost between all design arrangements tested.

Comparative statics has many limitations as an integrated technique. First, unless the process is repeated a number of times it is not possible to measure the benefits obtainable from design changes to accommodate alter-

[3]Techniques and symbols of flow diagramming are developed in Appendix A to this chapter.

native volume levels. Second, the range of designs tested is limited to those which the distribution analyst feels are acceptable alternatives. Third, facility locations must be assumed and held constant under any given design configuration. Thus, the interrelationship of facility location is not treated in design configuration. Finally, comparative statics is not able to handle trade-offs between customer service and cost requirements with the same degree of precision as other integrative techniques.

The limitations of comparative static analysis render it deficient for large-scale integrative studies. The technique is useful for evaluation of proposed modification to limited parts of an existing system. For example, comparative static analysis can be employed to check if a given market area has reached a sufficient volume to support replacement of direct shipments with a warehouse. The technique is fast and inexpensive, and it requires a minimum amount of technical expertise or computation capacity. If used with care and on specific types of problems, comparative statics can represent a useful short-range planning tool.

MULTIPLE ANALYSIS

The technique of multiple analysis was also introduced in Chapter 11 to illustrate the changing nature of total cost as a function of volume. Cost related to each system design can be divided into fixed and variable groupings. Each alternative system will have different cost functions in each category. Some systems will have higher fixed costs than others. The variable cost of handling more or less average shipments will also be substantially different between alternative systems. For any given volume one system will have the lowest combination of fixed and variable costs and therefore will be the lowest cost physical distribution alternative.

When using multiple analysis, an attempt is made to express variable cost relationships for each system in a formula. These formulas are linear in relationship and represent the variable cost of an additional average shipment to the market under study. Fixed costs are held constant. By testing alternative volumes of average shipments, it is possible to locate the level at which one system achieves lower cost than the next. The series of formulas represent the models of alternative systems under study.

Multiple analysis has many of the same limitations as comparative statics. Location is assumed, range of system alternatives is limited, and service cost relationships are lacking in multiple analysis. Because testing can consider performance at alternative volume levels, multiple analysis eliminates one of the main deficiencies of comparative statics.

Multiple analysis has limited usefulness as a planning tool. It is frequently utilized to aid operational decision making. For example, if alternative methods of direct distribution exist to service a given market, multiple analysis can be formulated on the bases of fixed and variable costs of each as a function of shipment size. Thus, given any particular shipment, it is possible to select the direct distribution alternative that should be utilized. Even if a warehouse exists in the service area, the multiple analysis model can provide valuable cost information to help decide if the shipment should be sent direct from the factory. Under certain conditions it may be less expensive to bypass the warehouse and ship direct. A multiple analysis simulator can be of great aid in daily management.

Thus, although comparative statics and multiple analysis provide techniques useful for limited research, training, and operational guidance, more powerful and comprehensive analytical tools are needed for tackling complex distribution system studies. Three such techniques are dynamic simulation, static simulation, and heuristics.

DYNAMIC SIMULATION

Dynamic simulation refers to a technique wherein all possible system designs are evaluated in the research process. Dynamic simulation is the most powerful integrative technique. However, it is also the most complex and requires the highest degree of expert capability. Static simulation and heuristics represent simplifications of dynamic simulation. As such, our discussion in order of (1) dynamic simulation, (2) static simulation, and (3) heuristics will move from the more general and complex to the most manageable forms of powerful integrative techniques.[4]

The dynamic simulation solution relies upon sequential tests of a system model. A study period, for example, one year's business, is held constant to test system capability. This business activity, called operational input, is used repeatedly to test design modifications. Each sequence in the simulation procedure results in an improvement in total system design. The final solution is determined when no additional worthwhile improvements can be made in the then-existing design. As such, dynamic simulation models are structured on a recursive relationship and rely upon numerical analysis for design solutions.

The models employed in dynamic simulation are mathematical and consist of four basic formulations: (1) initial condition, (2) system state, (3) operational relationships, and (4) feedback mechanisms. Each is briefly reviewed as they apply to problems of physical distribution system design.

Initial Conditions. Initial condition formulations consist of two types of data: (1) set and (2) flow. Each type of data is discussed in turn.

[4]For two discussions of simulation see John Dearden, *Computers in Business Management* (Homewood, Ill.: Dow Jones-Irwin, Inc., 1966), pp. 234–57; and Alfred A. Kuehn, "Complex Interactive Models," in *Quantitative Techniques In Marketing Analysis* (Homewood, Ill.: Richard D. Irwin, Inc., 1962), pp. 106–23.

Set data refer to a prevailing condition for the simulation process. To initiate the simulation procedure, it is necessary to define customers by location, size, and product demands. In addition, georeference coding is also required for raw material sources, suppliers, existing manufacturing plants, inventory accumulations, distribution warehouses, transport capacity, and all other factors involved in the existing distribution system. Set data also include parameter values for various managerial-determined constraints on system design. The degree of desired customer service is of critical importance as well as a statement of available resources. If any given facilities are considered beyond the scope of simulation study involvement, they are eliminated from the research procedure during development of set data parameters. Set data are of primary importance in the establishment of both system state and operating relationships.

Flow data represent the stream of demands to be placed upon the system during the study or planning period. At an ideal level, flow data will be constructed as a series of requirements for distribution activity by customers or other terminal locations. Such activity will be listed sequentially in order of occurrence for each time period under study. In seeking the best system design, flow data are held constant during the simulation period. The end result is a system status that will most effectively meet managerial-determined service policies at the lowest total cost expenditure.

System State.   System state refers to the value of all variables included in a system at any given time in the simulation procedure. In a physical distribution simulation, system state reflects the relationship among facility locations, inventory allocations, transport capacity, unit loading, and communication linkage. Each system state will have a service capacity and a related cost. Thus, reference to a system state is based upon a set of relationships among distribution activity centers in terms of expectations over a period of time.

The starting system state is defined by the set data formulated under initial conditions. Thus, although customer locations will not be specified in system state formulations, facility locations, transport capabilities, and other variable aspects of design will be sufficiently broad to allow all possible system configurations to be tested without geographical bias. Therefore, state formulations are developed on a georeference basis rather than on specific reference to a series of locational points. This range of system state possibilities is one significant difference between dynamic simulation and all other forms of simulation discussed later in this chapter.

Operating Relationships.   Operating relationships constitute a quantification of the interrelationship of all variables included in system design. In essence, operating relationships are behavioral, because they reflect the cost of change in system status. For example, the addition of a warehouse will result in substantial changes in transport, inventory, and communication demands upon a system. The operating relationship formulas provide a means for determining resultant changes in system state occasioned by the simulation process. As such, operating relationships are flow formulations, and system states are level equations.

In general, the development of operating relationships is the most complex task in dynamic simulation. This task is even more complex in geographically oriented dynamic distribution system simulation because these relationships can and do assume substantial value differentials based upon locational structure. By using this information, values for operational relationships may be constructed. Given an expression of regional differential, indices are constructed to reflect operational relationship values.

Feedback Mechanisms. Given an initial system state, flow input is processed to determine if an improved system state is possible. Such an improved system state results from analysis of operational relationships, tested over the study period. Dynamic simulation is distinguished from other forms of simulation by the way in which the time period relationships are treated.

For any prevailing system state, given a demand requirement, the system can be expected to have excess capacity, be adequate, or be deficient to the task at hand. These possible levels of capability and resultant influence on distribution system design were discussed earlier under static-dynamic relationships in modeling. Dynamic simulation derives its name from the capability of handling time-related performance penalities. The feedback mechanism formulations provide the structure for handling these delays. Under dynamic simulation, feedback is evaluated in terms of operational relationships and resultant system state. Thus, in addition to measures of capability and cost, the dynamic simulation process provides an approximation of system stability.

The Dynamic Simulation Process. To generalize, a dynamic distribution system simulation has the objective of designing that system which meets service requirements at lowest cost given managerially determined constraints. The initial conditions of the model provide set and flow data. Flow data are held constant and can be generated as many times as necessary to ascertain the best possible design. Each generation of flow data is called a study cycle. Initial condition set data are of two varieties. Data assumed constant by managerial preference or beyond managerial control constitute study parameters and are labeled set constants. The variety of set data allowed to respond to the study is referred to as set variables. During each cycle of the study, set variables will change; however, set constants remain the same throughout the total study or until managerially modified.

CHART 12–1   The Dynamic Simulation Process

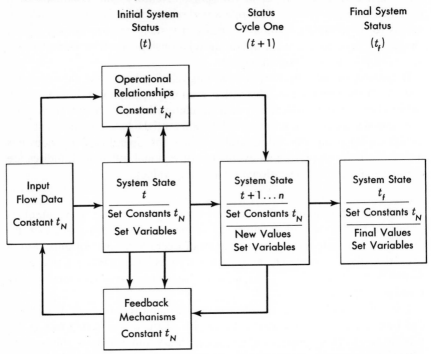

| | Initial System
Status
(t) | Status
Cycle One
$(t+1)$ | Final System
Status
(t_f) |

For each cycle of the study, a new system state will consist of set constants adopted as parameters and set variables developed as a function of operational relationships and feedback mechanisms for each segment of the study period.

This total process is generalized in Chart 12–1. The interrelationships of the simulation model are displayed so as to illustrate the recursion relationships. The initial study cycle results in a system state identified as $t + 1$. Operational relationships and feedback influence system state in two ways. First, for the initial cycle, the study period deficiencies in system capability are generated in terms of extra demand loads with related operational penalties. Second, given initial system status, deficiencies lead to modifications in system status, shown as $t + 1 \ldots n$. Such modifications are reflected as new values for system state set variables. This process is repeated until no improvement in system state is possible, and the system t_f (final system) has been structured.

The dynamic simulation process, if properly structured, should result in a configuration of physical distribution facilities ideal to support logistical requirements. Specifications concerning inventory allocations will be delineated for each facility. Perhaps the most beneficial result of dynamic simulation is a priority assignment of customers to specific supply facilities. The most desirable order processing and communications subsystem will be determined by the simulation. A final output of primary importance will be a transportation scheduling scheme, which will result in desired performance at lowest total system cost.

The experienced distribution manager may find the promise of dynamic simulation a little difficult to believe. His doubt is justified by the fact that it is highly unlikely that anyone has performed a dynamic simulation study as broad as described above nor will such studies become common occurrences in the near future. This lack of historical precedent should not be misinterpreted. Dynamic simulations have not been prohibited by a deficiency either of mathematical techniques or computer capacity to handle such problems. Rather, studies have compromised on less ambitious approaches because of inability to describe operational relationships and feedback mechanisms with sufficient precision and accuracy to obtain valid results. With time, such relationships will become quantifiable.

The dynamic simulation technique has the following advantages over other techniques: (1) all possible systems designs are evaluated in terms of managerial objectives and cost; (2) location is variable for all facilities unless held constant by managerial constraint; (3) the model is dynamic in structure providing a full impact of time relations common to business practice; and (4) the model is sufficiently broad to allow a full interplay of all operational factors. The disadvantages are (1) high cost of seeking perfect information in terms of data collection, analytical structuring, and computer capacity; (2) the overall complexity of the study often results in an inevitable communication barrier between technical and general management groups; and (3) extensive time is required to complete the study.

Dynamic simulation represents the closest approach to optimal modeling available for physical distribution system design. Although not a widely used tool, it does provide a normative guideline when more limited techniques are used.

STATIC SIMULATION

The static simulation procedure represents a modification of the dynamic process described above. Modifications are adopted at a sacrifice of optimum solutions to achieve a more workable model. Such modification results in simplicity, lower study cost, and faster solutions. In terms of the rapid rate of change in modern business, such "satisfactory solutions" may well be adequate for design requirements for a long time to come.

In static simulation the model is formulated around a group of plausible distribution facility locations. In the majority of cases, the type of facility is limited to distribution and plant warehouses with production capacity assumed constant. In addition, the model is often structured around finished goods distribution. Because the range of potential distribution facilities is limited, operational cost relationships are formulated on a point-to-point basis. This ability to work on a point-to-point basis overcomes the major hurdle of developing the all-encompassing operational relationships required in dynamic simulation. In static simulation, no attempt is made to structure the model to handle time-period interplay. Thus, because it is static rather than dynamic, problems related to feedback mechanisms are greatly simplified. The static simulation treats each operating period within the overall study period as a finite interval. Final results represent a summation of operating performance for each period in the study.

The static simulation procedure seeks the best network of facilities among those included in the study structure. The initial state of the system assumes that all plausible locations are included in the network. In subsequent cycles, distribution facilities are added and deleted on a trial-and-error basis until the best combination among the locations is ascertained. No assurance exists that the selection of facilities included in the study will represent the best possible range of alternatives.

The advantage of static simulation is that it is simpler, less expensive, and faster than dynamic simulation. Although the solution lacks unlimited design possibilities, it is sufficiently broad to include all apparent facility locations, transport alternatives, and communication subsystems. Inventory allocations are made based upon the network of distribution facilities included in each study cycle and service territories for each facility are delineated.

HEURISTICS

The heuristics simulation is designed to seek an acceptable solution similar to static simulation. Once again, a logical assortment of distribution facilities is assumed at the start of the study procedure. The total heuristic process attempts to keep reducing the problem into manageable size, allowing managerial intervention at critical points in the search process in order to guarantee acceptable results.

The heuristic process can be initiated from a number of different points of departure. The normal procedure is to select the minimum number of facilities among those available as a first approximation of system state. However, it is possible to start the process with only one facility. Because the total process deals with a maximum number of definable locations, it is possible to approximate actual costs for each proposed facility. In addition, transportation expense in terms of cost per ton-mile or some other constant measure can be introduced and maintained in the format of a data table.

The heuristic procedure is based upon aggregation of demand on distribution facilities. Given one or more facilities, demand over the study period is assigned on the basis of least cost to the available shipping points and the minimum inventory to service this demand is derived. The given network (system state) is then measured on the basis of cost and service capability.

This information is given to management for evaluation. The assumption is made that management has sufficient appreciation of realistic requirements not to eliminate a vital aspect of the problem. As a result of this evaluation, additional distribution facilities are added to the network by managerial discretion.

The modified system state is then evaluated once again aggregating demand to the available facilities. As new facilities are added, existing warehouses are reviewed in terms of continued desirability. The heuristic procedure includes a special bump-shift routine, which allows uneconomical distribution facilities to be eliminated. Once again results are compiled for managerial review. This process continues until the most acceptable network of distribution facilities is determined.[5]

The computer program for a heuristic simulation is developed in a manner that closely parallels the thought process of the human mind. This step-like procedure of adding facilities allows managerial review of system development with related explanation of logic at each step. Thus, the solution once derived requires little managerial interpretation.

Similar to static simulation, heuristics is faster, less complex, less expensive, and easier to understand than dynamic simulation. It has the added advantage of management involvement. The limitations of heuristics are similar to static simulation with two additional shortcomings. First, heuristics does not necessarily result in selection of the best network among those facilities that appear plausible. Static simulation does result in selection of the best network among the study array. Thus, although both represent less than optimum techniques, static simulation is more precise than heuristics. Second, although managerial intervention eases the process of understanding study results, the possibility of bias remains a constant danger.

Managerial Guide to System Design

Just as there exists no ideal physical distribution system suitable to the needs of all firms, procedures followed in the establishment of a design study vary extensively. As one would expect, the format for a dynamic simulation study would be considerably different than for a static comparison of two design alternatives. However, in the design process several definable steps should be taken in all studies. The purpose of this final section is to develop a managerial guide to the research process.

DISTRIBUTION AUDIT

The most important part of the total design process is the distribution audit. The audit is aimed at the development of information to be used in the design study. As such, all that follows centers around the search process of

[5]For greater detail see Kuehn and Hamburger, *loc. cit.*

data collection. Focal points in a comprehensive audit are divided as follows: (1) product profile, (2) market profile, (3) competitive profile, (4) existing facility profile, (5) measurement standards and cost profile. Each profile contains information for design and manipulation of the system model. It is surprising how few of the questions confronted in a distribution audit can be answered on the basis of existing corporate records. Thus, the typical audit will require considerable research effort to collect the necessary data. The following sections develop some basic types of questions a distribution audit should answer.

Product Profile.   The product profile is aimed at a complete delineation of products sold by a firm. The primary point of emphasis centers around those attributes of the product assortment which directly relate to the physical distribution process. Therefore, interest centers around (1) current packaging and physical attributes, (2) special handling requirements, (3) annual volume, (4) profitability, and (5) marketing congruity.

Packaging is of fundamental concern because of the protective aspects and size considerations that must be considered in distribution system design. Chapter 6 illustrated several of these factors in terms of handling throughout the distribution system. The physical characteristics of each product will determine the range of transport and storage alternatives available. To the extent that individual packages are commonly transported in larger pallet or container loads, special provisions will be required in the system design.

Special handling of products can be necessitated by size or perishable features. The handling of boats requires substantially different features than the handling of frozen-food products. It is essential that all special handling requirements be fully elaborated.

The annual volume of individual products in an assortment is of primary concern. In essence, volume relates to flow capacity in physical distribution system design. Perhaps the question of flow is best illustrated by two examples. Atomic generator distribution flow is very erratic with a few sold per year, each normally in a different geographical market. Baby food, in contrast, is bottled so fast that it is difficult to distinguish a single bottle on the production line with the naked eye. Unlike atomic generators, baby food demands a distribution network geared to mass volume, flowing on a continuous basis. In any product assortment, the flow characteristics among individual items will vary extensively. These characteristics must be calibrated on a seasonal basis in distribution system design.

Profitability of individual products on an annual basis is of extreme importance. Naturally, a firm desires to sell its most profitable products, and distribution systems must be designed so as to provide high performance levels for highly profitable products. However, products are seldom sold in isolation. Most products represent individual items in assortments and for proper measure in the system design, products should be grouped in terms of interdependence and assortment profitability.

Finally, for firms selling a wide variety of products, the question of marketing congruity must be quantified. The identical product may be marketed in widely divergent channels of distribution. Cooking oil, for example, may be sold to the consumer, institutional, foreign, and military markets. Although packaging will often differ, the product may be identical. However, a single firm will often market products so different that not even the similarities noted above exist. The question of divergent exchange channels is critical, because it represents a limiting factor in physical distribution system design. A great many economies of physical distribution are directly related to volume flow. To the degree that congruity is lacking, the volume flow of a firm is fragmented by individual channel demands for special services and alternative speeds of delivery.

The information required in development of a comprehensive product line profile is normally available within a firm. However, such information is often scattered about and not readily available except in fragmented degrees of detail. The purpose of the product profile is to develop reliable estimates of these various factors into a single information source.

Market Profile.   The market profile of a firm refers to a quantification of current and potential customer demands for individual products. Who are current customers? How much do they buy of each product? What is a reasonable estimate of future requirements? What special services do they require? Where are they located from a physical distribution viewpoint?

All of the above questions represent the type of information needed for system design. The question of location from a physical distribution viewpoint is of particular importance. A customer may purchase from one location and require delivery at any number of different locations. Most national retail chains are a prime example of this differential between purchase and delivery location. In physical distribution system design, both locations are critical. The purchase location is of prime importance from a communications network viewpoint, and delivery locations influence transportation, warehousing, and inventory allocations.

Requirements for special services also influence system design. Perhaps the best example of distribution system modification to meet special service requirements is found in the food industry. Although a few years ago it was common for processors to sell food chains solid carloads of a single or limited group of products, this procedure has altered radically. Today, large chains demand and get mixed carloads of a great many different products on a frequent basis. The retail chain, striving to increase the speed of product flow forced substantial changes in the distribution system design of processors. At one time processors could ship direct from plants; today most major firms have redesigned their systems to include a network of product-mixing distribution warehouse facilities. An improper evaluation of current and future special service requirements of customers could represent a critical error in future system design.

Although the market profile should develop exacting information on current customers, the potential of noncustomers is also of critical importance. To the extent possible, design of a system should strive to bring superior service to select prospects. Such capability can become a prime marketing tool. A common practice is to isolate a limited number of prime prospects who are located within the broad market area serviced by the firm. These target prospects can be included in design analysis with a resultant estimate of service cost and performance.

Competitive Profile.   Beyond an evaluation of competitors' customers who represent target prospects, the quality of service regularly offered by competitive firms should be appraised. Collection of this information will require some external research, but the payoff may be significant. In particular, what speed of delivery is provided by major competitors? How consistent is their service over a period of time? What level of in-stock performance is provided over a period of time?

Analysis of these and related questions can uncover some interesting information. Although most business propaganda seems to contain a degree of permissible puffery, logistical performance claims often lack reasonable proximity to actual performance. The critical issue is not only the opportunity such lack of competitive performance offers, but also the elimination of the danger of attempting to design a system to eliminate a nonexistent competitive advantage. The frequency of attempting to meet or beat a nonexistent competitors logistical advantage is not a rare occurrence in business. As strange as it may seem, top management is far more vulnerable to this trap than operating management.

Existing Facility Profile.   Each facility in the existing distribution system is unique and will have features that must be considered in system redesign. Such features include capacity, operating cost level, current mission, capabilities, condition, expansion possibilities, and degree of permanence. Information concerning these features of facilities is normally available; however, accumulation requires data collection from numerous departments.

In particular the degree of permanence is important to system design. Permanence is viewed in at least two ways: first, a financial expression of fixed capital committed in terms of depreciation schedules; second, the question of managerial willingness to incur penalities related to considering a given facility flexible for purpose of system design studies. The latter determines if a given facility will be included in a study, and the former develops cost estimates for use in design analysis.

The need for exacting facility analysis is very basic. How can a distribution system be modified if doubt exists regarding current and future potential capacity of existing facilities?

Measurement Standards and Cost Profile.   In Chapter 11 the question of isolating physical distribution costs was developed in detail. Among the various types of cost normally found in a firm, it is doubtful if all costs required for system analysis will be readily available. For a physical distribution study it is essential to develop cross-departmental cost measures as well as an approximation of the reaction of costs to different levels of throughput.

Only if a complete documentation of current costs is available can the proper accommodations to fit special requirements of the distribution analysis be developed and agreed upon. Determination of what costs will be affected, isolation of those that are significant, and application of consistent standards of costing are essential to the design process.

ESTABLISHMENT OF MANAGEMENT PARAMETERS

The second step in the distribution system design procedure is the development of management parameters. Alternative strategies to guide these policy formulations were discussed in detail at the end of Chapter 11. The actual statement of specific parameters falls into three categories: (1) output objectives, (2) design constraints, and (3) measurement standards.

Output Objectives.   Output objectives deal with cost and service expectations of the revised system. It is essential that such objectives be stated specifically in terms of measurable factors. A typical procedure at this stage in the study is to state specific service objectives but to set cost considerations aside until later in the study. Thus, the following is a typical format of service objectives: (1) the system will be designed to provide 95 percent inventory availability for category A products, 92 percent for category B products, and 87 percent category C products; (2) desired delivery of all customer orders will be within 48 hours of order placement for 98 percent of all orders; (3) customer service from secondary service points will be held to a minimum; (4) mixed commodity orders will be filled without back order a minimum of 85 percent of all orders; (5) back orders will be restricted to five days' aging; (6) the 50 most profitable customers will receive these minimum performance capabilities on 98 percent of all orders.

Given these statements of customer service, a system can be designed which will provide the desired performance. The total cost of such a system will be derived. To the extent that such cost does not meet managerial expectations, various levels of alternative performance can be tested.

An alternative approach to the statement of output objectives is to fix a maximum allowable total cost expenditure and then design a system to achieve the highest possible degree of service. Such cost-oriented objectives have the feature of practicality, because results will be within acceptable budget ranges. However, they lack the selectivity of the service-oriented approach to system design.

Design Constraints.   A second category of managerial policy deals with design constraints. From an analysis of the distribution audit, it is expected that management will place restrictions on the scope of permissible modifications. The nature of such restrictions will depend upon the specific circumstances of individual firms. However, two typical examples are provided below.

One restriction common to distribution system designs concerns the network of manufacturing facilities and the product assortment produced at each. To simplify the study, management may elect to hold existing manufacturing facilities constant in the system design. Although such constraints reduce the optimization of a study, they are justified on the basis of financial considerations and capacity for immediate change.

A second category of constraints deals with marketing channels and physical distribution activities of separate divisions. In firms with a traditional pattern of decentralized profit responsibility, management may elect to omit certain divisions from study consideration. Thus, some divisions may be managerially determined to be candidates for consolidated physical distribution operations, whereas other are omitted from consideration.

All design constraints serve to limit the scope of the study. However, as one executive stated the problem, "Why study things we don't plan to do anything about?" Unless there exists a reasonable chance that management is favorably inclined to introduce change, the subject in question should be structured as a study constraint. Once the model is developed, all such constraints can be evaluated at will with a minimum of structural change.

Measurement Standards.   In most situations the distribution audit will illustrate the need for managerial determination of measurement standards. Such standards will concern (1) the structure of synthetic costs, (2) the cost of performance penalties, and (3) the study period. Each of these categories of standards has been discussed previously. The essential point is that management must provide guidelines for each category as a prerequisite to the formulation of the system model. Once formulated such standards must be held constant throughout the design analysis. Although considerable managerial prerogative exists in the formation of standards, care must be exercised not to dilute the validity of the model and thereby subsequent study results.

MODEL DEVELOPMENT

Formulation of the system model requires substantial creative talent as well as analytical ability. This is normally the domain of the specialist. However, management still must play an active role in order to maintain control and to develop appropriate data into a usable format. Several steps are involved in model development: (1) technique selection; (2) input ordering; (3) model formulation and programming; and (4) validity checking and model calibration. Each is discussed in terms of managerial involvement.

Technique Selection.   The major responsibility of management in technique selection is to evaluate the recommendations of the specialist in terms of time and cost. It is to be expected that the specialist will be more concerned with development of broad gauged models requiring complex integrative techniques. Management must balance this desire for exacting answers and perfect information with related cost and time requirements. In addition, management must understand the capability and limitations of all proposed techniques. Although technical evaluation of problem requirements is an area of specialized talent, deciding if a firm can commit the necessary resources is a managerial responsibility. Neglect of this responsibility at an early stage of study development is perhaps the greatest cause for subsequent failure.

Input Ordering.   Given the study period, transactions must be developed for use as flow input and as set constants to the study model. The flow input represents historical records placed into a georeference code for study use. Set constants represent a restatement of managerial parameters in terms of the system model. The technical aspects of each of these input formulations is not a managerial responsibility. However, the validity of each must be checked prior to use.

Model Formulation and Programming.   Model formulation involves development of equations to handle system state, operating relationships and, to the degree utilized, feedback mechanisms. Programming consists of writing computer instructions to handle the required computations. Managerial responsibility in model formulation and programming is limited to a control of expense and constant review of progress. It is not unusual to have weekly briefing on development progress. Although excessive managerial pressures can be a deterrent to creativity, a lack of progress control can result in a substantial waste of resources.

Although beyond the scope of intent at this point, some significant techniques have been developed which can help management in project control. Program Evaluation Review Technique (PERT) and Critical Path Method (CPM) are two such techniques. Management may find either useful in control of model development, or the entire physical distribution study. These techniques are discussed in Appendix 13A.

Validity Checking and Model Calibration.   A critical managerial responsibility is checking the validity of the system model. Because mathematical model building and computer simulation is a complex task, the risk is always present that the technical expert will not understand or have sufficient knowledge of the specific business under study. Thus, before a model is used for system design, its validity must be tested. If the model is not a reasonable approximation to the situation under study, little in terms of improvements can be anticipated.

In development of a validity test two conditions are desirable. First, the original model state should be structured to simulate a known situation. As a start, the first system state is often structured as a replica of the existing system operated by the firm. Second, extreme care must be exercised to use all input flow data associated with the study period. Given these two conditions it is possible to test validity by appraising the model's capability to simulate results of a known situation.

Regardless of the care taken in testing model validity, an element of error remains a constant possibility. First, it is impossible to calibrate for all possible situations. This danger increases as the model becomes more dynamic. Second, it is never possible to eliminate or identify all compensating errors in a specific validity test. Although such errors may wash out in a validity test, their interrelation may become significant under alternate test situations. Every effort should be made to develop the best possible model, keeping in mind inherent limitations of the modeling process when evaluating results.

SENSITIVITY ANALYSIS

The process of sensitivity analysis provides a way in which management can test alternative distribution policies. In many ways the real payoff from an integrated distribution system study depends upon the range of sensitivity testing completed. Given a valid model, the simulation procedure will result in the best design possible in terms of managerial parameters. However, this does not mean the study is over. One of the greatest benefits of a system simulation is the ability to ask "what if" questions without taking a chance with the existing business.

In the simulation procedure, management parameters are introduced concerning output objectives, design constraints, and measurement standards. Each introduces an unknown degree of restraint on the simulation model. By holding all other factors constant, the influence of managerial parameters can be evaluated in service and cost results.

SYSTEM DESIGN AND IMPLEMENTATION PLANS

The most common question asked by business executives is, "What can I expect to see as the end result of a simulation study?" Unfortunately, unless considerable editing is completed and a report is prepared, the executive will see a voluminous stack of computer printouts. The mental barrier of approaching such a mass of data can greatly reduce the benefit gained from the study as a result of the need to "dig it out." Therefore, the best procedure is to develop a study summary report of significant findings. Such a report will contain the following information:

1. A statement of system customer service capabilities including an estimate of performance probability.
2. An estimate of total fixed and variable cost expressed as a percentage cost of sales for a specified operating period.
3. A comparison of service and cost projections for the redesigned system in comparison to the current system for identical time periods.
4. Estimated results of several alternative service policies and related costs of performance.
5. A format of required transport, facility, communication, and inventory capabilities under the integrated system.

The results of a distribution system simulation will contain infinitely more detail than the information listed above. Once management has selected a final system redesign, such detail is used to develop an implementational program. Prior to final selection of a system, a series of additional tests may be instituted.

It would be a rare firm that could move into an across-the-board revision of all elements in a distribution system. Thus, the simulation model becomes a valuable tool to select which steps will provide the greatest payoff if implemented at once. Thus, a five-year, or any desired time period implementation program, can be developed with a measure of expected results. Priorities and check points can be established to guide overall revamping of the existing system. The changing nature of business requires that constant checks be performed to test the continued validity of the system model.

Thus, from a managerial viewpoint a final system design never really exists. The redesign implementation plan is constantly being adjusted to take advantage of change. The firm that develops a distribution simulation, formulates an implementation plan, and then stops the simulation procedure, dissolves a powerful planning tool.

Chart 12–2 illustrates a flow diagram of the recommended managerial guide for distribution system design. Each of the major steps is noted with reference to areas of managerial concern. The left-hand side of the flow diagram illustrates the process of (1) sensitivity measurement and (2) continuous adjustment to change. The total process of distribution system design is a never-ending responsibility always subject to change with passing time.

Summary

In this chapter the reader has been introduced to a wide variety of techniques available to help in distribution system design. Emphasis throughout the chapter has been placed upon managerial responsibility rather than on

CHART 12–2   Flow Diagram — Managerial Guide to System Design

SYSTEM STEPS   MANAGEMENT RESPONSIBILITY

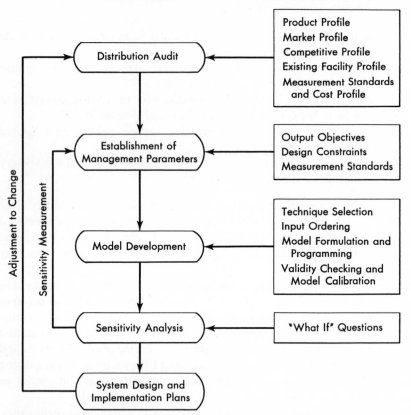

excessive technical detail. Particular attention was devoted to policy formation concerning system objectives and managerial responsibilities in system design. Attention in Chapter 13 now shifts to the area of administrative responsibility and organization of the physical distribution system.

Discussion Questions

1. Why would a firm set up its physical distribution so that it could utilize a number of different channels?

2. Why is there less control over support facilities than over fixed facilities? Why would a firm be more flexible if it used support facilities?

3. Why is it improbable that a firm could ever really achieve a truly optimum physical distribution system?

4. Are there any problems with the use of linear formulas in multiple analysis techniques?

5. What is dynamic simulation and where is its use in physical distribution management most appropriate?

6. Why is the distribution audit considered the most important part of the total design process?

7. What would be the penalties that a firm might face if it designed its physical distribution system to eliminate nonexistent competitive advantages?

8. Why, in a distribution audit, is it probable that data desired will not be readily available?

9. What is *sensitivity analysis*?

Appendix 12A
SYSTEM TERMINOLOGY AND FLOWCHARTING

Flowcharting of any type of a system represents the alignment of the steps followed by the system in performance of a specified activity. Flowcharts are widely used in automated data processing (ADP) for the purpose of outlining sequential steps in both general systems and computer programs. In distribution system design, the use of flowcharts provides a means by which the physical and the information flows can be visualized. To date no standardized set of symbols has been developed for use in specialized physical distribution flowcharts. The purpose of this appendix is to outline some standard symbols for use in physical distribution system flowcharting.

Standard Data Processing Flowchart Symbols

In the field of automated data processing standard symbols have been developed. In general, three basic symbols are used, and each is illustrated below:

Symbol *A* is the basic notation for an input or output of a given system flow. The symbol *B* is used to describe the direction of flow within a system. The direction is normally read from top to bottom and from left to right. It is not standard practice to use arrowheads, if the flow is in either of these directions. In the event flow is to the opposite or reverse direction, an open arrowhead is used to indicate this condition. Bidirectional flow is charted by broken or double lines. Symbol *C* represents the basic identification of a processing function. The processing symbol is used for the purpose of illustrating a major activity on the data flow. For example, the preparation of a payroll is indicated by a processing symbol.

These basic symbols are supplemented by a variety of special symbols that define in greater detail the type of input, output, or processing to be performed in a data-processing system. A great deal of effort has been centered on the development of these standard symbols. Both basic and special symbols are fairly interchangeable between major data-processing systems. When physical distribution systems are flowcharted for computer processing, these basic notations should be used. However, when flowcharts are developed for purposes of visualizing a physical distribution system, standard symbols used in ADP are too restrictive. Therefore, more descriptive symbols are desirable.

Recommended Physical Distribution Flowchart Symbols

Nine basic symbols are used to develop a physical distribution flowchart. Each is listed below wth a brief description.

Fixed Location
Activity Center

Symbol *A* is used to denote those physical distribution activities that are performed at a fixed location such as a distribution warehouse.

Transit Activity
Center

The transit activity center is noted by symbol *B*. It is useful to distinguish between fixed location and transit activity centers due to the wide range of alternatives in transit performance.

Input/Output

Symbol *C* is used to illustrate inputs and outputs of the physical distribution system.

Activity Centers
External to Physical
Distribution System

A great many activity centers of other areas of the corporation come into direct involvement with the physical distribution system. These external activity centers are indicated by symbol *D*.

Data Processing

Symbol *E* is used to indicate points of data-processing control. It is at these points that computer facilities are employed in the physical distribution system.

Management Activity

From time to time, special managerial action is generated as part of the overall system. Although such action is a part of almost every system segment, when special attention is desired symbol *F* is recommended.

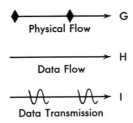

Physical Flow

Data Flow

Data Transmission

Three different symbols are used to illustrate flow in the physical distribution system. Symbol *G* is used to illustrate physical product flow. Symbol *H* is employed for information flow, and the special symbol *I* is used to denote the existence of data transmission equipment.

In addition to these nine basic symbols, any number of special symbols may be used to illustrate additional or more detailed physical distribution activities.

Example of a Physical Distribution System Flowchart

Chart 12A–1 illustrates a two-production plant–three-distribution warehouse logistical system. This system has the following characteristics: (1) each of the production plants ships to all three distribution centers;

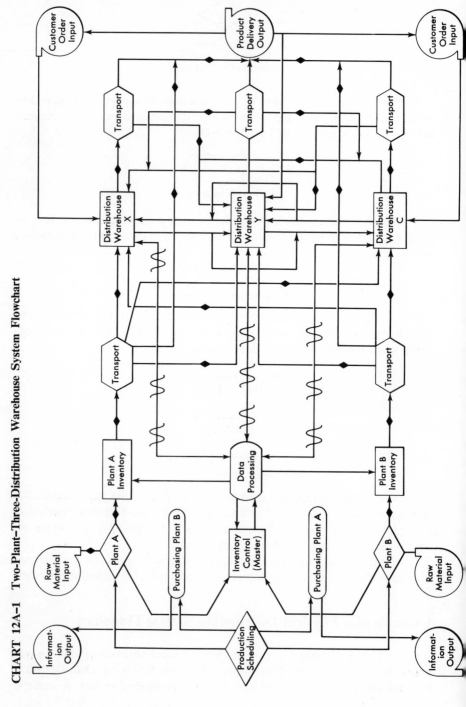

CHART 12A–1 Two-Plant–Three-Distribution Warehouse System Flowchart

(2) distribution warehouses have a communication capacity with each other and with central control; (3) distribution centers can interbranch transfer when the situation is warranted; (4) when conditions justify, shipments can be made direct from production plants to customers; (5) customer orders are routed direct to distribution warehouses for shipment if possible; (6) inventory and production control is maintained at the central inventory control location, which is linked to distribution warehouses by data transmission.

The system detailed in Chart 12A–1 represents a major simplification, because no detail is developed for major activity centers. In flowcharting a complete structure of a physical distribution system, the normal procedure would be development of diagrams for each subsystem.

CHAPTER 13 Distribution

Administration and Organization

GIVEN a physical distribution system design, the second broad area of managerial responsibility is administration. Physical distribution administration is concerned with the process of resource allocation and control of the five activity centers included in system design. Organization is the structure by which human resources are aligned in a particular physical distribution operation. Among the many subject matters of physical distribution management, the areas of integrated system administration and organization are the least understood. This lack of clearly defined principles is the result of the relative newness of integrated physical distribution systems and related performance measurement techniques.

This final chapter is concerned with system administration and organization for physical distribution management. The basic format is one of integrated management by objectives. It is through the establishment of clearly defined goals and continuous review of progress that administration is most effective. The first section of this chapter develops the basic concept of management by objectives and elaborates the planning process. Next, attention is directed to physical distribution control systems. Following is a discussion of organization for physical distribution management.

Management by Objectives

The essential concept of management by objectives (MBO) is the establishment of goals and controls. In MBO it is not the content of a job in terms of description which is important. Rather, the important facet is the objective for individual job accomplishment established for each administrative period. The job objective is the goal. Given a goal or a series of goals, physical distribution administration is concerned with control in order to measure progress toward goal accomplishment. Thus, the administrative task is one of planning and performance measurement. This section is concerned with planning, and the next is directed to physical distribution performance measurement.

OPERATIONAL PLANNING

Operational planning is of critical importance, because managerial talent is always in short supply. This deficiency is expected to become more acute in the future. Therefore, top and middle management cannot afford the luxury of becoming fire fighters bogged down in operational detail. One important technique for directing the efforts of an organization is the operational plan.

The operational plan for physical distribution administration is short range to the extent that it covers projected operations for months rather than years. The exact period of time covered will normally not exceed a single fiscal year. The operational plan covers a segment of overall system implementation program. The reader will recall that the system implementation program was the result of system design research outlined in Chapter 12.[1] Given a system implementation program (long range), operational plans (short range) must be developed to direct day-to-day work efforts. Long-range implementational programs represent a set of guideposts for short-range operational planning. The operational plan details expected accomplishments during a specified time period. Such accomplishments concern (1) facility adjustments and (2) performance.

Activity Center Adjustment. During any period, several adjustments in operating structure may be planned for implementation. For example, a firm may have a long-range system implementational program calling for the consolidation of 25 warehouses into 10 regional distribution centers. The full implementational program may cover a number of years and will therefore embrace several operational plans. The initial operating plan may call for a commitment to build or lease two of the regional facilities and to close a selected number of existing warehouses as a result of new customer service policies. Future operational plans may provide for the initial occupancy and use of these first two regional distribution warehouses, the commitment to building additional facilities, and the closing of other outdated warehouses

[1]See Chapter 12, page 337, for development of system design and related implemental programs.

scheduled for elimination. Physical distribution systems redesigns encompass a number of years, and consecutive operational plans will contain elements of the overall implemental program.

In consideration of activity center adjustments included in operational plans, two factors must be clearly understood. First, budget allocations must isolate the expense of initial set-up as well as once-and-for-all savings separate from day-to-day operational expenditures. Second, special efforts required to maintain customer service commitments during the period of activity center readjustment must be adequately programmed. Each of the above expenditures are a function of the long-range program for implementation of a new system rather than the operation of an existing system. As such, they are not expected to prevail between consecutive operational planning periods. Unless such one-time expenditures are isolated, the capability of comparative analysis of operational results from one period to the next is diluted.

The operational plan must provide for scheduled adjustments in activity centers. It contains an allocation of resources to accomplish the expected results and specifies a responsibility to achieve desired adjustments within the operational period.

Performance.   The bulk of the operational plan consists of a statement of management objectives for day-to-day operations and a commitment of resources to meet stated goals. Customer service objectives are outlined in detail. Thus, the goals are clearly stated for the total system. Each segment of the system is assigned specific responsibilities in terms of customer support, product line storage, and response time to meet marketing requirements. Such assignments are based upon a combination of forecasting and managerial judgment regarding future requirements. To meet these specified responsibilities, allocations of capital are made to each control unit in the total system.

Thus, the total operational plan provides the structure for meeting the physical distribution objectives. It assigns specific responsibilities regarding activity center adjustments and performance and allocates authorized resources. As such the total physical distribution effort is synchronized through the operational plan.

DEVELOPMENT OF THE OPERATIONAL PLAN

The operational plan can be developed in many different ways. Following is one approach to development.

Establishment of Planning Period Goals.   The goals specified for any planning period must be formulated at a top-management level. These goals should result from extensive system design studies. As indicated above, they relate to (1) system activity center adjustments and (2) day-to-day performance. Each category of goals for a specified operating period must be clearly stated.

Estimates of Expenditure. Given a statement of goals, the next step in the planning process is to estimate required expenditures needed to accomplish desired objectives. A typical procedure is to request budgets from individual management units. Thus, line management, given a statement of objectives, is asked to formulate a request for operational funds. The budgets once requested constitute each manager's financial estimates to achieve goals.

The review of individual budget requests is the critical juncture of physical distribution administration. Top management is concerned with the total performance of the system and not any one of the individual parts. Development of an integrated system provides top management with an estimate of the total dollars required to meet specified system objectives. The planning process at this point becomes one of reconciling individual budget requests with total system resources.

Budget desires of individual managers will almost always exceed funds required to assure good performance. This can be expected because no single unit manager is in a position to view the total system. A tendency also exists to view performance in any activity center on a unit cost basis. This bias in unit cost budgeting often forces uneconomic performance in one area without full evaluation of interrelationships to other areas. A traffic manager, concerned with unit cost, will tend toward low-cost transport selection, which he may only be able to achieve by delay of shipments.

The reader may ask, why are individual managers asked to formulate budget requests if we anticipate the above deficiencies? The answer is twofold. First, it is essential that the individual manager participate in budget formation in order to gain a complete understanding of the integrated nature of total system programming. Budget formation is one of the most potent training tools available to top management. Second, individual unit managers are often aware of factors, which must be considered in a specific operational plan and that have not come to the attention of top management. The greatest danger of total system planning is to develop a top-management complacency concerning the continued validity of the long-range implementation program. Cross participation between individual control center managers and top management is essential to the development of a realistic but demanding operational plan.

The Finalized Plan. The finalized operational plan provides a blueprint to guide short-range performance. The final plan should be in written format and contain a statement of objectives plus detailed cost budgets for each operational unit. The plan will focus on total system performance and objectives. The total budget package should be designed to combine all relevant cost centers into a single unified plan. By this method, each management specialist will be more likely to aim for his budget performance goal on an overall cost basis, because cost increases or decreases in one function are no longer relevant. It is the overall cost performance that counts. This concept of total accountability is one of the essential aspects of management by objectives. In order for the total system to accomplish the highest possible performance, all managers must assume correlative responsibiity for everyone else's job.

Plan Modification.   Once the final plan is developed, printed, and distributed, some aspect or element of the plan can be anticipated to be in need of modification. Thus, adjustments to the operational plan will be required throughout the total planning period. Such modification results from planning errors and by the need to adjust to unanticipated events.

Because the individual manager has participated in development of the integrated plan, he will be aware of the impact of his decisions upon other functional areas. In his day-to-day operations, he may also become aware of environmental changes that may adversely or favorably affect corporate distribution activities. Thus, a change in freight rates, packaging, material handling, and so on may come to the attention of an individual manager. As these changes occur, the individual manager is in a position to engage in planning and to recommend adjustments to the current operational plan.

Significant modifications to operational plans are encouraged, because results are obtained by exploiting timely opportunities. However, two rules must be followed in all such modifications. First, operational modifications must be formally requested prior to any deviation from planned operations. Second, it follows that all such modifications must be evaluated in terms of total system performance. Once proposed modifications are adopted, formal written amendments to the operational plan should be distributed to all managers engaged in physical distribution administration.

Summary — Operational Planning and Management by Objectives.   Management by objectives is dependent upon the development of a sound operational plan. The approved plan becomes the basis for performance measurement during the operating period. The process of developing an operational plan is time consuming and tedious. The problem is complicated by the need to view the total system on an integrated basis. Such integration often requires information beyond that normally available from a firm's standard costing or accounting systems.

Special emphasis should be made between the relationship of operational planning and total system implementation programs. The process of physical distribution system design results in an implementative program. Reference to Chart 12–2 highlights that the system design responsibility is a continuous process.[2] A feedback loop exists between the development of an implementational program and the distribution audit. This feedback loop exists to

[2]See Chapter 12, page 346.

allow for the advent of change upon system design. The need for such change is more often than not initially detected through the operational plan.

As noted earlier, consecutive operating plans represent short-range elements of the longer-range system implementational program. Therefore, physical distribution system design and administration are unified through the relationship between operational plans and implemental programs.

Physical Distribution Control

The operational plan provides the measurement base for control of physical distribution operations. The purpose of a control system is to assure that resources devoted to a specific goal satisfy managerial objectives. In this section the following aspects of physical distribution control are discussed: (1) nature of the control process, (2) types of control, (3) levels of control, and (4) control reports.

NATURE OF THE CONTROL PROCESS

Control of a physical distribution system is always relative to the operational plan. Without an operational plan, it is difficult, if not impossible, to measure performance. For example, in the retail field it is not unusual to purchase Christmas toys in early spring in order to realize special discounts and allowances. From a control viewpoint, such practices, although justified on a total cost basis, may result in significant temporary increases in distribution costs far in advance of the normal season. Such cost expenditures, when viewed in terms of the operational plan, cause little more than advanced planning for cash flow. When viewed without the benefit of an operational plan early expenditure for advanced physical distribution of Christmas merchandise could appear as an uncontrolled cost trend.

The basic concept of physical distribution control should be one of management by exceptions. The comprehensive and detailed nature of physical distribution requires that management review be limited to deviations from anticipated results. However, few managers are willing to sit back and wait for an exception to appear. The exception, by its very nature, is proof that a problem exists. Although solving such problems is a vital aspect of management, something more is needed. The something extra is a mechanism for system monitoring. The monitoring network exists for the purpose of reassuring management that the total system is tracking along the course desired. A deficiency noted from system monitoring should call for a diagnostic evaluation of causal factors. The advent of a significant exception means that a trend leading to a major deviation was overlooked during its formation stages.

To illustrate the relationship between system monitoring and exceptions, the following is a typical example from inventory management.

Dollars allocated to an open-to-buy program at a given point in a planning period may be near exhaustion. At the same time a critical item may be approaching a reorder point. Placement of the required order size as indicated by economic order quantity formulations could very well result in a commitment over and above authorized expenditures. One might assume that the individual merchandise controller would bring this situation to management's attention. If so, appropriate adjustments can be made.

However, if the original open-to-buy was sufficient to cover needs, the current deficiency of funds resulted from some past purchase decision made by the same controller in which he improperly allocated dollars. Therefore, resort to management means that the controller needs help to rectify his error. Unfortunately, too few individuals feel free to place themselves into open management scrutiny. This common fallacy of human nature is apt to cause the controller to gamble. In essence, he gambles that existing stock on the critical item will last until new funds are authorized at which time he plans to place a rush order. In reality he gambles a major segment of a firm's customer service policy by running a risk of critical item out-of-stock. Given their alternative, management may well select the choice of adding dollars to the open-to-buy over running the risk of an out-of-stock situation. The problem is that unless the firm enjoys a comprehensive monitoring system, management may never get the chance to express their choice until the out-of-stock turns up as an exception to stated policy.

In the case of inventory control, the monitoring system could be expected to signal that a critical item had reached and passed the inventory level of normal reorder without the issue of a purchase order. The inventory control manager would be expected to take appropriate action and if necessary request aid from higher management. The combined process of management is to prevent the monitored trend from becoming a full-scale exception.

From the above discussion, it is clear that management would rather prevent than correct exceptions. The monitoring system exists for this purpose. The exception reporting system exists to signal a breakdown within a segment of the organization that requires significant corrective action in order to prevent recurrence.

TYPES OF CONTROL

The control of a physical distribution system relates to expected level of performance and related expenditures. The overall operational plan calls for specified accomplishments in terms of performance and expenditure at two types of activity: (1) activity center adjustments, and (2) overall physical distribution performance. The control system should be capable of providing status reports concerning each type of activity.

Activity Center Control. As noted earlier, an individual operational plan may call for adjustments in the activity centers that constitute the physical distribution system. Such adjustments are planned, funds are authorized, and the actual implementation is placed on a time table. One function of the control system is to provide status reports concerning conformity to the agreed-upon plan. Such status or progress reports are for the purpose of anticipating problems that might occur if the implementational schedule is not met. A lag in development, which cannot be prevented, is more often more efficiently handled if rescheduled than overcome by the commitment of additional recources.

Reports concerning planned activity center adjustments are most often developed by middle management on a customized basis rather than from automated records. Care should be taken to see that such reports are provided on a regular basis and that they are sufficiently comprehensive to include all critical information. In one case of branch plant relocation, progress reports indicated that all was well. In fact, the new building was ahead of schedule. Appropriate plans were made to hire new workers. Personnel was transferred, and the product was stockpiled as scheduled in field warehouses to accommodate customers during the switch-over. The undetected problem was that a new series of automated finishing machines were not meeting specifications at the plant of a long-time, reliable equipment supplier. The final result was that a national branded appliance was for all practical purposes out-of-stock in the market place for well over three months. By the time the full problem was detected, the old facility had been closed down and equipment sold for salvage value. A deficiency in control reports placed this firm in a situation beyond the control of management. The final impact of this deficiency will not be known for some time to come, because of the serious void in market supply and its influence upon long-range market position.

Equally important to reports concerning planned activity center adjustments are those that indicate unplanned changes. Although it is difficult to visualize a situation where a plant or warehouse is added or deleted with pre-planning, inventories are subject to substantial changes over a single planning period. In general, the more variable the cost associated with a specific activity center, the more vulnerable is the center's unscheduled accumulation or depletion. The operational plan should specify maximum and minimum inventory levels by individual stocking location. One important aspect of total system monitoring is a current report concerning trends that could lead to unplanned modifications. Such deviations materialize over time and have a tendency to reach rather large proportions once the trend is fully developed. The causal force may stem from significant changes in sales patterns or from internally generated factors. In either case, such trends must be detected early to prevent serious readjustment problems and lags.[3]

[3]See Chapter 9, page 238, for additional development of this idea.

Performance Control.   Assuming all is well with basic activity centers, a critical need still exists for measurement of overall physical distribution performance. The control system of a firm must be capable of measuring efficiency and effectiveness of performance in comparison to the operational plan.

Efficiency is a dollar measure of expenditure to get a specific job done. A specified level of expenditure is authorized in the operational plan. Management is concerned with the relationship of authorized and actual expenditures. It should be noted that efficiency as developed here is concerned with the plan and subsequent performance. No attempt is made to state that the plan is the most efficient method for accomplishing the required physical distribution performance. That decision and related compromises were made earlier during system design. Given a design, a level of resource allocation is structured into an operational plan. Management, from an operations control viewpoint, is concerned with the efficiency of the authorized resource expenditure.

Effectiveness is a measure of accomplishment in terms of objectives. For example, if the objective is to never be out of stock at any location of a specific item, the system would not be fully effective if a single stock-out occurred. Effectiveness then is a measure of how well the integrated logistical system performs in term of goals. It would be a rare system that obtained 100 percent operating effectiveness over the total planning period.

In combination, measures of effectiveness and efficiency combine to provide performance controls. Effectiveness provides an indication of whether or not the desired job is getting done. Efficiency is a measure of the actual in comparison to planned cost for whatever level of performance the system is generating. For example, considering transportation expenditures, 95 percent of all orders may be arriving on time. However, the cost for the first three segments of the planning period may be 103 percent of the budget. In this example, effectiveness might well be within acceptable ranges; however, management may feel that steps are necessary to select more efficient transporation.

LEVELS OF CONTROL AND INFORMATION FLOW

The nature of system control requires that several different levels of information be developed within the corporation. As a general rule, the higher the level of management review in the organization, the more selective are the control information and the reporting. The following four levels of information are appropriate to physical distribution control systems: (1) direction, (2) variation, (3) decision, and (4) policy revision. At each level the information may be related to trend monitoring or exception correction.

Direction. At the level of direction, information flow and control is concerned with execution of the operational plan. A stream of transaction documents signals a need, and the action document commands that appropriate steps be taken to satisfy the need. For example, an order is received, credit is checked, the order is assigned to a distribution warehouse, picked, packed, and shipped. Upon shipment, the customer is billed in accord with the agreed-upon terms of sale. The order receipt is a transaction document, the remainder of the activities are generated as a result of action documents.

At specified time intervals, all transaction and action documents are combined in a series of status reports. Such status reports summarize individual activities in terms of existing capabilities to meet future transaction requirements. For example, total inventory usage may be summarized by each item in the product line, and a comparison is made to current inventories. As a result of status reports, additional action documents may be issued to replenish stock on specific items.

Two important features should be kept in mind concerning information flow and control at the direction level. First, information at the direction level is concerned with the day-to-day running of the business on an individual transaction basis. Selectivity of information at the direction level is limited to review of status in accord with predetermined decision rules. In total, information flow at the direction level is concerned with execution of predetermined programs.

The second feature of information flow at the direction level is that accumulation of records formulates a data bank for all other levels of control. It is from this data bank that all reports concerning effectiveness and efficiency are generated, all trends are monitored, and all exceptions are detected. Although managerial discretion at the direction level is limited, all that follows is based upon the accuracy of information processed and generated from transactions and action documents.

Variation. The variation level of control is concerned with accumulation of information that indicates all is not going according to plan. As indicated earlier, the variation level of control ideally results in interpretation of a trend which could lead to future trouble. However, the variation may very well first appear as an exception to the desired level of performance at the direction level.

At the variation level managerial discretion concerning the allocation of resources or capabilities first comes under consideration. The manager concerned must ascertain if the situation discovered is an isolated event or if it is symptomatic of a more serious problem. Second, the manager must determine if a solution to the problem is within the scope of his delegated authority or if it will require additional resources. Depending upon the manager's interpretation of these two questions, he will either issue corrective instructions to the direction level of operations or request assistance from the decision level.

It is important to realize that the scope of information reviewed at the variation level has been considerably reduced in comparison to the direction level. Management at the variation level is concerned with the broader issues of effectiveness and efficiency related to a series of transactions.

Decision.   Control at the decision level of management is concerned with modifications in the operational plan. In essence, situations have materialized at the direction and variation levels which require a reappraisal of the original operational plan. As the reader would expect, the assortment of information presented at the decision level will be very selective. It is significant to note that the decision level is the first control level at which a change in the operational plan is considered.

Such modifications will normally require allocation of additional resources. In accord with the format of control outlined here, the range of decision will never involve a modification of system objectives. In other words, customer service standards will not be changed if performance has been deficient. Rather, a greater expenditure will be authorized as required to meet system objectives. Managerial activities at the decision level must be evaluated in terms of total system consequences. As noted earlier, decisions that modify the plan must be relayed to all managers involved in total system performance.

Policy.   Control at the policy level relates to a basic change in physical distribution objectives of the firm. Once again, the areas of system design and administration merge when questions of policy are confronted. The level of concern becomes corporate-wide in scope and embodies all members of the corporation. The formulation of new policies will require an evaluation of planned system design as well as the required total cost of achievement. Requests for policy revisions may originate from any point within the total corporation. Thus far, this discussion of control has centered around information generated from the logistical data base and in general around deficiencies in either physical distribution performance or expenditure plans. However, policy situations may be occasioned from other areas of the corporation. For example, the marketing department may desire an overall upgrading of customer service standards.

To illustrate, assume that the current system is geared to servicing at least 90 percent of all customers at a 95 percent inventory availability within 60 hours of order receipt. Further, assume that the current physical distribution network is meeting these objectives at lowest total cost utilizing a seven-distribution-point system. However, marketing is not happy. Marketing management is of the opinion that service capability should be increased to the point where 90 percent of all customers at 97 percent inventory availability would receive 24-hour delivery. Top management is faced with a critical

CHART 13–1   Comparative Total Cost for Seven and Twenty Distribution Point Systems

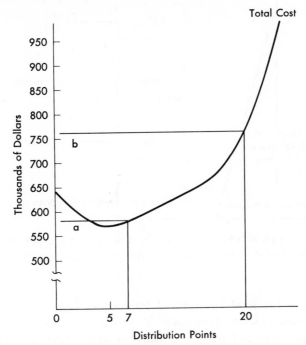

policy consideration. In accord with the steps of distribution system design, sensitivity tests are in order.

Chart 13–1 highlights results which might be isolated from such sensitivity testing. Marketing is requesting a 2-percent improvement in inventory availability coupled with a 36-hour improvement in delivery time. To achieve these goals, the existing network of distribution warehouses would have to be expanded by 13. The simulator, through sensitivity testing, determined that 20 facilities would be the lowest cost method for achieving the new service standards. The total cost of this expanded service capability is measured on the vertical axis of Chart 13–1 as the distance between Points *A* and *B*. Thus, the total cost of meeting the new managerial service standard will be $200,000 dollars per year greater than current expenditures. If the firm in question had a before-tax profit margin equal to 10 percent of sales, it would be necessary to generate additional sales of two million dollars to justify the added service on a break-even basis.

The policy decision of acceptance or rejection of the marketing proposal for increased service must rest with top management. Policy changes, once adopted, influence all other levels of logistical control. Regardless of source of origin — internal or external to the logistics sector — the formulation of new or modified policies will require a revision of implementational programs

CHART 13–2   Information Flow and Levels of Control

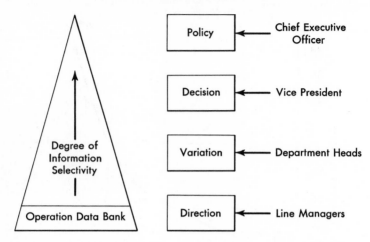

and operational plans. Once adopted, the new operational plan becomes the standard for control at the direction, variation, and decision levels of management.

Summary — Levels of Control and Information Flow.   Chart 13–2 will help clarify the four levels of control involved in physical distribution administration. Adjacent to each level, reference is made to a corresponding organizational rank within a corporation. On the left side of the chart, a data pyramid is developed to reflect the selectivity of information considered at each level of control. As noted earlier, each level is concerned with system monitoring as well as exception reporting. However, as information flows from the direction level to the policy level, the content of subject matter increases in importance to the welfare of the total corporation.

CONTROL REPORTS

The essential feature of all control systems is the quality of reports generated from the data bank. Unless available information can be presented rapidly, accurately, and on relevant subjects, little in the way of positive control will transpire. In general there are three types of reports used in a physical distribution control system: (1) status, (2) trend, and (3) special reports.

Status Reports.   As the name implies, a status report is designed to provide detailed information about some aspect of the physical distribution operation. One of the most common status reports is the Stock Status Report used in

TABLE 13-1 EXAMPLE OF A STOCK STATUS REPORT

ABC Company
Distribution Warehouse
Stock Status Report

Date 3-10-68
Controller A

			Unit Inventory		Forecasted				Inventory	Open Purchase Order Detail		
(1)	(2)	(3)	(4)	(5)	Avg. (6)	Back (7)	Suggested (8)	Dollars (9)	On Order (10)	(11)	(12)	(13)
Item	Location	Status	On Hand	On Order	Week Use	Order	Order Qty	On Hand		Date Placed	Date Due	Quan.
10-326-01	Detroit	Normal	183		25			457.50				
	Chicago	Out of Stock		365	40	45		0	912.50	2-15-67	2-26-67	365
	Atlanta	Expedite	29	145	15			72.50	462.50	3-1-67	3-12-67	145
	Newark	Over Stock	293		30			732.50				
	Tacoma	Order	55		10		75	137.50				
	Fresno	Normal	103		23			257.50				
TOTALS			663	510	143	45	75	1657.50	1375.00			530
10-327-05	Detroit	Normal										
	Chicago	Normal										
	Atlanta	Over Stock										
	Newark	Order										
	Tacoma	Order										
	Fresno	Order										
TOTALS												
10-365-00	Detroit	Normal										
	Chicago	Expedite										
	Atlanta	Out of Stock										
	Newark	Out of Stock										
	Tacoma	Expedite										
	Fresno	Expedite										
TOTALS												

inventory management. The stock status report is normally used to keep track of multiple item inventories at more than one stocking location. The amount of information contained on an individual report will depend upon the firm, its degree of inventory management sophistication, and the extent to which automated data processing is used. However, to illustrate a typical status report, Table 13–1 provides an example of an inventory stock status.

In the example, items of inventory are being controlled from one central management location for distribution warehouses located in Detroit, Chicago, Atlanta, Newark, Tacoma, and Fresno. The unit inventory of the ABC Company is being maintained on a computer using techniques of scientific inventory management. Individual items have been assigned to stock controllers who are responsible for inventory status at all six distribution warehouses. This particular report is for a controller referred to as A.

The individual item or unit number is printed in column 1. These item numbers do not appear in numerical sequence, because only items requiring controller attention are printed. However, if an item requires action at a specific distribution warehouse, status of that item in all other warehouses is also printed on the report. Thus, when a controller directs specific action concerning an inventory item he is able to view status at all stocking locations. The location is displayed in column 2 and status is reflected in column 3. Of particular interest is the printing of required action in the status column 3. Based upon the rules of the inventory control system, the controller is informed of the reason why the particular item appears on the stock status report. The remainder of the columns are for the most part self-explanatory. They provide the necessary information for the controller to direct the inventory procurement program.

Status reports exist for all physical distribution activity centers. Some relate to individual unit or transaction control; others are financial in nature. The purpose of the status report is to provide line managers with relevant information to fulfill their responsibility in the overall physical distribution system.

Trend Reports. Trend reports are normally used by administrators at levels of control higher than the line manager. In keeping with the flow of data outlined in Chart 13–2, trend reports are more selective in content than status reports. To illustrate, Tables 13–2 and 13–3 provide examples of trend reports that might be based upon the inventory stock status report.

Table 13–2, Daily Inventory Summary, provides an inventory recap for all items, controllers, and stock locations. This type of report is used by department heads for review of the overall inventory situation for the total physical distribution system. The data contained in the daily inventory summary is developed as a byproduct of the stock status report printed for inventory controllers. Thus, management is provided a quick recap of the total system and can evaluate overall performance.

TABLE 13–2   DAILY INVENTORY SUMMARY

	(1)	(2)	(3)	(4)	(5)
			Dollar Values Inventory		
Location	**Total Items Stocked**	**Percent In Stock**	**In Stock**	**On Order**	**Forecasted**
Detroit	1075	92	17,385	3,231	7,115
Chicago	1093	91	20,265	3,695	5,940
Atlanta	1041	88	15,197	3,780	8,201
Newark	1073	75	18,243	9,361	11,116
Tacoma	1075	89	23,116	5,143	4,307
Fresno	1026	90	19,450	2,184	1,993
Total System	6383	87.5%	$113,656	$27,394	$38,672

	(6)	(7)	(8)	(9)		
				Out of Stock by Class		
Controller	**Total Items**	**Percent In Stock**	**Percent Expedite**	**A**	**B**	**C**
A	1250	91	10	30	40	50
B	1300	89	09	36	71	38
C	1100	82	15	65	47	91
D	1275	85	09	15	81	95
E	1458	95	08	20	70	40
Total	6383	87.5%	10%	166	309	314

	(10)	(11)	(12)
	Items Out of Stock + 5 Days	**Items Over Stock**	**Orders Shipped on Schedule**
Detroit	12	31	96
Chicago	16	11	97
Atlanta	11	38	99
Newark	21	5	92
Tacoma	14	17	87
Fresno	19	0	94
Total	93	102	96%

TABLE 13–3   DISTRIBUTION PERFORMANCE RECAP

Performance Area	Week C-3	Week C-2	Week C-1	Current Week by Days				
				1	2	3	4	5
1. System In-Stock %	88.0	86.0	81.0	82.0	85.0	86.2	87.3	87.5
2. Weighted Performance %	83.8	84.2	10.0	79.8	83.2	84.0	86.3	87.0
3. Dollars Inventory	121,614	119,381	111,843	95,417	98,106	96,412	110,807	113,706
4. % Shipments on Schedule	99	97	98	99	96	97	98	96
5. Back Orders	365	691	780	193	217	238	165	101
6. Selected Data								
7. Other System								
8. Activity Centers								

Table 13–2 provides a variety of information. General performance is available on all locations as well as individual controllers. For example, the Newark Distribution Center is 75 percent in stock (column 1), 25 items have been out-of-stock greater than five days (column 10), and 92 percent of the orders scheduled for shipment were shipped as planned (column 12). From the viewpoint of a given individual, controller C is having problems. He is in stock on only 82 percent of his items (column 7), 15 percent of his items that are in stock currently require expedite efforts in order to prevent future out-of-stocks (column 8), and the items of which he is out of stock fall heavily into the critical area of a classified merchandise (column 9).

Armed with this information, the department head is in a position to review activities and take corrective action. If desired, he can request special reports, which will provide an abundance of detail to help further analyze a possible trend. For example, the department head in this case would probably desire more detailed information concerning the Newark facility and the activities of controller C. There is virtually no end to the selective information that can be generated from a data bank of the type maintained to develop Tables 13–2 and 13–3.

Table 13–2, Distribution Performance Recap, provides an executive summary of selected critical facts regarding inventory performance. Condensed information of the type presented in Table 13–3 would most often be used by executives at the vice-presidential or decision level of an operation (Chart 13–2). As noted earlier, it is a rare executive who is content to wait for exceptions to appear. Most executives would prefer to see the trend of performance in his areas of responsibility.

Table 13–3 covers a four-week period. The first three weeks are presented in aggregate; however, the fourth week is developed on a daily basis. Reports of this nature provide the basis for evaluation of trends and are useful in selecting areas for diagnostic activity. For example, the data in Table 13–3 points out that inventory performance over the past three weeks has deteriorated; however, performance on the most recent days indicates corrective action has been taken. Of particular interest in Table 13–3 is line 2, weighted performance. The weighted performance is a measure of stock availability in the quantities desired by customers. A system may enjoy a very high level of in-stock, but may be out of stock of the items most wanted by customers. Measures of weighted performance will normally run lower than measures of system in-stock.

The data presented in Table 13–3 provide inventory trend information, which is generated from the inventory stock status report (Table 13–1) and the daily inventory summary (Table 13–2). In all probability, the executive receiving the distribution performance recap would also be responsible for other physical distribution activity centers. Thus, the report could be ex-expanded to provide data on transportation, warehouse performance, order processing, material handling, and any other areas of concern. Because the information is selective and highly condensed, reports of this type can often be presented on a single standard-size page.

Special Reports.   Special reports may be created at any level of distribution administration and for a variety of reasons. Most often special reports are developed to provide detail on specific areas of performance. These general types of special reports are commonly utilized in distribution administration.

The first type is a diagnostic report, which provides detail concerning a specific phase of operations. For example, a report might be requested to provide greater detail regarding current backorders and corrective action which has been taken. If the firm in question operates a real-time system, special diagnostic reports may be obtained from either hard or soft copy by direct interrogation.

The second type of special report is a position paper. Given a current or anticipated problem, a report outlining alternative courses of action and expected consequences is often desirable. In terms of control levels (Chart 13–2), position papers are normally developed by line managers and department heads for use by executives at the decision level of the organization. Such position papers will often request additional resources and will, therefore, necessitate modifications to the operational plan if adopted. In accord with the levels of administrative control, position papers and related action may involve a greater allocation of resources to get a job accomplished. However, they will not involve changes in performance objectives.

The final special report is concerned with policy modification. Earlier in this chapter an example of a policy report was provided when the marketing department requested that customer service objectives be substantially improved or upgraded. Policy reports always are directed to or result from the chief executive officer of a given firm. Their content almost always involves areas of corporate activity beyond that normally responsible to the logistics sector of the firm.

Summary — Control Reports.   In conclusion, the content of control reports is highly customized to the individual firm, its organization, and the degree of automated information handling enjoyed. The content of reports should be geared to levels of administrative control. The higher the level of control, the more selective is the nature of information contained on the report.

Status reports for the most part are used by line managers for purposes of directing physical distribution activities in accord with predetermined operational plans. Trend reports are highly condensed and are used by executives at the variation and decision levels to monitor progress. The higher the control level, the more condensed and selective is the trend report. Trend reports prepared at the decision level should contain information related to all aspects of an integrated physical distribution system. Special reports are occasioned in response to a specific inquiry. Such inquiries may be initiated from any level of administrative control. It is useful to segregate special reports as to content of information. Special reports aimed to develop more data for day-to-day operations are classified as diagnostic reports. Those special reports aimed at decisions related to the operational plan are classified as position papers. The final category of special report is a policy paper.

The entire administrative control mechanism of a firm is directly related to automated information handling and organization. These two subjects are treated in the following sections.

Physical Distribution Information Systems

A corporation has four basic information systems: (1) financial, (2) marketing, (3) production, and (4) physical distribution. The content of each of these information sectors is concerned with the management of that particular aspect of the corporation. However, all information systems are highly interrelated and represent, in combination, the firm's total information system. The purpose of this section is to develop the physical distribution information system. However, the reader should constantly keep in mind that physical distribution information represents only one aspect of total corporate information.

COMPUTERS AND DATA TRANSMISSION

Central to the concept of information systems is the computer and data handling capacity. It is not the intent here to develop great detail concerning various computer systems. Rather, emphasis is placed upon some basic ideas concerning physical distribution information systems as they relate to computer capacity.

The types of control discussed in this chapter are beyond the capabilities of manual records or even so-called "tab card systems." The advent of multiple-level control systems did not become practical until the availability of high-speed digital computers. The speed of a digital computer enables tremendous amounts of information to be processed in a minimum amount of time. Such information concerning transaction and directive documents can be stored within the computer system for almost any period of time desired. In addition, information stored in a random access computer system can be retrieved with minimum time delay.[4]

In the physical distribution section of the firm, operations are carried on at widely separated locations. This geographical separation creates a need to

[4]For an expanded development see John Dearden, *Computers in Business Management* (Homewood, Ill.: Dow Jones-Irwin, Inc., 1966).

rapidly collect and disseminate information. Within the past decade substantial technological advances have been made in devices for data transmission. Technology has reached the point where combinations of data-processing and data-transmission equipment are available to handle most conceivable information system applications.[5]

Essentially three groupings of information flow can be identified based upon speed: (1) batching, (2) short-interval sequencing, and (3) real-time. Batching involves the groupings of data until sufficient volume is generated at a given location to justify entry into the tele-data processing system. Short-interval sequencing involves collection of information for a specific time period — for example, one day — with entry into the tele-data system at the end of the specified period regardless of volume. Real-time processing consists of a direct contact between all locations with immediate entry of information as generated. In a majority of physical distribution information systems, a daily sequence of data entry is adequate. At the present time the cost of maintaining a broad real-time information network is, in most cases, prohibitive.

Daily sequence of physical distribution data provides a continuous two-way flow of information between all activity locations and the point of central data bank maintenance. Thus, all transactions and records are stored in central data files from original documents. Status reports can be developed as desired, and selected trend or special diagnostic reports can be generated as frequently as necessary. The essence of a physical distribution information system is that all transaction documents are originated in a format which permits direct posting into data files. This posting results in a total information reservoir which contains relevant data in breadth as well as depth concerning logistical system status and performance.[6]

NERVE CENTER CONCEPT

Under the concept of total information systems, data are processed at speeds which allow discovery and interpretation of trends while they are forming. This information can be tapped at will by all levels of administrative control. At any given point in time all experience has been incorporated into the data bank. The potential exists to examine any control or design problem from all dimensions. The most appropriate structure for utilizing total information flow is likened to a control nerve center.

The control nerve center for a physical distribution system is similar to an air traffic control system. Central management has direct up-to-date status

[5]John Dearden, "How To Organize Information Systems," *Harvard Business Review*, March-April 1965, pp. 65–73; and Marshall K. Evans and Lou R. Hague, "Master Plan For Information Systems," *Harvard Business Review*, January-February 1962, pp. 62–103.

[6]For expansion see Donald J. Bowersox, "Total Information Systems In Logistics," *Business Logistics — Appraisal and Prospect*, J. L. Heskett ed. (Stanford, Calif.: Stanford University, 1965), pp. 107–122.

information concerning all units of the system. From the control center, interrogation of status and performance of individual units located at any geographic point may be initiated. Performance can be evaluated with respect to the operating plan allowing fast and efficient management response to any externally or internally generated change.

Organization

The potential of integrated control has caused dramatic change in theories and practice regarding physical distribution organization. The advent of total information systems has created strong forces for centralization of physical distribution policy and decision making. Because of the geographical scope of physical distribution activities a great deal of control has traditionally been decentralized. Thus, one main issue in organization is the degree to which operational control should be centralized or decentralized. A second issue in organization, centers around functional groupings. As indicated several times earlier, various phases of physical distribution responsibility have traditionally been scattered around the corporation and not under the control of any single executive.

Although the initial challenge of physical distribution centered around analytical developments, emphasis is now shifting to the vexing questions of administration and organization. Given identification of an opportunity to improve physical distribution performance, how is the desired degree of coordinated effort mobilized? Is reorganization desirable for achieving maximum control? What patterns of organization can be expected in the future? These and similar questions have become of prime concern regarding the management of physical distribution systems, In this section, traditional organization patterns are first reviewed. Attention is then directed to the case for development of an independent physical distribution organization. The final paragraphs deal with the relationships of line and staff and the issue of centralization. No model organization exists that will fit the needs of all firms. Therefore, at best the following comments on organization represent broad generalization.

TRADITIONAL PHYSICAL DISTRIBUTION ORGANIZATION

The responsibility of physical distribution management in a firm is to design and administer the logistical system. Regardless of organization groupings, this broad responsibility will engage the efforts of all departments of a corporation. Even if all operational responsibilities related to physical distribution are grouped into a single management unit, policies developed in finance, marketing, and manufacturing will continue to influence requirements and performance. Thus, physical distribution organization is at best a tool to assist in implementation of broader corporate policies.

In the early days, it was assumed that a firm *must* establish a so-called "distribution department" in order to implement physical distribution improvements. Many such departments were organized without full realization of the scope of integrated physical distribution activity. Although new in title, and often including activities formally headquartered in other organizational units, these early departments lacked proper corporate leverage to accomplish much improvement. What resulted from some of these early reorganizations was confusion between organization structure and philosophy or operation. Many firms established a formal organization, but management in general lacked a philosophy of integrated operations. Overall management lacked an appreciation of physical distribution requirements, capabilities, and economies.

The objectives of physical distribution normally stand in a degree of conflict to preferences of marketing, manufacturing, and finance. However, such conflict is desirable and in no way exclusive to physical distribution. Between marketing, manufacturing, and finance similar conflicts exist. The preferences of each major functional area must be reconciled to the prevailing corporate policies and objectives. Marketing, finance, physical distribution, and manufacturing represent subsystems to the total corporation. As such, trade-offs prevail between these organizational centers. The managements of each organizational unit must be sufficiently aware of their responsibility to develop an integrated capability, if maximum corporate efforts are to be mobilized.

Over the years the need for reconciliation has always existed between corporate activity areas. First, finance and manufacturing gained operational balance with recognition that financial policies and manufacturing economies often stand in sharp contrast for any given planning period. Next marketing, with a view toward market-oriented product development, challenged prevailing practices of financial and manufacturing planning. Once again, compromise was in order, and top management was forced to select the viewpoint that best met total corporate objectives. However, from each stage of development something better emerged. The corporation in total became better equipped for long-range survival.[7]

Physical distribution creates a new requirement for interdepartmental compromise. Although manufacturing traditionally desires long production runs and lowest procurement cost, physical distribution raises questions concerning the total-cost commitment of these independent practices. Finance, traditionally favorable to lowest possible inventories, is often confronted by physical distribution desires to increase inventory in an effort to reduce other

[7]John F. Varley, "Corporate Organization For Distribution Optimization," paper presented at Meeting of National Council of Physical Distribution Management, April 6, 1966.

distribution costs. In addition, physical distribution places on the accounting aspects of finance new requirements for total-cost measurement. In marketing, traditional preferences for finished goods inventory staging and broad assortments in forward markets often stand in conflict with total system economies offered by integrated physical distribution. Thus, new approaches to management, developed by physical distribution maturity, once again require compromise.

Physical distribution offers two main possibilities for improving total corporate effort. The first benefit is the potential of more exacting support from integrated control of material and finished goods flow. Through coordination of physical distribution efforts, most firms can look forward to better customer service without increasing appropriations. The second benefit is a potential for cost reduction. Such reductions are often realized in reduced fixed capital investments and day-to-day operational expenditures. However, physical distribution presents some special problems. Unlike some new developments in marketing, firms have been performing the physical distribution activities since inception. Special attention to physical distribution systems on the surface often appears redundant to traditional managers. Historical practices had resulted in the functions of physical distribution being neatly housed throughout the marketing, manufacturing, and financial organizations. The potential of operating these functional areas as an integrated system is easily overlooked. Chart 13–3 develops a traditional organization chart. Outlined are the activity areas of physical distribution traditionally performed by the marketing, finance, and manufacturing organizations. Each of these activities are of secondary importance to the major mission and responsibility of their parent organization. For example, transportation located in manufacturing results in little appreciation for high-speed, high-cost delivery in an acute marketing situation. Likewise, it is difficult for the marketing organization to appreciate holding customer orders in an effort to reduce transportation costs through larger volume shipments.

Because traditional organizations were capable of performing basic physical distribution activities, no general stimulant existed to encourage reorganization. Conversely, a barrier in terms of traditional organizational budgets and capital appropriation procedures did exist. Under traditional practice it would be a rare and broad-minded manufacturing executive that could envision an increase in transportation expenditure, accountable to manufacturing, in order to decrease inventory, accountable to finance, and improve customer service, accountable to marketing. Not only would the benefits of resources allocated to manufacturing go to other departments, the actual dollar expenditures would be committed to transportation, a secondary effort of the manufacturing department.

Regardless of planned reorganization, unless management of existing organizational units is able to recognize the corporate potential of integrated physical distribution not much will happen to improve the situation. Thus,

**CHART 13–3 Traditional Organization Chart and Selected
Physical Distribution Activities**

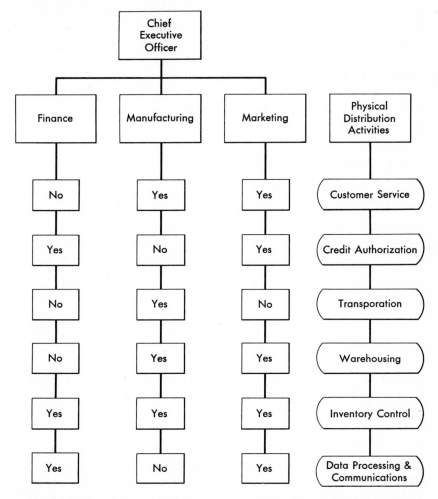

when proper philosophy of operations is lacking, little will be accomplished through reorganization. Conversely, when the proper philosophy of integrated operations does exist, firms are able to make substantial increases in performance and reductions in cost despite the lack of a special physical distribution organization.

It is interesting to note that, with rare exception, reorganization of physical distribution tends to follow a pattern of grouping responsibility within an existing organizational unit. For example, transportation is renamed physical distribution, and specified activities formally in marketing and finance are transferred to the new department. The new department, however, continues to report to manufacturing. Such shuffling, although often an improvement, fails to recognize the corporate-wide vested interest in integrated physical distribution. In fact, this form of reorganization presents evidence that the proper philosophy of integrated physical distribution operations is lacking. The real problems of expenditure, trade-off, and performance measurement continue to exist under such limited reorganization. Physical distribution remains a secondary concern of the parent organization. Little opportunity exists for presenting the physical distribution influence in corporate policy formation, because such considerations will often stand in conflict to primary responsibilities and objectives of the parent organization.

THE CASE FOR INDEPENDENT ORGANIZATION

Evidence seems persuasive that a case exists for independent organization of the physical distribution activities of the firm. By independent organization it is assumed that all activities related to performance of the physical distribution mission are assigned to a newly created management unit. Establishment of this new grouping is predicated on the following assumptions:

1. That there exists corporate-wide managerial recognition that the total physical distribution process consumes a substantial percent of each sales dollar.
2. That there exists corporate-wide managerial recognition that physical distribution must operate as a support unit to all other corporate activity centers.
3. That there exists corporate-wide managerial recognition that integrated control of the physical distribution system will supplement the efforts of marketing, manufacturing, and finance to create a stronger and more effective total corporate capacity.

Given these assumptions, it appears logical that a physical distribution organization should be afforded equal structural positioning as the other major corporate groupings. Chart 13–4 illustrates this structural positioning in the corporate chain of command. Included under each major division of the corporation is a chart of responsibilities. The current forces of business organization seem to be moving toward the pattern outlined in Chart 13–4. However, two traditional problems must be evaluated before the four major thrust groupings can become a reality. These problems center around (1) line and staff and (2) centralization versus decentralization.

Line and Staff Organization.   A traditional organization division is made between line and staff activities.[8] A line organization is generally conceived as performing operational activities directly related to the marketing and

---

[8]John F. Stolle, "How To Manage Physical Distribution," *Harvard Business Review*, July-August, 1967, pp. 93–100.

CHART 13–4 Independent Organization of Physical Distribution As One of Four Main Corporate Thrust Areas

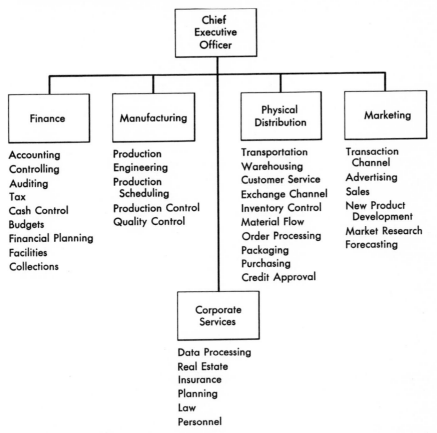

production of a firm's product or service offerings. A staff organization in contrast exists for purposes of developing new methods of achieving desired goals including assistance to line organizations in the accomplishment of specific responsibilities.

All traditional activities of the corporation — manufacturing, finance and marketing — consists of a combination of line and staff responsibilities. Although selling is a marketing line activity, marketing research, product development, and sales analysis are normally considered staff activities. These traditional distinctions can also be made in physical distribution. Chart 13–5 separates the line and staff responsibilities of physical distribution management. The development of a physical distribution organization is initially staff-oriented rather than line. The relative newness of physical distribution concept renders a need for substantial work of the staff nature prior to line reorganization. Thus, the separation of physical distribution staff activities from traditional departments, with subsequent formation of a line department, offers a convenient way to initiate and evaluate organizational change.

CHART 13–5   Physical Distribution Line and Staff Activities

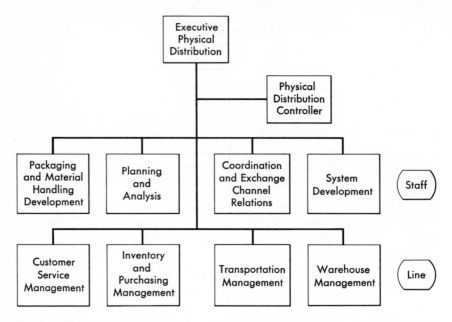

Under this arrangement, the new staff initiates research and development of system design, and actual supervision of the day-to-day line physical distribution activities remains with traditional departments.

In many cases establishment of a physical distribution staff department may constitute sufficient reorganization. The staff capacity provides internal consultants to aid in development of coordinated logistical performance. However, for the vast majority of companies such an arrangement, although perhaps sound on paper, has problems in performance. The staff group, lacking in authority and responsibility, may find substantial resistance to implementation of system modifications. The fact remains that, when retained in traditional departmental groupings, the line activities of physical distribution remain secondary activities to the primary mission of their parent organization.

Establishment of a line physical distribution organization eliminates the problems of secondary status as long as the responsible executive reports at an equal level with top managers of sales, finance, and manufacturing. As a general guideline, a physical distribution line organization should not be created unless supported by a competent staff. At the outset, the responsibility of physical distribution management was defined as that of design and administration of control systems. The design responsibility is staff in nature; the administrative responsibility is a line activity. The line organization will be of little value, unless critical issues of system design have been and continue to be evaluated at the staff level.

In summary, the responsibilities of physical distribution are conveniently divided between line and staff. In select cases reorganization at a staff level may be sufficient to achieve improved physical distribution performance. However, although staff activities may precede formation of line groupings, a combination of both will result in the most positive advancement in physical distribution capabilities.

Centralized Versus Decentralized Organization. An issue of sufficient magnitude is the question of centralized versus decentralized organization. Many firms are organized by division, each of which have a profit responsibility related to a specified product or service grouping.[9] Each of these divisions may in turn have marketing manufacturing, physical distribution, and finance.

The contrast between centralized and decentralized organizations is normally based upon the degree of direct operating responsibility over specified operations and not upon geographical locations. Two divisions of a given corporation may be located in the same building as the corporate headquarters and be classified as decentralized.

Corporations that are decentralized normally maintain corporate staff groups to assist in the coordination of separate divisional operations. Thus, although each division may have a marketing line and staff organization, corporate headquarters will also have a marketing staff. Under such organizational arrangements, the divisional staff will normally be of a limited size and function to assist in marketing of that particular divisions product line. Broader issues of marketing will be reserved for the corporate staff group.

Physical distribution line and staff operations can be fitted into this general structure of decentralized operations. However, unlike marketing and manufacturing, certain aspects of physical distribution encourage greater centralization. In general, economies of product flow are directly related to volume. Grouping of physical distribution line responsibilities of a number of different divisions into one centralized unit can result in elimination of duplicate facilities, economies of scale, and more effective performance.

The centralization of physical distribution responsibilities can result in the development of a single network of distribution warehouses, one order processing network, and the operation of a single transportation network. Thus, although decentralization may be the order of the day in marketing and manufacturing, physical distribution management may best be centralized. The degree to which multidivisional centralization of physical distribution is practical is limited by divisional size and congruency of marketing efforts.

Centralized physical distribution will benefit a company with small divisions, and it may only hinder the operation of a large division. The question of centralization is related to volume. The smaller the individual

[9]Robert Vernon Delaney, *Organization for Management of the Physical Distribution Function — A Case Study of the National Biscuit Company*, Master Thesis, Graduate School of Business Administration, New York University, 1966.

divisional volume, the greater is the tendency to centralize. Such centralization is limited by congruency of marketing effort. It is difficult to develop an efficient distribution system for two products sold through different channels to divergent markets.

Regardless of the degree of centralized line operations, divisionalized corporations normally find that physical distribution staffs gain an advantage in performance efficiency when grouped on a centralized basis. The planning of physical distribution activities can best be performed from the overall corporate vantage point where it is possible to evaluate multidivisional product flow in a single system design. Such centralization of staff responsibility allows maximum freedom in evaluation of needs and capabilities. In time, the most logical organization relationships is to find a mixture of centralized and decentralized line and staff operations among individual divisions in a multidivisional firm. The operations of a number of divisions will be centralized to combine volume and mixed product delivery, and other divisions will continue to be operated on a decentralized basis. Such combinations represent the prime objective of integrated physical distribution analysis.

The Distribution Controller.   Chart 13–5 illustrates a position referred to as the Physical Distribution Controller who reports directly to the top executive in the logistics sector of the firm. This idea is adopted from Dearden who predicts that the distribution controller will become common place in years to come.[10] The controller for physical distribution will have about the same responsibility as currently assigned to the financial controller. In essence, the controller will quarterback the operational plan for logistical activity and will supervise the flow of data and resources committed to its fulfillment.

This position of controller seems a necessity, if the many functions and activity centers of physical distribution are to be grouped under a single executive. The geographical separation between facilities common in large-scale physical distribution systems increase the need for exacting controllership.

Summary — Organization

The field of physical distribution management appears to be rapidly reaching the point where solution to organizational problems is required. Essential to reorganization is that all managers of a firm have a full appreciation of the benefits attainable from a fully integrated physical distribution system. Without an appreciation of the conflicts that exist and a belief that integration of physical distribution will lead to an improved total corporate effort, reorganization will be premature.

Successful reorganization must move physical distribution from the structure of existing departments with other primary responsibilities. Only

[10]Dearden, *op. cit.*

then will the benefit of integrated physical distribution be fully realized. The physical distribution department should stand parallel to marketing, finance, and manufacturing. To develop a successful organization, management will have to evaluate staff and line relationships. Although development of staff organization offers a way to get started, the degree of centralization of physical distribution desirable in multidivisional firms depends upon size and compatibility. In general, emphasis will be on centralized staff with line operations seeking a degree of centralization depending upon operational requirements. Regardless of final organizational arrangements, the full benefit of physical distribution organization will not be realized unless the management of such operations is afforded a voice in corporate planning and policy formation.

Appendix 13A
LINEAR PROGRAMMING

Linear programming is a quantitative aid for more effective business decision making. Ferguson and Sargent[1] define linear programming in the following manner:

Linear Programming is a technique for specifying how to use limited resources or capacities of a business to obtain a particular objective, such as least cost, highest margin, or least time, when those resources have alternative uses. It is a technique that systematizes for certain conditions the process of selecting the most desirable course of action from a number of available courses of action, thereby giving management information for making a more effective decision about the resources under its control.

Linear programming is currently being used in many areas of business. For the physical distribution manager, linear programming is useful in the following situations:

1. Determining the shipping mix of products to maximize cube utilization and weight.
2. Determining optimal location for plants and warehouses to minimize transportation costs.
3. Determining the sources of plant supply to minimize transportation costs.

Thus, the physical distribution manager in using linear programming as a management tool is benefited by better decision-making capabilities that allow a more thorough insight into a wide range of solutions.

Several modifications of linear programming are available. For purposes of illustration, the transportation method is used.

[1]Robert O. Ferguson and Lauren F. Sargent, *Linear Programming: Fundamentals and Applications* (New York: McGraw-Hill, 1958), p. 3.

Linear Programming — The Transportation Method

The transportation method is a linear programming model designed to minimize a single function referred to as the objective function. The basic method is applicable to many situations and derives its name from its early use in transportation scheduling.

To illustrate the transportation method, a hypothetical case for the ABC Automobile Company is developed.[2] This illustration will proceed in a step-by-step manner integrating the basic procedures of the transportation method and the ABC Automobile Company. In this illustration the Company (ABC) wants to minimize transport costs between four part suppliers and three final automobile assembly plants.

First, the problem is framed by collecting all pertinent information. To comply with this step, the physical distribution manager needs three sets of data: (1) weekly demand of parts for individual assembly plants, (2) weekly supply of parts provided by individual parts suppliers, and the (3) transportation cost per unit from suppliers to assembly plant. Each set of data is illustrated in Tables 13A–1, 13A–2, and 13A–3.

Second, to facilitate the programming processes, a matrix should be developed. This matrix arranges the supply, demand, and transportation cost data.[3] However, the matrix must maintain a balance between supply available and parts demanded. This is accomplished by inserting an "other" column,[4] which will absorb the supplier's capacity not specifically needed by the ABC Automobile Company.

Third, an initial solution is determined. Initial solutions can be determined by using four methods: (1) existing assignments, (2) present lowest cost solution found by inspection, (3) managerially preferred method, and (4) the Northwest Corner Rule (NCR). The NCR method is used in this illustration to provide a systematic and logical initial solution that determines the routing quantities. The procedures for initiating the NCR are as follows:

a. Start in the upper left hand or northwest corner of the matrix and compare the demand needs in the column with the supply provided in the row. Then place the smaller of these two values in the column. If this fills the plant's demand, move right to the next column in the same row and fill this plant's demand. This is continued until the supply has been exhausted for the row.

b. Moving to the next row, again compare the plant's demand with the supply available and select the smaller of the two amounts. If this smaller amount is too large, use the quantity that will balance the column. Then move to the next column and follow the same procedure.

---

[2]For a complete discussion of this method see Nyles V. Reinfeld and William R. Vogel, *Mathematical Programming*, (Englewood Cliffs, N. J.: Prentice Hall, Inc., 1958).

[3]Edward H. Bowman and Robert B. Fetter, *Analysis for Production Management* (Homewood, Ill.: Richard D. Irwin, 1961), pp. 113–116.

[4]"Other" column is a dummy column.

TABLE 13A–1 WEEKLY DEMAND FOR PARTS FOR INDIVIDUAL ASSEMBLY PLANTS

Plants	Demand Units
X	5,200
Y	19,600
Z	12,000
Total	36,800

TABLE 13A–2 WEEKLY SUPPLY OF PARTS PROVIDED BY INDIVIDUAL PARTS SUPPLIERS

Supplier	Capacity Units
A	20,400
B	10,400
C	4,800
D	4,400
Total	40,000

TABLE 13A–3 TRANSPORTATION COST FROM SUPPLIERS TO INDIVIDUAL PLANTS PER CWT*

Supplier	Plant X	Plant Y	Plant Z
A	$20.00	$17.00	$18.00
B	15.00	14.00	16.00
C	10.00	13.00	12.00
D	10.00	11.00	9.00

*F.O.B. Shipping Point.

c. After completing the second row, move to the third and fourth row, etc., following the above steps.

Matrix II (Table 13A–5) illustrates the Northwest Corner Rule upon completion.

Fourth, the initial solution is evaluated for more economical alternatives. Matrix II is now evaluated to determine if the least-cost solution has been discovered. By analyzing each vacant square in the matrix, a better solution may be found. This is accomplished by varying the combination of supply and demand within the established supply-and-demand constraints.

To evaluate the vacant squares in Matrix II, the following steps should be taken:

a. Select a vacant square. This square, it should be remembered, represents a new combination of supply and demand.

TABLE 13A–4   MATRIX I

Supplier	Plant X	Plant Y	Plant Z	Other	Total Supply
A	$20.00	$17.00	$18.00	$0	20,400 units
B	15.00	14.00	16.00	0	10,400 units
C	10.00	13.00	12.00	0	4,800 units
D	10.00	11.00	9.00	0	4,400 units
Weekly Assembly Plant Demands In Units	5,200	19,600	12,000	3,200	40,000

TABLE 13A–5   MATRIX II

Supplier	Plant X		Plant Y		Plant Z		Other	Total Supply
A	(5,200)	$20.00	(15,200)	$17.00	—	$18.00	$0	20,400
B		15.00	(4,400)	14.00	(6,000)	16.00	0	10,400
C		10.00		13.00	(4,800)	12.00	0	4,800
D		10.00		11.00	(1,200)	9.00	(3,200)	4,400
Weekly Assembly Plant Demand In Units	5,200		19,600		12,000		3,200	40,000

b. Trace a path in the existing matrix. This path starts and ends in a vacant square, with all intervening squares having a quantity supplied in them. These quantities are in parentheses. Then to keep the evaluation simple, move or transfer one unit into the vacant square while making appropriate adjustments to maintain the system's balance. The same path should again be traced analyzing costs. Place a plus sign before those costs added and a minus sign before those costs deleted. Remember, only right angles are permitted.

c. The total of plus and minus costs in the path should be found and the difference should be placed in this vacant square.

d. This process of evaluating each square is continued until all vacant squares have been assigned a positive or negative value. If all the results are positive, the best system has been found. If one or more of the routes is a negative number, a better solution exists for the system.

Using the above guide, Matrix II can be analyzed. An example of the steps above can be shown by selecting vacant square A-other. Matrix III traces through the addition of one unit to vacant square A-other. This results in adding +0 to square A-other. To offset the movement of one unit, one unit must be subtracted from D-other with a cost reduction of −0. Now row D is out of balance so one unit is added, increasing transportation costs by $+9$. This process then goes to BZ or a -16 reduction, to BY for a $+14$ addition, and to AY for a -17 reduction. The process is now complete, and this portion of the matrix is balanced. The result is a $10-per-unit savings in transportation by reassigning in path A-other.

TABLE 13A–6   MATRIX III

Supplier	Plant X	Plant Y	Plant Z	Other	Total Supply
A		$-(17)$		$+(0)$	-10
B		$+(14)$	$-(16)$		
C					
D			$+(9)$	$-(0)$	

The remaining vacant squares in Matrix II have the following results:

Square	Change in Cost	Net Change
AZ	$18 - 16 + 14 - 17$	-1
A-Other	$0 - 0 + 9 - 8 + 14 - 17$	-10
BX	$15 - 20 + 17 - 14$	-2
B-Other	$0 - 0 + 9 - 16$	-7
CX	$10 - 20 + 17 - 14 + 16 - 12$	-3
CY	$13 - 14 + 16 - 12$	$+3$
C-Other	$0 - 0 + 9 - 12$	-3
DX	$10 - 20 + 17 - 14 + 16 - 9$	0
DY	$11 - 14 + 16 - 9$	$+4$

In Matrix IV (Table 13A–7), these results are indicated in their respective vacant squares. The total transportation cost in Matrix IV is $558,400.

TABLE 13A–7   MATRIX IV

Supplier	Plant X		Plant Y		Plant Z		Other		Total Supply
A	(5,200)	$20	(15,200)	$17	-1	$18	-10*	$0	20,400
B	-2	15	(4,400)	14	(6,000)	16	-7	0	10,400
C	-3	10	$+3$	13	(4,800)	12	-3	0	4,800
D	0	10	$+4$	11	(1,200)	9	(3,200)	0	4,400
Weekly Assembly Plant Demands In Units	5,200		19,600		12,000		3,200		40,000

*Highest negative transportation cost.

Fifth, the review process determines the desirability of moving a quantity in parentheses to one of the negative values just found. If more than one negative value exists for a quantity in parentheses, the highest negative value should be selected first.

In determining the value in parentheses that should be moved to the highest negative value in the review process, the path in Matrix IV that was used to determine the highest negative value should be retraced. In Matrix IV, it is the path used to determine A-other's value. Then the lowest positive quantity should be inserted in the square with the highest negative value. In this instance, 1200 units is the lowest quantity in parentheses in path A-other. This value is placed in square A-other. Remember column and row totals must be balanced after such adjustments.

Sixth, after reallocating the quantities in parentheses, the vacant squares are again analyzed for the highest negative transportation cost. This is the fourth step that was discussed previously. Then the fifth step is repeated. The fourth and fifth steps are continued until there are no negative transportation costs. This then gives the optimal system. Matrix IX is the optimal system having the lowest transportation cost.

TABLE 13A–8   MATRIX V

Supplier	Plant X		Plant Y		Plant Z		Other		Total Supply
A	(5,200)	$20	(14,000)	$17	−1	$15	(1,200)	$0	20,400
B	−2	15	(5,600)	14	(4,800)	16	−7*	0	10,400
C	−3	10	+3	13	(4,800)	12	−3	0	4,800
D	0	10	+4	11	(2,400)	9	(2,000)	0	4,400
Weekly Assembly Plant Demand in Units	5,200		19,600		12,000		3,200		40,000

*Highest negative transportation cost.

The total transportation cost in Matrix V is $576,400.

TABLE 13A–9   MATRIX VI

Supplier	Plant X		Plant Y		Plant Z		Other		Total Supply
A	(5,200)	$20	(14,000)	$17	−1	$18	(1,200)	$0	20,400
B	−2	15	(5,600)	14	(2,800)	16	(2,000)	0	10,400
C	−3*	10	+3	13	(4,800)	12	+4	0	4,800
D	0	10	+4	11	(4,400)	9	+7	0	4,400
Weekly Assembly Plant Demand in Units	5,200		19,000		12,000		3,200		40,000

*Highest negative transportation cost.

The total transportation cost in Matrix VI is $562,400.

TABLE 13A–10   MATRIX VII

Supplier	Plant X		Plant Y		Plant Z		Other		Total Supply
A	(2,400)	$20	(16,800)	$17	−1	$18	(1,200)	$0	20,400
B	−2*	15	(2,800)	14	(5,600)	16	(2,000)	0	10,400
C	(2,800)	10	+3	13	(2,000)	12	+4	0	4,800
D	+3	10	+4	11	(4,400)	9	+7	0	4,400
Weekly Assembly Plant Demand in Units	5,200		19,600		12,000		3,200		40,000

*Highest negative transportation cost.

The total transportation cost in Matrix VII is $554,000.

TABLE 13A–11   MATRIX VIII

Supplier	Plant X		Plant Y		Plant Z		Other		Total Supply
A	+2	$20	(19,200)	$17	−1*	$18	(1,200)	$0	20,400
B	(2,400)	15	(400)	14	(5,600)	16	(2,000)	0	10,400
C	(2,800)	10	+3	13	(2,000)	12	+4	0	4,800
D	+3	10	+4	11	(4,400)	9	+7	0	4,400
Weekly Assembly Plant Demand in Units	5,200		19,600		12,000		3,200		40,000

*Highest negative transportation cost.

The total transportation cost in Matrix VIII is $549,200.

TABLE 13A–12   MATRIX IX

Supplier	Plant X		Plant Y		Plant Z		Other		Total Supply
A	+2	$20	(18,800)	$17	(400)	$18	(1,200)	$0	20,400
B	(2,400)	15	(800)	14	(5,200)	16	(2,000)	0	10,400
C	(2,800)	10	+3	13	(2,000)	12	+4	0	4,800
D	+3	10	+4	11	(4,400)	9	+7	0	4,400
Weekly Assembly Plant Demand in Units	5,200		19,600		12,000		3,200		40,000

The total transportation cost in Matrix IX is $548,800.

No negative values exist in Matrix IX. This matrix, therefore, is the lowest cost method of shipping parts to the ABC Automobile Company.

Appendix 13B
PERT AND CPM

Until recently, physical distribution managers had no formal means of managing projects of a nonrepetitive nature. Previously each physical distribution manager devised his own system of organizing nonrepetitive projects. For the most part, these systems were insufficient to handle the complexity of interrelationships associated with large scale projects.

In the mid-1950's, several industries characterized by their large, complex, development-type projects found a need for sophisticated project planning and progress evaluation techniques. These programs would enable better control over the 4 M's — manpower, money, materials, and machinery. Thus, critical path concepts were devised.

Critical path concepts include two types of programs and their variations. The Critical Path Method (CPM) was a concept jointly developed by the E. I. de Nemours Company and Sperry Rand for scheduling, planning, and coordinating new engineering projects. The other concept, Program Evaluation Review Technique (PERT), was developed by the United States Navy Special Projects Office, and the Lockheed Missiles and Space Company as a management tool for the Navy's Polaris Program.

Before PERT or CPM were developed, project managers found it difficult to effectively organize the countless tasks comprising large projects. Due to the mind's inability to effectively cope with this complexity and their interrelationships PERT and CPM were developed. These two concepts became management planning and analysis tools that could coordinate total project development without dividing the work into independently managed portions.

The basis of PERT and CPM rests in the critical path network concept. In this appendix characteristics common to each are first reviewed. Then, peculiarities of PERT and CPM are examined in separate discussions.

Developing the Network

The backbone of CPM and PERT lies in its graphical presentation for project management. This graph is basically developed from Gantt or bar charts, which were designed to control the time elements inherent in any project. They include starting and finishing times as well as the current status of the project.

CPM and PERT Networks go further than Gantt charts. They add to the project network the dependencies and interrelationships of the activities and define the unique activities in greater detail. Because of this more detailed delineation of activities, a graphical network is developed.

The Network

The PERT and CPM network is a flow chart of events that are joined by lines illustrating their interrelationships and interdependencies. These networks consist of two basic elements, events and activities. Events are depicted on the network as squares, circles, rectangles, triangles, and so on, and are called nodes. The activities connecting the events are symbolized as solid or dashed lines and are called arrows.

The event is an occurrence whose accomplishment is known as a specific point in time. These represent the achievement of some goal and they signify the start or completion of at least one activity.

Activities are of two types: real and dummy. Real activities represent the necessary work that must be completed to progress from one event to another. These activities expend men, machinery, money, and materials. They are represented by solid lines beginning and ending at nodes. Dummy activities are constraints representing the dependency of one event upon another. They are illustrated as dotted lines representing zero time, or involve lead or wait time. Dummy activities do not involve expenditure of men, money, materials, or machinery.

Reality:	Event	Activity (Real)	Event	Activity (Dummy)	Event
Symbol:	1	———————	2	··············	3
	Node	Arrow	Event	Arrow	Event

Estimating Expected Activity Times

A project manager must have some knowledge of the times needed to complete the individual activity and the total project. To do this, he has available two methods. PERT uses variable times, whereas CPM uses deterministic times as expected times for completion of activities. It is in using these two different time estimates, variable and deterministic, that the fundamental differences arise between PERT and CPM.

Using variable times, PERT estimates activities that have never been performed before (new construction, research, and development). Because of this, there is a considerable chance that an accurate estimate of the performance times is not available. Thus, a large variance is introduced into the performance times.

CPM uses deterministic times. These are time estimates whose mean value is accurately known and whose variance in performance time is small. These activities generally are quite repetitious (maintenance, assembly, and so on).

Performance Time Estimates for PERT

PERT programs assign performance times to each activity in the network. Due to the large variances inherent in projects using PERT, three time estimates are used. These three time estimates, optimistic, most likely, and pessimistic, allow for the uncertainty involved with performance times.

Optimistic time estimate denoted by the symbol a is the *minimum time* the activity will take if everything goes right. The most likely time estimate is noted by the symbol m, and it is the *normal time* an activity would take if the activity was done repeatedly. Finally, the pessimistic time estimate denoted by b is the *maximum time* an activity would take when done under adverse conditions.

To find the mean elapsed time in a PERT program, the above three time estimates are used in the following equation:

$$t_e = \frac{a + 4m + b}{6}$$

This equation gives the most likely time a weight of 4 and the optimistic and pessimistic times a weight of one each.

Using the mean elapsed formula, the mean elapsed time (t_e) for each activity in the construction of a warehouse can be calculated.

After completing the calculation, the t_e are placed below their respective activity as illustrated in Table 13B–1 for the construction of a warehouse.

Knowing the mean elapsed time (t_e), total mean elapsed time (T_E) can be calculated to determine the time needed to accomplish the project. However, there are many paths that lead to the project's completion. In PERT, though, the longest path or the largest T_E is used to establish the expected completion date. No project is complete until all activities leading into the last event are finished. Table 13B–2 lists a few of the many possible paths; the most critical path is indicated by an asterisk.

In selecting path 1–2–8–10–14–19–20–21 a T_E of 192.3 hours is established as the total elapsed time from the beginning of Event 1 to the completion of Event 21. The project then cannot be completed until all activities along path 1–2–8–10–14–19–20–21 are complete. If the project must be speeded up to utilize a trade-off between cost and time the program manager should increase the flow of men, money, and machinery into activities on this path. However, as this occurs, the total elapsed times change and so do critical paths. Thus, it may be deemed necessary to establish a new critical path where the trade-off between time and cost again occurs.

Knowing the longest path and thus the longest span of time, the project manager may determine the largest allowable time for completion of the project. Dates, however, for individual situations can be determined independently of the network.

TABLE 13B–1 WEIGHTED AVERAGE t_e's FOR VARIOUS PATHS

Activity	Pessimistic	Most Likely	Optimistic	t_e
1–2	15	10	4	9.8
1–3	9	5	0	4.67
2–8	10	60	90	61.67
3–4	7	5	0	4.5
4–5	22	20	15	19.5
5–6	18	15	13	15.
5–7	40	30	22	30.3
6–9	35	30	20	29.16
7–8	13	10	7	10.
8–10	28	20	15	20.5
9–10	17	15	11	15.16
10–11	10	5	0	5.
10–12	35	30	20	29.16
10–14	11	5	0	5.16
11–18	65	60	45	58.3
12–13	18	15	12	15.
13–14	11	10	8	9.83
14–15	12	10	7	9.83
14–16	17	15	10	14.5
14–19	64	42	38	45.
15–19	40	30	20	30.
16–19	25	20	10	19.16
17–19	9	5	0	4.83
18–19	7	5	0	4.5
19–20	21	20	17	19.67
20–21	12	10	5	9.5

TABLE 13B–2 PATH AND ELAPSED TIME

Path	Activity Mean Elapsed Time	T_E
*1–2–8–10–14–19–20–21	9.8 + 61.67 + 20.5 + 29.16 + 42 + 19.67 + 9.5	= 192.3
1–3–4–5–7.8–10–14–19–20–21	4.67 + 4.5 + 19.5 + 30.3 + 10 + 20 + 20.5 + 29.16 + 19.67 + 9.5	= 147.80
1–3–4–5–6–9–10–14–19–20–21	4.67 + 4.5 + 19.5 + 15 + 29.16 + 15.16 + 29.16 + 42 + 19.67 + 9.5	= 188.32
1–3–4–5–7–8–10–11–18–19–20–21	4.67 + 4.5 + 19.5 + 30.3 + 10 + 20.5 + 5 + 58.3 + 4.5 + 19.67 + 9.5	= 182.44
1–2–8–10–12–13–14–16–17–19–20–21	9.8 + 61.67 + 20.5 + 5.16 + 15 + 9.83 + 14.6 + 19.16 + 4.83 + 19.67 + 9.5	= 189.72

*Most Critical Path

CHART 13B-1   Warehouse Construction PERT Network with Mean Elapsed Time

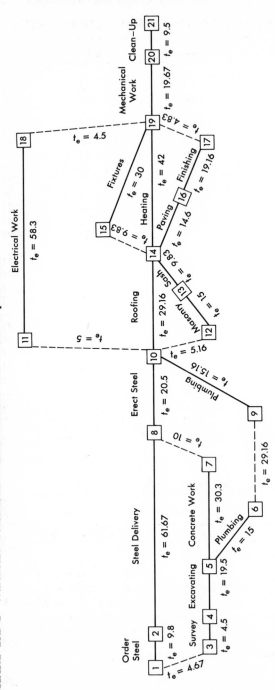

PERT as previously mentioned uses variable times rather than deterministic times. These variable times introduce large variances, which can be calculated by the following formula:

$$V = \frac{(b - a)^2}{6}$$

a = Optimistic Time Estimate
b = Pessimistic Time Estimate

The variances can then be used to determine the probability[1] of meeting the scheduled date of any given event or project. However, the technical validity of such formulation is controversial and questionable and its formulation is achieved through the use of a computer.

The Most Critical Path

The most critical path is the path taking the longest time to traverse from Event 1 to Event 21. In this instance, the most critical path is Path 1–2–8–10–14–19–20–21 because it places the greatest time constraint on completion of the project's final event.

The completion time of the most critical path is found by adding the mean activity elapsed time (t_e) to arrive at the total mean elapsed time (T_E). If any of the activities on the critical path are delayed, the total mean elapsed time (T_E) is increased. On the other hand, if mean activity times are decreased, the completion of the project may be hastened. However, the critical path may change to another path, once the present path becomes shorter than some other path. For instance if Path 1–2–8–10–14–19–20–21 is shortened to 189 hours from 192.3 hours, Path 1–2–8–10–12–13–14–16–17–19–20–21 may become the critical path provided the activities are not rearranged. If they are rearranged, a completely new network is necessary.

All other paths excluding the most critical path are classified as slack paths. The slack these paths are allowed is measured as negative, zero, or positive. Positive slack indicates the project is ahead of schedule in this path; zero slack indicates on-schedule; and negative slack indicates behind-schedule.

When negative slack occurs, the total activity time is greater than the time available to complete the project as scheduled. This situation may make the slack path longer than the present most critical path. This path then becomes the most critical path and the scheduled completion time may be delayed.

[1]See *Systems Analysis, A Computer Approach to Decision Models* by Claude McMillan and Richard F. Gonzalez (Homewood, Ill.: Richard D. Irwin, Inc., 1965), pp. 189–210, for a discussion on probability and PERT.

TABLE 13B–3   DIFFERENCES BETWEEN PERT AND CPM PROGRAMS

Feature	PERT Class	CPM Class
(a) Forward and backward passes, slack computation	all	all
(b) Random event numbering	most	few
(c) Multiple initial and terminal events	most	apparently none
(d) Scheduled dates	most	very few
(e) Calendar dates	most	few
(f) Optional output sorts and formats	most	several
(g) Network condensation	very few	none
(h) Activity orientation	several	all
(i) Statistical analysis	all[1]	none[1]
(j) Cost optimization	very few	several
(k) Cost control	very few	very few
(l) Resource allocation	very few	very few

[1]In this text this is true by definition, as stated in the discussion of feature No. 12, Statistical Analysis.

Interpretation of Results

PERT, CPM, and their variations have critical paths upon which management should focus its attention. The critical path analysis, if the interpretations are correct, can illustrate how planning, scheduling, and coordinating critical activities can reduce expenditures for men, material, money, and machinery. Also, the critical path illustrates where time-cost trade-offs are possible and desirable. For instance, the physical distribution manager should consider the trade-off of construction cost of a warehouse due to acceleration of the building program against cost of storing merchandise elsewhere.

Other Differences in PERT and CPM Programs

The basic difference between PERT and CPM lies in the time estimates and PERT's probabilistic approach. Table 13B–3 shows further distinctions in the two classes of critical path programs.[2]

Benefits of Critical Path Concepts

PERT, CPM, and their variations pass through a basic number of common steps although each step may vary with the particular concept. Briefly the

[2]Moder, Joseph J., and Phillips, Cecil R., *Project Management with CPM and PERT* (New York: Reinhold Publishing Corporation), p. 249.

steps are (1) establishing a network diagram, (2) estimating the expected activity time, (3) developing the critical path, and (4) using the results.

PERT, CPM, and their variations greatly assist the project manager. They allow for better planning, scheduling, and control of the specific project. This enables the project manager in having a system for documenting and communicating the project plans, schedules, completion times, and project costs. Also, the concepts focus management's attention on the 10 to 20 percent of the project that is most constraining to results. The critical path analysis illustrates the effects of technical and procedural changes on the overall project schedule.

Ending Appendixes

APPENDIX E1 Simchip I—

A Physical Distribution Game

Simchip I is a physical distribution management decision simulation based upon four firms supplying five market areas with potato chips. Each firm produces potato chips in one-pound size bags and distributes to the five areas in the week following production. The overall objective of the simulation is to make maximum gross distribution profits for a time period specified by the umpire. Product sales results in revenue generation. Warehouse and inventory costs, production costs, transportation costs, and distribution costs result in expense generation.

The general purpose of Simchip I is to demonstrate to the student the basic interrelationship between several important elements of the physical distribution task. The game has not been designed to present all possible alternatives in a dynamic setting, but rather to focus on those key elements of the task in such a manner as to provide important background perspective for the student.

In order to focus on the physical distribution task, some simplifying assumptions have been made. These assumptions include a simplified market structure, a limited product line, and the elimination of promotional and advertising decisions.

The explanation of Simchip I is divided into three general parts. The first part entitled "Information on Key Variables" presents detailed data on all of the variables used in the simulation. The second part entitled "Explanation of Forms and Procedures Used by the Student" explains the forms and procedures used in actually playing the game. The third section illustrates the forms utilized by the players in recording decisions.

The game may be played for as many periods as specified by the umpire. The student should carefully review all materials in the appendix and thoroughly understand the simulation procedure before completing any decision forms.

Information on Key Variables

MARKET DATA

Consumer demand for the product is the key determinant in the firm's sales. Each firm starts the simulation with an equal share of the total market. Consumer demand based on past sales history fluctuates ±15 percent. As the simulation develops, each firm's market share will vary depending on the efficiency of production and physical distribution.

RAW MATERIALS

	Cost	Package	Pounds Per Cubic Foot
Potatoes	$ 4.21/cwt	100# Bags	6.66
Salt	1.735/cwt	100# Bags	12.50
Oil	16.21/Drum	50 gal. Drum −400#	44.44
1# Bags	22.00/M	1000 Bags −260#	9.64

WAREHOUSE AND INVENTORY

Each firm has two types of warehouse facilities available for Raw Materials Storage.

Private.   12,500 sq. feet 20′ clear
80% usable cube = 200,000 cubic ft
Warehouse overhead charge = $1443/wk
Warehouse operation = Throughput = Total receipts + Total Production
  (from Status report) ÷ 2 × $.16/cwt

Public.   A public warehouse will be used after 200,000 cubic feet have been placed in private warehouse.

Cubic Feet	Cost/Cubic Feet
0–100,000	$.015
100,000–500,000	.010
500,000–and above	.005

(Note: Cost includes delivery from warehouse to factory.)

RAW MATERIAL INVENTORY CARRYING COST

Ending raw material inventory (at cost) × 10% ÷ 52
Finished Goods Inventory Carrying Cost = Waste × Unit Wholesale Price × 20% ÷ 52

CHART E1–1   Simchip I — Market Structure

MARKET STRUCTURE

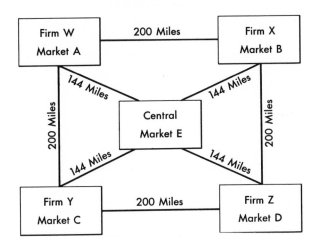

PRODUCTION CAPACITY

Capacity. Each firm operates a cooking plant located at their home market location (see Chart E1–1). This plant has a cooking capacity of 20,000 pounds per day normal, 5,000 pounds per day overtime, and an additional 20,000 pounds by scheduling Saturday production. Production must be completed in the week prior to the following week's anticipated sales.

Production Overhead. Fixed overhead charge regardless of production — $3750/wk. A portion of this overhead is for the reusable cartons utilized in delivery.

Cooking Costs. The production of finished potato chips requires raw potatoes, oil, salt, and bags. Costs are incurred as raw materials are converted to chips.

COOKING CONVERSION — 1000# FINISHED CHIPS

Potatoes	4370#	$183.970
Salt	50#	.868
Oil	400#	16.210
Bags	1000#	22.000
		$223.048
	Total	Cost/lb.
Total cost	223.05	.223

COOKING COSTS — REGULAR

Basic (Lbs.)	Per/Lb./Day	Saturday Per/Lb.
10,000	.220	.319
11,000	.215	.319
12,000	.210	.319
13,000	.205	.319
14,000	.200	.319
15,000	.195	.283
16,000	.190	.283
17,000	.185	.283
18,000	.180	.283
19,000	.175	.283
20,000	.170	.283

COOKING COSTS — OVERTIME

Basic (Lbs.)	Per/Lb.
0–2500	.284
2501–5000	.246

TRANSPORTATION COSTS (INBOUND RAW MATERIALS)

Transportation of raw materials is accomplished by rail, common carrier motor truck, and private trucks. All raw materials are received from Central City.

COMPANY TRUCK (No Lead Time)

	Capacity (lbs)	
	Truck A	Truck B
Potatoes	60,000	24,000
Salt	50,000	20,000
Oil	96,000	38,000
Bags	10,000	4,000

	Cost	
	Truck A	Truck B
Basic	$100/week	$65/week
Per Mile	$ .15	$ .10
Average Mile/Hour	40	45
Loading/Unloading Time	4 hours	4 hours
Driver's Wages	$6/hour	$6/hour

CENTRAL CITY — RAIL (2 Weeks Lead Time)
(No Maximum)

0–480,000 lbs	$ .15/cwt
480,000–960,000 lbs	.13/cwt
960,000–1,440,000 lbs	.125/cwt
1,440,000–Any Q lbs	.120/cwt

CENTRAL CITY — Truck (1 Week Lead Time)

	LTL	TL
Potatoes	0–30,000 lbs $.50/cwt	30,000–50,000 lbs* $.35/cwt
Salt	0–25,000 lbs $.55/cwt	25,000–60,000 lbs* $.35/cwt
Oil	0–48,000 lbs $.30/cwt	48,000–96,000 lbs* $.20/cwt
Bags	0–5,000 lbs $.85/cwt	5,000–10,000 lbs* $.65/cwt

*Maximum weight/shipment.

DISTRIBUTION COSTS (FINISHED PRODUCT)

COMPANY TRUCK

	Truck A	Truck B
Per Mile	$.15	$.10
Average Mile/Hour	40	45
Unloading Time	1 Hour	1 Hour
Driver's Wages	$6/Hour	$6/Hour
Capacity: Cartons	1,620	600
Pounds	9,720	3,600

COMMON CARRIER

	LTL 0–9,000 lbs	TL Over 9,000 lbs
Central (144 Miles)	$3.50/cwt	$3.00/cwt
Adjacent (145–200 Miles)	$3.90/cwt	$3.40/cwt
Distant (Over 200 Miles)	$4.20/cwt	$3.80/cwt

DISTRIBUTION IN MARKET AREA — Basic Cost/Market $250.00*

	Cost/cwt
Under 2,000	$ .27
2,001–5,000	.26
5,001–10,000	.25
10,001–15,000	.24
15,001–20,000	.23
20,001–25,000	.22
25,001–30,000	.21
Over 30,000	.20

*This cost is added once each decision period for each market in which distribution is made. This cost represents storage in transit and distribution in the various market areas.

Explanation of Forms and Procedures Used by the Player

STATUS REPORT

The status report provides the basis for planning each period's actions and aids in preparing the Operating Statement. It is filled out by the umpire. The form contains your company's share of each market and the amount of waste you had last period. You are to assume that you will sell the amount proposed if you produce and distribute that amount to each market. The percentage share may be compared to past percentages to get an idea of your distribution in each market as compared to the other companies. Waste is the amount produced and distributed to each market that was not sold.

Remember, this is a physical distribution simulation and your score will be determined by how well you control your logistic system. Coordination among team members is of prime importance!

DECISION-RECORDING FORM

Production Schedule.   This schedule will be completed showing production for each day and the total for the week.

Raw Material Inventory Status.   Beginning inventory and purchase orders due will be provided by the umpire at the start of the simulation. After this, you will be responsible for completing this form in duplicate and returning one copy to the umpire each period. The starting inventory will be the same figure as last period's ending inventory. Usage (obtained from the production worksheet) and receipts (obtained from the warehouse worksheet) are applied to beginning inventory to obtain ending inventory.

All new orders placed and those placed in previous periods and not received during the period are deleted.

Distribution Schedule.   This schedule is provided in three parts:
Total Distribution.   This form is to be filled out completely showing the market and the day of distribution. Total (q) will show the daily distribution; Total (p) will show the total distribution to each market. These two totals must be equal.

Company Truck Distribution.   This schedule will show your truck schedule for each day of the week and the total pounds distributed. If the truck is used for raw materials pick up, the route will be entered in the market column and miles recorded. (Example: Your firm is located in market B. You make a raw materials pick up in Central (E). Market column would show B-E-B-; miles, 288; pounds and distribution stops, blank. If you loaded your truck with 9,000 pounds of chips and delivered 4,500 to market

D and 4,500 pounds to E, and then picked up the raw materials the form would be Market, B-D-E-B, miles 488; pounds, 9,000; distribution stops 2.)

Common Carrier Distribution. This schedule will show the daily distribution by market and pounds when using common carrier.

Note: The combined totals of parts 2 and 3 must equal the total distribution in part 1.

OPERATING STATEMENT.

The work sheets provided are cross-referenced to assist you in preparing your operating statement.

GENERAL

The decision recording form and the operating statement will be completed and turned in to the umpire on the day announced by your instructor. Fill out these forms completely and accurately as they are subject to audit at any time during the simulation. File each period's work sheets so that you will be able to support your figures.

STATUS REPORT

COMPANY_____   END OF PERIOD _____

Market	Proposed Demand in pounds	% Share Last Period	Waste Last Period in #
A			
B			
C			
D			
E			

TOTAL   _____ _____ _____

SALES COMPUTATIONS:

Total distribution in $ = distribution last period × .845¢
Total waste in $ = waste last period × .845¢

TOTAL DISTRIBUTION LESS TOTAL WASTE = TOTAL NET SALES

$_____ − $_____ = $_____

DECISION RECORDING FORM

COMPANY_____   END OF PERIOD_____

Production schedule:

M	T	W	TH	F	S	S
#	#	#	#	#	#	#

Raw materials inventory status:

	Potatoes #	Oil #	Salt #	Bags #
Starting Inventory				
Usage (−)				
Receipts (+)				
Ending Inventory				

Order due

#	period				
_____	_____				
_____	_____				
_____	_____				
_____	_____				
_____	_____				
_____	_____				
TOTAL COMMITTED					

DISTRIBUTION SCHEDULE:

1. Total distribution:

	M	T	W	TH	F	S	TOTAL (p)
Local							
Mkt							
Mkt							
Mkt							
Mkt							
Total (q)							

2. Company truck distribution:

	TRUCK A				TRUCK B				
	Routing	Miles	Pounds	Stops	Routing	Miles	Pounds	Stops	Total #
M									
T									
W									
TH									
F									
S									

TOTAL   ____ ____ ____   ____ ____ ____ ____

3. Common carrier distribution:

	MARKET	POUNDS	MARKET	POUNDS	MARKET	POUNDS	TOTAL #
M							
T							
W							
TH							
F							
S							

OPERATING STATEMENT

A. Sales (In Dollars) $ _____

B. Warehouse and Inventory Costs
    B-1. Warehouse Overhead $ 1443 _____
    B-2. Warehouse Operations $ _____
    B-3. Extra Warehousing (Public) $ _____
    B-4. Raw Material Inventory Carrying Cost $ _____
    B-5. Finished Good Inventory Carrying Cost $ _____
    Subtotal $ _____

C. Production Costs
    C-1. Overhead $ _____
    C-2. Cooking Conversion $ _____
    C-3. Cooking Costs – Regular $ _____
    C-4. Cooking Costs – Overtime $ _____
    Subtotal $ _____

D. Transportation Costs – Inbound Raw Materials
    D-1. Company Truck
        Fixed Charge $ 165.00 _____
        Variable Charge $ _____
    D-2. Common Carrier – Rail $ _____
    D-3. Common Carrier – Truck $ _____
    Subtotal $ _____

E. Distribution Cost – Outbound (Finished Product)
    E-1. Company Truck Variable $ _____
    E-2. Common Carrier Truck $ _____
    E-3. Distribution in Market $ _____
    Subtotal $ _____

        Total Cost $ _____
            Profit for Period $ _____

B-1. Warehouse Overhead (Private) $ _____

B-2. Warehouse Operations (Raw Material Handling)

Raw Material Receipts During Period

	#	Order No.
Potatoes	_____	_____
Salt	_____	_____
Oil	_____	_____
1 # Bags	_____	_____

TOTAL RECEIPTS (a) _____

Raw Materials Used
During Period (#)
(Production Worksheet) (b) _____
TOTAL (a) & (b) _____ $\div 2 \times .16$/cwt = _____

B-3. Extra Warehousing (Public)

Cubic Ft. Used During Period   _____
× Appropriate Rate   _____
Extra Warehousing Cost for Period $ _____

B-4. Raw Material Inventory Carrying Cost

Beginning Raw Materials Inventory

Potatoes	_____	× 4.21/cwt	= _____
Oil	_____	× 4.05/cwt	= _____
Salt	_____	× 1.735/cwt	= _____
Bags	_____	× 22.00/Bale	= _____

TOTAL (a) $ _____

Ending Raw Materials Inventory

Potatoes	_____	× 4.21/cwt	= _____
Oil	_____	× 4.05/cwt	= _____
Salt	_____	× 1.735/cwt	= _____
Bags	_____	× 22.00/Bale	= _____

TOTAL (b) $ _____

TOTAL (a) and (b) $ _____ $\div 2$ = (c) $ _____
(c) _____ × 10% $\div 52$ =
Period Raw Material Inventory Carrying Cost $ _____

B-5. Finished Goods Inventory Carrying Cost

Period Waste (Status Report) _____
× Unit Wholesale Price $ _.845_____
$ _____ × 20% $\div 52$ =
Period Finished Goods Inventory Carrying Cost $ _____

C. PRODUCTION COSTS:

C-1. Overhead .... $ _3750_____

C-2. Cooking Conversion

Quantity cooked this period _____(finished)

Potatoes	_____ × $.0421/lb =	_____
Salt	_____ × $.0017/lb =	_____
Oil	_____ × $.04/lb =	_____
Bags	_____ × $.022/bag =	_____

TOTAL CONVERSION COST _____

C-3. Cooking Costs — Regular

Quantity cooked   ×   rate/lb   =   total cooking cost

M _____ × _____ = _____

T _____ × _____ = _____

W _____ × _____ = _____

TH_____ × _____ = _____

F _____ × _____ = _____

S _____ × _____ = _____

TOTAL _____

C-4. Cooking Cost — Overtime

Daily output in excess of 20,000 lb × rate

_____ × _____ =

_____ × _____ =

_____ × _____ =

TOTAL _____

D. TRANSPORTATION COSTS:

Inbound Raw Materials:

D-1. Company Truck . . . . Fixed Charge $ _____

    * Total Mileage per Period × Rate

Truck A _____ × _____ $ .15 _____ = _____

Truck B _____ × _____ $ .10 _____ = _____

(Driving time + Loading time) × Drivers Wages

(_____ + _____) × $6 = _____

                                    TOTAL _____

*Separate truck mileage between raw materials hauling and finished goods delivery.

D-2. Common Carrier — Rail

Total lbs × Rate

_____ × _____ ×

_____ × _____ ×

_____ × _____ × _____

                    TOTAL _____

D-3. Common Carrier — Truck

	TOTAL LBS/ SHIPMENT	× RATE (LTL OR TL)	
Potatoes	_____ ×	_____ =	_____
Salt	_____ ×	_____ =	_____
Oil	_____ ×	_____ =	_____
Bags	_____ ×	_____ =	_____

                                  TOTAL _____

E. DISTRIBUTION COST:

Outbound Finished Product

E-1. Company Truck

*Total Mileage Per Period × Rate

Truck A _____ × _____ $ .15 _____ = _____

Truck B _____ × _____ $ .10 _____ = _____

Driving Time + Unloading Time × Drivers Wages   =

(_____ + _____) × $6.00   = _____

TOTAL _____

*Separate Truck mileage between raw materials hauling and finished goods delivery.

E-2. Common Carrier — Truck:

MARKET	POUNDS	×	RATE (LTL OR TL)	
_____	_____	×	_____	= _____
_____	_____	×	_____	= _____
_____	_____	×	_____	= _____
_____	_____	×	_____	= _____
_____	_____	×	_____	= _____
_____	_____	×	_____	= _____

TOTAL _____

E-3. Distribution In Market

No. of markets in which distribution is made × fixed distribution charge =

_____ × _$250._____ = _____

Pounds delivered in Market:

Rate/cwt

A _____ × _____ = _____

B _____ × _____ = _____

C _____ × _____ = _____

D _____ × _____ = _____

E _____ × _____ = _____

TOTAL _____

APPENDIX E2 Plant

Location Factors

Current economic literature contains many contributions aimed at developing a general theory of industrial location. Several such contributions were reviewed in Chapter 4. These theoretical studies address the problem of explaining geographic distribution of plant capacity. The main criterion permeating the majority of published works is the rational allocation of scarce resources. Thus, most location literature has been devoted to explaining socially acceptable goals generated from classical competitive economics.

However, the principle of free economic action and profit maximization may lead to personal goals inconsistent with social goals. Given imperfections in social and economic organization, individual entrepreneurs may find profit opportunities derived from astute location decisions. It may appear that economic theory and applied business practice are, therefore, incompatible. This view is quite incorrect. The function of location theory is to abstract from practice so that all elemental forces affecting location may be identified. Once these forces are appropriately defined, they implicitly form the foundation of public policy, which is aimed at achieving maximum economic welfare. One result of location theory is, therefore, the formation of adequate public policy to guide the nation's economic welfare. Given this orientation, the complete acceptance of general location forces for the purposes of solving an individual location problem may be inappropriate. However, theory aids in the identification of fundamental forces affecting location and thus assists in the organization of an applied method for locating a specific plant. Applied methodology can be developed within the guideposts so conveniently developed by economic theorists.

Least-Cost Location Factors

The contributions of location theorists point out that all location factors can be grouped and summarized under three broad categories: (1) least-cost factors, (2) profit maximizing factors, and (3) intangible factors. To select a proper plant location, a complete evaluation of the influence of each category of factors on a particular location problem is necessary. Thus, it is important that all location factors be clearly understood. This and the following two sections are devoted to a detailed discussion of each category.

Location cost factors may be divided between transfer costs and production costs.[1] Transfer costs are defined as the costs that result from the movement of raw materials to the proposed plant site and those that are incurred by shipping finished products to market.[2] Production costs include all other costs related to plant operation. To achieve the least-cost location, the sum of all transfer costs and production costs must be minimized.[3] Intangibles may be defined as those elements affecting costs which may not be classified in transfer or production accounts.

TRANSFER COSTS

Transfer costs as a factor in plant location have traditionally been considered by assuming that all other location influences are negligible.[4] Such an assumption tends to minimize important location forces and, therefore, should be employed with considerable caution. On the other hand, this approach allows a detailed and unrestricted treatment of this very important factor. Transfer costs frequently are a dominant element in plant location. Because they are readily quantifiable, transfer cost analysis provides a convenient starting point for solving location problems. In Appendix 10A, an analytical technique is developed which may be employed to arrive at the geographical point of least transfer costs. However, it is essential to keep in mind that transfer costs are only one of many location influences. The point of least transfer cost will normally have to be amended to accommodate other location elements in selecting the profit-maximizing plant site. Five principal

---

[1]Professor Hoover presented as the core of his thesis two influential cost categories — transfer and process. Although not utilized in a similar manner, these cost categories have been adopted for the present treatment. See Edgar M. Hoover, *The Location of Economic Activity* (New York: McGraw-Hill Book Co., 1948).

[2]Transfer costs are defined to include all cost components as developed in the total cost discussion. For a complete discussion of all costs included in transfer costs, see Chapter 4.

[3]Only costs that vary between alternative locations are influential in plant location. For example, the cost of raw materials, per se, is not important unless this basic cost is geographically variable.

[4]For example, see D. Philip Locklin, *Economics of Transportation* (Chicago: Richard D. Irwin, 1947), p. 43.

methods of movement are available to transport raw materials and finished products. These are rail, truck, air, water, and pipeline. The particular method capable of solving a given movement problem depends upon the commodity to be moved, distance, weight, size of shipment, speed required, cost, and so on.[5] Given the alternative methods capable of moving a particular commodity, the specific method or combination of methods employed is selected on the basis of cost and type of service required. Cost in all cases should be held to a minimum under the standards of service necessary to satisfy market requirements. Thus, when service requirements are satisfied, the combination of methods that results in the lowest total transfer cost may be determined by utilizing the total cost techniques introduced in Chapter 11. The combination of transfer methods and resultant costs can be materially altered by the geographic point at which the production plant is located. Consequently, in selecting a plant location, it is necessary to isolate the one best geographical point from which service requirements may be satisfied at the lowest total transfer cost.

Intercity transfer costs may be divided into two components: the costs associated with accumulation of raw materials and those related to product distribution. Accumulation costs result from the movement of raw materials or semifinished products to the point of manufacture. Distribution costs are derived from shipment of finished products to the final market through all intermediary steps. A particular plant location may be pulled toward the market or toward the source of raw materials depending on which location minimizes the sum of accumulation and distribution costs. In some cases, as will be shown, a location between the market and the source of raw materials may yield the lowest total transfer costs.

MATERIALS-ORIENTED INDUSTRIES

The plants in a particular industry may be located near the source of raw materials because of the unique location of the raw material or because of a great weight loss in the process of production. Extractive industries as characterized by agriculture, mining, and lumbering must be located at the point where raw materials are available in economic quantities. In agriculture, the supply and quantity of land suited to particular crops plays the dominant role. In mining, it is the location of deposits; in lumber, it is the location of forests.

Industries in which, because of the nature of the product, great weight loss is experienced in production tend to locate plants near the source of raw

[5]The capabilities and limitations of various modes of transport are discussed in greater detail in Chapter 6.

materials.[6] Sugar beet refining and cotton ginning are excellent examples.[7] The net result of such locations is to reduce total transfer costs, because the weight shipped to market is significantly less than the weight of raw materials. A third element causing plant locations near raw materials is the perishability of the materials. Many agricultural canning and freezing processes are examples. The great canning and freezing complex in central New Jersey with its vast fresh fruit and vegetable acreages and large processing centers illustrates this condition. To some unmeasurable extent, this location factor is offset by technological improvement in transportation equipment, for example, refrigerated cars and trucks.

In summary, several major forces influence transfer costs for particular industries, thereby making the point of least transfer cost one in close proximity to the source of raw materials. These forces are (1) great loss of weight in raw materials during processing or production, (2) availability of raw materials for extractive industries, and (3) perishability of the raw material.

MARKET-ORIENTED INDUSTRIES

Industries that add weight during the production of finished products, experience large differentials in rates between raw materials and finished products, or produce a highly perishable finished product, tend to locate plants near the market.[8]

A typical weight-gaining process is found in the beverage industry. Water, a major ingredient in the final product, causes substantial weight gains during production. Because adequate water supplies are found in most potential locations, it is economically desirable to ship concentrates rather than finished products. The weight added to the final product by the addition of water causes transfer costs to be lowest when it is added near the market.[9]

It is interesting to note that in the total marketing effort of the firm, advertising may somewhat modify the impact of transfer cost factors. If

[6]J. Russell Smith and M. Ogden Phillips, *Industrial and Commercial Geography* (New York: Henry Holt and Company, 1950), p. 48.

[7]For example, about one-sixth of the weight of sugar beets is retained in the extracted sugar. This is also important in cane sugar production; the mature cane is about 10 percent fiber, 18 percent sugar, and 72 percent water. Stanley Vance, *American Industries* (Englewood Cliffs, N. J.: Prentice-Hall, Inc., 1955), p. 557.

[8]There is considerable confusion in current literature regarding whether perishability, service, and so on are location forces requiring a market orientation as a result of transfer expense, or location forces requiring a market orientation due to consumer preferences. Unquestionably, both forces are important. A clear separation could be obtained only by studying specific industrial location problems.

[9]In some cases where other than "any quantity" rates prevail, for example, if rates in carload lots are lower than rates on less-than-carload lots, it may be possible to increase weight without increasing total costs. Furthermore, within a limited range, increased weights may decrease cost. See Locklin, *op. cit.*, p. 55.

advertising can develop a product image allowing a higher price to be commanded, this increased revenue may sufficiently absorb the added transfer expense associated with a location at a point distant from the market. This is of particular importance to firms selling to a national market in which the production process does not allow the use of concentrated syrups. In the beer industry, for example, the accepted meaning of a "premium beer" is that it sells at a price above that of the locally brewed products. Although there may indeed be quality difference, it is not the only foundation for classifying a beer as premium for marketing purposes. However, the basic market orientation rule is not greatly influenced by this special case. If concentrates can be employed, the location impact of advertising may be channeled toward more productive sources while lower transfer rates are enjoyed. Primary examples of such physical distribution decisions are the policies followed by the major soft drink producers.

Even when weight differentials between raw materials and finished products are negligible, the plant may be attracted to a market location. A general characteristic of rates is that lower rates are placed upon cruder materials with the rate increasing as the product reaches final stages of fabrication.[10] Therefore, transfer rates tend to increase with the stage of manufacture. Historically, this condition reflects the value of the service principle in rate-making. That is, in some loose way it was assumed that the higher the value a commodity could command, the more easily it could absorb a higher freight rate. The monopoly position enjoyed by the railroads up to the 1930's allowed such discrimination to be practiced. Newer modes of transportation in competition with the railroads have readily impaired the railroad's ability to continue such practices. Value of service, under modern rate-making theory refers to the rate that may be charged by a competing form of transport equivalent service.[11] Under this new concept, the spread between raw materials rates and finished product rates is likely to diminish in the future. To the extent that this differential diminishes, such discrimination will become of lesser consequence in plant location.

If the final product is characterized by extreme perishability, there may be additional reasons why a market-oriented location should be selected. Special handling and the requirement for extreme speed may tend to increase the cost of transferring such commodities. Under such conditions, production close to markets minimizes such transfer expense, for example, baked goods, ice cream, and delicatessen foods.

In summary, transfer forces pulling plant locations to a market proximity are (1) weight gains during production, (2) differential freight rates between raw materials and finished products, and (3) perishability of the finished product.

---

[10]Locklin, *op. cit.*, p. 47.

[11]For an excellent discussion of competition in rate making see Joel Dean, *Proceedings Railway Systems and Procedures Association*, 1959, Fall Meeting, Chicago.

LOCATION AT OTHER POINTS

A third goup of industries has traditionally been labeled "foot-loose" industries. This is because the transfer costs related to their particular manu-facturing process allow selection of a plant location either at markets, at raw materials, or at some intermediate point. If a particular industry is truly "foot loose," transfer costs may play a small role in determining plant location. For example, research and development firms are quite independent of the transfer forces under consideration.

But this is not true for all the firms that select plant sites at points separated from raw materials or markets. In some special cases, a plant located at an intermediate point represents the least-cost transfer location. The earlier discussion illustrating why plants are attracted to materials or markets was based upon the assumption that freight expense for a through movement was less than the expense incurred from movements to and from an intermediate point. Although this is normally true, there are some notable exceptions.

Probably the best known exception to the general rule is the granting of in-transit privileges by the transport companies. Among in-transit privileges, the most widely utilized are milling and fabrication. In both cases, the raw material may be shipped to a production point, then to final destination at a combined cost slightly higher than the through rate. Utilization of this artificial removal of the "diseconomy" of short hauls is particularly influential when the pull of the materials and the pull of the market are otherwise almost equal. Examples of in-transit privileges can readily be found in the grain and steel industries. The impact of in-transit privileges is to allow management considerably more freedom in selecting plant sites. The net effect of in-transit privileges is to promote the dispersion of industry.[12]

Intermediate location may also stem from the use of trans-shipment points. Location at trans-shipment points can be highly beneficial to industries processing raw materials, which have low transport costs, into final products normally associated with high transport costs. In such cases, location at junction points may greatly reduce aggregate transport costs. Water facilities are among the cheapest methods of movement and may economically be used for transporting bulky raw materials. Processing may then take place during the rehandling operation. This has the net effect of reducing unneces-sary rehandling cost. Location at such junction points means that raw mate-rials may move via water transportation, and finished products may be shipped via the cheapest satisfactory means of reaching the market. The importance of Pittsburgh and Youngstown as steel centers may be attributed in part to the availability of water transportation facilities.

Additional factors that pull plants to intermediate locations result from the need to utilize several raw materials or serve several different markets. A firm

[12]Truman C. Bigham and Merrill J. Roberts, *Transportation* (New York: McGraw-Hill Book Co., 1952), p. 25.

that utilizes a number of raw materials in processing can usually realize lowest transfer costs by locating at collection points. A collection point is a location that has minimum aggregate accumulation costs for various raw materials. On the other hand, a distribution point is a location that has minimum distribution costs to various markets. When one material or one market cannot be identified as the primary determinant of lowest transport costs, an acceptable compromise location at intermediate least-cost points may be the alternative.

In summary, if an industry can be categorized as truly "foot loose," plants may be located at any point, and transfer costs may not be a dominant location element. Particular industries tend to locate plants at intermediate points depending upon certain economic forces. In these special cases, transfer costs will be minimized at an intermediate location.

DISTORTING INFLUENCES

The transfer factors indicated above combine to point out the one best location that results in lowest total transfer costs for each plant. Several factors may act to displace the least-cost location based only on minimum transfer costs. Processing costs, competition, and intangible elements that displace this location will be considered shortly.

At this point, some additional transfer factors of institutional nature must be considered. One such element is simply the availability of transportation facilities. Extensive industrial development of the Northeastern United States may be attributed in part to this condition. At one time, no geographical point within this region was further than ten miles from a railroad.[13] The influence of topography and its resultant effect upon transportation facilities cannot be overemphasized. Waterways are restricted to rivers, valleys, lakes, bays, and relatively level areas where canals can be constructed. Other natural barriers influence the character of various modes of transportation. The transportation network is a powerful element that limits the availability of locations to points along the current configuration of transfer routes.

Rate discrimination among commodities and geographic areas will also modify location decisions. Utilization of base point pricing or uniform blanket rates may completely distort the influences of transportation costs. In addition, rate policies of the various carriers can greatly influence the location of industries. Although rates are subject to regulation, the point must be kept in mind that effective rates are set by the carrier. Close proximity to facilities does not necessarily mean lowest rates. Another important point is that published rates do not necessarily reflect the rate at which freight actually moves. It is necessary to make a detailed study of rates under which relevant commodities actually move rather than to accept published rates.

[13]Locklin, *op. cit.*, p. 49.

In conclusion, transfer costs as location factors can attract plants to the point of raw materials, markets, or to some intermediate point. Which prevails will depend upon the service necessary to meet individual market requirements and the cost of achieving this service at alternative locations. Because of the general importance of transfer costs in plant location, techniques that minimize this factor offer convenient starting points for solving location problems.

PRODUCTION COSTS

Production costs consist of all expenses necessary to convert raw materials into finished products. The production costs related to any given manufacturing process are geographically variable. Such geographical differences may be directly traced to forces of immobility. To the extent that any factor necessary for production of a product is mobile, it will tend to move to the geographical area of greatest reward.[14] From the viewpoint of production costs, the most economical location is one that combines the cheapest critical immobile factors with the necessary array of inexpensive mobile factors. Major production costs may be grouped into three categories each of which are, in varying degrees, important location factors. These are (1) rent, (2) labor, and (3) power.

Rent. In broad perspective, rent includes the following production costs: land, taxes, and capital.

Land Cost. Land prices may reflect wide regional differences. These cost differences result from the immobile characteristics of land and the wide variation in the natural endowment of individual sites. Variations in costs among specific sites stem primarily from scarcity. The general rule is that the more intensive the demand for land in a given area, the greater will be the cost. Normally, land cost diminishes as distance increases from the city center. Although the cost of land within the central city may be high, it usually offers certain economies that offset this high purchase price. Among these advantages are more adequate transport supply and a more flexible labor market. The price of a parcel of land must, therefore, be considered in light of other location advantages it may provide.

For any manufacturer, there are two classes of plant sites. First, sites with existing structures may be purchased or rented. Although vacant plants are found in abundance, the adaptability to specific location requirements may be limited. Because the average life of a real estate improvement is often in

---

[14]Hoover adequately summarizes the influence of mobility on location in the following quote: "The price of a freely mobile factor would be the same everywhere and would not affect the location of production or other factors at all." See Hoover, *op. cit.*, p. 69.

excess of 60 years,[15] this quality of durability results in a standing stock of plant facilities that have limited adaptability to individual tenants. The second alternative is to purchase vacant land. Construction normally requires a substantial capital outlay that tends to bind the firm to a permanent location thus decreasing mobility. Whether to rent or buy is primarily a financial question to be considered in light of company policy.

Tax Cost. The influence of tax cost on location decisions is elusive, to say the least. Common knowledge dictates that a firm will attempt to locate at the point of least aggregate tax cost. It also follows that the 50 bodies of state tax laws, not to mention uncounted community ordinances, will render distinctly different tax assessments in various geographical areas. Yet numerous empirical studies point out that tax costs are, at best relatively unimportant, secondary influences in location. Greenhut reviews four studies, which all agree that the incentives offered by lower taxes were not the determining factors in locating industries.[16] The location influence attributed to taxes was concluded to be of primary concern only in selecting between various sites within a particular area. Additional support is given to this conclusion by a study completed by Stopler concerning the influence of taxes on plants locating in Michigan.[17] He concluded that taxes rank far down the list of factors influential in location decisions.

These observations also agree with the study of taxation effects on industrial location completed by Floyd.[18] In discussing the theory that higher-than-average industrial taxes in a community will restrict its industrial growth, he concluded that tax considerations are only influential in selecting between alternative sites situated under different taxing jurisdictions when a firm finds such sites satisfactory in all other respects. A study completed by Bergin and Eagan support these findings. Only 32 out of 272 respondents mentioned a favorable tax structure as an important location factor.[19] Normally, few firms will relocate because of high taxes. Taxes may play a minor role in the decision to relocate, but the combined role of these and other costs cast the influence. Tax costs are especially influential when political boundaries, such as state lines, separate the communities under consideration. In addition, taxes are primary cost factors for firms with a high proportion of assets, which are taxable under state and local ordinances. For example, if a firm requires a large acreage of land to undertake produc-

[15]Ernest M. Fisher and Robert M. Fisher, *Urban Real Estate* (New York: Henry Holt and Company, 1954), p. 162.

[16]Melvin L. Greenhut, *Plant Location in Theory and in Practice* (Chapel Hill: University of North Carolina Press, 1956), p. 126.

[17]Wolfgang Stopler, *Special Study for Michigan Legislature*, Michigan House of Representative State Printing Office, Lansing, 1958.

[18]Joe Summers Floyd, Jr., *Effects of Taxation on Industrial Location* (Chapel Hill: The University of North Carolina Press, 1952).

[19]Thomas P. Bergin and William F. Eagan, "How Effective Are Industrial Development Programs," *Michigan Business Review*, Volume XII, January, 1960, p. 25.

tion, property taxes may become important location elements. In such cases, the firm tends to move toward areas offering comparatively lower property tax levies.

Capital Costs.   The cost of capital is an important factor in plant location, but this does not mean that the manufacturer must be geographically near the source of funds. Capital is the most mobile of the elements influencing location. The major significance of capital rests upon availability and cost. In order for a business to grow, it must have ready access to capital at reasonable cost. Neither of these two requirements is directly related to location. Availability is more nearly connected to the financial status of the firm requesting loans and the character of executives employed by the firm than it is to location. The cost of capital is a direct result of the money market, although this too may depend upon the intrinsic character of the firm. Historically, capital has been considered an influential factor in location. Today, financial requirements are rarely, if ever, critical determinants. The decline of the influence of capital upon location is generally attributed to the rise in mobility of capital funds.

Labor.   The location influence of labor affects various manufacturing firms in different ways. These variations tend to pull the location of particular industries toward the geographical point that will best satisfy labor requirements. Although the accumulative influence of labor upon location is difficult to measure, for some companies it is the greatest single influence motivating plant relocation.

Granted that there are great variations in labor requirements between different industries, a number of firms are attracted by the presence of low labor rates. Traditionally, wage levels in the United States have been lowest in the southern states. Accordingly, many firms that are labor intensive and operate on low margins locate in the South to take advantage of large numbers of low-wage, unskilled workers. Wages paid are important determinants of location but only one aspect of the labor cost factor. From the viewpoint of the employer, productivity, skill requirements, stability, and labor legislation also must be considered.

Location advantages of an area that offers low wage rates may be offset by low productivity rates. Hoover points out that high wage rates do not necessarily attract job seekers or repel employers.[20] Low production costs may be found in areas with relatively high wage rates. The essential concern for the manufacturer is the productivity of labor and labor's response to maintaining low overhead costs. Hot climates are normally considered to be areas of low productivity. Although this statement has not been substantiated, to the extent that it is true, the low wage advantages of the South may be offset by decreased productivity.

[20]Hoover, *op. cit.*, p. 103.

Firms that require highly skilled labor normally locate in close proximity to the areas that offer such skill. When other critical factors force manufacturers to move from areas of skilled labor, this loss may be offset by bringing skilled operators to train the local unskilled labor force. Such a procedure was followed by shoe manufacturers when they first located their processing facilities in St. Louis.[21] It is possible to offset the lack of skilled workers, but this is a costly and time-consuming process.

Regardless of the planning and analysis taken prior to locating in a particular area, low labor costs will not be realized if the local labor force proves unstable. High labor turnover is expensive. Retraining and loss of productivity are cost factors that cannot easily be recovered.

Labor laws can also cause cost differences between geographical areas. Virtually all industries are subject to state labor laws. Workman's Compensation insurance rates normally are applied against payrolls at rates varying substantially among the states. Although not a limiting factor to some firms, compensation charges may represent a substantial cost to the manufacturer when a large work force is employed.

The size of the necessary labor force can also limit location possibilities. Those manufacturers who require large work forces normally are restricted to densely populated areas. In any community, the available supply of labor is basically represented by the workers unemployed. Response of labor to geographical wage differences is often restricted due to movement expense. Although the mobility of labor may be somewhat "sticky," migration can materially affect the local labor supply in times of increased demand.

Power. Historically, the location of power resources has been an outstanding factor in the selection of plant sites. But power, like capital and labor, has gained mobility throughout the years. For some early industries, the most attractive sites were located at the fall lines of navigable streams. At this point, water could be harnessed to turn power wheels at minimum cost.

Technological developments have greatly altered the location influence of both power and fuel. Although some plants are still attracted by the availability of cheap and abundant power, in most industries the cost of power as a percentage of total cost is small. Aluminum reduction plants are examples of firms attracted to water-power sites. Natural gas, in the production of glass, and accessibility to coal and coke in steel production are other examples of power-oriented industries. On account of its more or less uniform availability, the location of the average plant will not be chosen solely because of power or fuel cost differentials.

In summary, the various location factors of rent, labor, and power can materially influence the cost structure of a plant located at different geographical points. To the degree that production factors are immobile,

[21]Smith and Phillips, *op. cit.*, p. 51.

costs will be geographically variable. Thus, to find the point of least production cost for a given plant, it becomes necessary to evaluate alternative cost structures resulting from different potential locations. To a large extent, these geographical cost differences result from forces of external economies of location. Therefore, prior to concluding the discussion of location cost factors, attention is briefly directed to external economies of location.

EXTERNAL ECONOMIES OF LOCATION

External economies of location refer to cost reductions which result from the geographical clustering of plants.[22] The forces of concentrations explain to a large extent why the least-cost location for many plants tends to congregate within a few industrial areas. For particular plants such cost reductions may be direct or indirect. Direct cost reductions evolve from the increased demand for interchangeable factors of production and transportation resulting when a large number of plants locate within a single industrial complex. Indirect cost reductions stem from other benefits realized from location in close proximity to an industrial population.

Examples of direct cost reductions are (1) lower total transfer costs resulting from better transport facilities, (2) reduced production costs due to a ready supply of technically trained labor, and (3) specialization of supplies allowing lower unit costs for materials, supplies, and services. These direct cost reductions explain to a large extent the forces underlying least-cost analysis.

Indirect cost reductions are not as easily qualified. Greenhut refers to this category of influences as a group of generally neglected location forces.[23] He points out that indirect cost-reducing factors may be separated from basic cost factors, because they emphasize the relationship between physical distance and costs in terms other than those of transfer and labor costs. Insurance is an example of a cost factor reduced by locating in an industrial community. A particular type of insurance may be available, because of better protective facilities or familiarity of an insurance company with local hazards. Although the cost of insurance is a direct expense, the reduction in cost resulting from excellent protection represents the influence of indirect economies of concentration. Advertising costs can also be reduced by location in highly populated areas. Lower expense may be incurred to achieve equal population coverage.

[22]External economies of location as used here are similar to the forces referred to by Weber as agglomerative. He defined an agglomerative force as "An aggregate cost reducing influence resulting from spatial interdependence." In external economies of location, economies of spatial interdependence are considered from the viewpoint of direct and indirect reductions. The original discussion of agglomerative forces did not develop this distinction in great detail. See Carl J. Friedrich (trans.), *Alfred Weber's Theory of Location of Industries* (Chicago: The University of Chicago Press, 1928), p. 134.

[23]Greenhut, *op. cit.*, p. 168.

The combined influence of external economies of location is to attract plants to industrial complexes. Individual firms attempt to locate plants in close proximity to other plants in order to enjoy mutual benefits of spatial concentration. To a large extent these same forces may influence a particular firm to centralize individual plants in order to realize maximum benefits from external economies.[24]

TOTAL LEAST-COST LOCATION AND MARKET AREA

Thus far, the two main categories of costs influencing plant location have been identified as transfer and production costs. Thus, influence of industrial concentration upon these two cateogories of cost has been discussed. The contributions of plant location theory point out that the sum of all costs must be minimized to arrive at the geographical point of least-cost plant location. This is an important concept, which requires additional expansion.

If one accepts that many costs are geographically variable and that the market to be serviced is rigidly defined, the location problem simply consists of finding the one point within the market area which offers the lowest total cost. When considering transfer costs, it was pointed out that various mathematical techniques may be employed to determine the least transfer cost location for a given plant within a defined market area. At this location, the lowest possible total transport expense would be experienced. Similarly, it is analytically possible to determine the least production cost location within this same market. It is highly probable in any location problem that these two low-cost points considered separately will be geographically different. Thus, the final solution is one of isolating a compromise location that offers the lowest total cost of meeting market requirements.

It is important to note that rarely, if ever, can a firm statistically define its market area. It may be possible to define distribution points within these markets and then locate a plant to minimize the total cost of production and movement to these points. But a market must always be considered an area, and if such areas are accepted as also being geographically variable, many complications enter the concept of total least-cost analysis. Therefore, the assumption of a fixed market area should be given additional consideration.

In reality, market areas are at least geographically variable in terms of size, population density, purchasing power, consumer preferences, and competitive activity. In order to maximize profits, the firm must adjust its total market effort to accommodate the character of each market served. In the next section, the discussion of location factors is expanded to consider the impact of geographically variable markets and competitive offerings.

[24]Hoover expands this consideration to include individual benefits realized by centralizing all plants owned by an individual firm. See Hoover, *op. cit.*, p. 80.

However, first, the impact of cost concepts alone upon market size is examined to illustrate the theoretical importance of selecting the total least-cost location for a plant.

If the assumption of a fixed market area is replaced with a market variable in size, the location problem centers upon selecting a plant location consistent with the market objectives of the firm. If the firm's target is to capture as large a market as possible, total least-cost concepts must be adjusted to demand elasticity for the product under consideration.[25] In order to isolate the single relationship between least-cost and market size, the location case of a spatial monopolist is developed. Although this location case is unrealistic and abstract, it illustrates the impact of total least-cost concepts upon market size under assumed conditions.

In this illustration of a spatial monopolist, the assumption of a fixed market area is replaced by one of an area characterized by a uniform geographical dispersion of customers[26] and freight rates linear with distance. These customers are assumed to have identical preferences for the product offered, limited by their indifference to the product which is based solely upon price. When the total price of the monopolist's product reaches this level, the customer is no longer willing to purchase the product offered. Because of the lack of competitive forces, the monopolist is free to locate his plant at any geographical point that offers the total least-cost combination of production and distribution consistent with capturing the largest market possible.

It is theoretically defensible that, under the assumed condition, the monopolist will sell his product in all directions until he reaches a point where he equates revenue cost with marginal revenue. Therefore, the market area that evolves will be a circle around the plant location. The final area contained within the circle will be determined by marginal conditions and customer price indifference limits. This does not mean, however, that the area of the market circle will remain constant regardless of plant location. Under the conditions of uniform dispersion of consumers, the monopolist can vary his location point. If geographical differences in total costs of product creation and distribution are experienced by such location variance, it logically follows that marginal costs are geographically variable. Under such conditions, the monopolist will find it economically beneficial to adjust his plant location to a point from which he can capture the largest market area. This probably will not be at the point that affords least transfer costs or at the point that represents least production costs related to a given market area. Rather, only at the point of least total cost can the area of the market be maximized.

[25]Without elaboration, it appears sufficient to point out that there are a number of theoretical situations in which other economic forces may limit the market objectives of the firm.

[26]The reader should note this is not a step toward reality. The market is still assumed to represent geographically uniform population density, purchasing power, and consumer preferences. The only change has been the redefinition of the area the firm is willing to service.

CHART E2–I   Least-Cost Market Relationships

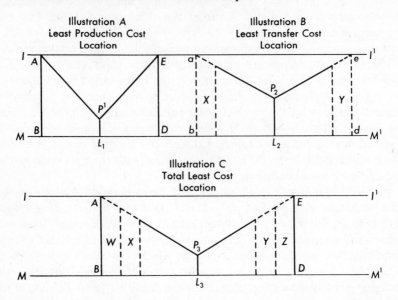

Chart E2–1 illustrates the location forces developed above. The assumptions are the same as stated previously, although certain theoretical considerations have been omitted[27] to concentrate upon the variables cited. In illustrations A and B, the total market area available to the monopolist is represented by the base line MM'. Consumer indifference is assumed to be at a level indicated by the horizontal line II'. Within the limits imposed upon the problem, the objective of the monopolist is to capture the largest market area possible. Note the illustrations A and B represent two alternative locations within the one market MM'. These locations are labeled L_1 and L_2.

If the monopolist locates his plant at the geographical point L_1 (illustration A), he has selected a location that offers the lowest total cost of production within the given market area indicated by L_1P_1. At this point, however, his distribution costs, shown by the slope of the lines AP_1 and EP_1, are very high. The combination of costs results in a market area defined as BD. From location L_1, the monopolist can only satisfy market BD before he reaches the point of consumer indifference to his total offer. However, he has the alternative of selecting the point of least transfer cost identified as L_2 (illustration B). If he selects this location, after adjustments in production costs, L_2P_2, and distribution costs, once again illustrated by the sloped lines, the market BD can be captured. Note at location L_2 the monopolist has increased his market area by the two areas, X and Y, indicated by broken lines. This market expansion is possible because the geographical variation

---

[27]Namely, FOB pricing is assumed, and the free manipulation of scale economies upon production costs is assumed without reference to an actual production function.

in transfer cost more than offsets the variation in production cost after adjustments for increased volume. Given a selection between these two alternatives, the location L_2 appears to be most consistent with the monopolist's objectives.

Reference to illustration C points out that the one best location still has not been selected. Given similar problem limits, a location at L_3 allows the monopolist to capture the larger market BD (illustration C). Once again making scale economy adjustments and taking into consideration geographical variation in production and transfer costs, the monopolist finds he can increase his market area by the four areas, $WXYZ$, over a purely production cost location, and by two areas, W and Z, over a purely transfer cost location. Thus, location L_3 represents the total least-cost location for the proposed plant, which, under the assumed conditions, also results in profit maximization.

The assumptions necessary to illustrate least-cost market area relationships minimize the practical value of the above location illustration. However, it does develop a basic relationship under consideration and indicates a few forces that underlie the ideals of spatial monopoly. It is now desirable to explore the complications that evolve from intense competitive rivalry and a consideration of other geographical variations in market patterns.

Profit-Maximizing Location Factors

The problem of selecting a plant site requires broader consideration than simply total least-cost analysis. The fact that new plants are not located within a competitive vacuum may cause considerable amendment of a purely least-cost location.

In the American economy, most firms compete under imperfect conditions falling between the classical definitions of pure competition and pure monopoly.[28] This is the highly competitive area in which product differentiation, price variation, advertising, sales promotion, and brand preference are among the many strategies employed to obtain maximum revenues. Additionally, individual markets vary extensively in terms of wealth and consumer density. In such markets, variations in consumer preferences are the rule rather than the exception. To maximize profits under imperfect conditions, among other marketing tactics, the concepts of physical distribution becomes a competitive weapon. Assuming that the objective of the firm is profit maximization, adjustments must be made in purely least-cost locations to accommodate competitive and market forces. The final location should represent the geographical point allowing the highest spread between

[28]If one is willing to accept pure competition and pure monopoly as polar examples, the forms of imperfect competition under consideration would consist of monopolistic competition and the various types of oligopoly.

total cost and total revenue. This location is referred to as the profit-maximizing location for a given plant. At least two categories of forces can be isolated as determinants of profit-maximizing locations. These are market requirements and competitive location decisions.

MARKET REQUIREMENTS

Earlier, it was determined that some firms are basically market oriented as a result of least transfer cost factors. A plant may also be attracted to a particular market if, for other reasons, increased revenues will more than offset increased costs. For each plant, a profit-maximizing location offers the highest spread between total cost and total revenue. For small plants, this may be a location from which a small segment of the total market can be served at greater consumer convenience than large firms can profitably provide. For large firms, adjustments to market service requirements may require the location of branch plants or warehouses. In total, consumer requirements for prompt service attract plants to locate in close proximity to the market, although this may not represent the lowest total cost location.[29]

When consumer demand is extremely erratic, those forces attracting the plant to the market may be intensified. If consumers purchase a product in variable quantities and follow a somewhat unpredictable purchase pattern over time, producers must be in a position to adjust rapidly to market trends. Under extreme conditions of erratic demand, the only profitable alternative for meeting market requirements may be a small plant located within the market area. The forces of market service will be considerably more important if the final product sold in an industry is characterized by little or no brand preferences among consumers. To the extent that definite loyalties are displayed, brand preference may partly offset the forces of erratic demand. If the consumer is willing to wait a reasonable time prior to switching brands, the firms enjoying such loyalty have some degree of freedom from the above-mentioned location factors. However, brand loyalty, like many other market phenomena, represents a rather temporary advantage, although location is a more rigid aspect of a firm's total market offer. The case of "premium quality" beers noted earlier is an example in point. Regardless of the increased revenues these selected brands have commanded in the past, some producers have expressed preferences for decentralizing their production facilities.

In many cases, the quality of the product may influence plant location. Regardless of cost structures, market success of firms dealing in perishable products is directly related to their ability to reach consumers prior to product

[29]The point can be argued that the quality of service is in reality a cost factor, because it may determine the actual amount of potential demand realized. In this discussion, the quality of service is viewed as a location factor, which pulls location away from the least-cost transfer point.

deterioration. The impact of perishability was considered in the discussion of transfer costs; therefore, additional elaboration is not necessary at this point.

Manufacturers who supply materials and technical service normally find a location close to their customer's plants beneficial to sales. Close proximity to customers means that breakdown and change-over requirements can be satisfied with minimum time delays.

And finally, the mere fact that markets are geographically variable in terms of income and population density means that some markets have inherent location appeal. A manufacturer offering a multiple product line may find that the total market offering of his firm can only be maximized within large and wealthy markets. Such markets offer the variety of consumer preferences necessary to profitably support an entire product line.

In summary, the force of market requirements is an important determinant of a profit-maximizing location. If a plant located within a market complex attracts revenues greater than the increased costs associated with this location, it becomes economically sound to select such a geographical point. However, to a large extent, competitor's plant locations determine the location from which a new plant in the industry can maximize profits.

INFLUENCE OF COMPETITOR'S LOCATIONS

Historically, the influence of competition upon plant location has been considered in a manner similar to that employed in the discussion related to Chart E2–1. Assumptions are made of undifferentiated products, equal geographical distribution of consumers, identical consumer preference, and so on. The market pattern obtained for particular plant locations is then traced through a variety of configurations finally resulting in a hexagon or honeycomb pattern of market areas.[30] When linear illustrations are employed, the assumptions are retained. The influence of competition is then examined by observing the resultant market divisions as additional producers enter the market. In these theoretical presentations, price is the sole determinant of competitive rivalry.[31]

In the discussion relevant to Chart E2-I, the assumptions of identical production costs and transfer costs were replaced by ones of geographical

---

[30]The development of hexagon space relationships is generally attributed to the works of Losch, as noted in Chapter 6. For a detailed discussion of this theoretical phenomenon in translated form, see Stefan Valavanis, "Losch on Location," *American Economic Review*, Vol. XLV, 1955, p. 637; or John A. Howard, *Marketing Management* (Homewood, Ill.: Richard D. Irwin, Inc., 1957), p. 390, or Greenhut, *op. cit.*, p. 141; or Walter Isard, *Location and Space Economy* (New York: John Wiley, 1956); or August Losch, *The Economics of Location* (trans.), 2nd ed. revised (New Haven, Conn.: Yale University Press, 1964).

[31]For a discussion of linear development of demand influences upon location decisions, see Greenhut, *op. cit.*, Chapter 6. For a discussion of the resultant market composition as new firms enter a lineal expressed market see Arthur F. Smithies, "Optimum Location in Spatial Competition," *Journal of Political Economy*, Vol. XLIX, pp. 423–439.

variation, and the impact of these changes upon market area was partially pursued. Although all such examinations have theoretical importance, they are not directly related to the current objective. The relevant perspective for selecting plant sites is one of the individual firm seeking a profit-maximizing location.

Under conditions of imperfect competition, competitive forces may influence new plants to select locations spatially separated from current plants in the industry or, under some conditions, locations in close proximity to existing plants. As noted earlier, if the products offered by firms in a given industry are similar, the net effect may be a decentralization of locations in order to differentiate products by virtue of high service standards. The general effect, therefore, may be a dispersion of plants over the entire market. This is particularly true when production costs related to a given product show little geographical variance. As a theoretical insight, the above generalization is a valid explanation of a basic rule underlying the concepts of spatial monopoly.

Under conditions of imperfect competition, however, this general rule may be temporarily reversed by individual firms seeking locations which minimize uncertainty. If the particular industry is characterized by highly differentiated products supported by intense promotional efforts, consumer preferences for particular brands may tend to geographically disperse a firm's total sales. Under such a condition, rather than each firm commanding a small market segment by virtue of price and service, the industry will be characterized by a large number of firms competing within overlapping markets.

The net effect may render it impossible for a large-scale plant to be located in order to enjoy a degree of spatial monopoly. Therefore, all large-scale plants within the industry may be attracted to the one area allowing total least-cost operations. From geographically concentrated locations, each firm within the industry is able to serve the entire market at a speed and cost similar to those of competitors. Product prices tend to equate among the different firms' products and the industry settles down to intensive forms of nonprice competition. To some degree, the early stages of the automobile and appliance industries represented such concentration of industrial capacity.

These concentrations have at least two important effects upon long-range competitition within the industry. First, locating production plants within a relatively small geographical area tends to introduce warehouses as an important part of physical distribution systems. As particular firms are able to intensely cultivate certain market segments, volumes may increase to the point where warehouses and later branch plants can be economically justified. At this point, the implications of spatial monopoly once again become relevant.

Because warehouse and branch plant installations tend to reduce costs, and at the same time allow increased customer service, the concentration of

CHART E2–2 **Example of an Economically Justified High-Cost Location**

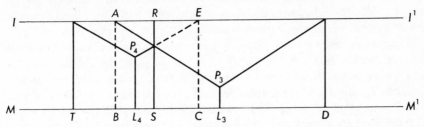

industry plants can be influenced. Earlier, as the plants within the industry generated to a given location area, the ability to render a high level of service was equalized among firms. With the introduction of warehouses and branch plants, it becomes possible for individual firms to gain a competitive advantage by virtue of increased customer service. Warehouses normally are justified on the basis of cost reductions achieved by consolidated shipments into a market area. To the extent deemed competitively wise, such savings tend to allow the firm considerably more latitude in price variation. Therefore, to some extent, price competition can also be undertaken as a means of increasing market share. To some unmeasurable degree, both the ability to render a high quality of service and the pricing latitude may offset the marketing advantages of differentiated products. Thus, although the plants within an industry are initially geographically concentrated for competitive reasons, the advantages of decentralization in the long run are often shifted to warehouse or branch plant locations. Such currently appears to be the case in the automobile and cereal industries and in certain parts of the soap industry.

The second important effect of industry concentration is to allow small marginal firms to operate profitably from high-cost locations. The small firm operating in the hinterlands may be able to overcome some technological advantages of larger producers with highly differentiated products merely on the grounds of price and service. To briefly illustrate this point, the case of the spatial monopolist is reproduced once again in Chart E2-2. Note, retaining the earlier assumptions accompanying Chart E2-1, a second small-scale plant has entered the MM' market and is located at L_4. Although the production costs, L_4P_4, at the new location are substantially greater for the smaller volume of production, the market TS has been captured. Theoretically, it can be argued that L_4 is not the best location for the new plant; granting this, it is interesting to observe that the market area BS has been captured from the plant located at L_3.

If the plants located at L_3 and L_4 produce similar products, the line of consumer preference between the two firms is represented by the vertical line RS. At this point the sloped lines P_4E and P_3A intersect and each firm offers the product at the same total price. However, it was noted that product differentiation is the rule rather than the exception under conditions of imperfect competition. If the assumption of similar products is dropped, new limits enter the competitive situation represented in Chart E2–2. The area labeled $ABCE$ becomes the market within which the two plants compete for consumer preference. Although the line RS represents the point of equal product price, theoretically plant L_3 could sell to the limits of its original market (broken line AB) and the firm, L_4, could penetrate the market area of L_3 as far as the broken line EC. Only when the points A and E are reached by firms L_3 and L_4 does the total product price reach the level of consumer indifference. Regardless of brand preference, the areas TB for plant L_4 and CD for plant L_3 remain spatial monopolies. Although this illustration greatly abstracts from many implications of nonprice competition, the potential of a profitable fringe location is illustrated.

In summary, the market requirements and the stage of industry competition can substantially affect location decisions. Competitive forces may tend to decentralize or concentrate plants depending upon product characteristics and stage of industry development. In successful plant location, the ultimate site selected should represent the combination of cost, market, and competitive factors that results in profit maximization for the particular firm.

Intangible Location Factors

A final group of location forces influencing site selection is often classified as intangible factors. Intangible factors may be divided into two categories for discussion purposes. The first category contains cost-revenue influencing factors that result from personal contacts of company executives. The second group is personal preferences that influence site selection.

COST-REVENUE INFLUENCING FACTORS

Plant locations may be altered to capitalize on the personal contacts and influences of management. Such factors may directly influence the availability of materials, capital, and sales. The availability of capital may be related to personal friendships and confidences that exist between management and creditors. Special requests for rush materials or spare parts in order to eliminate production bottlenecks may be given urgent consideration if friendly relations exist. Last of all, additional sales may be realized by community contacts developed by executives.

All of these intangible factors influence the cost-revenue structure of a particular firm. Without this aspect of personal consideration, location forces are impersonal results of cost and competitive factors. With consideration of personal influence, locations may be altered to increase profitability. Obviously, this influence is most paramount to small manufacturing firms, which in rare cases may find their only economic justification based upon such personal relationships.

PERSONAL PREFERENCE

Personal preferences influence plant location as a result of adjustments made to accommodate human needs and desires. A particular community may be selected, because it offers desirable types of recreation, housing, or educational facilities. A particular region may be selected, because it offers an enjoyable climate. Although such factors cannot be conveniently analyzed within the framework of economic analysis, the fact remains that purely personal considerations can be important determinants of plant location.

The net effect of intangible considerations is to alter the ideal economic location. The range of freedom available in selecting sites to fit intangible specifications is somewhat narrow if profit-maximization principles are strictly employed. For any particular firm, these factors may only be influential in selecting between communities located within close proximity to each other.

APPENDIX E3 The Effect

of Scale Economies on Plant Locations

THE degree to which the analysis in Appendix E2 is applicable in actual cases depends, in part, on the economic characteristics of the industry in question. The unique economic characteristics of individual industries may be illustrated by drawing from economic theory and economic geography.

The theoretical factors that account for differences in the impact of physical distribution principles on the spatial relation of plant and distribution facilities largely revolve around scale economies. Reference to any standard economic geography text shows considerable variation in the spatial distribution of plant capacity by industry categories. For example, the baked goods industry is characterized by a wide distribution of plant capacity generally following population patterns. At the opposite end of the scale, the steel industry appears to be relatively concentrated. In the industries noted above, a singular difference of fixed capital requirements is apparent. In the steel industry a high degree of fixed capital is required as a condition of economic production, whereas in the baked goods industry a relatively low degree of capital investment is required.

Degrees of capital investment in any industry are closely connected to the extent of the market. Generally, the more efficient a distribution system of a country and the larger the market, the more likely large-scale enterprise will result. The existence of production scale economies in an industry depends, to a considerable degree, on the availability of an efficient and economical distribution system.

In the economic theory, industries may be classified into three cost categories: (1) increasing cost, (2) constant cost, and (3) decreasing cost. These three cost conditions are indicated in Chart E3–1.

CHART E3–1   Increasing, Constant, and Decreasing Unit Cost Schedules

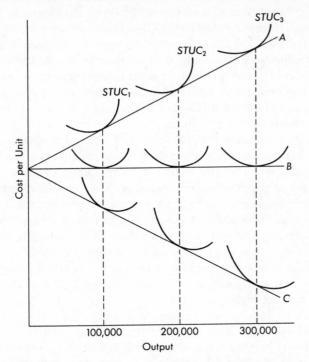

Line *A* in Chart E3–1 shows that unit costs of production rise as the scale of plant increases. At the smallest scale of plant, production costs are shown to follow the total unit cost curve indicated by $STUC_1$. The optimum output for this scale of plant is found at the point where the short-run cost curve $(STUC_1)$ is tangent to the long-run cost curve (A). Output at the optimum level is 100,000 units. When the scale of plant is increased to an optimum output of 200,000 units, the production costs follow $STUC_2$. Finally, at the largest scale of plant with 300,000 units, optimum costs follow $STUC_3$. In each case, as the scale is increased, the whole schedule of costs rises.

Line *B* in Chart E3–1 illustrates an industry which experiences constant costs as the scale of plant increases. This is indicated by the horizontal long-run cost curve (B). Line *C* shows costs declining as the scale of plant increases. This is the familiar cost curve associated with the economies of mass production.

A number of recent economic studies have been designed to measure scale economies of different classes of industry.[1] Generally, the studies have concentrated on balance sheet and profit-and-loss statements. The professed

[1]For example, see T. O. Yntema, "An Analysis of Steel Prices, Volume and Costs: Controlling Limitations on Price Reduction," United States Steel Corporation, *T.N.E.C. Papers*, New York, 1940, Vol. I.

orientation of these studies has been to determine the production efficiencies of firms of different sizes in a variety of industrial classifications. However, the aggregative nature of balance sheets and profit and loss statements makes it extremely difficult, if not impossible, to separate production costs and distribution expense. Conceivably, a firm that may appear inefficient from an overall operative and distribution point of view may be, in part, highly efficient in production and inefficient in distribution. Only when production costs are separated from distribution costs can the real nature of production scale economies be measured realistically.

A clear case illustrating the relationship of physical distribution expense and spatial distribution of plant and distribution facilities is in the industries with decreasing unit cost. By assuming distribution cost to be zero, any industry experiencing increasing economies of scale to infinite output levels will result in a single plant serving all consumer needs. When a firm in this cost category institutionalizes its position in the market, it appears unlikely that new competing firms can successfully challenge its economic dominance. A new competing firm most likely must establish a capacity of a smaller size in order to establish its position in the market. A new firm with smaller capacity and output, as compared to the established firm in the industry, can only experience higher unit cost.

In Chart E3-1 this condition is shown in Line *C*. If a firm achieves the size of plant associated with a 300,000-unit optimum output, its cost will be at the lowest possible level. A new firm entering in competition under these conditions will have a higher cost schedule than any established firm. If distribution expenses are zero, no new firms can compete with the established firm unless production is scaled immediately to the levels of the established firm.

The best example of this condition is the public utility industry such as the electric power, gas, and telephone companies. In this industry, a service monopoly is granted to a single firm in its market territory. This legal monoply is firmly based on the existence of scale economies in each of the companies cited above. Because of this economic fact, a single firm in the above industry in its appropriate market will result in a lower unit cost and, consequently, more economical satisfaction of existing consumer demand than if competition were allowed.

Legalized monopoly depends on the existence of adequate public control. The function of cost control over public utilities rests upon state and federal commissions or on the competitive force of substitution of service. According to traditional views, competition through substitution is a weaker force in cost control for socially desirable ends than competition of the classical variety. However, because it is highly unlikely that competition in the public utility industry results in optimum allocation of resources, legal monopoly becomes an acceptable alternative public policy.

The above argument may also be used to explain the spatial distribution of various segments of a vertically integrated industry. In part, the real impact of physical distribution principles on location decisions appears in bolder relief when a single vertically integrated industry or firm is analyzed than when a series of firms integrated in a horizontal fashion are so treated. A vertically integrated firm with some degree of competition will be subjected to competitive pressures, which generally force it toward an objective of maximum efficiency. One aspect of overall efficiency in such an industry is the spatial distribution of various segments in the hierarchy of vertical integration. Generally, in those segments of the firm with substantial scale economies, a single or small number of plants will be sufficient to supply all needs. The automobile industry illustrates this point. Historically, the automobile industry has been largely concentrated in the Northeastern United States — particularly Michigan.[2] This concentration may be due, in part, to the fact that the early engineering and financial innovators concentrated their attentions in this area. However, the availability of steel in this area, the major ingredient in auto manufacture, was of equal persuasiveness. The large concentration of a variety of suppliers may have also played a role. Finally, the abundance of population in this area assured a high concentration of sales in close proximity to plant locations. In short, Weber's agglomerative force appears to have been important in this case.

As distribution expense, including transportation costs, increased, the economic validity of original location decisions was laid open to market pressures. The further complication of population shifts increased the relative importance of markets formerly of little consequence. The explosive economic growth of the Far West, especially California, is a case in point.

These cost increases and differential growth rates of spatially separated markets combined to raise the total costs of service. As these factors tended to force distribution costs up, profit margins in the peripheral markets tended to diminish. Eventually, rising costs forced margins in these markets to unsatisfactory levels. This was especially true in situations where demand elasticities prevented a rise in prices to cover these additional costs. To avoid margin reductions to unduly low levels, changes in the spatial distribution of plant and distribution facilities may become necessary. However, it was not desirable to shift these facilities indiscriminately. Generally the first segment of the firm likely to be shifted is the portion that has clear increasing or constant cost characteristics. In the auto industry, scale economies are not as dominant in the assembly operation as they are in some of the parts divisions. The construction of motor blocks, for example, has reached a highly mechanized state, which suggests scale economies of some possible significance.[3] Therefore, it is likely that the number of locations where motor blocks are manufactured may remain small. On the other

[2]Charles W. Boas, "Locational Patterns of the Michigan Passenger Automobile Industry: 1900–1957," *Papers of the Michigan Academy of Science, Arts, and Letters*, Vol. XLIV, 1959 (1958 Meeting).

[3]George Maxcy and Aubrey Silberston, *The Motor Industry* (New York: Macmillan Company; London: Allen and Unwin, 1959). Optimum outputs for different segments of the auto industry vary from 100,000 units in the body and panel-stamping operations.

CHART E3–2   Increasing Unit Cost Curve

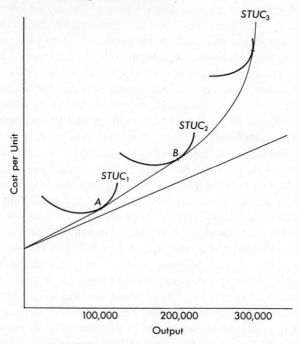

hand, the shipment of finished automobiles from assembly locations suggests high distribution expense. As volumes in specific markets increase, the
number of assembly plants may also increase.

Industries of Increasing Cost

Chart E3–2 illustrates the increasing cost portions of the firm's production
schedule. The chart indicates that the production cost per unit increases as
output increases. The curves labeled *STUC* indicate alternative scales of
plant that may be built. This is characteristic of an industry of increasing
cost or decreasing returns to scale. The straight line indicates the distribution
expense added to the production expense in order to find total unit cost.
Distribution cost increases at an exponential rate with output. It assumes
this characteristic when a single market, each segment of which is growing
at a differential rate, tends to increase the average length of the movements.
The increase in the lines of supply causes distribution expense to assume
this characteristic. Although production cost per unit may be linear in nature,
the total unit cost, including distribution expense, may take a nonlinear
character.

Considering the above cost conditions, it is desirable, in the interest of
overall efficiency, for the firm to serve each local market with the smallest

CHART E3–3   Decreasing Unit Cost Curve

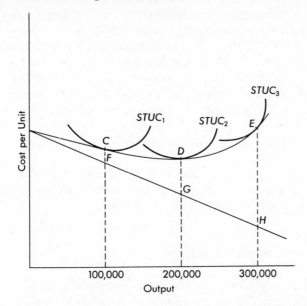

allowable scale of plant. Of course, the market must be sufficiently large to support the minimum scale of plant in the industry.

The growth of the firm may be visualized as resulting from the increased size of the sales territory of the plant. As the sales of the plant increase from 100,000 to 200,000 units, it is necessary to move to the next largest scale of plant ($STUC_1$ to $STUC_2$). But this results in an increase in both production and distribution costs. The average total costs at the optimum output of the scale are B compared to A at $STUC_1$. Therefore, savings may accrue to the amount of $B - A$ per unit if a new plant is constructed to serve the added 100,000 units of sales. This will result in pushing production costs down the cost curve to $STUC_1$ and an output of 100,000 units at two plants instead of 200,000 units at one plant. Production economies are thus maximized, and distribution costs are minimized. Industries of increasing costs will tend toward a large number of relatively small firms more or less widely dispersed.

Industries of Decreasing Cost

Chart E3–3 shows the production unit costs declining steadily as the scale of output increases. At the optimum output (100,000 units) at minimum scale ($STUC_1$), production unit costs are at F. Distribution costs are FC resulting in total unit costs equal to C. Increasing output to scale 2 ($STUC_2$) shows that at 200,000 units production unit costs are G and distribution costs are DG resulting in a total cost equal to D. Because total costs have declined, the added demand from 100,000 units to 200,000 units may be more economically served by expansion of plant facilities at the existing location.

At scale 3 ($STUC_3$), production costs drop to their lowest level of H per unit at 300,000 units of output. The distribution expense at this level is HE resulting in a total cost equal to E. Although demand exceeds 200,000 units, it appears desirable to maintain production at existing locations. When demand exceeds 200,000 units it appears that the better alternative is to locate a plant nearer to the growing portion of the market. By this action the overpowering impact of distribution expense on peripheral markets will be partially overcome.

Under conditions of decreasing unit production costs, the number of plants is likely to be smaller than under conditions of increasing costs. They are also likely to serve larger market territories.

Industries of Constant Costs

The last cost condition is one of constant returns to scale. That is, as output increases, unit production costs remain constant. Under these cost conditions, the distribution expense plays the dominant role in determining the number and geographic distribution of plant facilities. Production costs in this last case, will tend to play a passive role.

Charts E3–1 to E3–3 may now be used to analyze further the automobile industry. Freeing the mind of traditional marketing-oriented analysis will enable one to conceive of the problem the industry faces. The end product, of course, is the automobile sold to the final consumer. Primary emphasis here is on the sale of the individual unit to single consumers so as to avoid the problems of fleet and industrial sales.

However, concentration on the sale of the finished car should not necessarily blind one to alternative routes to final delivery, which is, in large measure, the physical distribution function. Considering a car from the physical distribution point of view quickly leads one to the limits of shipment varieties. These limits are either to ship a car completely assembled at a production point to the market or to ship the same car completely unassembled.[4]

In the automobile industry, the selection of the proper physical distribution system depends, in considerable part, on the distribution savings that may accrue in each case compared to economies of scale in production. Those segments of the industry having especially good consolidation potential in transport, resulting in distribution economies, and having scale

---

[4]The locational patterns developed here may be altered by the economic impact of the multi-level railroad car as the industry reevaluates and relocates assembly plants. The logic remains valid.

economies inherent in production, are likely to reflect some degree of stability in the number of plants and their location. Examples of such components are motor blocks and spark plugs. The highly automated techniques in these segments of the industry, combined with the relatively large proportion of fixed investment, result in the spawning of large numbers of units of finished products from a relatively small number of plants.

On the other hand, the shipment of finished cars results in considerably increased physical distribution expense, because consolidation potential in transportation here is rather limited. Inferior utilization of transport results in a substantial increase in cost.

Assembly plants located nearer to significant market segments are a means of achieving rational selection of various segments of the total production efforts vis-à-vis their spatial arrangement. Because of the relatively large proportion of labor expense in this segment of the industry, it is unlikely that significant scale economies may be experienced. The combination of a relative lack of scale economies in assembly operations, as compared to other operations in the production process, results in considering the assembly operations as the first of the production processes subject to increased distribution expense with its concomitant relocation result.

APPENDIX E4 Plant Location –

General Procedure and Checklist

General Procedure

Plant location procedure consists of an organized development of location factors within a working framework. Selection of a plant site is a compromise among various location forces. Because location is conceivably possible at an infinite number of geographical points, the final decision requires an orderly elimination of undesirable locations until the one best plant site is selected. Fortunately, the natural and logical process of plant location provides a satisfactory location procedure, which consists of plant analysis and field analysis.

Plant Analysis

The first step in applying location theory to practice is an appropriate evaluation of the three categories of location factors as they apply to the individual plant location problem. This stage of evaluation is referred to as plant analysis. For plants currently operating, one purpose of plant analysis is to determine if relocation is desirable. With the assumption that a new location is desirable, careful analysis of all location elements will determine what specifications the new location must meet. Similarly for new plants, analysis must be completed to isolate relevant location specifications.

444

It is during plant analysis that the contributions of location theory can be applied to the specifics of an individual problem. The critical cost factors for the new plant should be identified, and a detailed cost study of current operations should be completed. This will allow comparative cost analysis between the current location and potential new sites. In most cases identification of cost factors requires extensive data collection. The net result is ideally a number of specifications that can be transposed into dollar costs. For example, the amount of labor required, the point of raw material procurement, the power requirements, and the many other factors noted earlier should be quantified in order to guide field research. A detailed study of market areas and competitive forces should be completed in order to determine what general geographic areas appear to contain a profit-maximizing location. Finally, the impact of intangible elements should be given complete analysis.

The final result of extensive plant analysis is a set of location specifications designed to guide the process of site selection. If one or two location factors evolve as critical, they should be identified during plant analysis. Only after the location problem has been analyzed in the magnitude here indicated is field analysis ready to be undertaken.

Field Analysis

Field analysis consists of three steps necessary to reduce the geographic area of concern to a few potential locations. Evaluation of location alternatives should be completed at the regional, community, and site levels of consideration. Field analysis procedure is not viewed as a limiting process. Selection of the one best community need not be made prior to conducting a search for satisfactory factory sites. Several search areas can simultaneously be considered, including their alternative communities and respective factory locations.

Individual states are not considered focal points of attention. Beyond doubt, some states offer advantages for location while others have distinct disadvantages. The potential geographic territory included in a search area is indifferent to political boundaries. Consequently, several different states may simultaneously be considered as location prospects.

REGIONAL EVALUATION

The first step in selecting a specific site from a potential geographic area is regional evaluation. The task at this stage of selection is to determine what areas qualify for detailed field examination. The total area under consideration will vary according to the specifications of individual firms. In cases where cheap labor is the primary location influence, regional exam- ination may be limited to Southern states. If proximity to markets is a primary requirement, regional possibilities will be in the general locale of major market areas. Extreme competitive or intangible influence may limit the regional areas to a few in number. Whatever the specifications, the first step is to identify the geographic areas which meet the broad location requirements.

The second step is to determine which of the alternative regions will be most economical for achieving location objectives. Consideration begins with the assumption that all costs are regionally variable. Each potential region is evaluated by examining the expense of satisfying location require- ments. The differential in cost between alternative regions will vary with particular industries. For any particular firm, regional evaluation will identify geographic areas that will satisfy location requirements at least cost. The regions that present possibilities for most economic operation be- come the search areas for particular communities.

COMMUNITY EVALUATION

Up to this point, the firm considering plant location has, by the process of elimination, selected a few general areas within which communities capable of satisfying location requirements must be identified. Community evaluation should include the availability of necessary facilities. Such factors as availability of utilities, adequate labor force, and transportation must be examined. If a particular community appears to have the necessary charac- teristics in this respect, a more detailed investigation is undertaken.

Detailed investigation consists of measuring all facilities in terms of potential costs of manufacturing. If all facilities are available at a reasonable cost, investigation is extended to include intangible characteristics of the community. The character of local politics and the community's attitude toward industrial development must be considered. Of primary concern is the question of compatibility between the firm and the community. For example, will the proposed building and manufacturing operations meet with the approval of the community? Not understanding all implications of such intangible factors can result in a serious and expensive mistake on the part of the firm. The firm must also consider if the community fulfills the environmental desires of the personnel to be transferred. Living conditions must be examined in terms of such factors as recreational facilities, cost of living, and adequate housing. If the community offers incentives, complete details should be examined. Analysis of these and all other factors of im- portance will point out which communities are the best potential locations for conducting manufacturing operations. Evaluation of potential sites still remains.

SITE EVALUATION

Evaluation of available sites represents the last step in plant location. Only if the community meets all other requirements will the search be necessary. Selection of a site to construct a new plant can normally be completed in all industrially minded communities. In location problems where a ready constructed plant is sought, evaluation of sites may be necessary prior to community delineation.

In selecting a site, attention must once again be directed to cost analysis and consideration of intangibles. In addition, physical requirements and topographic features must be considered. Naturally, the direct cost of procurement is one governing factor. Other costs such as obtaining rail sidings, utility hook-ups, and highway access also require evaluation. From the intangible aspect, the firm must determine if the neighborhood is consistent with the desired image of the firm. For some firms, location in close proximity with "linked" industries may be desirable.

Only after satisfactory plant sites have been determined is the location process near completion. At this point, the firm's executives are armed with the necessary facts to make an intelligent location decision. Sufficient information should now be available to determine which area, what community, and the particular site which offers the best plant location.

Because all location factors have been under consideration throughout plant and field analysis, the forces of cost, market competition, and intangible location factors have guided the selection procedure. To aid in selecting between alternative sites, comparative cost analysis is helpful. The total costs of operation at each potential site should be compared to total costs experienced at the old location. Such cost analysis will clearly point out the benefits gained from relocation.

Plant Location Check List

I. Plant Analysis
  A. Distribution Analysis
    1. Distribution System Analysis
      a. Current Production Points
      b. Current Warehouse Locations
    2. Long-term Expansion Plans and Policies
    3. Primary Transfer Requirements
    4. Modes of Transportation Capable of Satisfying Transfer Demands
      a. Raw Material Movement
      b. Finished Product Movement

B. Production Analysis
1. Raw Material Requirements
    a. Present Point of Purchase
    b. Quantity Purchased
    c. Alternate Purchase Points
2. General Characteristics of Production Process
    a. Special Factors Dependent upon Location
3. Labor Requirements
    a. Number of Skilled and Unskilled
    b. Degree of Labor Organization Acceptable
    c. Number of People to be Transferred
4. Power and Utility Requirements
C. Market Analysis
1. Geographical Location of Major Market Segments
2. Competition Analysis
    a. Production Locations
    b. Major Markets Serviced and Relative Strength in Each
D. Managerial Location Preferences
E. Location Specifications for New Plant
1. Distribution Requirements
2. Production Requirements
3. Market Requirements
4. Managerial Preferences
F. Cost Analysis at Present Manufacturing Location
1. Transportation
2. Production

II. Field Analysis
A. Regional Analysis
1. Least-Cost Transfer Location
    a. Arrival at Alternative Points Using Different Raw Material Purchase Points
2. Selection of Region(s) to be Given Detailed Analysis
3. Analysis of Location Factors Variable Between States
    a. Legal Structure
    b. Political Environment
    c. Corporate Laws and Tax Structures
    d. Labor Laws and Labor Conditions
    e. State Financial Status
    f. Industries Currently Located in State
    g. Cost-of-Living Index
4. Selection of State(s) to be Evaluated in Detail Based upon Regional Analysis and Location Specifications

B. Community Analysis
1. General Description of Community(s)
2. Population and Growth Patterns
3. Industrial Climate
   a. Existing Industry
   b. Local Laws
   c. Labor Situation
   d. Community Attitude Toward Industry
   e. Amount of Cooperation Available
4. Supporting Facilities and Services
   a. Transportation Facilities
   b. Utilities
   c. Municipal Services
5. Living Conditions
   a. Cost of Living
   b. Housing Conditions
   c. Educational Facilities
   d. Recreational Facilities
   e. Character and Quality of Local Government
6. Selection of Community(s) on the Basis of Location Specifications to be Evaluated for a Plant Site

C. Site Analysis
1. Geographical Considerations
   a. Size
   b. Soil Content
   c. Drainage
2. Utility Availability
3. Availability of Required Transportation Facilities
4. Costs
   a. Procurement
   b. Landscaping, etc.
5. Selection of a Site(s) Based upon Location Specifications

III. Final Location Selection
A. Proposed Costs at Alternative Sites
1. Continuing Production and Distribution Costs
2. Initial Establishment Costs
B. Comparative Analysis of Proposed Costs with Costs Experienced at Current Location
C. Final Selection of New Location Based upon Least-Cost Comparison

Selected Bibliography

Chapter 1

ALDERSON, WROE. *Marketing Behavior and Executive Action*. Homewood, Ill.: Richard D. Irwin, 1957.

CONSTANTIN, JAMES A. *Principles of Logistics Management*. New York: Meredith, 1966.

DRUCKER, PETER F. "The Economy's Dark Continent." *Fortune* (April 1962).

HESKETT, J. L., ROBERT M. IVIE, and NICHOLAS A. GLASKOWSKY. *Business Logistics*. New York: Ronald, 1964.

MAGEE, JOHN F. *Physical Distribution Systems*. New York: McGraw-Hill, 1967.

MOSSMAN, FRANK H., and NEWTON MORTON. *Logistics of Distribution Systems*. Boston: Allyn, 1965.

"New Strategies to Move Goods." *Business Week* (September 1966).

STAUDT, THOMAS A., and DONALD A. TAYLOR. *A Managerial Introduction to Marketing*. Englewood Cliffs, N.J.: Prentice-Hall, 1965.

TAYLOR, FREDERIC W. *Scientific Management*. New York: Harper, 1957.

Chapter 2

BULLEN, H. JAY "New Competitive Selling Weapon — Physical Distribution Management," *Sales Management* (May 7, 1965).

FORRESTER, JAY W. *Industrial Dynamics*. Cambridge: M.I.T. Press, 1961.

HOWARD, JOHN A. *Marketing Management: Analysis and Planning*, rev. ed. Homewood, Ill.: Richard D. Irwin, 1963. See especially Chap. 8.

"New Strategies to Move Goods," *Business Week* (September 1966).

STERN, MARK E. *Marketing Planning: A Systems Approach*. New York: McGraw-Hill, 1966. See especially Chaps. 7 and 8.

STEWART, WENDELL M. "Physical Distribution: Key to Improved Volume and Profits," *Journal of Marketing* (January 1965).

Chapter 3

ALDERSON, WROE. *Marketing Behavior and Executive Action.* Homewood, Ill.: Richard D. Irwin, 1957.

COMMONS, JOHN R. *The Economics of Collective Action.* New York: The Macmillan Company, 1950.

COX, REAVIS. *Distribution in a High-Level Economy.* Englewood Cliffs, N.J.: Prentice-Hall, 1956.

DAVIS, KENNETH R. *Marketing Management.* New York: Ronald Press, 1961.

McCARTHY, E. JEROME. *Basic Marketing: A Managerial Approach,* rev. ed. Homewood, Ill.: Richard D. Irwin, 1964.

STAUDT, THOMAS A., and DONALD A. TAYLOR. *A Managerial Introduction to Marketing.* Englewood Cliffs, N.J.: Prentice-Hall, 1965.

STEWART, WENDELL M. "Physical Distribution: Key to Improved Volume and Profits," *Journal of Marketing,* January, 1965.

VAILE, ROLAND, E. T. GRETHER, and REAVIS COX. *Marketing in the American Economy.* New York: Ronald Press, 1952.

Chapter 4

GREENHUT, MELVIN L. *Plant Location in Theory and Practice.* Chapel Hill: University of North Carolina Press, 1956.

HOOVER, EDGAR M. *The Location of Economic Activity.* New York: McGraw-Hill, 1948.

HOWARD, JOHN A. *Marketing Management: Analysis and Planning,* rev. ed. Homewood, Ill.: Richard D. Irwin, 1963. See especially Chapter 8.

ISARD, W., *et al. Methods of Regional Analysis: An Introduction to Regional Science.* New York: John Wiley, 1960.

LEWIS, RICHARD J. *A Business Logistics Information and Accounting System for Marketing Analysis,* Unpublished Ph.D. Dissertation, Michigan State University, 1964.

LOSCH, AUGUST. *The Economics of Location.* New Haven, Conn.: Yale University Press, 1954.

TAFF, CHARLES A. *Management of Traffic and Physical Distribution,* 3rd ed. Homewood, Ill.: Richard D. Irwin, 1964.

WOYTINSKY, W. S., and E. S. WOYTINSKY. *World Commerce and Governments.* New York: Twentieth Century Fund, 1955.

ZIMMERMANN, ERICH WALTER. *Introduction to World Resources,* ed. by H. L. Hunker. New York: Harper and Row, 1964.

Chapter 5

GOGOL, ARTHUR E., and L. C. SCHMETZER. "Reducing Transportation Costs," *Small Business Administration,* April, 1962.

JONES, ROSS E. "Physical Distribution Management: Functions and Practices," in Dirksen, Charles J., Arthur Kroeger, and Lawrence C. Lockley, eds. *Readings in Marketing.* Homewood, Ill.: Richard D. Irwin, 1963.

LAZER, WILLIAM. "A Systems Approach to Transportation," *Distribution Age,* September, 1960.

MAGEE, JOHN F. "The Logistics of Distribution," *Harvard Business Review*, July–August, 1960.

STANTON, WILLIAM J. *Fundamentals of Marketing*. New York: McGraw-Hill, 1964. See especially Chapter 17.

STAUDT, THOMAS A., and DONALD A. TAYLOR. *A Managerial Introduction to Marketing*. Englewood Cliffs, N.J.: Prentice-Hall, 1965. See especially Chapter 19.

STERN, MARK E. *Marketing Planning: A Systems Approach*. New York: McGraw-Hill, 1966. See especially Chapter 7.

Chapter 6

"An Appraisal of the Petroleum Industry of the United States," *Industry of the United States*, United States Department of Interior (Washington, D. C.: Government Printing Office, January, 1965).

BAIER, MARTIN. "ZIP Code — New Tool for Marketing," *Harvard Business Review*, Vol. 45, January–February, 1967, pp. 136–140.

BELEN, FRED. "ZIP Codes — Bonus for Business," *Business Topics* (East Lansing, Michigan: Michigan State University), Spring 1967, Vol. 15, No. 2, pp. 19–25.

Big Load Afloat, American Waterways Operators, Inc., Washington, D. C., 1965.

BUGAN, THOMAS. *When Does Title Pass?*, 2nd ed. Dubuque, Iowa: W. C. Brown Company, 1951.

KING, CHARLES W. "How Total Costs Affect Ratemaking," *Distribution Age*, December, 1965, p. 25.

MEYER, *et al. Economics of Competition in the Transport Industries*. Cambridge, Mass.: Harvard University Press, 1964, Appendix D.

National ZIP CODE Directory, United States Post Office Department, Publication 65 (Washington, D. C.: Government Printing Office, January, 1966).

1963 Census of Transportation, Commodity Transportation Survey, Part I, Commodity Groups, U. S. Department of Commerce, Bureau of Census (Washington, D. C.: Government Printing Office, January, 1966).

ROBERTS, MERRILL J. *Economics of Consolidated Transport*. Pittsburgh, Pa.: University of Pittsburgh Press, 1967.

ROBERTS, MERRILL J., and Associates. *Intermodal Freight Transportation Coordination: Problem and Potential*. Graduate School of Business. Pittsburgh, Penn.: University of Pittsburgh Press, 1966.

TAFF, CHARLES A. *Management of Traffic and Physical Distribution*, 3rd ed. Homewood, Ill.: Richard D. Irwin, 1964.

Chapter 7

Explanation of the Development of Motor Carrier Costs with Statements as to Their Meaning and Significance, ICC Statement No. 4-59, Washington, D. C., August, 1959.

LONGMAN, D. R., and MICHAEL SCHIFF. *Practical Distribution Costs*. Homewood, Ill.: Richard D. Irwin, 1955.

McCARTHY, E. JEROME. *Basic Marketing: A Managerial Approach*, rev. ed. Homewood, Ill.: Richard D. Irwin, 1964. See especially Chapter 20.

MOSSMAN, FRANK H., and NEWTON MORTON. *Logistics of Distribution Systems*. Boston: Allyn and Bacon, 1965. See especially Appendix to Chapter 2.

Chapter 8

ALFORD, L. P., and BANGS, J. R. *Production Handbook.* New York: Ronald Press, 1958.

BOWMAN, EDWARD H., and FETTER, ROBERT B. *Analysis for Production Management.* Homewood, Ill.: Richard D. Irwin, 1961.

BROWN, R. G. *Smoothing, Forecasting and Prediction of Discrete Time Series.* Englewood Cliffs, N.J.: Prentice-Hall, 1962.

LEWIS, RICHARD J. "A Business Logistics Information and Accounting System for Marketing Analysis," Unpublished Ph.D. Dissertation, Michigan State University, 1964.

MAGEE, JOHN F. *Physical Distribution Systems.* New York: McGraw-Hill, 1967.

Physical Distribution Management: The Total Systems Route to New Profits, Programmed Instruction for Management Education 100. New York: American Management Association, Inc., 1967.

PUDER, R. W. "Containerization: One Shipper's Problems, Solutions, Needs," *Management of the Physical Distribution Function,* A. M. A. Management Report No. 49. New York: American Management Association, Manufacturing Division, 1960.

WELCH, E. W. *Tested Scientific Inventory Control.* Greenwich, Conn.: Management Publishing Corporation, 1956.

Chapter 9

ANDERSON, O. KELLEY, JR., *et al. Information Management: An Analysis for Businessmen.* Cambridge: Harvard Graduate School of Business Administration, 1962.

DEARDEN, JOHN. *Computers in Business Management.* Chicago: Dow Jones-Irwin, 1966.

FISK, GEORGE. *Marketing Systems: An Introductory Analysis.* New York: Harper and Row, 1967. See especially Chapters 9 and 12.

GENTLE, EDGAR G., JR., ed. *Data Communications in Business: An Introduction,* Published for the American Telephone and Telegraph Company. New York: Publishers Service Company, 1965.

KOTTLER, PHILLIP. *Marketing Systems.* New York: McGraw-Hill, 1967.

McCARTHY, E. JEROME, and J. A. McCARTHY. *Integrated Data Processing Systems.* New York: John Wiley, 1966.

McLUHAN, MARSHALL. *Information Technology and Survival of the Firm.* Chicago: Dow Jones-Irwin, 1966.

"Management Information," *Special Reprint Series, Harvard Business Review,* 1967.

Chapter 10

ACHTER, STEPHEN B. "A Practical Way of Allocating and Controlling Warehousing Costs," *N.A.A. Bulletin,* February, 1960.

BRIGGS, ANDREW J. *Warehouse Operations Planning and Management.* New York: John Wiley, 1960.

ENEBORG, C. G. "How to Plot the Ideal Location for a Warehouse," *Management Methods,* January, 1958.

FREDERICK, JOHN H. *Using Public Warehouses*. Philadelphia: Chilton Company, 1957.

GREENHUT, MELVIN L. *Plant Location*. Chapel Hill: University of North Carolina Press, 1956.

HOOVER, EDGAR M. *Location of Economic Activity*. New York: McGraw-Hill, 1948.

LOSCH, AUGUST. *The Economics of Location*. New Haven, Conn.: Yale University Press, 1954.

"New Nerve Centers of Distribution," *Dun's Review and Modern Industry*, June, 1963, Part 2.

TAFF, CHARLES A. *Management of Traffic and Physical Distribution*. Homewood, Ill.: Richard D. Irwin, 1964.

Chapter 11

"The Dillon Study," *Progressive Grocer*, May 1960, p. D-18.

LANDIS, EUGENE J. *TELSCAR: An Industrial Approach to Rail Transport Quality Control*, Proceedings: Railway Systems and Management Association Meeting, Chicago, Illinois, August, 1964.

LAKASHMAN, ROBERT, and STOLLE, JOHN R. "The Total Cost Approach to Distribution," *Business Horizons*, Winter 1965, Vol. 8, No. 4, pp. 33–46.

LEWIS, HOWARD T., and CULLITON, JAMES W. *The Role of Air Freight in Physical Distribution*. Boston: Harvard University, 1956.

RAYBURN, L. GAYLE. "Setting Standards for Distribution Costs," *Management Services*, March–April 1967.

RIGGS, BRUCE J. "Sales, Production and Transportation Factors on Plant Location," *Transportation and Distribution Management*, October, 1961.

United Air Lines' Profit Analyzer. Chicago: United Air Lines, 1961.

Chapter 12

BOWMAN, EDWARD H., and ROBERT B. FETTER. *Analysis for Production Management*. Homewood, Ill.: Richard D. Irwin, 1961.

BRYAN, STANLEY E. "How to Use Linear Programming," *Purchasing*, September 9, 1965.

DEARDEN, JOHN. *Computers in Business Management*. Homewood, Ill.: Dow Jones-Irwin, Inc., 1966.

FERGUSON, ROBERT D., and LAUREN F. SARGENT. *Linear Programming: Fundamentals and Application*. New York: McGraw-Hill, 1958.

FORRESTER, JAY W. *Industrial Dynamics*. Cambridge: The M.I.T. Press, 1961.

JOHNSON, RICHARD A., FREMONT E. KAST, and JAMES E. ROSENZWEIG. *The Theory and Management of Systems*. New York: McGraw-Hill, 1963. See especially Chapter 8.

KUEHN, ALFRED A. "Complex Interactive Models," in *Quantitative Techniques in Marketing Analysis*. Homewood, Ill.: Richard D. Irwin, 1962.

KUEHN, ALFRED A., and MICHAEL J. HAMBURGER. "A Heuristic Program for Locating Warehouses," *Management Science*, July, 1963.

SHYCON, HARVEY N., and RICHARD B. MAFFEI. "Simulation — Tool for Better Distribution," *Harvard Business Review*, November-December, 1960.

Chapter 13

ALDERSON, WROE, and STANLEY J. SHAPIRO, eds. *Marketing and the Computer.* Englewood Cliffs, N.J.: Prentice-Hall, 1963.

BOWERSOX, DONALD J. "Total Information Systems in Logistics," in J. L. Heskett, ed., *Business Logistics — Appraisal and Prospect.* Stanford, Calif.: Stanford University, 1965.

DEARDEN, JOHN. *Computers in Business Management.* Homewood, Ill.: Richard D. Irwin, 1966.

DEARDEN, JOHN. "How to Organize Information Systems," *Harvard Business Review*, March–April, 1965.

DELANEY, ROBERT VERNON. *Organization for Management of the Physical Distribution Function — A Cast Study of the National Biscuit Company*, Master Thesis, Graduate School of Business Administration, New York University, 1966.

EVANS, MARSHALL K., and LOU R. HAGUE. "Master Plan for Information Systems," *Harvard Business Review*, January–February, 1962.

STOLLE, JOHN F. "How to Manage Physical Distribution," *Harvard Business Review*, July–August, 1967.

VARLEY, JOHN F. "Corporate Organization for Distribution Optimization," Paper presented at Meeting of National Council of Physical Distribution Management, April 6, 1966.

Index

Notes

Notes

Notes

Notes

Notes

Notes